W9-AEW-157

EDUCATION LIBRARY
UNIVERSITY OF KENTUCKY

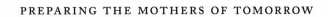
PREPARING THE MOTHERS OF TOMORROW

PREPARING THE
MOTHERS OF TOMORROW
Education and Islam in Mandate Palestine

ELA GREENBERG

UNIVERSITY OF TEXAS PRESS
Austin

Educ.

LC
2410
.P19
G74
2010

Copyright © 2010 by the University of Texas Press
All rights reserved
Printed in the United States of America
First edition, 2010

Requests for permission to reproduce material from this work should be
sent to:
    Permissions
    University of Texas Press
    P.O. Box 7819
    Austin, TX 78713-7819
    www.utexas.edu/utpress/about/bpermission.html

♾ The paper used in this book meets the minimum requirements of ANSI/
NISO Z39.48-1992 (R1997) (Permanence of Paper).

LIBRARY OF CONGRESS CATALOGING-IN-PUBLICATION DATA

Greenberg, Ela.
Preparing the mothers of tomorrow : education and Islam in mandate
Palestine / by Ela Greenberg. — 1st ed.
    p.   cm.
Includes bibliographical references and index.
ISBN 978-0-292-72119-7 (cloth : alk. paper)
1. Muslim women—Education—Palestine—History—20th century.
2. Muslim girls—Education—Palestine—History—20th century.
I. Title.
LC2410.I74G74   2010
371.828'29709569409041—dc22

                          2009020091

Dedicated to the memory of my father,
G. Robert Greenberg,
a biochemist who really wanted to be a historian

CONTENTS

ACKNOWLEDGMENTS

Although I often felt I was working in a bubble, numerous people that I have met over the ten years of researching and writing this book have offered support, advice, and friendship. I could not have seen this book through from start to finish without the encouragement and assistance of Ruth Roded, mentor and friend. For a decade already, she has listened to me work through my research ideas, has patiently read drafts, and has provided me with moral support whenever needed.

I especially want to thank my friend and colleague, Khader Salameh. Khader first gave me the idea of researching the education of Muslim girls when he brought me a microfilm of a list of pupils for the Islamic Girls' School in Jerusalem, and convinced me to have a look at it. He also was the one who told me about the archives in Abu Dis and who accompanied me there on my first visit. Over the years, Khader has endured my bantering about "my school," and girls' education; I could not have written this book without him. Erika Lindensmith, Tali Shinhav, Laila 'Abed Rabho, Noga Efrati, Abigail Jacobson, Liat Kozma, Wasfi Kailani, Awad Halabi, and Hillel Cohen have all been there in some way or another when I needed them. Ellen Fleischmann, in particular, has been supportive of my work, gave me insightful comments on earlier drafts, and graciously shared her interviews with me, while Maria Småberg kindly sent me her doctoral dissertation when I could not find it in Jerusalem. In the final stages of this project, Nissim Rejwan provided much-needed encouragement, as well as endless cups of "Iraqi tea," while Mona Hajjar Halaby, Laura Schor, and John Harte have shared with me their own projects on education in late Ottoman and Mandate Palestine, providing me with renewed inspiration and support.

I am most grateful to the women interviewed for this project and to those who assisted me in interviews. Suʿad Stratton, whose name I incidentally came across on an Internet petition, eagerly shared with me her educational experiences as well as those of her sisters. She and I have remained in touch ever since, clearly one of the joys of doing this kind of research. I also would like to thank Saʿid al-Husseini and Nadia and Teddy Theodorie for allowing me to reproduce here photos from their private collections.

I am particularly indebted to the director and staff of the *Muʾassasat ihyaʾ al-turath wa-l-buhuth al-islami* in Abu Dis for welcoming and assisting me in my research there from early 1999 until the outbreak of the Second Intifada in September 2000. Indeed, my fondest memories of the years of researching this book were spent sitting in this archive, drinking coffee and talking to the employees and other scholars who used the archives. I am most grateful to Faiza Ahmad, Lubna Suliman, and Asmahan Edhidl, who made me feel welcomed and shared with me tidbits of their lives, and, of course, green almonds; Muhammad Safadi, Jamal Ghoshieh, and Ghassan Muheibish, who retrieved container after container of documents; Bassam Quttine (Abu Sami), who arranged interviews and accompanied me to them; Muhammad Rumman (Abu Murad) and the late Musa Abu Rumi (Abu Thaʾir), who shared their office with me, as well as their infectious enthusiasm for the villages of Suba and al-ʿIzariyya, respectively; and the librarian Muhammad Halaseh, who has remained in e-mail contact over the years and who together with Jamal searched the archives for photographs for this book, but to no avail. Thanks are also due to Fahmi ʾAnsari, who welcomed me into his own personal library in East Jerusalem when the political situation made it very uncomfortable, and to Nabil ʾAnsari, who helped by finding some otherwise inaccessible Arabic sources.

I appreciated the assistance of the staffs at the Jewish National Library, the Israel State Archives, the Central Zionist Archives, Yad Ben Zvi Library, the Sophia Smith Collection at Smith College in Northampton, the Middle East Centre Archives at St. Antony's College, and the Library of Congress in Washington, D.C. I especially would like to thank Debbie Usher of the Middle East Centre Archives, who graciously found photographs for this book; Reuven Koffler of the Central Zionist Archives, who assisted me in locating photographs as well; and Laura Kells and Barbara Bair of the Manuscript Division of the Library of Congress, who helped me find documents related to the Islamic Girls' School and to the American Colony.

For much of the time spent on this research, Hebrew University of Jerusalem served as a second home. There I found support and encouragement from Amnon Cohen, Haim Gerber, Reuven Amitai, and Ruth Kark. Ruth Kark, in particular, urged me to consider the missionary aspects of education and provided me with very useful comments on some chapters. Ami Ayalon of Tel Aviv University also read an earlier draft of this work, and motivated me to see it through to the end. Lastly, I am indebted to Rashid Khalidi, who first introduced me to the idea of working on Palestinian history while still an MA student at the University of Chicago, and whose own work has been inspiring.

The research for this book would not have been possible without funding from various sources. I am indebted to the Truman Institute for the Advancement of Peace for funding me as a doctoral student and then as a postdoctoral researcher, and to the Institute of African and Asian Studies at Hebrew University of Jerusalem, which awarded me with the Bartov Prize, in addition to other grants over the years. I also thank the Yad Ben Zvi Institute and Yad Orah for their support, as well as the Sophia Smith Collection Library, which provided me with travel funds to research in its archives. Year-long postdoctoral fellowships at the Department of Middle Eastern History in the School of History at Tel Aviv University and at Hebrew University also enabled me to complete this work.

My gratitude goes to some of the students whom I have met over the years and who have assisted me in various ways: Adina Gerver, Noaz Cohen, Rachel Levy, Miri Golub, Aviva Birkenstadt, Mollie Gerver, Lauren Simons, Stacy Lee, and Hanadi Dabash for their help on this project or other endless projects, which enabled me to devote myself to this book.

Thanks are also due to Jim Burr, the Humanities Editor at the University of Texas Press, for his interest and assistance in producing this book. I would also like to thank Christopher D. Chung for his help in the copyediting stage.

My family has been supportive of my academic endeavors all along. My parents, Susan J. and G. Robert Greenberg, understood that my visits home always included a stop at the University of Michigan Graduate Library, followed by a visit to Kinkos' Copy Shop. My father, especially, took time to read and question earlier incarnations of this work. Although I regret that he was not able to see this final product, his guiding influence remains until today. Amir Cohen, husband, partner, friend, and "Abba," has encouraged me to research and write, not give up, and to complete this book. I also thank his parents for being supportive and for spending perhaps more afternoons with their granddaughters than they had expected. Finally, my daughters Einav and Alma Greenberg Cohen have provided much joyous relief from endless writing and rewriting, and they can finally stop saying, "Finish your book!"

LIST OF ABBREVIATIONS

AUB	American University of Beirut
CMS	Church Missionary Society
CZA	Central Zionist Archives
IIRHR	Institute for Islamic Records and Heritage Research
ISA	Israel State Archives
J&EM	Jerusalem and East Mission
JNL	Jewish National Library
MECA	Middle East Centre Archives
PRO	Public Records Office
SSC	Sophia Smith Collection
SMC	Supreme Muslim Council
SPFEE	Society for Promoting Female Education in the East
WTC	Women's Training College

NOTE ON TRANSLITERATION

In transliterating from Arabic, this book follows the system used in the *International Journal of Middle East Studies*. Diacritical marks have been omitted, but the *ayn* (') and *hamza* (') have been retained for Arabic terms not found in an unabridged English dictionary. I chose not to transliterate place names, leaving them as they are commonly rendered, and some personal names that appear in English-language sources, even if they deviate from the system of transliteration. For transliteration of Hebrew titles and names, I have relied upon the fifteenth edition of *The Chicago Manual of Style*. For the sake of clarity and brevity, I chose to translate the titles of Arabic press articles into English.

PREPARING THE MOTHERS OF TOMORROW

INTRODUCTION

In 1930, on the pages of *Filastin*, a daily Arabic newspaper issued in Jaffa, a law-yer by the name of Najib al-Hakim penned the following: "We won't achieve independence and we won't awaken unless the woman is given a nationalist education," noting that, "Of course, girls are the mothers of tomorrow. They are the other half of men. Indeed, they are the pillar of nationalist life, lest we not say, they are the total pillar." Yet according to this author, the foreign schools in Palestine sought to thwart the nationalist education of young girls by replacing "our inherited Eastern morals and customs with western customs and morals. We forget the past. These schools make us forget our language, even in our homes." The implication was that young girls educated in these schools would not be able to raise their children properly: "Child experts say the home is the first school and the mother is the teacher. The baby is the plant which the mother nurses with honorable water when she is honorable. How can she nurse the baby with honorable water when she is ignorant of the meaning of honor? How is this possible when she is prepared for this principle but she is unable to learn this in the colonialist schools?"[1]

This vision of girls' education as contributing to the next generation of nationalists was particular neither to time nor to place. From the late nine-teenth century onward, men and women throughout the Middle East dis-cussed, debated, and negotiated the roles of young girls and women in pro-ducing modern nations. Lisa Pollard has argued that Europeans in Egypt were among the first to link this notion of nation to the home and family, as they produced travelogues and other writings full of negative images of de-bauchery, perversion, and female denigration within Egyptian homes, giving impulse to the British occupation of 1882. Creating a modern Egypt through reform of the home and family, particularly by eradicating polygamy and the seclusion of women, both prominent among the upper ruling class, thus became central to British policies in Egypt,[2] and echoed throughout writings by missionaries in the region as well. Muslim reformers and later Arab nationalists also debated the reform of the home and the family, at its crux the question of borrowing from Europe, and the degree to which the East should adopt and adapt the culture of the West.[3] Early twentieth-century Arab nationalists also appropriated a variety of metaphors of the "modern family" to combat the negative image created and promulgated by the West, with the image of the modern family used for mobilizing the public in pursuit of nationalist goals, as Beth Baron has shown in her important work.[4] Similarly, Afsaneh Najmabadi has elucidated how in late nineteenth-century Qajar Iran, modernists reconfigured the role of a woman from being a woman of the household, that is, one of several wives or concubines within a multigenerational harim, to being upheld as wife, as her husband's companion, as household manager, and as nurturer and educator of the next generation of male citizens.[5]

The question of girls' education became central to this discourse. Lebanese educator and early nationalist Butrus al-Bustani (1819–1883) believed that women should be educated so that they could run their households, and care for their children,[6] echoing ideas put forth by the eighteenth-century French philosopher Jean-Jacques Rousseau.[7] Some thirty years later, in 1872–1873, the influential Egyptian thinker, writer, translator, and educator Rifaʿa Rafiʿ al-Tahtawi (1801–1873) published a textbook called *al-Murshid al-amin lil-banat wa-l-banin* (Guiding truths for girls and boys). In his *al-Murshid*, al-Tahtawi departed from al-Bustani's vision of womanhood by linking girls' education with the stability of the nation. Female education would cement the bonds of marriage and the family, seen as the building blocks of the nation and markers of stability. Education would also provide women with proper leisure activities and training for appropriate work.[8] Al-Tahtawi's ideal of education was similar to, if not influenced by, that of European philosophers such as the German Johann Gottlieb Fichte (1762–1814), who urged his countrymen to use education in order to build a strong state and create a patriotic generation of men and women in the wake of ongoing military struggles between Prussia and France.[9]

The end of the nineteenth century and the beginning of the next was marked by an ever-growing debate over women's roles. As Beth Baron has shown, the women's press in Egypt that flourished from the 1890s onward, primarily focused on the middle-class domestic ideal of conjugal marriage, with the mothers raising their children and running their own households. At the center of this emerging ideal was support for girls' education.[10] While the women's press was influential among female readers inside and outside Egypt, and gave rise to similar publications in Beirut and Damascus, the writings of Qasim Amin (1865–1908) transformed the debate into a far more vocal one. A French-educated, upper-class lawyer and judge in the British administration in Egypt, Amin presented ideas in his *Tahrir al-mar'a* (The emancipation of woman, 1899) and *al-Mar'a al-jadida* (The new woman, 1900) that were felt for decades to come. Inspired by Europe, as was characteristic of the Ottoman Egyptian elite to which he belonged, Amin believed that the West held the key to progress and advancement. Like the women's press, he supported girls' education in order to uplift and reform the family and the nation, while he called for an end to women's seclusion and to their wearing of the face veil, claiming that both undermined and at times prevented girls' education.[11]

In both the women's press and the works by Amin, women's roles as mothers were paramount. The caring mother as educator gained significance in advancing notions of modernity and nationalism. As Baron writes, "Maternal imagery proved particularly prevalent in nationalist literatures across the world," with Egyptian women identifying themselves and being identified by others as "the mothers of the nation."[12] Baron points out that "those who emphasized the role of women as 'Mothers of the Nation' argued that the nation would only advance with girls' education and women's progress. Only educated mothers would imbue their sons with love for the nation."[13] Thus the education of girls as future mothers was essential to the progress of the nation and to its depiction and acceptance as being a "modern" nation. Although this notion traversed administrative boundaries throughout the Middle East, particularly thanks to the Arabic press, the discourse appears to have varied somewhat according to the context. While the rhetoric of the "mothers of the nation" recognized the pioneering role that elite, educated Egyptian women had in constructing both the family and the nation within Egypt, at the same time, it reflected their influence and position in leading the Arab nations. In contrast, the phrase "mothers of tomorrow" (*ummahat al-ghad*) was commonly used within the Arabic press in Palestine. It referred to the anticipated role that young, educated women in Palestine would have not only in creating new, modern families but also in determining their country's future.

The standard histories of Palestinian nationalism and Palestinian society until 1948 paid little attention to women and gender until the publication of Ellen Fleischmann's work on the contribution of Palestinian women to their nationalist struggle before 1948.[14] Researching and writing in the wake of the First Intifada (1988–1993), in which Palestinian women were visible participants, Fleischmann showed that primarily elite Palestinian women during the British Mandate also were mobilized to work on behalf of the nationalist struggle. She stresses the significance of their education, which provided them with the skills needed to create a movement of women, and which influenced them to enter the male-dominated public sphere. *Preparing the Mothers of Tomorrow* builds upon Fleischmann's work by exploring the development of girls' education as integral to the nationalist and modernist narratives in Palestine from the late Ottoman period through the end of the British Mandate. It examines how girls' education in government, missionary, and private local schools sought to transform Muslim girls into the "mothers of tomorrow," meeting both modernist and nationalist expectations of gender. Class and religion were equally significant to both educational provision and quality of education.

Markers of nationalism and modernity had already begun to manifest themselves in various ways in Palestine by the end of the nineteenth century. The effects of the Ottoman Tanzimat or "reordering" reforms issued during the last half of the nineteenth century replaced traditional Ottoman government, religious, legal, educational, and social institutions with "modern," early-nationalist institutions by the turn of the century. Rashid Khalidi eloquently describes how following the Tanzimat, the traditional religious bureaucracy and education "ceased to confer prestige and status in society as it once had," being replaced by western methods of scholarship.[15] Palestine's cities also were transformed during this time. The port cities of Jaffa and Haifa expanded as they accommodated foreign missionary and merchant communities, who were granted official privileges to reside throughout the Empire. New spacious neighborhoods developed outside the familiar city walls, serving the Arab elite and rising middle-class families, as well as small foreign Christian communities.[16] The grand, often ostentatious Arab homes became markers of modernity, representing the way Arab elite and middle-class families wished to live, as well as how they wanted to be identified.[17] In the years preceding World War I, electricity, phonographs, and even cars had become apparent in Palestine's urban centers.[18]

The Arabic press in Palestine had a significant role in promoting a modern vision of a Palestinian nation. Although Arabic newspapers had been published elsewhere, in Palestine they appeared only after the Young Turk Revolution of 1908, which marked the restoration of the Ottoman constitution, the end of the sultan's autocratic rule, and the beginning of an era of pluralism and freedom of speech. During 1908, some fifteen newspapers appeared in Palestine, heralding the new era, while some thirty-four newspapers were in existence by World War I.[19] Although individual newspapers were smaller and less developed than those emanating from the more cosmopolitan and larger cities of Cairo, Beirut, Damascus, and Alexandria, Ami Ayalon's meticulous study of the Arabic press shows that they circulated far beyond their place of production.[20] Already before World War I, the newly founded Arabic press in Palestine expressed its indignation toward Zionism, settlements, and the idea of Palestine as a Jewish homeland. An even livelier press emerged following the war, in which opposition to Zionism remained a central theme, together with resentment toward the British Mandate. The transition from weekly newspapers to daily ones following the crisis of 1929 gave the press an even more prominent and stronger voice in mobilizing the reading public in the nationalist struggle.[21] At the same time, however, the two most important Palestinian newspapers, *Filastin* and *al-Difaʿ*, both issued in Jaffa, promoted the idea that Palestine was "modern" and had a place in the modern world by running advertisements for "the most important accoutrements of modern life," including items of clothing, household furniture, electric goods, and automobiles. Although Mark LeVine claims that these advertisements were marketed to members of the elite bourgeois in Jaffa,[22] the fact that these newspapers were distributed throughout Palestine meant that these notions of modernity extended far beyond the confines of the middle and upper classes in Jaffa. As Ayalon has argued, the Arabic press in Palestine was transmitted orally in public spaces, such as the local coffee shops,[23] where illiterate members of the urban and rural population were exposed to nationalist and modernist ideals to which the underprivileged may have also aspired.

Women's roles and gender issues also were discussed on the pages of the Palestinian press, reflecting the women's awakening (*al-nahda al-nisaʾiyya*), the flourishing discussion of women's roles that Baron brought to our attention in her work on the Egyptian women's press. The women's awakening articulated both progress of and possibility for women in both the national and domestic spheres, which took place throughout the region at the end of the nineteenth century, and continued through the twentieth century. Although existent issues of *al-Nafaʾis al-ʿasriyya*, one of the first Palestinian periodicals to be published in 1909,[24] discussed the women's awakening, it was only after the war and on the pages of the daily newspapers that a regular discourse about women in Palestine appeared. According to Fleischmann, the 1920s should be seen as the beginning of the "virtual outpouring of heated, contentious articles on gender issues."[25] The Haifa-based *al-Karmil* and Jaffa's *Filastin* both published regular columns about women for its readers, as did the Haifa newspaper *al-Nafir* and the short-lived Jerusalem newspaper *al-Hayat*, which appeared only in 1931. In particular, these newspapers articulated the significance of girls' education both to being modern and to building the nation. The press followed and praised the accomplishments and achievements of educated women in both the West and the East, particularly those who challenged gender norms and entered previously all-male spheres and professions.[26] For example, *Filastin* wrote that "the awakened woman in Egypt and Beirut has formed organizations and published newspapers and spoken in clubs and gatherings, all for advancing her cause, and the result of her awakening has been that public opinion in Egypt and Lebanon has begun to sympathize with her cause," while it added that "the Palestinian woman is almost ready to show her true colors."[27] Palestinian women were praised for their scholastic abilities, in particular, with the press publishing the names of female graduates from specific schools each year, most likely penned by the schools themselves in order to advertise their achievements.[28] From the end of 1929 onward, marked by an Arab women's congress in Jerusalem and the subsequent creation of the Arab Women's Association, which enabled women to engage in nationalist activities,[29] the press began to run articles about women's "firsts," that is, records of the first-time accomplishments of individual Arab women inside and outside of Palestine. Fleischmann posits that these were attempts to construct a "positive, active image of the 'modern' (elite) Arab woman," with both journalists and women themselves "acutely aware of Western, negative portrayals of Arab women as backward and degraded."[30] Yet, in parallel to the press's emphasis on the first-time accomplishments of individual women, the women's columns urged female readers to devote themselves to their husbands, children, and homes.

This discourse of domesticity manifested the triad of nationalism, modernity, and girls' education. This was illustrated well by the discussion of breast feeding in a number of newspapers published in Palestine. Mother's milk was described as the "best nourishment," and a "total natural meal," as well as being essential to the child's health.[31] *Al-Karmil* asserted that mother's milk transferred the positive traits of the mother to the child, and helped to shape the child's character. One article associated nursing with the nation, stating that a mother "nurses her son with the milk of love for the nation," while another connected nursing with creating a stable family life, considered key to building the nation.[32] Women were told to adhere to strict feeding schedules and to nurse their babies only according to specific times, which varied by author.[33] Similarly, they were urged to begin weaning their infants anytime between five and nine months, much earlier than the two years prescribed in the Qur'an.[34] The underlying message was that many Palestinian women did not breast-feed their children, but rather had begun to use animal milk as well as powdered formulas, such as Nestlé, a British infant formula advertised in the local Arabic newspapers.[35]

Girls' education was pivotal to discussions about motherhood. Their education was seen as having the potential to transform the family so that it could meet both modern and nationalist expectations. As Pollard writes within the context of colonial Egypt, it was "in the classroom [that] the habits and customs of modernity were shaped, the sins of the domicile purged, and the mores of the new nation articulated."[36] Schools would produce "reformed, educated, rational" mothers, who were constructed as essential to raising boys who would be able to run the affairs of the state along modern lines. According to Pollard, "women's education became a project not only of creating educated, literate women but of producing mothers who could lead the home and national family into a new era."[37] Although these visions of girls' education were created by both elite, upper-class men and women, they were not just restricted to them; the vision of teaching girls to be proper and nationalist mothers was extended to all social classes.

The opening of girls' schools in the late Ottoman period and through the British Mandate did not develop in a vacuum; rather, it had its foundations in the indigenous form of schooling known as the *kuttab* (pl. *katatib*), which throughout the late nineteenth and early twentieth centuries was condemned as being a pre-modern, antiquated institution. Originating in the early Islamic periods of the Umayyads and Abbasids, the *katatib* provided children with religious training, rudimentary knowledge, and religious socialization. Most *katatib* were composed of a single teacher, usually an elderly male religious scholar, who taught the basics of reading, writing, arithmetic, and religion. Pupils completed their studies as soon as they could recite the Qur'an from memory (*hifz*), a feat that was marked with a public ceremony of recognition.[38] Often located near the local mosque, or in the home of the teacher, the *katatib* were supported financially by the *awqaf*, properties endowed for religious, educational, or charitable purposes for the benefit of the Muslim population, thus giving them a prominent position within Muslim communal life. Although the *katatib* provided generations with a basic education and knowledge of Islam, attempts to replace them with modern schools led to their neglect within the historiography of the region. Moreover, as Ami Ayalon has noted, many autobiographical accounts have depicted learning in the *kuttab* as a rather unpleasant experience, with authors recalling poorly trained teachers, dilapidated physical conditions, the difficult task of having to commit the Qur'an to memory, and the frequent use of corporeal punishment with the teacher beating the soles of the pupils' feet with a cane.[39]

Although the *katatib* were aimed primarily at young boys, there is anecdotal evidence that girls also attended them. In a middle-class neighborhood of Cairo in the late nineteenth century, Edward Lane observed girls in a local

A kuttab *in al-Bireh, early twentieth century. Note the little girls sitting in the back.*
From the Prints & Photographs Division, Library of Congress, LC–DIG–ppmsca–10621.

kuttab, where they sat separately from their male peers and refrained from
interacting with them.[40] The famous Egyptian singer Umm Kulthum also
attended a *kuttab* with her older brother in their small village along the Nile
south of Cairo, along with a few other girls, around 1910.[41] There is also some
indication that separate girls' schools, funded by the *awqaf,* existed as early
as the sixteenth century in Anatolia and in the larger cities throughout the
Ottoman Empire by the eighteenth century,[42] suggesting sufficient demand
for gender-segregated education for girls. In the Shiʻa cities of Iraq, rudimentary *katatib* for girls from the middle strata were established during the
Ottoman period so that they could learn to read the story of Husayn ibn ʻAli
in the battle of Karbala, who became the first Shiʻa martyr.[43] This evidence,
although far from complete, suggests that girls' formal education was already
in existence by the time the Ottoman state and the missionaries began to set
up their schools during the nineteenth century.

We do have evidence that some girls were educated in informal settings.
Using al-Sakhawi's biographical dictionary of leading figures of the fifteenth-
century Mamluk period, Jonathan P. Berkey found that young girls from
families of ulama, Muslim religious scholars, were taught by fathers, brothers,
or grandfathers, or were allowed to sit in on lectures or private teaching circles
in the mosques, although they were excluded from the *madrasa,* the institution of higher religious learning.[44] As Berkey argues, the ulama "took special
care to educate their female offspring," aware that all Muslims, both men and
women, had to be cognizant of religious practices and behaviors in order to
maintain their community's well-being. Moreover, the ulama recognized the

importance of providing young girls with knowledge that regulated women's rituals, hygienic practices, and purity.[45] By the nineteenth century, this practice had altered somewhat, with upper-class Muslim families hiring unrelated male and female tutors to teach their daughters in the privacy of their homes. Huda Sha'arawi (b. 1879), the future leader of Egyptian feminism, was tutored in Arabic, Turkish grammar, and calligraphy by Arab religious scholars, while she learned French and piano from an Italian woman. As the daughter of a wealthy provincial notable, and whose mother was from the Turco-Circassian elite, Sha'arawi's upper-class social status dictated that she be kept out of the public eye and remain in the harim;[46] thus private tutoring in her home was most suitable. In contrast, the hiring of European women to serve as private tutors in foreign languages, arts, and music also evoked notions of modernity deemed crucial to upper-class identity at the time.[47] In contrast, middle-class pubescent girls who had reached the age of marriage were often apprenticed to older local women, known as *mu'allimat* (teachers), who taught the intricacies of domestic arts, including embroidery and sewing,[48] as this was thought to give them better chances of getting married. John H. Melkon Rose, for example, tells how his aunt, along with other Armenian girls in late Ottoman Jerusalem, studied for a few months with a woman who trained them in needlework and cooking in preparation for married life.[49]

By the early twentieth century, it was no longer enough for young girls to be educated by mature, knowledgeable older women, male tutors, or within the *kuttab*. Rather, the political circumstances in the nineteenth century, the growing western economic presence within the Ottoman Empire, loss of territory to Europe, and the discontent felt among many religious and ethnic minorities, all of which were perceived as threats to the Empire's unity, propelled a series of reforms intended to modernize and strengthen the Empire. The creation of a network of state-supported schools was part of these reforms, with the idea that schools would not only educate the Empire's youth, but also indoctrinate them to be loyal citizens, unified by a shared Ottoman identity.[50] The vast distance of the Arab provinces from the Empire's center and the linguistic and ethnic diversity between its Arab and Turkic provinces, however, meant that notions of local patriotism, that is, an almost innate identification with the place in which people lived and to their immediate surroundings, were also nurtured.[51] What Benedict Anderson has argued for print capitalism, namely the production of an imagined kinship and sense of belonging to a greater collective through the medium of the printed language,[52] can also be said of education. The provision of schools, together with the curricula, school celebrations, alumni associations, school sports, and so forth, all provided a means for creating national identification and "imagined" communities.[53] In addition to cultivating loyalty and a shared identity, the Ottoman state schools sought to imbue a kind of modernity among its people, especially in the face of western Orientalism that portrayed the Empire as backward and far from being "modern." Yet this modernity did not mean secularism, as Benjamin C. Fortna has convincingly argued, as Islam remained a central component in shaping Ottoman education, identity, and modernity, and played a significant role in binding together the citizens of the Empire.[54]

The Ottoman state schools were established as missionary schools throughout the region also began to develop. Scholars of gender and colonialism in particular have focused on the British and American Protestant missions and their provision of education to Arab girls throughout the region. The missions especially were a site where issues of gender and modernity, as well as questions of religious and national identity, collided.[55] Some scholars have also explored the French, Italian, and German Catholic orders, all of which had a strong presence in the region and created popular schools and health clinics.[56] Much of the existent literature on missionary education tends to focus on the provision of education to the Christian communities, among whom American and British missionaries especially hoped to convert from what they considered to be "nominal" Christianity, whose religious practices they found "appalling," "ossified," and "backward," to a more "correct" form of Christianity, namely Protestantism.[57] In contrast, it seems that the failure of the missionaries to convert Muslims to Christianity also has been construed as their inability to provide education to the Muslim community, an idea that Heather Sharkey refutes in her important study of the activities of the Church Missionary Society among Muslims in Sudan.[58] Sharkey's additional work on Christian missions in Egypt as well as that of Mahmoud Haddad on the responses of Muslim intellectuals and religious reformers to missionaries in nineteenth- and twentieth-century Syria shed light on the need to examine those communities where the missionaries may not have been successful in conversion, but were accomplished at educating.[59]

While the focus of works on missionary education has raised questions about identity, the scholarship on education during the British Mandate over Palestine has emphasized the nationalist struggle between British colonial officials and the local population for control of their education.[60] Several scholars have argued the role of boys' education in Palestine, as in the works on the Arab Government College, the male teachers' training institution established by the British in 1918 in Jerusalem, as being central to the nationalist narratives of Palestine.[61] Unlike in other higher schools in Palestine, Arabic rather than English was the language of instruction, and it had an all-Arab staff, including known educators Khalil Totah and Ahmad Samih al-Khalidi. *Preparing the Mothers of Tomorrow* complements these works, while acknowledging the suggestion of Julia Clancy-Smith to reconsider "approaches to, and narratives of, education in the colonial context which only view the question through an institutional and national—indeed merely a nationalist—lens," as it has tended to privilege the education of upper-class boys. Her argument is that scholars have downplayed girls' education as well as educational experiments, as they "do not fit neatly into the nationalist trajectory; thus they have been consigned to collective forgetfulness."[62] Yet as this book posits, girls' education was just as central to Palestinian nationalism as it was to modernity.

Although both Christian and Muslim girls in Palestine were the beneficiaries of education, *Preparing the Mothers of Tomorrow* focuses on the provision of girls' education to the Muslim majority. Palestine's Muslim and Christian populations often lived in the same neighborhoods, shared many of the same norms and customs, and worked together politically in the nationalist struggle; the differences arose, however, when it came to schooling. While the Ottoman state provided education for the Muslim majority population throughout the Empire, it recognized the Empire's non-Muslim minority communities as autonomous religious communities, and gave them the right to control their own religious, judicial, and administrative matters, including education. Known as the *millet* system,[63] this gave rise to separate education for various religious communities throughout the Middle East. Although highly critical of the Ottoman rule, the British continued to apply the *millet* system to the non-Muslim denominations in Palestine, while they assumed responsibility for the Muslim majority, including the provision of education. Thus, the educational opportunities open to Muslim girls tended not to be the same as those available to Christian girls in Palestine, with the exception of the missionary schools and a single government teachers' college where there was some overlap between the Muslim and Christian populations.

This book also seeks to correct the idea that Muslim girls were less likely to be educated than their Christian counterparts, an idea that has shaped the historiography, even though Islam and its canons affirm the right of Muslim women to be educated. This idea was rooted in the West's representation of the East as inferior, downtrodden, and in need of controlling and taming as a means of asserting its dominance and power. Orientalism, which shaped the writings and images produced by travelers, missionaries, photographers, and British officials alike, cast Muslim women as idle and "shackled," while Christian women were portrayed as being more free, liberated, and receptive to modernity.[64] Palestinians themselves were not immune to this way of thinking. Muhammad Bahjat and Muhammad Rafiq al-Tamimi, educated Palestinians who were also officials of the Ottoman administration, expressed an "internalized form of Orientalism"[65] in their important survey of the Beirut province on the eve of World War I, in which they differentiated between Muslims and non-Muslims. Upon visiting the mixed town of Safad in Palestine, they remarked that the Muslims there were "indifferent to matters of education, while the non-Muslim peoples, they are more enlightened and awakened as in other places."[66]

As a result of this dichotomizing between Arab Christians and Muslims, an educational hierarchy was created. The official publications of the Department of Education during the British Mandate, for example, regarded missionary schools as the apex of education, which catered primarily, although not exclusively, to the Christian population, while the same reports described the schools primarily attended by Muslim children, namely the British-administered government schools and the locally founded institutions, as being of lower standards and encountering difficulties because of the population they served.[67] Even if some of the missionary schools were better schools, I argue that this hierarchy of education has caused a lopsided understanding of education, in which we know far more about the missionary schools and their pupils, who came primarily from Christian denominations, than about the educational opportunities of the Muslim majority. This hierarchy also helped to efface the *kuttab* from the historiography because of its association with "non-modern," rote methods, with the *kuttab* only recently being reconsidered by scholars.[68]

The prevailing notion that the missionary schools were the best schools has also contributed to the relative scholarly neglect of locally initiated private schools founded throughout the late Ottoman and British administrations. Demands to control education and create schools free of foreign, government, and/or religious influence were one of the main forces driving the establishment of these schools. The pioneering works by Donald J. Cioeta and Martin Strohmeier have shown that these schools in late Ottoman Beirut emphasized a modern education appropriate to the needs of the local people, which included instruction in their own religious rites as well as in the Arabic language, mirroring Arab demands for self-determination and sovereignty.[69] Similarly, Rashid Khalidi has highlighted the role that several of the privately founded boys' schools in Palestine played in shaping local patriotic and Muslim identities.[70] As this book shows, locally initiated schools in Palestine transcended issues of social class in the name of nationalist and religious unity, while also adding gender to the equation.

Little attention has been given to Islam as a factor in girls' education despite its prominence in Palestinian nationalist politics. The Supreme Muslim Council (SMC), appointed in 1922 by the British colonial administration, oversaw the affairs of the Muslim community, and used Islam as a means to gain supporters. Controlling the *awqaf,* or religious endowments, the Supreme Muslim Council restored *al-haram al-sharif,* the third most important site within Islam, home to the al-Aqsa Mosque and Dome of the Rock, in addition to its many other projects benefitting the Muslim population. By the 1930s, the SMC began to portray the struggle for Palestine not only as a nationalist struggle, but also as a religious one.[71] The popularity of Muslim preacher 'Izz al-Din al-Qassam, who mobilized Palestinian villagers in the revolt of 1936–1939 against both British and Zionist targets, also gave Islam political legitimacy.[72] Islam, alongside nationalism, also played a decisive role in shaping the identities of young Muslim boys in Jerusalem's Rawdat al-ma'arif School, founded in 1906 by members of Jerusalem's ulama, and later administered by the Supreme Muslim Council.[73] As I argue in chapter three, Islam was equally significant in shaping relations between teachers and their female pupils in Palestine's two Anglican schools and in complicating issues of identity. In chapter four, I continue to examine identity within a private Muslim girls' school in Jerusalem.

As this book shows, especially in chapters one and two, this new modern education for girls remained circumscribed by class, religion, and geographic location. Disparities existed between urban and rural areas, with towns enjoying access to girls' education far more than villages. Religion also shaped access to education. Members of the Christian communities in Palestine had not only greater opportunities for education than the Muslim majority, but access to a higher level of education. Ayalon posits that "Christian institutions were wealthier and better equipped, their teachers more numerous and better trained, and they often enjoyed the powerful backing of a mother organization abroad."[74] As a result, Christian girls were the main beneficiaries of secondary and post-secondary female education, while for the majority of Muslim girls, their education came to an end after, at most, six or seven years of elementary education if they lived in the cities, and three or four years in the villages. Although some of the Muslim upper and middle class sent their daughters to a few years of post-elementary school as it became available, for the majority, regardless of social strata, elementary education was considered sufficient, as their chances of advancing to secondary school and beyond were circumscribed by gender norms, economic considerations, and the sociopolitical reality of Palestine during this time period.

Certainly by the end of the Mandate period, however, girls' education in Palestine had become a means of social mobility for mainly middle class and even lower-middle-class families. Rashid Khalidi has made a similar argument for the rising middle classes in Ottoman Syria, who saw the development of modern boys' schools as a vehicle for their advancement. Just as boys' education gave rise to new professions that had previously been unknown in the region, namely medicine, pharmacy, law, and journalism,[75] so did girls' education. I contend in the final two chapters that girl's education in Palestine, even though it aimed to create modern mothers, also opened doors for non-elite Muslim women to pursue careers primarily in teaching, as well as other occupations, in addition to giving rise to social, charitable, and political associations of primarily upper- and middle-class women.

Chapter 1

Educating Girls in Late Ottoman Palestine

The literary journal *al-Nafaʾis al-ʿasriyya*, published by Khalil Baydas, was one of the earliest publications in Palestine. It first appeared in January 1909, several months after the Young Turk Revolution of July 1908 and the reinstatement of the Ottoman constitution, an era characterized by promises of press freedom, educational reform, and equality.[1] In April 1911, *al-Nafaʾis al-ʿasriyya* published an article, by a writer with the initials Kh. S, most likely referring to the renowned Arabic teacher, educator, and inspector of schools, Khalil al-Sakakini. The article took the form of a dialogue between a woman and her servant, a situation that on its own raises questions of authority. The two discuss the problems of the available schools throughout Greater Syria, which included Palestine, as well as the importance of girls' education.

> Servant: What is your news today, oh Juhaina?
>
> Juhaina: I have all kinds of news. Which especially do you want?
>
> Servant: Give me what you have concerning our national (*wataniyya*) schools.
>
> Juhaina: You already have played a melancholy tune . . . What a great sorrow it is that we see our youth being trained to love everything that is foreign. The Jesuit schools and other French schools teach sciences in French while the American schools teach them in English and so forth. Every language is spreading in our country except for Arabic. You will see that the best of our young men is not good at expressing his ideas in the language of his land. How can he contribute if he is a stranger in his language and a stranger to the ideas, the aspirations, and nationalism? Because the one who studies in the language of his people will share their thoughts and aspire to their aspirations . . . he will yearn for their nationalism . . . There-

fore, you will find most of our Syrian people are foreigners, all foreigners. Foreigners in their language, in their thoughts, in their nationalism, in their food, their clothing, their belongings, and all the rest. They have no nationalism except their names.

Servant: But the blessing of our national schools, oh Juhaina, is that they revive without a doubt the nationalist character and the Arabic language because it is for these aims they were established.

Juhaina: I have visited these schools one by one . . . all of them are imitations, and not nationalist in the meaning that we understand, but rather, they devote most attention to foreign languages. If the nationalists want these schools to do a real service, they must encourage them to change their ways and return to strengthening the Arabic language in order to give these schools a nationalist character for which they will be known, especially when these schools show concern for the morals of the pupils and prepare them to be the men of the future . . .

Juhaina: And you, what is your opinion [of the girls' schools], oh Servant?

Servant: If only most of the girls' schools among us were forward thinking, then I would be proud of them.

Juhaina: What do you mean by that?

Servant: I mean that our girls' schools rarely are concerned with properly preparing the girl so that she can undertake a future profession. The medical schools encourage their pupils to be doctors, and the engineering schools graduate their pupils in the art of engineering. . . . As for our girls' schools, they do not take into consideration the future profession of the girl and prepare her for it. You will see that the hundreds of our girls who graduate from school are limited in knowledge . . . The woman raises her children and is their teacher and her home creates the men of the future and his women. How can she prepare men who are enlightened about the nation when she does not learn this art in school? If only the Syrian girls' schools had begun a long time ago by teaching the art of household management and teaching the girls how to care for their homes and how to raise their children, we already would have among us a proficient number of women doctors. . . . As for their education, it is limited to languages, the piano, handicrafts, and the principles of some of the luxury sciences which the pupils forget once they leave the door of the school . . .

Juhaina: So what is the remedy for this malady?

Servant: The curative remedy is to create nationalist schools whose first goal will be to prepare girls, teaching them the rules that they will need, and to train them in managing the house and educating the men in the school of the home before the school of the teacher. As for the foreigners, they are not concerned with what concerns us, and we do not have to ask them to plant nationalist principles in the minds of our sons and daughters . . .[2]

The above dialogue was typical of this period; similar arguments could be found in neighboring journals throughout the region, particularly in Cairo and Beirut. What makes this article significant is that it is one of the earliest existent discussions of girls' education within the nascent Palestinian press, and by 1911, it reflected many of the problems that plagued girls' education in Palestine as well as throughout Greater Syria, to which it refers. In particular, it underscores the important status that the foreign schools, namely the Catholic and Protestant schools, had assumed throughout the region. Moreover, it highlights the linkage between girls' education and their future as mothers, wives, and homemakers, with the implication that uneducated women were incapable of caring for their families. As Pollard has shown in the case of Egypt, the family and domestic life had become central to the discourse about education in British-ruled Egypt, just as it had in late Ottoman Palestine.

The above dialogue also emphasizes a growing interest in "nationalist" schools, that is, schools that manifested the desire for cultural and political independence of the Arab provinces, including Palestine. Although nationalist schools specifically for girls did not fully develop in Palestine until the British Mandate, the fact that they were mentioned already in the late Ottoman period indicated a real concern that the popularity of the Catholic and Protestant schools, especially among girls, would produce generations of Arabs who did not know Arabic and who knew little about their own cultures and history. Moreover, demands for nationalist schools and the lack of reference to the Ottoman government schools underlined the deep dissatisfaction with the government-funded schools, particularly in the years following the Young Turk Revolution. This chapter examines the growing availability of education for Muslim girls in late Ottoman Palestine, through the Young Turk Revolution and culminating with World War I. During this period, girls were no longer circumscribed to being educated informally or in the rudimentary *kuttab* school, but had access to foreign Christian schools and Ottoman-funded education, as the future of the modern nation was increasingly linked to providing formal domestic education for young girls.

FOREIGN SCHOOLS IN THE SERVICE
OF EVANGELIZATION

From the mid-nineteenth century onward, hundreds of Christian missionaries, belonging to numerous and diverse Catholic orders and Protestant missions, arrived in Palestine where they engaged in spiritual, educational, welfare, and medical work. The Catholic orders, dominated by the French, were motivated by the anti-clerical atmosphere in post-revolutionary France.[3] The Catholic orders first came to Palestine and to other parts of the Ottoman Empire in the mid-nineteenth century in order to spiritually nurture and protect the indigenous Latin Catholics, following the reinstatement of the Latin Patriarch in Jerusalem, a position that had been abrogated for five hundred years.[4] Unlike the Catholic orders that had ties to the local Latin churches, the various Protestant missions were inspired by a religious and evangelical fervor taking place in their home countries. At midcentury, they arrived in Palestine and other parts of the world eager to spiritually convert the "heathens" as well as to transform their societies, which they characterized as "primitive" and "backward," and in need of enlightening. The majority of the Protestant missions worked among Christians from the Eastern churches, whose practices they deemed unorthodox, and whose Christianity was seen as only nominal. By the late nineteenth century, many of the Anglo-American Protestant missions also began to express an increasing interest in serving the Muslim population.[5] From 1864 onward, however, the Ottoman government issued a policy that allowed them only to settle and open schools in places with a considerable Christian population, thus severely limiting their access to predominantly Muslim towns and villages.[6]

Members of the Greek Orthodox Church were especially receptive to the Catholic and Protestant schools and other institutions, as their own struggle to Arabize the church, especially its Hellenic-dominated clerical hierarchy, had created a situation where the majority of Arab Orthodox boycotted their own church, with the exception of using it in an official capacity for baptisms, marriages, and funerals.[7] Until the end of the century, the Greek Orthodox Church did little to advance the education of its constituency,[8] which further alienated the people from the church; as a result, Greek Orthodox children had little choice but to attend Protestant and Catholic schools, with many leaving the church in the process. The absence of schools within the Greek Orthodox community, compounded with the frustration at the clerical hierarchy, led to the church's decline; while in 1847, the Greek Orthodox formed 90 percent of the Christian population in Palestine, by 1880, they were only 67 percent.[9]

Both the Catholic orders and the Protestant missions identified indigenous women and girls as the primary target of their missions. As Fleischmann has argued in her work on American Protestant mission schools in Syria, indigenous women were seen as being particularly susceptible to religious teachings, because of innate characteristics such as compassion, sensitivity, and nurturing. Their role as mothers was recognized as an important pillar of missionary ideology, which linked "proper mothering" with the ability to nurture Christian ideals as well as morality in the next generation.[10] That is, women, if trained to be "proper wives and mothers," were the key to transforming the home, both spiritually and physically. Rosa E. Lee, who was involved in the Quaker Friends' Mission in Palestine, wrote before World War I that "there is not much hope for a nation if its women are kept in ignorance and degradation . . . One of the best ways to overcome such conditions is to place the child in a healthy Christian home."[11] Schools, along with welfare and medical work, thus became essential components in the missionary project of instructing girls and women in creating the "healthy Christian home." According to Fleischmann, the missionaries saw their schools as having the role of "taming" the girls, and removing them from their familiar Arab culture, deemed improper, to what was seen as a more appropriate, westernized environment within the walls of the schools.[12]

Targeting women as the subject of their mission was facilitated, if not motivated, by the large number of western women who found a place for themselves in both women's Catholic orders that were created in the early part of the nineteenth century and in the Protestant missions, which began to accept single, unmarried female missionaries from the 1860s onward.[13] By the end of the nineteenth century, more women were engaged in Protestant missionary work than men,[14] with Willy Jansen having made similar claims for Catholic women's orders in the Middle East.[15] A number of factors contributed to the increase in women missionaries. Like men, women also saw themselves as "servants of God," and sought to evangelize throughout the world. As Joan Jacobs Brumberg argued in her work on American missionary women, many of them were middle class, whose lives had developed around their churches and doing charitable work. The development of women's roles within the foreign missions especially was aided by the publishing of missionary journals aimed at middle-class female readers.[16] The entry of women into higher education in both North America and Europe also contributed to the rise of women missionaries; for example, Mount Holyoke Female Seminary in New England, one of the earliest colleges for women, prepared its students exclusively for missionary work overseas.[17] In addition, the development of early feminism and the growing acceptance of travel overseas among the educated middle class also facilitated the entry of female missionaries into the field.[18] Some women saw missionary work as an extension of feminist expression, believing that they were working to uplift native women, while at the same time they were fulfilling their own sense of self by creating a role for themselves in the male-dominated missions. The male-dominated missionary hierarchies, however, continued to see the role of female missionaries as a maternal one, namely that of teaching local native girls.[19] The dominant numerical presence of women in the field, however, enabled them to expand beyond educational work into activities that included industrial workshops, medical clinics, and social welfare, all run by women primarily for women. The expansion into other fields, however, was not always satisfactory; in some cases, women left the organized missions and became independent missionaries, such as Frances E. Newton, who had served as a missionary in an organized mission for twenty-five years, and resigned from her post when her male supervisor refused to let her make decisions because of her gender.[20]

In contrast to the Protestant female missionaries who often felt restricted by the dominant male voices within the missionary organizations, the female Catholic orders in Palestine had the support of the church hierarchy to carry out their work. Monsignor Joseph Valerga, who served as the Latin Patriarch in Jerusalem from 1847 until 1872, and his successor Monsignor Vincent Bracco, both saw the French Catholic women's orders as key to revitalizing the Latin church in Palestine, and recognized girls' schools as essential to strengthening the local parishes.[21] The Sisters of St. Joseph of Apparition (*Rahibat mar yusuf*) were the first to arrive in 1848, having previously worked in Algeria and Larnaca. Between 1848 and 1905, with the financial assistance of the Latin Patriarch, the Sisters established schools, orphanages, and medical clinics in Jerusalem, Jaffa, Bethlehem, Ramallah, Ramla, Bayt Jala, Nazareth, Nablus, and Abu Ghosh. In 1855, they were joined by the Sisters of Notre Dame de Sion (*Rahibat siyyun*), who set up schools in Jerusalem, Nazareth, Haifa, Acre, and Shefa 'Amr. Another order, the Sisters of Notre Dame de Nazareth (*Rahibat al-nasira*), also arrived in 1855; their work was centered initially in Nazareth, and later expanded to Haifa, Shefa 'Amr, and Acre between 1858 and 1864, and to Tarshiha in 1946.[22]

Whereas the Catholic missions had the financial and moral support of the Latin Patriarch, facilitating the establishment of schools and other institutions that continue until this day, the early Protestant missions struggled to establish themselves in Palestine as well as elsewhere throughout the Empire. The lack of an infrastructure that they encountered upon first arriving in the region meant that their first attempts at creating schools were irregular and ephemeral at best, pioneered by wives of the early missionaries.[23] Missionary

Henry Harris Jessup tells about a Mrs. Whiting, the wife of an early missionary to Jerusalem, who in 1834 and 1835 gathered a dozen or two Muslim girls in her home to instruct them in reading and sewing. Mrs. Whiting, in a letter sent to Jessup, wrote that although the local women were accessible and hospitable toward her, they were reluctant initially to place their daughters under her instruction. Jessup implies that the families had to be persuaded with financial inducements before they would allow their daughters to study with Mrs. Whiting.[24] Local suspicions and particularly, the distrust of the local clerics, who viewed the Protestant missions as a threat to their religious communities, often undermined their efforts. Jeremy Salt has shown that Eastern churches frequently ordered their followers to avoid interactions with the Protestant missionaries, or face excommunication from the church, which would translate into social and economic anathema in particularly close-knit communities.[25] Rumors that the missionaries had "evil designs," including the kidnapping of young girls to serve as concubines in the Ottoman harim or to be sent off to the West,[26] not only served as implicit critiques of those families who chose to send their daughters to missionary schools, but also stirred up fears among local residents, who questioned the intentions of the missionaries in working among young girls and women.

Not having the support of a local church hierarchy as the Catholic orders did, the Protestant missions developed methods for winning the trust of the local population. One way was by requiring the missionaries to learn Arabic in order to interact and work with the local population in their own language, as emphasized by Jessup. Another method was the hiring of Arab women, both local and non-local, to work as "native teachers," nurses, and as "Bible readers" in their institutions. Both the London-based Society for Promoting Female Education in the East (SPFEE)[27] and the Church Missionary Society (CMS)[28] hired Arab women who had been educated in early Protestant schools to work as teachers in their schools.[29] As Murre-van den Berg notes, "These women have played important but largely undocumented roles in the spread of evangelical modernity in the Middle East."[30] These women represented a model for young Arab girls of women who had been transformed from "heathens" or nominal Christians into believing Protestants. By employing local Protestant women and by using Arabic as the language of instruction, both the schools of the SPFEE and the CMS presented an image of being "less foreign" and more indigenous.

The decision of the SPFEE and CMS to focus their efforts in providing schools to more rural parts of Palestine was replete with obstacles that the urban-based Catholic schools did not face. Frances Newton, who served as a missionary with the CMS, and whose job was to supervise ten village schools in the Nazareth area, wrote that the difficulties of getting young girls especially to attend school were great. The schools adopted the practice of providing "a gift of a print frock to each village child once a year. It encouraged good attendance, for village life makes demands on a child's time."[31] That is, in the villages, households were heavily dependent upon their daughters to perform daily chores, which caused their tardiness or overall absence from school. This was in contrast to girls from the urban upper- and even middle-class families who hired household help, usually men and women from neighboring villages.[32] Village schools also closed their doors during the harvesting season, with Newton writing that "this is the most important moment of the year . . . whole families leave their village homes and camp in the plains for weeks at a time."[33] The reality of the villages took its toll on many of the schools. As Tibawi pointed out, "outside Jerusalem, it was difficult to organize schools for girls,"[34] because there were few trained or capable women teachers at that time, but also because of the role that girls and young women were expected to fulfill within their households. According to a report by a German missionary, however, some girls' schools outside of Jerusalem were relatively successful at attracting pupils, including Muslim ones. The CMS school in Nablus, for example, reportedly was attended by fifty girls, half of whom were said to have been Muslim; a CMS school in Gaza, then a small town of 2,000 Muslims and only a small minority of Greek Orthodox, had fifty to seventy Muslim girls enrolled.[35] Similarly, a missionary doctor and a longtime foreign resident of Nazareth claimed before World War I that nearly all the educated Muslim girls in that town had attended the CMS day schools.[36]

Like the CMS, the English and American Quakers' Society of Friends opened a successful girls' school in Ramallah in 1869, followed by some in nearby villages. According to local lore, a young teenage girl, Maryam Karam, encountered a Quaker missionary couple in the street and asked them to open a school for girls. When asked who would teach in the school, Karam declared that she would, as she had been educated for three years at the German Protestant Talitha Kumi School in Jerusalem. In 1889, the American Society of Friends assumed full responsibility for the schools in the Ramallah area, and transformed the existing girls' school into the Girls' Training Home, a boarding school, whose first class was composed of twelve girls. By 1912, the school had expanded not only in number, but also had fee-paying students, indicating the growing acceptance of the school by the local population. The aims of the school were to provide a Christian religious education according to Quaker beliefs; to train girls to become teachers; and to improve the health and domestic conditions of the villages, in addition to teaching the geography and history of Palestine. The Training Home had strict entrance requirements, requiring certificates from former schools, and the passing of an entrance exam, apparently in order to attract only the brightest pupils.[37]

The Girls' Training Home educated some 140 girls between 1889 and 1909, with the average stay being five years. The high-level entrance requirements and the school's location in Ramallah, rather than in the more populous Jerusalem, may have limited the enrollment. Of the 140 girls in the school at the end of the nineteenth century, 45 were from Ramallah, 33 were from Jerusalem, 12 from outside of Palestine, and the remainder from other parts of Palestine. Until after World War I, most of the girls at the Friends School were Greek Orthodox, Protestant, or Catholic, reflecting the religious composition of the town and the surrounding villages.

Toward the end of the nineteenth century, the American Quaker Friends also opened day schools in several villages in the area of Ramallah, following the success of the Girls' Training Home. The village day schools were all run by graduates of the boarding school, and were entirely conducted in Arabic, in contrast to the school in Ramallah, where the language of instruction was English. Mornings were spent learning basic reading, writing, arithmetic, and scriptures, while the afternoons were devoted to gender-specific curricula, with girls learning to sew and embroider, and boys learning English, a coveted language reflecting the growing rise in immigration among men from Ramallah and surrounding villages to North America. Rosa E. Lee, one of the founders of the Quaker mission in Palestine, noted that girls brought their younger siblings to school, having been entrusted to care for them during the day,[38] indicative that the Quaker missionaries were willing to work around what others would have seen as an obstacle in educating village girls.

Lee believed that the real significance of these village schools was not the education, but rather the role that they assumed in transforming children's hygienic habits, writing that "the effect of these day schools is not so much the little book learning which the children receive as the cleanly habits and high ideals which the teachers try to instill into them."[39] Lee noted the decrease in eye infections among children as an example, and linked it to their education and improved hygienic habits. That is, the Quakers, as well as other missionaries who established schools in the villages, saw themselves as having to teach village girls how to be "modern," before they could even consider book learning. As Lee wrote, "In the village . . . every woman went barefooted. Not a single family had plates. All ate from a big bowl with their hands except a few of the richest who had wooden spoons . . . Bedsteads were unknown. All slept on straw mats on the floor."[40] Village education was changing all this;

according to Lee, "a village girl who has been educated in our school is more likely to be given a word or choice as to marriage and with clean, industrious habits formed in the school, she is prepared to make a happier home."[41]

While the Protestants initially based their missions in the more rural areas, the Catholic orders were more urban-based, and focused at first on providing relief through education to impoverished girls from the lower classes. The Sisters of Zion, for example, opened its school in Jerusalem in 1862, taking in a total of twelve pupils.[42] Nearly twenty years later, as Shahin Makarius reported in *al-Muqtataf,* an early Egyptian newspaper, the school had some 150 girls, mainly orphans and impoverished Latin Catholics, who learned French, Arabic, housework, and needlework.[43] The poverty found within the urban areas of Palestine, the terrible health conditions, and the inability of families to support all of their children contributed to the popularity and legitimacy of these schools, especially as they provided poor students with a free education, in addition to food, clothing, and school utensils.[44] By teaching practical skills, these schools enabled young girls to work as domestic help or seamstresses, in attempts to improve their socioeconomic position.

The religious diversity of the urban areas enabled these schools to open in predominantly Christian neighborhoods, without offending the Muslim community, while concurrently they opened their doors to small numbers of Muslim pupils. In the 1870s, the Sisters of Zion decided to establish a separate class for Muslim girls within its school, so that the Muslim girls would not be exposed to undue religious teachings, although the numbers in this class are not known.[45] By the end of the nineteenth century, the Sisters of Zion also ran a boarding school for some twenty-five girls from elite families, among them Greek Orthodox, Armenians, and Protestants, as well as eleven Jews and four Catholics. From time to time, a few girls from Muslim families attended, including the "daughters of the Pacha," revealing the elite social composition of this institution.[46] In 1880, at the age of thirteen, Khadija Hadutha al-ʿAlami entered this school; her father was a shaykh and from one of the prominent Jerusalem Muslim families.[47] Zahiyya Nashashibi, from another Muslim notable family of Jerusalem and active in the Arab Women's Association in the late 1920s and 1930s, also attended the school around World War I.[48] The Sisters of Zion boarding school taught languages, history, geography, math, music, drawing, and embroidery, subjects that had once been taught to girls privately in their own homes, while the pupils were also expected to engage in weekly charitable activities,[49] all suggestive of the school's elite character. As Mona Hajjar Halaby noted in her study of the Sisters of Zion school, Arabic was not part of its upper-class education,[50] reflecting upper-class beliefs that young girls should not know to read and write in Arabic.

The decision of the Catholic orders to open its doors to upper- and middle-class Muslim girls was the result of several factors. French scholar Victor Guérin, who traveled in Palestine several times between the 1850s and 1880s, correctly believed that the differences between Catholics and Muslims were collapsing as "all want to learn French and apply it with ardor."[51] Like elite Christian families, upper- and middle-class Muslim families began to realize that they had to provide their sons and daughters with a modern education in order to maintain their social status. Although most initially sent only their sons to these schools, western-educated sons may have also influenced the enrollment of their sisters and other girls within the private Christian schools. Moreover, competition and rivalry with upper-class Christian families also influenced elite Muslim families to enroll their daughters in the Christian schools, as it was no longer enough to instruct them at home or to send them to primarily Muslim, Ottoman government schools. In her work on Alexandria from the mid-nineteenth century onward, Naguib has argued that elite Muslim families perceived the discipline and morality of the Catholic schools in particular as protecting their daughters against promiscuous behavior, with the nuns being models of upright moral behavior, modesty, self-control, and self-discipline.[52] That is, whereas in the past, elite Muslim families instructed their daughters at home in order to protect their reputations, they could now send their daughters to the Catholic schools. The acquisition of the French language also had a class appeal and was considered an appropriate language for young upper-class girls to learn, mimicking patterns of the upper classes in Europe.[53] Interest in educating Muslim girls was also fueled by competition between the French Catholics and the Protestants themselves, who were actively competing for influence within the same communities.[54]

A number of Protestant missions also created schools in urban areas. In the port city of Jaffa, Jane Walker-Arnott, a Scottish Presbyterian woman, established the Tabeetha Mission School in 1863. Walker-Arnott, who came from an upper-class background, was not trained as a missionary nor was she affiliated with any recognized and organized mission. Considered an independent missionary, she was motivated by religious convictions as well as by the difficult environment of late nineteenth-century Palestine. She commenced her school with fourteen girls in the spring of 1863, and by the following summer, she had fifty-some pupils, most of whom were poor and orphaned. In 1875, with financial support from Thomas Cook and Son, the famous travel agency, she was able to build a new school building, one of the first outside

Girls doing calisthenics at the Tabeetha Mission School in Jaffa, also known as "Miss Arnott's school," end of the nineteenth century. From the Prints & Photographs Division, Library of Congress, LC–DIG–ppmsca–10706.

Jaffa's old city walls.[55] In addition, supporters in England and the United States paid the tuition fees for the girls, while a number of graduating pupils were contracted as teachers and were required to teach for one year upon completing their education. By the end of the century, the "Tabeetha Mission" had expanded significantly to include the "Home school" with forty free boarders and forty paying day pupils from upper-class families, as well as two day schools, one for Muslim girls in the north of Jaffa, and another for Christian girls in the southern part of Jaffa.[56] The fact that elite families began to send their daughters to this school, despite the large number of French Catholic schools in Jaffa, suggests that some members of the elite had begun to sense the importance of learning English, most likely linking it to the peak of British imperialism at the end of the nineteenth century.

Similarly, the Jerusalem and East Mission (J&EM), founded in 1887 by the Anglican Bishop of Jerusalem for advancing Anglican interests in Palestine, established separate schools for both upper- and lower-class girls in Jerusalem. In 1888, it created "St. Mary's Home," a boarding school with the aim "to train a girl socially and religiously, and to fit her to support herself when she leaves school."[57] According to Inger Marie Okkenhaug, St. Mary's Home reportedly started with ten Jewish girls, who received room, board, and clothing free of charge. Threats of excommunication (*herem*) by members of the Jewish community caused many of the Jewish girls to leave the school;[58] they were replaced primarily by Christian girls and a few Muslims. As Okkenhaug points out, the school "had a clear class profile," and sought to attract middle-class girls, from "good families," who could pay the tuition fees, or girls who were on scholarships provided by foreign donors.[59] By 1904, the official publication of the J&EM reported that applications for St. Mary's Home were "constant" from "all parts of Palestine and Syria."[60] By 1911, the school was full, with some thirty boarders who paid ten pounds per year, plus a charge for uniforms, and another twelve day students, who were described as "better class children," who paid two pounds a year; six reportedly were Muslim girls.[61]

Next door, the J&EM ran a separate day school, which provided a gratis education to around one hundred girls, numbering sixty Muslim girls and forty Jewish girls in 1900. According to Okkenhaug, the day school pupils learned reading, writing, and math, in addition to Arabic, English, and needlework, while a "central part of the education was scripture reading, both in Arabic and English," even in the youngest grades.[62] It also offered a class for older girls, focusing on sewing skills, which reportedly "supplied a real want, as it raises the status of a girl (in this country so desirable) if she can earn money by her needle."[63] Although the J&EM occasionally encountered antagonism from both Jewish and Muslim circles, the fact that the day school persisted with its mixed student body suggests that the various communities were not as agitated when daughters of the urban poor were educated in Christian missionary institutions as when upper-class girls were. As Okkenhaug writes also, the fact that the day students did not have to board at the school may have made it more attractive to Muslim families.[64]

While the J&EM appealed to girls from different religious backgrounds, the schools belonging to the Russian mission known as the Imperial Orthodox Palestine Society were an anomaly in the history of Christian schools in Palestine. The Imperial Orthodox Palestine Society was not an evangelizing mission, but rather saw its position as one of safeguarding the Greek Orthodox population in Palestine, and protecting them from the proselytizing efforts of the Catholic and Protestant churches,[65] a position that they could claim by virtue of the capitulations that the Ottomans had made with Russia. The local Greek Orthodox community welcomed the Russian mission, mainly because they were undergoing a process of alienation from their own church over the struggle to Arabize it against the Hellenic clerical hierarchy. By promoting the use of Arabic in their schools, the Imperial Orthodox Palestine Society believed that it would attract pupils and diminish the influence of both the Protestants and the Catholics.[66]

The Russian mission opened schools primarily in Greek Orthodox villages in the Galilee, far from the scrutiny of the church's hierarchy in Jerusalem, and also in villages where Protestant and/or Catholic schools had already opened,[67] reflecting the degree of competition that existed between the various missions. As part of its competition with the Catholic and Protestant missions, the Imperial Orthodox Society also advanced girls' education beyond the primary level by establishing a female teachers' training school in Bayt Jala in 1890, which other missions did not do until well into the Mandate period. Girls entered the school for eight years, graduating between the ages of eighteen and twenty, with one-fifth of the eighty women who had graduated from the school in 1898 having become teachers in the Society's schools.[68] The Mandate government schools as well as the nationalist schools employed a number of women graduates of this seminary, as they were well versed in the Arabic language.

With the exception of the schools run by the Imperial Orthodox Society, most of the Catholic and Protestant mission schools in Palestine did not teach in Arabic, but rather in French, English, Italian, or German. In particular, French language schools were most popular in late Ottoman Palestine, the result of growing economic and commercial ties with France (see Table 1).[69] The Francophone schools in Palestine also steadily grew during the late Ottoman period, increasing from fifteen schools in 1860 to forty-eight in 1912. In 1912, some 3,587 girls reportedly attended French language schools in Jerusalem,[70] while a report issued by the University of St. Joseph before 1915 indicated that some 5,800 girls and 2,400 boys in Jerusalem were enrolled in French Catholic schools,[71] indicating their significant role in promoting education in that town.

From 1908 onwards, with the introduction of the press in Palestine, observers began to question the education of youth in foreign schools. An article in the Jaffa newspaper *Filastin,* about an association that helped orphaned Greek Orthodox girls, proclaimed that although girls' education was a main priority, "we will not be forced to send our children to foreign schools where they teach them foreign customs and persist in rites not like our own."[72] The author was fearful that Palestinian Arab children would forget their own traditions and culture if educated in the Protestant and Catholic schools. A resident of Jaffa warned readers of *Filastin* that "the foreign schools are many and they work at dividing our minds for the sake of knowledge, just as they have divided our kingdom in politics."[73] Outsiders also commented upon what they saw as the dangerous effects of foreign education among Palestinian children. O. Eberhard, a German school inspector who in 1906 had visited a number of schools in Jerusalem, asked, "What is the sense of all this veneer, glittering half education which only creates superficiality and makes the folks unhappy . . . Isn't it better to have good Arabs than bad Europeans?"[74] In the Catholic Frères School, a boys' school in Jerusalem open to all confessions, he found that "all the teaching, except the teaching of Arabic, is conducted

TABLE 1. FEMALE PUPILS IN FOREIGN CHRISTIAN SCHOOLS IN LATE OTTOMAN PALESTINE

Location	School	# Pupils c. 1896	# Pupils 1900/1901
French Schools			
Acre	Sisters of Nazareth	220	250
Shfa Amr	Sisters of Nazareth	150	X
Haifa	Sisters of Nazareth	250	150
Nazareth	Sisters of Nazareth	210	150
Nazareth	Sisters of St. Joseph	110	60
Jerusalem	Sisters of the Rosary	20	X
Jerusalem	Sisters of Zion	187	150
Jerusalem	Sisters of Charity	20	X
Jerusalem	Sisters of St. Joseph	395	120
Bethlehem	Sisters of St. Joseph	445	272
Ramallah	Sisters of St. Joseph	110	X
Jaffa	Sisters of St. Joseph	220	X
Ramleh	Sisters of St. Joseph	70	X
German Schools			
Haifa	German Catholics	X	30
Jerusalem	Talitha Kumi	X	118
Jerusalem	Schmidt's College		
Jerusalem	German orphanage	X	34
English Schools			
Nazareth	English, intermediate	X	98
Nazareth	English, primary	X	83
Acre	English	X	150
Kafr Yasif	English	X	70
Haifa	English	X	150
Nablus	English	X	30
Jaffa	Tabeetha	X	69
Lod	Unspecified Protestant	X	60
Ramla	Unspecified Protestant	X	60

Sources: Data for 1896 from Cuinet, *Syrie Liban et Palestine;* Data for 1900/1901 from *Salname nezaret-i ma'arif 'umumiye,* 1321 (1903).

in French." In this school, Eberhard noted with concern that "the pupils here speak French even during the intermissions,"[75] indicating that the students had been so thoroughly immersed in the French language that they felt more at ease speaking French among themselves than Arabic. Arab-Ottoman officials Tamimi and Bahjat expressed similar concerns that even teachers who were able to teach in Arabic did not inculcate in the pupils any shared nationalist unity, writing that the relationship to "the Ottoman nationalist education" (*al-tarbiyya al-wataniyya al-ʿuthmaniyya*) of several women teachers who had been trained in the schools of the Imperial Orthodox Society "is completely lost."[76]

The popularity of the foreign Christian schools, especially among girls, may have been related to language acquisition. Autobiographies by non-Palestinian, elite Arab women born at the turn of the century indicate that many elite families did not want their daughters to learn *fusha*, the literary Arabic, and often preferred that they learn a foreign language.[77] *Fusha* was seen as the language of men and of public affairs, and inappropriate for girls, especially upper-class girls, to master. One common reason given was that if girls could write in Arabic, then they would pen love letters to neighboring boys; while this concern illustrated the growing fascination with romance and courtship emanating from the West,[78] it also represented a much greater fear that teaching women and girls to read and write Arabic might upset the gendered division between men and women, in addition to providing women with a means to improve their social and political status. Keeping girls and women ignorant of *fusha* was, in Eric J. Hobsbawm's words, "a reminder of their lack of knowledge and power."[79] Little did they understand, however, that it did not matter so much whether or not upper-class girls learned Arabic or a foreign language, as it was their education, and not necessarily the language taught, that provided them with the skills needed to improve their social and political status.

Despite the relative success of the Protestant missions and Catholic orders in promoting girls' education in Palestine, religious antagonism, proselytizing, and cases of conversion within various schools often tarnished their reputations, as well as their relations with the local population. The story of the suicide and attempted suicide of two female boarding students at the English Orphanage in Nazareth in late 1872 and early 1873 led to what Nancy L. Stockdale has called a "dramatic scandal," in which the local Protestant Arab community in Nazareth accused the British headmistress of beating and enslaving the girls, and depriving them of food and water. In the charges that they wrote to both the headmistress and to the SPFEE in London, which administered the school, they also threatened to remove their daughters and place them in the competing Catholic schools.[80] Jansen has claimed a possible link between the scandals in the English Orphanage and sightings of the Virgin Mary a year or two later by Sultane Maryam Ghattas, a young Arab woman from Ayn Karim, who had been educated by the French Catholic Sisters of St. Joseph. Similar to the visions of the Virgin Mary as seen in Lourdes in 1858, the Virgin Mary was said to have called upon Ghattas to establish a native congregation of sisters who would work for girls' education. Jansen suggests that Ghattas's apparitions of Mary should be seen as part of the local Palestinian resentment toward the Protestant missions, magnified by incidents such as the one in Nazareth, as well as the traditional rivalry between the Catholics and Protestants. The appeal to create an indigenous religious female order devoted to girls' education also evinced the dichotomy between foreign education and a local Arab one.[81] These visions of Mary may have also added to the popularity of the French Catholic schools among the local Christian and Muslim population, as both saw Mary (Maryam) as an exemplar and model of piety and obedience.[82]

Similar tensions took place between the missionary schools and the Muslim community, almost always fueled by conversions, however negligible, and rumors of conversion. Jaussen, a French Franciscan cleric and an early ethnologist who had lived in Palestine from the turn of the century onwards, wrote about one such case that shook Nablus at the end of World War I. The Sisters of St. Joseph, who administered a school and medical clinic in Nablus, a town considered conservative and "hostile" to outsiders,[83] were accused of having helped one of their former pupils, a young Muslim woman and the daughter of the head of the town's municipality, to run away from her family. According to Jaussen, the father accused the Sisters of having converted his daughter and of hiding her in the school, where they supposedly dressed her in the habit of a sister in order to disguise her identity; these accusations quickly turning into a local campaign to close the school. When the girl eventually turned up in the Syrian Orphanage in Bethlehem, she admitted that she had been angry at her father for having taken two additional wives, and had run away, but denied receiving any help from the Sisters of St. Joseph. The accusations against the Sisters of St. Joseph need to be understood within the context of suspicions among the Muslim population toward the aims of the Christian schools and the lack of control that parents evidently felt over their children's education; many were published as tracts against the missionary schools circulating throughout the region.[84] These accusations also need to be understood within the context of an ongoing power struggle between the municipality and the Sisters, which began during the First World War, when the municipality unsuccessfully tried to confiscate the building of the Sisters of St. Joseph as "enemy property," and to exile the nuns into Asia Minor.[85]

That a runaway Muslim woman found shelter in an orphanage run by German Protestant Christians was perhaps not exceptional. Already in the 1850s, a number of foreign missionaries began to work among orphans, as well as abandoned and runaway children, by offering them food, shelter, and training. The missions were facilitated by the fact that communal and state structures for dealing with these children were either absent or not entirely functional. The German Protestant Ludwig Schneller founded the Syrian Orphanage in Jerusalem initially for Maronite Christian children who had survived the inter-communal violence of Mount Lebanon in 1860.[86] Missionaries may have seen orphans especially as primary candidates for conversion because of the absence of parental concern and control. 'Abd al-Ra'uf Sannu, in his research on nineteenth-century German Protestant missions in Palestine, posits that Talitha Kumi, a Protestant boarding school founded in 1851 by the German Kaiserwerther Diakonissen in Jerusalem, successfully converted a number of orphaned Muslim students. To avoid creating friction with the authorities or with the Muslim population, Muslim pupils who converted to Christianity were given western names and upon completing their studies, often went to work as domestics in European homes or in other missionary institutions in the region. After 1884, the number of Muslim orphans at Talitha Kumi dropped considerably, as local authorities threatened to punish those who enrolled girls in this school, even if they were needy and orphaned.[87]

Despite the vulnerability of some of the young girls who attended missionary schools, the number of converts to Christianity was minimal. Richter had noted that there were only 30,000 Protestants throughout the entire Middle East in 1908,[88] with most of the converts having belonged to the Eastern churches. Heather Sharkey similarly has claimed that there were very few Muslim converts to Christianity, despite evangelizing attempts by American and English Protestant missionaries from the 1880s onward.[89] While local efforts to thwart the influence of the Catholic orders and Protestant missions played a role in limiting the number of conversions, the relationship between the Ottoman government and the missionaries, which Jeremy Salt has described as being "one of mutual suspicion and mutual dislike,"[90] also was a contributing factor. The Ottoman government imposed restrictions on the missions, many of which played out in the various education laws promulgated in the mid-nineteenth century.

THE OTTOMAN EMPIRE AS AN EDUCATOR STATE

Given Ottoman suspicions and fears toward the foreign Christian schools, by midcentury, the Ottoman government began to take small steps toward promoting state-sponsored education. Following the Crimean war, as a continuation of the reforms that had been inaugurated earlier in the century, the Ottoman state issued the Reform Decree of 1856, which recognized the right of the non-Muslim *millets* to establish their own schools, as long as those schools came under Ottoman supervision.[91] Although this decree denied the *millets* of some of their autonomy, it also spurred the development of additional schools. In particular, these schools were established in response to the growth of the Catholic and Protestant schools and the rising fear within the non-Muslim religious communities that they would lose their young people to the missionary schools through conversion, excessive westernization, or migration. From 1891, for example, the Greek Orthodox Patriarchy in Jerusalem embarked on a policy of establishing schools for its constituency throughout Palestine, so that by the eve of World War I, the church had established some eighty-three schools throughout Palestine,[92] with an all-female *Jam'iyat 'add al-yatimat al-urthudhuksiyyat* (Association for Helping the Orthodox Orphans) in Jaffa financing a handful of Palestinian Greek Orthodox girls to attend schools in Jaffa and Beirut.[93]

In 1869, the Ottoman state issued the ambitious Law of Public Education (*Ma'arif-i 'umumiye nizamnamesi*), although it was only implemented a decade later during the reign of Sultan 'Abdul Hamid II (1876–1909). Under the new law, elementary education was to be compulsory for all children under the age of twelve. Each provincial capital had to organize educational councils for the administration, supervision, and financing of government schools. Every town and village, or at least every two villages, was to have a separate primary (*ibtida'iyya*) school for Muslim children and a separate one for non-Muslims. Village residents were expected to pay for the cost of the school buildings and their upkeep, as well as to cover the teachers' salaries. The four-year curriculum included reading and writing in Turkish, math, sciences, geography, and history, and the relevant religious instruction. Intermediate level schools (*rushdiyya*), providing an additional four years of education for youth between the ages of ten to fifteen, were to be opened in towns with more than 500 homes.[94]

The Law of Public Education officially recognized the need for girls' education, stipulating that primary schools had to be separated by gender if a community could financially support two schools, and if not, schools were to be coeducational.[95] Ahmad Samih al-Khalidi, a Palestinian educator, recalled later that it was not uncommon, at least in the years before World War I, for girls to attend boys' schools at the elementary level, when the number of girls in a given area was too few to justify the establishment of a separate school, or in cases where the conditions simply were not met.[96] The willingness to accommodate mixed-gender schools in many ways originated with the *kuttab*, which also was attended by a minority of girls.

The legislation also recognized that girls should be able to pursue their education beyond the primary level, stipulating that towns had to establish all-female *rushdiyya* schools, which would enable girls to acquire at least an intermediate level education. In addition, government-supported high schools (*i'dadiyya*) were to open in each provincial city, providing an additional three years of education. Unlike the lower-level schools, the *i'dadiyya* level schools were intended to integrate Muslim and non-Muslim pupils. *I'dadiyya* schools for women, however, never materialized; the only exception was a single institution established in Istanbul in 1880, which closed after two years due to low enrollment, and would not reopen again until 1911.[97]

The 1869 law also stipulated that a teachers' training school for girls (*Dar al-mu'allimat*) be established, reflecting the ambitious state project of expanding girls' education at all levels, and of enabling women to enter the government workforce as teachers. Founded in Istanbul in 1870, *Dar al-mu'allimat* admitted girls as long as they agreed to teach for a number of years following their graduation, and accepted whichever post was offered to them.[98] To keep up with the expansion of education in the provinces, and to enable girls to study closer to home, the Ottoman state pledged to establish teachers' colleges throughout the provincial capitals from 1882 onward, although this pledge was never realized.[99] The lack of provincial government teachers' colleges proved a stumbling block in increasing the number of girls' schools throughout the Empire, with the teachers mainly coming from the Turkish speaking provinces of the Empire and finding it difficult to integrate into the Arab provinces. It was only after the 1908 Constitutional Revolution that *Dar al-mu'allimat* actively began to recruit young women from the Arab provinces. An announcement in *Filastin* appealed to those Palestinian women who wanted to "join the community of teachers," noting that "assistance" was available for graduates of the *rushdiyya* schools, including those from the non-Muslim *millets*, on condition that they knew Turkish well.[100] The school's distance from Palestine and instruction in Ottoman Turkish, however, surely dashed the hopes of many girls who wanted to train as teachers, giving more appeal to the local missionary schools that had begun to also offer career training. Although we know very little about the Arab women who did attend *Dar al-mu'allimat*, most likely they were the sisters of men who were studying in Istanbul or the daughters of Ottoman officials, such as the Beirut-born Su'ad al-Asir al-Husayni, who entered *Dar al-mu'allimat* in 1910 when she was only fourteen, and graduated in 1917, after which she taught first in Beirut and then in Jerusalem.[101] It was only toward the end of Ottoman rule, in 1916, that *Maktab Jamal Pasha,* a teacher's college for women, was opened in Beirut in order to increase the number of Arab women teachers in the Ottoman government schools; Afifa Malhas, a young Palestinian woman from Nablus, was among its pupils.[102]

As both Ben Fortna and Selim Deringil have argued, the 1869 Law of Public Education, especially given its emphasis on girls' education, as well as subsequent educational legislation, should be understood partly as an attempt to unify the empire both religiously and nationally; state-supported schools constituted a defensive tactic for battling the growing influence of the Catholic and Protestant missionary schools throughout the Empire, which were seen as being a divisive force.[103] By providing state-supported education, the law was seen as protecting the Muslim population from depending upon the Catholic and Protestant schools for their education, while it also drew the non-Muslim religious communities back into the folds of the Empire by providing government-supported schools for them as well. As Deringil has shown, the law also reinforced Ottoman control over education of its citizens, by stipulating that all non-Muslim private schools within the Empire had to submit their curricula and teachers to public inspection, building on an earlier law from 1858 that required these schools to be subject to licensing and to the regulations of the Ministry of Education. In 1880, the Ottoman state further extended its control over the non-Muslim private schools by creating local educational commissions to supervise the textbooks and curricula that they were using, with an inspectorate for non-Muslim and foreign schools appointed in 1887. In 1894, the Ottoman state also legislated that Turkish had to be taught in non-Muslim schools, with Turkish teachers being assigned and paid by the Ottoman government.[104]

Despite the legislation, the laws applying to the non-Muslim schools were not always enforced. Local Ottoman officials approached these institutions with caution, knowing full well that they enjoyed the support and backing of the different foreign consuls.[105] As Tibawi has argued, the foreign consuls had enough clout in order to defy Ottoman orders and to influence the appointments of Ottoman officials, who would be more sympathetic to the foreign schools. The recommendation of James Finn, the British consul in Jerusalem, in 1853 to remove a particular mufti who had reportedly incited the Greek Orthodox community to attack a Protestant school in Nablus, and to appoint a successor who was on friendly terms with the Protestants, is illustrative of the power that the consuls had, and of their close relationships with the missions. In other cases, the foreign consuls reportedly bribed local Ottoman functionaries to remain silent about missionary activity. Even when the foreign consuls tried to intervene and impose Ottoman sanctioned restrictions, the missionaries were often defiant.[106]

In addition to serving as defensive bastions against the missionary schools, Ottoman state schools should also be understood as part of the much greater competition between East and West in terms of modernity and progress. Imperial photographs of schools and their pupils, collected in elaborate albums and presented to heads of states, manifested both the modernity and progress of the Empire, and the integral role played by schools and children in its realization.[107] In her study of cartoons in the Ottoman Turkish press, Palmira Brummett has further argued that the Empire promoted "Ottoman exceptionalism," referring to a sense of superiority that the Empire sought to maintain, despite western Orientalist charges of a crumbling, fraying Empire, and despite the political, economic, and social realities that it faced. "The monarchy, the idea of a multiethnic empire, longevity, past military glory, Islamic law, and certain presumptions about class and gender" were posited as the basis of this superiority,[108] with schools, like cartoons, being one vehicle of its dissemination.

The application of the 1869 Law of Public Education in Palestine in the early 1870s reflected the role of government schools, particularly for girls, both in challenging the already tangible Catholic and Protestant influence in the region, and in unifying Palestine with the rest of the Empire by teaching schoolchildren notions of Ottoman belonging and superiority. The Ottoman government opened a girls' school in Nablus as early as 1873, followed by schools in Acre, Haifa, Nazareth, Tiberias, and Safad between 1875 and 1895.[109] By the end of the nineteenth century, higher level *rushdiyya* schools for girls had been established in Jerusalem, Hebron, Gaza, Jaffa, Haifa, and Acre, each instructing between fifty and one hundred girls.[110]

Although the history of the Ottoman schools in Palestine has yet to be documented, we know that by the early twentieth century, the town of Nablus had a significant number of government elementary schools for girls, as well as boys—in fact, more than any of the other districts in the province of Beirut to which it belonged.[111] Nablus and its surrounding villages differed from other towns in Palestine in that it was mostly Sunni Muslim, with small numbers of Greek Orthodox, Catholics, Protestants, and Samaritans. The town's geographical isolation and mountainous terrain contributed to its relative homogeneity, as well as to the preservation of its autonomy, rendering Ottoman control over Nablus and the surrounding villages nominal. Perhaps because of its isolation and autonomy, the town developed into a center for religious learning among local and rural families. As Mahmoud Yazbak has shown, many families from Nablus sent their sons to continue their studies in the religious colleges of Damascus, Istanbul, and at the famous al-Azhar in Cairo.[112] The limited opportunities for religious scholars, however, together with the town's growing commercial and industrial importance in the mid-nineteenth century,[113] encouraged some young Nablus men, including those who descended from ulama and the merchant elite, to attend Istanbul's law and medical schools, as well as the school for civil servants.[114] The establishment of Ottoman government schools may have been the result of the growing influence of these newly educated men, who, as Yazbak has argued, returned to their hometown as products and agents of state education.

While the decision to open government schools throughout Palestine often served as a challenge to already existing missionary schools, this was not the case in Nablus. David Kushner has argued that the isolation of Nablus and its lack of exposure to western outsiders, who bypassed the town because it had neither sites of Christian pilgrimage nor a significant non-Muslim population, led local residents to harbor suspicions and express open hostility toward the few outsiders who did venture into the town.[115] Protestant missions had tried to operate in Nablus as early as the 1860s but were forced to keep their activities to a minimum because of the animosity of local residents, including both Muslims and Greek Orthodox.[116] Only toward the end of the nineteenth century did Nablus become more open to outsiders, especially with the acceleration of its economy, and with increasing Ottoman control through the stationing of troops and the development of roads and communication systems.[117] It was at this time that the Sisters of St. Joseph were able to establish its hospital, and then, reportedly at the request of local residents and the municipality, the order opened a girls' school. The London-based Church Missionary Society also set up a small Protestant girls' school, attended by fifty girls in the 1890s.[118] In both cases, the Ottoman girls' schools predated the missionary ones.

Whereas Nablus had a government girls' school by the 1870s, the government girls' school in Jerusalem was opened only in 1884/1885.[119] Although the history of its first dozen years has been undocumented, Isma'il Bey al-Husayni, head of the local department of education in Jerusalem, turned to the American Colony to administer the school in 1897.[120] Nineteen-year-old Bertha Spafford Vester, the daughter of the founders of the American Colony, took on the responsibility together with the assistance of Miss Brooke, an older woman who had taught at the American Colony and in English mission schools. Vester administered the school until 1904, followed by her sister

Grace for a few years. In a draft of her memoirs, Vester described the school before she took over its administration as a *kuttab* style school, where "the pupils had sat on straw mats cross legged, where they swayed back & forth & repeated the Koran by rote."[121] The school itself was located in a *waqf*-endowed building called *al-Dawardariyya*, bordering the northern side of *al-haram al-sharif*.[122] According to Vester, it "had the appearance of a ruin," and she added that "it was quite shocking to think that children had been confined for hours in these dark, airless rooms and expected to study under such conditions."[123] Although it is difficult to contest Vester's description, it constitutes an implicit criticism of Ottoman state education and "Ottoman modernity." This criticism—that, despite the reforms, the Ottoman schools remained low-level, poorly equipped, *kuttab*-style institutions—may have been propagated by the missionaries themselves, as a means of deprecating the Ottoman educational system, while also buttressing their own. The writer Asma Tubi, who was born in Nazareth in 1905 and educated in missionary schools, also voiced similar criticisms, writing that "the Ottoman state did not move to create educational institutes in this country. All it did in the beginning was to open elementary *katatib* schools. It collected the little children in them and [standing] before them a shaykh would give lessons on Qur'anic verses and the principles of the Arabic language . . . Just as it also opened *katatib* for girls, which were managed by old women."[124]

At Vester's insistence, the school was transformed from a *kuttab* to a "modern" institution, in terms of its physical presence, its teachers, and its curriculum. The school's building was renovated, notably by adding windows and enlarging existing ones, and partitioning larger rooms into smaller spaces. Books, copybooks, lead pencils, and slates were ordered from Syria, while blackboards, tables, desks, and benches were built by local carpenters. The older teachers were slowly replaced by young women from the American Colony and trained Muslim women teachers from Beirut, who were supplemented by a few volunteers, educated girls who had studied at the Sisters of Zion School and at St. Joseph's. Vester noted that the "Board of Directors were anxious to introduce parlor tricks and accomplishments; they wanted French & English, piano and drawing, more specially painting to be taught," the same kinds of topics emphasized in the more prestigious Catholic and Protestant schools. Vester, however, insisted that "the girls must first grapple with elementary reading, writing, and arithmetic."[125] She also introduced sewing into the school's curriculum, based on the assumption that few Muslim women knew how to sew, and later added other handicrafts including "fine embroidery."[126] Rozsika Parker has argued that the incorporation of embroidery into the formal education of girls was in part intended to differentiate girls' education from that of boys, thus creating greater acceptance of girls' education.[127] While sewing and embroidery may have been regarded as gender appropriate subjects, the girls also used these skills to produce handmade items to sell at bazaars in order to raise money for the school, whose budget, according to Vester, was insufficient and far less than that of the government boys' schools.[128]

Three hundred and fifty girls reportedly registered on the opening day of the newly renovated school, while others were turned away for lack of space. They represented the various social strata of Jerusalem's Muslim community. Vester wrote that the school had become a cause for curiosity as "whole families accompanied their daughters to inspect the school house," as well as the new "Christian teachers,"[129] as if their presence was representative of a modern transformation. Without additional research on girls' education throughout the Empire, it is difficult to say whether or not the Ottoman girls' school in Jerusalem was an anomaly in that it was a combined effort by both government and foreigners to provide a sound education. As noted by Eberhard, the German who visited the school in April 1905, giving the American Colony responsibility for the Ottoman girls' school in Jerusalem was a means of elevating its educational level.[130] The incorporation of two foreign administrators in a government school was a means of appealing to upper-class Muslim girls who had attended the Catholic and Protestant schools, and who, without the intervention of the two westerners, may have been reluctant to switch to an Ottoman government school.

GIRLS' EDUCATION ON THE EVE OF WORLD WAR I

In September 1914, Khalil al-Sakakini visited the same Ottoman girls' school in Jerusalem that Bertha Vester had once administered, and revealed mixed feelings about the school's progress:

> We tested the older class in Arabic reading, the class that was taught by my sister, and we found that the girls had improved at reading, and they understood what they read and what they said, and they were able to inflect as they read. And then I ordered one of the girls to change the story from masculine to feminine, and she did so, which pleased me. But Shaykh Hassan was not content with this . . . and he began asking the girls questions in grammar according to the old way, and when they did not understand his intention, he said, they do not know anything. Then we asked them about arithmetic and geography and we found them very weak, because their

teacher was very weak too, if not ignorant in the subject that she taught
. . . Then we entered the remaining classes and we found them overcrowded
with girls of different ages, and none of them knew anything.[131]

While al-Sakakini's account focused on generational differences between
the teachers and the inspectors in what the girls should learn and which
methods should be used, as well the difficulties of finding qualified women
teachers, his criticisms also expressed dashed expectations for educational reform following the 1908 Young Turk Revolution.

The revolution had instilled hope for the Empire's future, especially given
the rhetoric of constitutionalism, reform, and citizenship rights transcending borders as well as ethnic and religious divisions. The emergence of the
Committee of Union and Progress (CUP), a pro-constitutional organization,
as the leading political force, and its emphasis on education as a tool for reforming and enlightening the Empire, was welcomed by many as a positive
change. Just as a nascent Palestinian press emerged, local educators established a small number of private schools in the spirit of the CUP reforms.
Khalil al-Sakakini's *al-Madrasa al-Dusturiyya* (the Constitutional School),
founded in Jerusalem in 1909, was one such institution; it reflected the promises and the optimism of the era by teaching Arabic language and literature,
by accepting boys from different religious and social backgrounds, and by
doing away with corporeal punishment.[132]

The optimism was, however, short lived. The pro-Turkic tendencies of the
CUP, and its decision immediately after the 1908 revolution to make Turkish the language of instruction in elementary schools, caused concern among
Palestinian Arab nationalists.[133] The nascent Palestinian press was full of
criticisms of the post-1908 educational reforms, and the lack of any visible,
tangible change. The journalist Butrus al-Shihadeh lamented on the pages
of *Filastin* that despite "dreaming about life in the era of the constitution,
we continue wearing the clothing of the previous one . . . they are outdated
clothing, irreparable, while before us are new clothes," which, in his eyes,
were unattainable. He continued writing that "ignorance is being raised in the
void, despite that you say it is an era of freedom, constitution, and equality. It
is the most dangerous illness for this country. . . . The most important books
for the uplifting of the nation are schoolbooks. The pupils do not have any
books . . . and the nation remains as it was."[134] Over a year later, a student at
one of the higher government schools for boys in Beirut also wrote in *Filastin*
that "this is the fourth year [since the reinstatement of the Constitution] and
the nationalist travels about and does not see Palestine wearing a new robe
or advancing in its enlightenment." Embedded in this statement was implicit

criticism of the pro-Turkic tendencies of the ruling CUP and the indifference of the CUP at this time toward teaching in Arabic in the schools. Regardless of the language in which children were being taught, the level of the schools was not sufficient; the same young author retorted, "You see the graduates of these schools, especially the *rushdiyya* schools, hanging their diploma in a corner of their homes, while working as carpenters or blacksmiths."[135]

In 1913, the Ottoman government passed a provisional law for elementary education, again raising expectations. The 1913 law stipulated that state-funded elementary education was to be compulsory and free of charge for children from the age of six. The law specifically mentioned that education segregated by gender would continue, with every village or urban neighborhood having to provide a girls' school if there were more than fifty girls under the age of six. The law also acknowledged the need to expand teacher training and rural education. In addition, greater administrative, financial, and pedagogical responsibility over elementary education was given to the local government authorities. Part of the decentralizing of government education meant that local communities, both urban and rural, were to assume the financial burden of providing buildings, furnishings, and materials for the elementary schools, as well as some of the salaries of the teachers. The new law also stipulated that Arabic could be the language of instruction in the government elementary schools within the Arab provinces, as long as Turkish also was taught, reflecting a changing attitude of the ruling CUP party toward non–Turkish speaking inhabitants of the Empire and a growing recognition of Arab cultural and nationalist aspirations.[136] The new legislation also gave greater government control over private schools, including the foreign Christian schools and those administered by the local religious communities, projecting concerns that these schools did not cultivate any kind of patriotism nor allegiance to the Empire, as illustrated by the dialogue that began this chapter.

Muhammad Rafiq al-Tamimi and Muhammad Bahjat were critical of the overly ambitious 1913 law in their impressions of the Ottoman government schools that they visited during their tour of northern Palestine around 1915–1916. Al-Tamimi and Bahjat observed crowded classrooms, and noted the effects of poor budgets that did not enable the schools in both towns and villages to provide adequate education, despite promises of free and compulsory education. A teacher who administered a kindergarten in Nablus, attended by one hundred girls between the ages of four and six, complained about the "loss of pencils and educational utensils needed for the kindergarten art," which, in the past, she had been able to provide because the school had charged a tuition of a single *majidi* (a silver Ottoman coin worth twenty piasters) to the children of wealthy families. The implication was that by no longer allowing schools to charge tuition fees, the teacher did not have enough government financial support to run the kindergarten according to "modern" standards.[137] The lack of utensils and tools meant that the kindergarten had become nothing more than a day shelter for young children.

Al-Tamimi and Bahjat were particularly critical of what they believed to be the ignorance and poor skills of the Ottoman government teachers, in many ways faulting them for widespread illiteracy and ignorance. Upon visiting the girls' school in Tiberias, attended by some fifty girls, they wrote that "a Christian woman who knows English, Arabic, and French administers this school. As for the head teacher, she is a graduate of the intermediate-level school in Acre, but she is ignorant to the degree that she does not know all the numbers, while the second teacher is not bad even though she does not know Turkish."[138] Without well-trained teachers, the establishment of schools would have little effect. Overall, al-Tamimi and Bahjat concluded that many of the schools were "very distressing and sad, their teachers completely ignorant, without any strength, inclination, and competence to educate the villages and teach them proper behavior."[139]

The poor, dismal condition of Ottoman schools, however, was not entirely the fault of the Ottoman government, with poverty also playing a significant role, particularly in the enrollment of girls in the government schools. In Salfit, while the boys' school had one hundred pupils, the girls' school had only ten pupils, even though the government elementary schools were free of charge. Al-Tamimi and Bahjat concluded that the reason "for the neglect of the matter of education is hunger," noting that the living conditions had deteriorated as a result of locusts that destroyed crops the previous year, "and [the people] are, as the village *mukhtar* (village head) told us, in a state of struggle and demise."[140] As it was mainly girls who were not being educated, it can be inferred that the poverty and the loss of crops compelled families to keep their daughters at home, where they cared for their parents and younger siblings in their struggle to survive. In many cases of poverty, girls were also sent to boarding schools belonging to the Christian missions where they were fed and clothed.

Regardless of the problems, and the inability of the Ottomans to fully implement educational reform in Palestine, the establishment of girls' elementary schools, even the most rudimentary, served as the basis for the continued development of girls' education for nearly three more decades under the British colonial administration. In the first years of British rule, the British government educational reports described girls' education as being virtually "non-existent," implying that the Ottomans were too "backward" to establish schools; this paternalistic view helped to justify the British Mandate over Palestine, and the notion that the primarily Muslim inhabitants of Palestine were in need of colonial tutelage. In reality, though, the British built their girls' schools on the very same foundations as their Ottoman predecessors, while taking credit for planting the seeds of girls' education that already had been germinated during the late nineteenth century.

Chapter 2

Removing "the Long-Standing Prejudice against Girls' Education"

GOVERNMENT SCHOOLS AND
MUSLIM GIRLS DURING THE
BRITISH MANDATE

In September 1935, some sixty residents of Safad sent the High Commissioner for Palestine the following petition:

> We, the undersigned *mukhtars*, merchants, elders and farmers of Safad town, hereby beg to point out the crisis now prevailing in the Government schools of Safad and particularly in the girls' school, the only one in the town, which has only 9 classes and 8 teachers and most of the classes contain more than 50 pupils. There should be more than one school in such a large town as Safad. The boys' schools still reject many children. It is unjust, therefore, in such a century of civilization as the twentieth century and under the British Mandate over Palestine, that our sons and daughters should remain ignorant while the Government Treasury is loaded with funds. We appeal to Your Excellency to kindly solve this problem, which should concern you more than it concerns us, by opening more schools or by increasing the number of teachers and classes as circumstances require.[1]

Two years later, several people from Safad, including two village leaders (*mukhtar*), sent another petition, insisting that Safad, although located "far in the north" and isolated from other places, should not also be deprived of education. This petition noted that "existing schools are not sufficient to take in all the children of school age and can barely absorb 60 pupils although those who apply for admission exceed 400. Most of the children are rejected, and remain ignorant, roaming about the streets. The city is also stricken with poverty and cannot afford to establish private schools." The petition again begged the government to expand the existing boys' and girls' schools, and to establish a proper kindergarten. Noting that the Scots College, a secondary school run by the Scottish Mission, had closed and moved to Haifa, the petitioners requested that the government increase the number of secondary classes in the government schools so that pupils could continue their studies.[2]

The experience of the Palestinians under Ottoman rule, and especially the slow speed of reforms, had a considerable impact on the way in which they perceived the British vis-à-vis education. Not only did Palestinians consider the twentieth century an era of progress and enlightenment, especially in sharp contrast to the previous centuries, but they also saw the British Mandate as a vehicle for advancement and change, and the harbinger of a new era, significantly different from its Ottoman predecessor. The writers of the first petition had high expectations of the British, especially in terms of education, as they brought to Palestine an expertise that they had acquired in other colonial administrations. By the late 1920s and through the mid-1930s, their expertise came under scrutiny by the very people who believed they would benefit from British rule. Even though it was written only two years later, the second petition already indicates a growing despair and anger toward the British administration, as their pleas had still not been answered.

With the demise of the Ottoman Empire, this chapter focuses on the role of the British colonial administration in promoting girls' schools, and the relationship that developed between the Arab population and the British administration vis-à-vis its educational policies. The collapse of the Empire, however, did not mean an end to its influence, as the foundations for education had developed during the late Ottoman period. While defending the Empire and challenging the missionary influence were the pillars of the Ottoman educational policies, class, religion, and location emerge as key to the British colonial policies toward girls' education. While missionary education becomes central to the education of girls from the Christian elite, the government schools cater primarily to the urban, middle- and lower-class Muslim strata. Although the British relied heavily on the Ottoman infrastructure, they also introduced teachers' colleges primarily intended to train Muslim women to serve as teachers in what the British promoted as an "expanding" system of education.

COLONIAL POLICIES TOWARD
URBAN GIRLS' EDUCATION

In December 1917, when the British army first marched into Palestine, they found a country that that had been shaken economically, politically, and socially by World War I, and whose schools were barely functioning. During the war, the Ottoman government expelled foreign citizens of the enemy (allied) countries, European Jews and Christians alike, and sequestered their property, thus forcibly closing many of the Catholic and Protestant schools.[3] Although A. L. Tibawi claimed that Ottoman government schools were not affected by the war and continued to function,[4] the shortage of funds was surely felt. The economic crisis emanating from war-torn Europe was tangible in Palestine, as foreign banks closed down, and as local banks ceased to sell gold and provide credit.[5] The British blockade of the Syrian coast, poor agricultural conditions, inclement weather, and the inability of the Ottomans to supply provisions caused a famine in Greater Syria that spread as far south as Jerusalem by 1917. Although we do not know how many Palestinians were affected, an estimated 500,000 people throughout the region died from hunger by the end of the war in 1918.[6] Conscription into the Ottoman army also mobilized about three-fourths of the adult Arab male population, with some never returning from their military service.[7]

The position of women and children in Palestine following the war was particularly grave. Khalil al-Sakakini noted that in the aftermath of the war, female-headed households became common, and as the family support dwindled, the number of children placed in orphanages or left without supervision grew.[8] Helen Bentwich, a social worker by profession and the wife of Norman Bentwich, who served as attorney general in the British administration, acknowledged that the acute poverty following the war pushed many girls into prostitution, stating that it was the "only way the girls can help their families to live."[9] As Margalit Shilo argues in the context of Jerusalem, "there was nothing new about the phenomenon of prostitution in the Holy City, yet its scope after the British army's entry into the city in December 1917 was exceptional, evoking considerable attention and anxiety."[10] The presence of British troops, mainly in Jerusalem, Jaffa, and Haifa, who ensured the establishment of the British military administration, later to become a civilian one, only exacerbated fears of prostitution, exploitation, and other dangers threatening young girls. Former missionary Frances E. Newton echoed these fears, claiming that the war had led to the "breaking down of many protective fences in the social code," and called on British women in Palestine to mobilize on behalf of the most difficult cases involving young Arab girls.[11]

The American Colony in Jerusalem responded to the situation by creating the "Christian Herald Orphanage." Short biographies of those resident in the orphanage, appearing as appeals for donations within church publications, indicated that in many cases, the children had been orphaned of one parent, either father or mother, with the surviving parent unable to care for them. For example, one biography reads "Erfat Ersas, aged twelve, is a little motherless Mohammedan, whose father Hafiz Ersas, was impoverished by the war."[12]

Girls playing at the "Christian Herald Orphanage," administered by the American Colony in Jerusalem, 1918. From the papers of John D. Whiting, Prints & Photographs Division, Library of Congress, LC–DIG–ppmsca–13291–00122.

Another biography reads "Faruze Saallah, age five, is a Mohammedan. Her father, Abed Saallah, died from nephritis caused by lack of food and exposure in the Turkish Labor Corps. Her mother, Nazerie, has two boys to support, one an epileptic and helpless."[13] Not only did this biography suggest the humanitarian crisis during the war, but it also indicated that this girl's mother was willing to place her daughter in the care of Christian missionaries but not her sons, perhaps reflecting the mother's inability to protect her daughter from the post-war threats to young girls.

Women from the Palestinian elite, as well as some of the western residents, responded to this post-war situation by creating charitable organizations, adding to the few already existing organizations that had been founded at the turn of the century.[14] The Social Service Association, formed in 1918 by British, Jewish, and a few Arab women, blamed the Ottomans for having left "pestilence and famine everywhere, and what was worst of all, a great deal of immorality."[15] It opened up a shelter for wayward girls, where they were "trained in housework and sewing and taught to read and write," so that they could later find employment.[16] In May 1918, Katinko Deeb, a young Palestinian woman from Jerusalem who had worked as a teacher for a few years before marrying, together with other members of the Greek Orthodox

Church, founded *Jam'iyat tahthib al-fata* (The association for training the girl), to assist girls in their community to pursue an education,[17] despite the poor economic situation. A little more than a year later, a group of Muslim women in Jerusalem formed *Jam'iyat nahda al-fatat al-'arabiyya* (Association for the awakening of the Arab girl), to provide Muslim girls with a "more honorable living," by teaching them sewing and embroidery.[18]

The British administration also understood that promoting education was one of the ways to protect young girls from the vices associated with the war. In order to return Palestine to a degree of normalcy, it allowed most of the former Ottoman government schools to reopen, which were "located for the most part in the same place, and often in the same building as the Ottoman regime."[19] Local educational committees, formed at the end of the Ottoman rule, were able to resume their tasks of supervising lower elementary schools, including the appointment and dismissal of teachers. In addition, the new administration allowed missionaries, religious communities, and other individuals whose schools had closed at the outbreak of World War I to reopen them.[20] The British also maintained the gendering of education that the Ottomans had instituted, making an exception only in the 1930s for young boys between the ages of four and seven to attend kindergartens attached to urban girls' schools.[21] In August 1918, the British appointed Hilda Ridler, who had worked with the colonial administration in Egypt, as the girls' school inspector and advisor for female education.[22] The British military administration also formed a special committee on girls' education in early 1919, which included Sultana al-Sakakini, a former teacher and the wife of Khalil al-Sakakini.[23]

In late 1920, at a meeting of the Advisory Council, a committee made up of British officials, Arabs, and Jews, Director of Education Humphrey Bowman stated that "it is proposed to put into force [elementary education] for all children in Palestine with the exception of those of the nomad tribes or of outlying districts." In the same meeting, he acknowledged that "the training of girls is perhaps the most important function of education, the primary end of which is to train up good citizens of the country, and the Department of Education intends to cooperate with the people of Palestine, irrespective of creed or sect."[24] Despite the lip-service to expand elementary education, the British administration dutifully noted the difficulty in removing "the long standing prejudice against girls' education,"[25] which, whether or not it was truly tangible, came to inform the British policy of not advancing girls' education beyond the status quo.

By reopening the former Ottoman schools, the British administration gave the impression that it was not making any real transformations, but rather

Hilda Ridler, headmistress of the Women's Training College and inspector of girls'
education in Palestine, December 1944. From the G. Eric and Edith Matson Photograph
Collection, Prints & Photographs Division, Library of Congress, LC–DIG–matpc–00643.

was continuing the status quo. As Abigail Jacobson has argued, the British maintained the Ottoman system as much as possible in terms of administrative areas and units, of which public education was one.[26] Undoubtedly, earlier colonial experiences influenced these decisions, with the majority of those who joined the British administration having had years of experience working in Egypt and Sudan, including Bowman and Ridler in the Department of Education. As Tibawi writes, "experience gained in India and Egypt opened the eyes of educational administrators to the futility and dangers" of promoting education that did not meet the needs and demands of the local population.[27] It is difficult not to draw comparisons between this unwritten policy of maintaining the status quo in Palestine with British experiences in Sudan, where attempts to create girls' schools were met with resistance, causing the British to completely neglect girls' education, and preferring to "channel their limited resources into forms of education that would garner more public support," namely the education of Muslim, Arabic-speaking males from Northern Sudan.[28] Given that Bowman, the first director of education in Palestine from 1920 to 1936, had previously served as an educational official in Sudan, it is not surprising that his administration approached the education of Muslim girls in Palestine rather cautiously.

Similar to the social hierarchy created in Sudan, which affected access to education, the British reinforced an already existing educational hierarchy that kept the Muslim population dependent upon government provision of education, while they left the responsibility of educating the Christian population to the Catholic orders and Protestant missions, with whom the Department of Education developed friendly relations. It must be noted that although government schools were open to Christian students, their numbers remained marginal, primarily because of the wide availability of private Christian education, as well as the refusal of the Department of Education to provide Christian religious instruction when there were not enough students.[29] In places where the Christian population was significant, such as in Nazareth, reports circulated that Muslim families found it impossible to admit their children into the government schools, as the heads, who were Christian, "naturally prefer to accept [Christian] sons over poor Muslim ones."[30] Throughout the entire Mandate period, however, the percentage of Christian children in government schools stood at about 10 percent. By the end of the Mandate, the number of Christian girls in government schools had reached no more than 2,000, most of whom were daughters of government officials or who lived in areas where government schools were the only available educational institutions.[31]

During the first few years of the British administration, the Department of Education focused on establishing government girls' schools in urban areas only, a formula already developed in Egypt and Iraq. In the 1924–1925 scholastic year, a total of nineteen government elementary schools, which began with kindergarten and continued through the sixth-grade class, had been opened for girls in towns throughout Palestine, in contrast to the ten schools for village girls.[32] Most of the urban schools were overcrowded, understaffed, and had poor infrastructure and physical conditions. The policy of locating government schools in former Ottoman public buildings and in rental properties was ill conceived, as many of these buildings were in dilapidated condition and were too small to accommodate the number of pupils seeking admission.[33] As a result of the physically inadequate conditions of the schools, many pupils were denied admission, especially as more children began to attend school by the 1930s. In September 1932, for example, 59 percent of girls applying to the urban government schools for the first time throughout all of Palestine were refused admission.

The district of Hebron especially lacked educational options for girls. A single government girls' school served the entire district, which included the town and the surrounding villages, and over 70,000 inhabitants.[34] The demand, however, was much greater than the available room, with 77 percent of its applicants being turned away.[35] Local demands that the school add a sixth-grade class fell on deaf ears, with the director of education claiming that expansion of the school would not be economical, since only nine girls attended its fifth and highest class.[36] As a town that was almost entirely Muslim, with the exception of a small Jewish community, Hebron also did not have any private Christian schools providing residents with an alternative to government education.

In the mid-1930s, partially in response to the overcrowding, the British administration embarked on plans to create new urban schools. The New Mamuniyya Girls' School, built in the Shaykh Jarrah neighborhood of Jerusalem, and not to be confused with the original Mamuniyya Girls' School, was meant to serve as a model girls' school.[37] The British administration and the local population, however, had different gender and cultural expectations regarding the school buildings. In Ramallah, despite requests to build boys' and girls' schools at different locations on the "grounds of morality," it was decided that "such an objection should not be taken too seriously and that the local authorities should not sacrifice the best sites or pay more money merely for such a reason."[38] The refusal to accommodate the requests of local Ramallah families, however, may have cost the school some of its pupils. The district commissioner complained that in Hebron, the buildings of the girls' school were "scattered, and on the main roads," while the "exposure of the girls to the public" gave "rise to bitter criticism from the local inhabitants." As a compromise, the director of education proposed that the administration rent property where they would create a "central girls' school," at a total cost of £11,000, instead of building a new girls' school. Yet rather than foot the entire expense, the British demanded that the municipality of Hebron pay half the costs, even though its budget was inadequate and it could not finance such projects.[39] The refusal of the British to pay for the cost of new buildings, and the insistence that the local population partake in the expenses, meant that schools, especially for girls, were never enlarged, or never built at all. The government girls' school in Hebron remained overcrowded and scattered about on the main roads, with many pupils turned away well into the late 1930s. Similarly, a girls' school in Tiberias planned in the 1930s was never realized,[40] while the building of a girls' school in Beersheba was delayed until 1946.[41]

Although the Department of Education reported in its published annual reports that nearly every town had a government girls' school, the town of Haifa did not have one until 1934.[42] According to the Department of Education, Haifa did not have suitable rental accommodations, making it impossible to open a girls' school there. Yet the real problem was the Department's struggle with the Muslim religious community heads over the control of *awqaf mundarisa* properties. These were *awqaf* properties whose revenues, having ceased to benefit their original beneficiaries, had reverted to the Ottoman Ministry of Education as part of the Ottoman reforms of the religious endowments. According to Uri M. Kupferschmidt, nearly all the urban schools in Palestine, some twenty-eight buildings in all, fell into this category.[43]

During the late Ottoman period, many of these properties passed to the local educational committees, which were entrusted with opening and managing the government schools, and whose role recommenced under the British administration. In Haifa, however, the local educational committee apparently had ceased its activities in the early years of the Mandate, and transferred its properties to Haifa's Islamic Society, which used the government girls' school building to house its own private school for Muslim girls.[44] The stance of the Islamic Society, which worked in tandem with the Supreme Muslim Council, was that the Muslim community had the right to use the building, as it had been *awqaf mundarisa*. Throughout the Mandate period, the Supreme Muslim Council, as the highest representative of the Muslim population, battled the Department of Education for the return of all of the *awqaf mundarisa* properties and their revenues; that is, they claimed that the majority of the urban government school buildings belonged to them, and that the revenues were intended exclusively for the education of Muslim children.[45] The question over who was legally entitled to use the former Ottoman school buildings placed the Department of Education in a precarious position, as it challenged the very right of the Department of Education to provide education for Muslim children.

In addition to buildings, opening schools also required teachers. In order to supply women teachers for the government girls' schools, the Department of Education established the Women's Elementary Training College in Jerusalem in the summer of 1919. Although its aim was to train teachers so that the Department of Education would not have to import teachers from Egypt and Syria (which they did anyway in small numbers), de facto, it became the only government institution that offered a full secondary program for girls. In 1924, the school dropped the "elementary" from its name, becoming known as the Women's Training College (WTC), reflecting its changing role and dual status as providing both teacher training and secondary education. The school's curriculum also was altered to reflect these needs. Initially, the WTC provided a four-year program, the last year related to pedagogy and practice teaching; in 1941, the program was expanded to five years, enabling students to prepare and sit for the Palestine Matriculation exam.[46] While no complete figures are available for the number of women who actually graduated from the WTC, in 1930, it was reported that out of 145 women employed as government schoolteachers, 94 of them had completed the WTC.[47] That number, however, does not include the women who chose not to teach at all, or who left teaching not long after finishing their studies at the WTC.

Through the mid-1920s, twice as many Christian pupils as Muslims attended the WTC. Ruth Woodsmall, the general secretary of the international YWCA, visited the WTC in 1928 while collecting material for her book on women in the Middle East. She remarked that the school had a difficult time recruiting Muslim girls, and "in the beginning it was necessary to take the Moslem students free and urge them to come."[48] Part of the problem may have been that the WTC required all pupils, even those from Jerusalem, to reside within the school, which did not allow parents much control over their daughters. Moreover, girls were only permitted to leave the school one day a month accompanied by a parent or guardian, while visits by family members were also limited.[49] Although Muslim families had all kinds of reasons why not to send their daughters to the WTC, the British understood this reluctance as an expression of resistance on part of Muslim families in allowing their daughters more than just a rudimentary education. Ridler, the principal of the WTC and inspector of girls' education, also believed that Christian women would make better teachers, as they presumably "led freer lives, and the attendance at mission schools had accustomed them to leave the seclusion of the home."[50] The notion that Christian students were more liberated together with the perceived opposition of Muslim families in educating their daughters set the tone for the admission and subsequent imbalance between Muslims and Christians in the school.

Only in the late 1920s did the school's student body begin to shift in favor of the Muslim pupils, when the number of Muslim applicants reached more than half. In part this was the result of increasing government efforts to expand government girls' education within the urban areas. It may have also related to a growing reluctance of Christian women to train as teachers for the government schools, as a result of occasional religious tensions between Muslim girls and their Christian teachers, as well as difficulties that urban women had when having to teach and live in the predominantly Muslim villages.

As the WTC began to cater to more Muslim women, it also adopted a "distinctly harim atmosphere," in the words of Woodsmall. By imposing "harim conditions," British officials may have been trying to replicate colonial experiences in India, where upper-class Muslim and high-caste Hindu women were educated within the zenana, the gendered, inner compartments of homes where they spent their time.[51] According to Woodsmall, strict gender segregation "followed a very conservative policy . . . carefully avoiding any criticism of promoting social freedom," in order to convince families that their daughters would continue to uphold conservative values even as they trained to become teachers.[52] Thus, the WTC held all-female events, refrained from photographing the students in order to maintain their modesty, and did not allow men in the school. On those occasions when male officials visited the school, "some of the teachers veil[ed] as well as the older girls," and when the shaykh came to give religious lessons to Muslim pupils, the teachers and girls were instructed to cover their faces as well.[53] Woodsmall suggested that this was all just a façade, writing that "although the Training College carefully avoids promoting social or religious ideas, it is steadily laying the foundation for a future social freedom which seems inevitable," in reference to the social freedom that women felt as they embarked upon teaching careers.[54]

Admission to the WTC was not easy. Only the top students in the sixth-grade class (later becoming the seventh grade) of the government town schools were selected to sit for the WTC's oral and written entrance exam. Acceptance was awarded to only a dozen or so girls each year.[55] In 1929, for example, one hundred girls sat for the exam, which included fifty-nine Muslims; out of all those applicants, only eighteen won acceptance.[56] Girls who did not get accepted charged the school with discriminating, with Fleischmann noting that "young women linked their ability to obtain an education with their economic welfare."[57] One disappointed applicant charged the school with elitism, as she was from an impoverished family in Nablus, while a father with a large family on a meager pension expressed surprise that his daughter, who would have been one of the only Druze students at the school, was not admitted.[58] There may have been some truth to these charges. Although in the early years, the WTC covered the tuition and boarding fees as a means of attracting students, a method that had been tried and tested in colonial Egypt, by 1924, the WTC began to accept paying students alongside students on scholarships. Charging between £21 and £24 per year, the school was able to increase the number of paying students, who quickly outnumbered those on scholarship. In 1930, for example, nineteen pupils were "scholars," while another forty-five paid for their education.[59] Paying fees, according to Lord Cromer in the context of Egypt, was believed to be the "best test" of whether or not a people "really desire to be educated."[60] As Fleischmann has argued, the imposition of school fees, "which could represent a significant percentage of a family's income," made the WTC into a "select establishment for the elite."[61]

In recognition of the limitations of the WTC, the British provided a small number of scholarships for Arab women to attend teacher training schools abroad. With assistance from the Egyptian government, two Christian girls who completed their studies at the WTC in 1922 were sent to attend Bulaq Teachers' Training College in Cairo, and were joined by two Muslim girls in 1924.[62] Through the 1920s, a few Muslim women were also sent to the lower-level Primary Teacher's College in Helwan, a southern suburb of Cairo.[63] That the Muslim women came from some of the more notable families of Palestine may have been a means of convincing other elite Muslim families to allow their daughters to train as teachers.[64] As the WTC became increasingly Muslim, the Department of Education also began to send mainly Christian women to England to study for teaching training degrees. Most were graduates of the Anglican-administered Jerusalem Girls' College, such as Fahima Nasser, who completed a one-year program at the London Day Training College in July 1931, and then taught at the Women's Training College.[65] Only in 1938 were two Muslim women sent to England on a government scholarship for teachers' training. They were Sa'ida, a graduate of Schmidt's College, and Madiha Adib Nusaiba, who had completed her studies at the Jerusalem Girls' College, both from elite Jerusalem families.[66]

Throughout the entire Mandate, the WTC remained the only government institution in Palestine where girls could get a full secondary education. In part, limiting access to secondary education was the stance of the first director of education, who believed that secondary education created a "half educated, unemployed class," a lesson learned in India and Egypt.[67] As Fleischmann has argued, the Department of Education focused its elementary school curriculum with the "central goals of creating good wives and mothers" while discouraging government-supported studies beyond the elementary level.[68] As was the case with the British Department of Education in Iraq, the official attitude in Palestine was that the government had to sufficiently meet the needs of primary education for girls before it could begin to develop secondary education,[69] a task that took the British nearly three decades to undertake.

Only in the 1940s did the administration begin to acquiesce to demands in Jerusalem, Nablus, and Jaffa for secondary classes for girls.[70] Jerome Farrell, who succeeded Bowman as the director of education, saw the provision of secondary education as creating Palestinian support for the British Mandate, while he dismissed missionary education as being too foreign, and nationalist schools as having a "marked political bias."[71] By this point, adding a few secondary classes to urban government girls' schools was seen as a benign, almost trivial overture to the Arab community. It could be seen as an attempt to mend relations, especially following the six-month Arab strike and subsequent armed rebellion against the British, which began in April 1936 and was only extinguished in 1939. Despite local demands and the willingness of the administration, girls' enrollment was significantly lower in the government secondary classes than in the elementary classes, and progressively dropped with each grade.[72] In the 1944–1945 school year, the last year for which statistics were found, 226 girls total were registered in government secondary classes, including the WTC,[73] a relatively low number, especially when compared to the numbers who graduated from the Protestant and Catholic schools.

The decision of the British administration to add secondary classes to the government girls' schools came a little too late, however, as the private Christian schools already had a monopoly over secondary education in Palestine. As they did elsewhere, private schools in Palestine filled the educational vacuum left by the colonial administration. Statistics from 1926–1927 show that 153 girls, without reference to religion, were studying in post-elementary classes in Catholic schools throughout Palestine and another 204 girls in Protestant ones, with the British administration providing secondary education for girls only at the WTC.[74] Two decades later, the private Christian schools maintained their monopoly over secondary education, with 1,193 girls, compared to the 226 girls in the government secondary classes.[75] Although the statistics do not break down the numbers enrolled by religion, we know that Christian students outnumbered Muslims in the Protestant and Catholic schools. That these schools were in urban areas, with Jerusalem offering more opportunity for private secondary education than other towns,[76] made them somewhat accessible for Muslim girls. It was not uncommon for families, particularly from the Muslim urban elite, to send their daughters to board in one of the many private Christian secondary schools in Palestine's cities and towns. The mufti of Nablus, for example, sent his daughter to the German Catholic Schmidt's College in Jerusalem to complete her education,[77] while Yusra Salah, also from a Muslim family in Nablus, attended the Friends' School in Ramallah.[78] Nonetheless, secondary education remained a "luxury," primarily appealing to the elite, as it was dependent upon the ability to pay the tuition fees.

The limited choices for education, especially secondary education, led some girls to pursue their education outside of Palestine, with Beirut being the favored destination since the late Ottoman period. Some schools even advertised in the Palestinian Arabic press, such as the Nationalist College, a private, coeducational school in Shweifat, near Beirut, and a coeducational Quaker school in Brummana, a village in Mount Lebanon, both preparing pupils for admission into the first year at AUB. Both announced that school representatives would be travelling around Palestine in order to register students.[79] An undocumented number of Palestinian girls, whose names appeared in school publications, attended the British Syrian Training College in Beirut, which provided classes through the eighth grade, in addition to college preparation and teacher training.[80] Fluency in English was required, indicating that the girls who attended the school most likely already attended one of the local English-speaking missionary schools.

VILLAGERS DO NOT WANT TO EDUCATE THEIR DAUGHTERS

As they did in other colonial contexts, the British had a different policy for the villages than for the urban areas. Their policy toward the villages was shaped by "the belief that only a few should be permitted to continue beyond elementary school [and which] accorded with the department's efforts to preserve the existing differences between rural and urban populations so as to maintain a balanced occupational structure."[81] One of the main concerns of the director of education was that too much education in the villages would disrupt the social fabric and lead to migration and unemployment; rather, he believed that the right kind of education would contribute to agricultural development and improving rural conditions.[82] These sentiments were strikingly similar to those uttered in 1905 by Lord Cromer, the British Consul General in Egypt, who warned that "any education, technical or general, which tended to leave the fields untilled, or to lessen the fitness or disposition of the people for agricultural employment, would be a national evil."[83] Thus fitting with these attitudes, the Department of Education, in conjunction with the Department of Agriculture, saw the main purpose of the village schools as providing agricultural instruction over a period of four years, which, as Roza I. M. El-Eini points out, was both "the minimum time necessary to achieve permanent literacy, and the 'maximum which social conditions in the villages allow[ed] to the majority of pupils.'"[84]

In order to minimize expenditure, the Department of Education adopted a policy that required villagers to finance the building of the school, costing anywhere between £100 and £700, depending on the size of the school and the building conditions. In return for financing the building, the Department of Education provided the salary of the teachers, whom it also appointed, transferred, or dismissed. The schools were to be built on sites chosen outside of the villages, according to a model plan that would allow "expansion from one room to two or more," and which would include a garden for agricultural work. Exceptions were made "if the village [was] poor, or if there has been a bad harvest," with the Department of Education willing to accept "an existing building instead of erecting a new one," but this was "generally regarded as a temporary measure."[85] This policy requiring villagers to finance the construction of their own buildings departed significantly from British policy in Egypt, where the British administration had begun to take control of many of the village *kuttab* schools, and to supervise their curriculum, while giving grants-in-aid to additional *kuttab* schools in return for government inspection.[86]

The British insisted that villages not only finance the building themselves, but also construct separate boys' and girls' schools, departing from Ottoman educational law that recognized the utility of building coeducational schools in thinly populated villages. This idea that the village schools had to create gender-segregated schools also digressed from the British experiences in the Egyptian provinces, where they refused to create separate schools for girls, in the belief that girls could attend the lower-level *katatib* schools alongside boys if they truly sought an education.[87] The attitude of the British administration in Palestine was just the opposite: that if the villagers wanted to educate their daughters, they would build them separate schools. This imposition of gender segregation, that is, the creation of "harim conditions" and the refusal to allow coeducation, reflected very conservative assumptions of Islam and Muslim society, shaped by British experiences with the elite upper classes in India and Egypt. While upper-class Palestinian Muslims tended to practice strict gender segregation, its imposition in village schools, however, was rather ironic, especially as village boys and girls from a very young age worked together during the harvesting.[88]

The policy of creating two gender-separate schools at village expense negatively affected the spread of girls' education, leading Bowman to believe that there was widespread "prejudice against female education."[89] Although Herbert Samuel, the High Commissioner for Palestine, had approved a four-year plan in 1920 to create 300 rural elementary schools for boys and girls, by the time he had relinquished his post in 1925, the government had not yet reached its goal, with only 265 village schools having been opened, of which 98 were in new buildings, and only 10 were for girls.[90] Having to construct two separate schools for boys and girls was not always financially possible. Villagers in al-Bireh sent a petition, stating that they were unable to meet "the request of a minority of villagers to build a school for girls in the village," not because they opposed the girls' education, but rather "because of the distress and poverty and inability to pay taxes."[91] It should be noted that boys were also deprived of a school, as in the case of al-Khadder village, near Bethlehem, where village males were unable to contribute one hundred mils each toward a new boys' school.[92] By the late 1940s, "to circumvent limitations of size, [villagers] proposed the establishment of joint village schools," thus combining girls' elementary schools with boys' secondary schools, both of which were in demand.[93] It is not clear, however, if the British authorities accepted this idea.

Villages may have also been reluctant to invest in girls' schools because investment alone in the building did not guarantee the opening of girls' schools. The Department of Education forcibly closed the girls' school in the village of Mujeidil near Nazareth when attendance in the higher grade (fourth grade) was low, despite village protests and despite the estimate of some 150 girls between the ages of six and twelve in Mujeidil who could have attended the school.[94] The Department of Education justified the closure by writing that a "village school which fails to develop a fourth class is a waste of public funds."[95] The lack of female school attendance in Mujeidil could be explained by the central roles that girls assumed in agricultural work. The centrality of girls in village households was pervasive throughout Palestine even until the 1940s. One woman from the village of Silwan near Jerusalem recalled that her older sisters attended school for only a few years in the 1940s because "we lived from agriculture. We would go to sow land. . . . My sister, who studied until the fourth class, at age fifteen, would go to the land at Khan al-Ahmar to help with the sowing. We would go to pick the wheat. We worked in the land. The fellahin would take the girls to work the land with them."[96]

The development of schools in certain villages over others may have also depended on the intervention of middlemen and their proximity to government officials. Ylana N. Miller has identified three groups of officials who played important roles in the villages. The highest-ranking Palestinian administrators in the villages were the district officers who initially were responsible for matters of taxation, security, and welfare and whose control extended over a number of villages, clustered into sub-districts. In order to gauge village sentiments, they worked closely with the *mukhtar*, whose position had begun to wane during the Mandate period.[97] Throughout the Mandate period, to be a district officer was a coveted position held primarily by men with family and political ties. By the 1930s, the district officer had become increasingly instrumental in transmitting village demands to the government and in implementing government policy. As Miller points out, male teachers also used their positions of authority and their ties to the Department of Education to petition the government for favors.[98] The clustering of the initial village girls' schools in the Acre sub-district, specifically in the villages of Abu Snan, Kafr Yasif, al-Rama, and Tarshiha, suggests that its district officer, most likely aided by the village leaders and male teachers, was influential enough in order to convince the villagers and the Department of Education of the necessity for girls' schools in that area. Some of these villages, such as Kafr Yasif and al-Rama, were already familiar with girls' education, as a result of the various missionary schools founded in these villages at the end of the nineteenth century.

One village that was not serviced by the government, despite a long educational history, was al-Zib. The Ottomans had established an elementary school there in 1882,[99] and some time after 1930, the British had opened a boys' school, which by the late 1940s included over a dozen female students.[100] The presence of female students in the boys' school, however, did not move the British. In 1947, the Palestine Arab Workers' Society (PAWS), the oldest trade union in Palestine, which had recruited members from al-Zib, mostly small farmers, merchants, and day laborers, tried to intervene. It petitioned the Department of Education, writing that "there is good spirit in the village for education of girls, and the people have requested several times from the government to open a girls' school, but their request has not been answered. In the village there is a proper building for this aim, therefore we present the suggestion of opening a girls' school and the appointment of teachers."[101] Even though the village expressed demand and had a readily available building, its request went unanswered.

Even if a village was able to create a girls' school, it still faced the obstacle of finding women teachers. For women who trained to become teachers, the majority of whom grew up in the cities and towns, the villages often came as a real shock. Most found it impossible to set up a household on their own, and had little choice but to live with other teachers, siblings, or elderly mothers. When their households broke up, the women teachers found themselves also having to ask for transfers elsewhere. Health and sanitary conditions were also inadequate, if not lacking altogether. Village teachers frequently reported health problems, such as malaria and pyrexia. Teacher Wadia Bulus complained to one official that "my life in Kafr Yasif is very difficult and it is not in my ability to remain any longer and here my health has diminished. As for in Acre, I can live with my relatives and my living there would be much easier as I would be close to my town and my family."[102] Although Mustafa al-Dabbagh, a government school inspector, believed that teachers were expected to not only teach and create a bond with pupils, but also to edify the villagers by pointing out their wrongdoings,[103] women teachers, in particular, found the validity of their actions constantly being questioned. Hilda Zeibak complained about her work in the village of Abu Snan, near Acre, and felt that she "could not do much in the village as a whole because the teacher is criticized unmercifully in this region."[104] The personnel files of women teachers employed in villages are also full of accusations of indecent behavior, the consequence of being unmarried, working women without family members to protect them. As a result, the majority of women sent to teach in the villages did not stay for more than a few years, either transferring to more urban positions, or marrying, which brought an end to their teaching career.[105]

In 1931, a commission led by Sir Samuel O'Donnell, former secretary to the British government in India, whose purpose was to examine and report on the revenue and expenditure of the British administration in Palestine, set the tone for the next few years, causing expansion of rural education to come to a standstill. Even though the O'Donnell Commission acknowledged that the "fellahin believes vaguely that a school is a good thing," economic circumstances and need for additional labor compelled parents to withdraw their children before their education was complete.[106] Past experiences in India, where high-caste Hindus resisted British attempts to expand education into rural areas, had a strong influence on the commission.[107] Believing that the similarities between the rural areas of Palestine and India were great, the commission report concluded that village education in Palestine was a "waste of money and time," an attitude that was supported by the treasury as well.[108] Rejecting the comparisons between India and Palestine, Bowman, then the director of education, believed that inefficient and poorly educated teachers contributed to the stagnation of village education, and he urged the expansion of village schools, in conjunction with improving the teacher training.[109] Nonetheless, Bowman explicitly favored the expansion only of boys' education, writing that "no considerable extension of female education in villages is yet practicable, but advantage will be taken of any opportunity which may present itself for the establishment of a village girls' school wherever possible."[110] That is, the administration should not impose education on village girls, but rather develop schools when the villages demonstrated both a need and a financial ability to provide for a school building.

Departing from the overall freeze on girls' education, Sir Arthur Wauchope, the high commissioner for Palestine from 1931 to 1938, announced in 1935 his intention to open six more village girls' schools and a center in al-Bireh, then a village near Ramallah, to train Muslim village girls as teachers.[111] The establishment of the Rural Teachers' Training Center that same year represented the admission by the Department of Education that employing urban women in village schools was a complete failure. Its creation also reflected official recognition that village girls should be able to complete a full elementary education. Having completed the fourth elementary class in a village school, girls could then continue their studies in the Training Center for two more years, later expanded to three. The curriculum covered subjects taught in the rural schools, including gardening, poultry raising, and bee-keeping, in addition to classroom management and simple pedagogy. In conjunction with the idea that teachers should bring relief and progress to the villages, the pupils learned basic social welfare work and health work, supplemented by visits to the local infant welfare center and eye clinic.[112] Although the Rural Teachers' Training Center filled a large gap in rural education, colonial personnel files reveal that the school also played a significant role in educating Muslim women from urban areas of Palestine. Balqis Ahmad al-Shaykh was born and raised in Acre, and graduated from the Rural Teachers' Training Center in 1941. Khadija Kilani, in the same class, was from Jerusalem. Nazmiyya Muhammad Hassun, who graduated the following year, hailed from Haifa.[113] Their attendance in the school suggests that urban girls, who were unable to secure admission to the WTC, would continue their studies at the Training Center. As these women were not from the Muslim elite, opening the doors of the Training Center to urban, non-elite Muslim girls also may have been a means of diverting them from the WTC, and enabling the WTC to maintain its elite image.

Despite the training of rural women teachers, and occasional overtures at expanding girls' education in the villages, the British continued to refuse to open village girls' schools. Finances played a key role in limiting girls' education, and echoed British policies in Egypt, where Lord Cromer said that "want of money . . . was the first obstacle in the way of rapid progress."[114] According to Tibawi, the education budget dropped from £130,000 in 1921–1922 to £97,279 in 1923–1924, leading to the curtailment of all educational expansion until 1933. Although the British cited the economic depression as the cause of the financial stringency, Tibawi claims that the state revenue

Teachers and students (?) at the Rural Teachers' Training Center, al-Bireh, 1946.
Photograph by Anna Riwkin-Brick, CZA PHR/1174725.

had increased by over a million pounds from 1921 to 1931. Rather than invest in education, the colonial administration chose instead to give one-third of the budget to public security, with the rest divided between other services in order to maintain minimal development of Palestine. Although the budget was increased in the mid-1930s, by the end of that decade, the British again had diminished its educational expenditure, with their financial resources funneled into thwarting the Arab Revolt, before being financially drained by World War II.[115]

Toward the end of the war, the British increased the educational budget in Palestine, enabling some growth in the number of village girls' schools. In 1944–1945, there were forty-six girls' schools throughout the villages of Palestine. The numbers, however, are rather misleading, as only two provided a full elementary program through the seventh elementary class, while the others reached the fourth elementary class or less. In comparison to the town schools for the same year, twenty out of a total of thirty-four town schools or 59 percent of them offered the full elementary cycle.[116]

For lack of other options, some girls attended the local village boys' school. In 1929–1930, more than fifty girls, primarily Muslim, were enrolled in boys' schools throughout villages in the sub-districts of Ramallah, Beersheba, Nablus, Tul Karim, Jenin, and Safad, a phenomenon that continued over ten years later.[117] In 1942, the educational committee, elders, and notables of Malha, a village near Jerusalem, appealed to the Department of Education that, having already built a boys' school, their "desire to give the same chance to our girls grew so strong during the last seven years that some of us put their girls in the boys' school. This desire is reaching its peak and is almost causing us a problem. The boys' school is becoming crowded, the number of girls wishing to go to school is highly increasing, and in such an embarrassing condition we find no way except to request from Your Honour to help us in establishing a girls' school."[118] Similarly, the *Rabitat al-shabiba al-ramiyya* (al-Rama young men's union), representing the mixed Greek Orthodox, Druze, and Muslim village of al-Rama, alerted the Department of Education that several girls, having completed the fifth grade level in the local girls' school, were admitted to the higher-level boys' school. As the petition noted, "the majority of girls, being unable to use this privilege, were, therefore, left semi-illiterate."[119] In both cases, the petitions illustrated that British-imposed gender norms helped to prevent pre-pubescent and pubescent village girls from attending school, and, in some cases, from continuing their education. For some village girls, however, the opportunity to be educated was far greater than maintaining the "harim conditions" that the British administration had dictated.

In the 1940s, about 6 percent of village girls continued their education in the urban government girls' schools, which offered a higher level than the village schools. It was not easy for village girls to attend town schools. Some girls were compelled to leave home and move in with relatives or acquaintances, just as women teachers did, as well as other professional women.[120] Others traveled daily from their villages to nearby towns, accompanied by older brothers who also attended nearby high schools or with their fathers. From the village of Suba, several girls from a single family walked on a daily basis to attend school in Jerusalem, some ten kilometers away, with their father, who worked in the city as a baker.[121] Not all girls were so lucky. The daughters of the Abu Rish family were not allowed to walk the three miles from their village of Izariyya to Jerusalem with their brothers in order to continue their education.[122]

The failure of the British to open girls' schools, as well as boys' schools in all the villages, also gave impetus to the *kuttab* schools to continue to function as well, as a means of informal education. In 1931, some 28 urban-based *katatib* were recognized by the Department of Education as educating 1,023 boys and 148 girls.[123] In the 1930s in Bayt Safafa, a village near Jerusalem, some twenty-five to thirty-five children attended the *kuttab* of Shaykh Jabbar, with girls sitting in the front of the room and boys at the back. Each child remained in the *kuttab* just long enough to master reading, writing, and memorizing the Qur'an. 'Aliyye, a former pupil of Shaykh Jabbar, recalled that "the boys afterwards would go to school. There were not any schools in Bayt Safafa, only in Jerusalem. The girls did not go. My brothers studied with me with the Shaykh. I was better than them. After they finished, they went to school, and I did not . . . They went to school in Jerusalem and I stayed at home." Na'ame, also from Bayt Safafa, actually claimed that the opening of a government boys' school in the village in 1935–1936 caused all the boys to leave the *kuttab*, leaving only the girls to study with Shaykh Jabbar.[124]

'Aliyye relayed that while her mother had encouraged her to attend the *kuttab*, that was the extent of her formal education. She continued to learn informally with the help of her brothers and a Jewish neighbor who offered to teach her some English. She remembered that

> we had cows and I would take them to graze and the Jewish neighbor would come and visit me when I brought the cows to graze. She said to my mother, "How can a mother allow her son to study and not the daughter?" I stood by her. She said, "Come to me, I want to teach you English." I went to her and she taught me the alphabet in English. I learned English from this neighbor. When I took the cows to graze, I would take a notebook and a pen without my mother knowing where I went, so I could study with the neighbor. When I would return home, I would open the notebook to study, but as soon I realized my mother was home, I would hide the notebook.[125]

ACCUSING THE BRITISH OF "INEFFECTIVE LITERACY" AND "DELIBERATE ILLITERACY"

The colonial limitations of girls' education did not go unnoticed by the public. While individuals and local committees regularly petitioned the Department of Education, demanding the establishment or expansion of a school, the most visible, public battle against British policies toward education was launched by the local Arabic newspapers from the late 1920s onward. The newspaper *al-Karmil*, published in Haifa by Najib Nassar, often ran articles on the front page censuring the department's limited provision of education. For several years, Nassar published a series of field reports based on his own visits to government schools throughout the country. While Nassar often praised the British administration for spreading "progress" and "modernity," he also criticized it for not meeting the people's demands for education. Nassar and his newspaper led the campaign to open a girls' school in Haifa, calling upon the director of education to open a school so that "our daughters do not loiter in the streets, whose morals will be lost from social relations with boys of the alleys."[126] The same article argued that a government school would solve the financial difficulties facing many families who could not pay the tuition fees of the private schools in Haifa, especially when they had several daughters to educate. When the school was finally opened in Haifa some fifteen years after the British Mandate in Palestine had begun, *al-Karmil* reminded readers that the struggle was not yet over, writing that "many women and men came to us, not believing that their daughters were refused a seat . . . those refused have increased more than before. The people are in a growing crisis and have waited every day for the opening of a school for their daughters."[127] In the opinion of *al-Karmil,* opening a girls' school in Haifa was not sufficient if the school could not accommodate all those who sought admission.

Nassar also published a series of articles addressing the problems of village education. Nassar contended that the village schools did not truly fulfill their aims in educating youth to remain in the villages. He complained that "limiting the education of our children to reading and writing makes them believe that they will become *effendiyya* [westernized, middle class] and that it is disgraceful for them to engage in agriculture. They demand [bureaucratic] positions, which they do not get, and [then] they become a burden upon their fathers and their country, and they sell their land and their houses in order to eat bread, wear pants, and sit at the coffee shops, sharing their political views."[128] Similarly, his wife Sadhij Nassar, a journalist in her own right, disparaged the British Mandate for not developing girls' education within the villages. Like many others, she believed that village girls needed practical agricultural training, writing: "Country girls are not like the city girls who fear dirtying their hands from work. Rather, they work all the time in the fields and orchards. It is essential, I think, that they have some knowledge of agriculture and of raising birds and livestock in order to enlighten them."[129]

Although both Najib and Sadhij Nassar criticized the British for not doing enough to develop agricultural education, their attitudes echoed that of the director of education, who favored practical, manual instruction over an "ineffective" literary education, perceived as useless to Palestine's progress.[130] Moreover, their views were typical of urban Palestinians, who tended to perceive the villagers as different, backward, and capable only of working in agriculture. The word for peasant, *fallah* or *fallaha,* even was considered a disparaging term, referring to a person who was uncivilized or lacked sophistication.[131] Given the role that *al-Karmil* played in inculcating nationalist sentiment throughout Palestine, it becomes clear that both Najib and Sadhij Nassar believed that the village schools, with their emphasis on agricultural skills, were essential to the Palestinian struggle in remaining on the land and in preventing land sales to the Zionist movement. As Najib Nassar had mused repeatedly in several articles, a literary education would lead only to lost hopes, idleness, and forfeiture of land.[132]

Palestinian criticisms of the policies of the Department of Education were particularly scathing by the mid-1930s, reflecting the growing discontent with the colonial administration as well as the intensifying of Palestinian nationalism. In July 1935, Jamal al-Husayni, representing the newly founded Palestine Arab Party,[133] submitted a petition to the British Parliament, alleging that "illiteracy is a common enemy that is being developed among the Arabs by the negligence of the Government." He charged the British with deliberately not developing schools, despite Arab demands, in order to keep the Arabs ignorant and politically disorganized. He contended that the claim "that the Government does not find teachers enough to carry out its original programme in doing away with illiteracy is foundless [*sic*]," noting that the Department of Education could have imported teachers from Syria or Egypt, and that Palestine was actually exporting teachers to Iraq and Transjordan. Al-Husayni also challenged British claims of not having enough finances to fund education, pointing out that the British increased the budget of the police and prisons, and had "floated loans . . . for all purposes except education." Finally, al-Husayni accused the British of not enabling the Arabs to control their own education and of allowing them to remain uneducated because of the British commitment to Zionism, which he believed "thrives much better when confronted by an Arab population three quarters of whose members are illiterates and consequently ignorant."[134]

During late 1936 and early 1937, these claims were heard again before the Royal Commission, which came to Palestine to investigate the reasons for the six-month-long Arab-led economic strike beginning in April 1936, followed by an armed revolt against both British and Zionist targets. Hearing testimonies of Arabs, Jews, and British officials, educator Khalil Totah, who spoke on behalf of the Arab Higher Committee, was most direct, stating that the major grievance of the Arabs was that they did not have any control over their own education and as a result, it did not reflect their nationalist aspirations. British control over Arab education, he concluded, was "either designed to reconcile Arab people to this policy [of creating a Jewish national home in Palestine] or to make the education so colourless as to make it harmless and not endanger the carrying out of this policy of the Government."[135] Like Jamal al-Husayni, Totah also accused the British of failing to eradicate illiteracy, especially among women, by not opening enough girls' schools. In his testimony before the Royal Commission in January 1937, Totah decried the British provision of education, noting that in all of Palestine, there were only fourteen village girls' schools, with only fifteen girls having reached the seventh elementary class.[136] Following the release of the Commission's findings, which confirmed the charges leveled at the British administration, the Jaffa newspaper *al-Difa'* asked cynically in reference to five hundred children who were refused admission into the government schools if "the Department of Education want[ed] to leave this number wandering the streets," or did "the administration [have] any remorse, in light of the accusations of the Royal Commission that it had committed injustices against the Arabs for not showing enough concern for girls' education."[137]

Illiteracy was especially tangible within the Muslim community. The 1931 census revealed that only 3 percent of Muslim women and 25 percent of Muslim men were literate, with literacy defined as the ability to read or write in any language among inhabitants aged seven and up. The other religious communities in Palestine were somewhat better off. The missionary schools contributed to the higher literacy rates within the Christian community, where 44 percent of Christian women and 72 percent of Christian men were counted as literate, while the Jewish community had reached 93 percent literacy among its male population, and 78 percent among its female population. In terms of geographic distribution, Muslim women in Jerusalem, at 23 percent, were more literate than their sisters in Haifa and Jaffa, at only 10 percent. Jerusalem also had the highest rate of literacy among Christian women at 65 percent, compared to only 51 percent in Jaffa and 50 percent in Haifa.[138] The relatively high level among women in Jerusalem, Muslim as well as Christian, was a direct result of the city's well-established schools.

The low levels of literacy in general especially among women can be explained not only by British policy, but also by reading as primarily a male pursuit, at first limited to the ulama, and later expanded to include the male elite who benefited from the development of modern education. Literacy was a sign of having acquired an education, which conferred prestige and status upon the ulama and later on the male elite.[139] As Ayalon points out, "most Arab Palestinians were excluded from the 'literate community,'" no matter how it was defined, with more men receiving an education than women, and with Christians having better access to education than Muslims. For those who were literate, books and the ability to read became a symbol of modernity and progress, with Graham-Brown and others having noted that books began to appear as props in photographs of youth, boys and girls who were being educated, as well as of male and female intellectuals already in the late Ottoman period.[140]

Village girls suffered from the highest rates of illiteracy, because of the obstacles both in creating schools for them and in keeping them in school. As Tibawi points out, "the Department [of Education] was all the time trying to achieve permanent literacy with four years of schooling, with incompetent teachers and inadequate equipment, and in areas with sharply different social environments."[141] In a study about village education, Mustafa al-Dabbagh, an inspector of education, wrote that one of the main problems in maintaining literacy among village pupils was that their families removed them from school before completing the full four years of village education,[142] usually because of economic reasons. Government statistics reveal that the number of girls enrolled in village schools significantly dropped from the first to the fourth elementary grade. In the 1943–1944 school year, 872 girls were enrolled in the first class of the village schools, but only 282 girls were in the fourth grade class; that is, enrollment in the fourth and usually highest grade in the village decreased by 70 percent. In contrast, enrollment from the first to the fourth grade in the urban schools diminished by only 37 percent. In the urban girls' schools, the real decrease occurred after the sixth grade,[143] with families tending to remove their daughters once they reached puberty.

Literacy was seen as being essential to promoting nationalist goals. Although Beth Baron has shown within the Egyptian context that nationalism does not require literacy in order to thrive,[144] leading members of the Palestinian nationalist movement did draw a connection between literacy and nationalist consciousness. In particular, they used the press to rally the public, although the degree to which it really influenced the illiterate segments of the population is questionable. Fleischmann has argued that the press "may well have played a socializing and politicizing role disproportionate to its size and official readership figures in the intensely political atmosphere of mandatory Palestine," pointing out that the British carefully monitored and censured the press, as they understood its mobilizing potential.[145] Weldon C. Matthews has shown how one political party, the Istiqlal party, used its official newspaper to articulate Arab nationalism, to criticize British policies, to create dissent among readers, and to mobilize the population in civil disobedience tactics against the British.[146] Certainly for the younger generation within the nationalist movement, who had received a western-style education and had developed modernist views, illiteracy was seen as not being conducive to nationalist consciousness and to nation-building. It is difficult to determine if the British deliberately sought to keep the Palestinians illiterate, as local nationalists claimed. British experiences in Sudan, with young Northern Sudanese educated at Gordon College, an elite colonial institution, who began to subvert British rule through their nationalist writings and demonstrations, may have negatively shaped British attitudes toward expanding literacy in Palestine.[147]

Women writing within the press saw female literacy not only as meeting nationalist needs, but also as imperative for reforming the country. Subhiyya Maqdadi, a young girl from Tul Karim who attended the Friends' School in Ramallah and later entered AUB, argued that when "a woman learns reading and writing . . . she will form opinions and she will reject superstitions and idle talk destroying the minds of women."[148] While she saw women's literacy as expanding their knowledge and providing women with a voice, her argument also evoked the modernist approach of eradicating popular female practices that were considered superstitious, from exorcising spirits from the body to wearing charms to ward off the evil eye. In contrast, Fatima Fahmi underlined the notion that girls should only learn to read and write so that they could acquire religious knowledge.[149] The link between girls' literacy and religious knowledge was also illustrated by the Haifa-based *Jam'iyat tahthib al-fatat*, which held a "party for ladies" in 1920 during which they read the story of the birth of the Prophet Muhammad, in addition to giving speeches about the importance of girls' education.[150]

The wish of the British to "remove long-standing prejudices against girls' education" by providing the Palestinian Muslim population with a system of government education was far from being realized by the end of the British Mandate. The last set of available figures from 1944–1945 shows that the government administered only eighty girls' schools in all of Palestine, with a total attendance of 15,303 pupils. While the British may have made inroads in terms of spreading boys' education, having opened 398 boys' schools attended by 56,359 pupils,[151] the government provision of girls' education was poor in comparison. By the end of the Mandate period, Arab girls formed only 21 percent of all the pupils in the government schools. Numbers give evidence to the disparity in education that was created by the British, with urban girls as well as boys having had a higher likelihood of becoming educated than rural children. Only 7.5 percent of the girls in the villages received an education, while roughly 60 percent of their urban sisters did. This disparity meant that the majority of the Palestinian female Muslim population, which overwhelmingly resided in villages, was not educated, in contrast to a minority of girls who resided in Palestine's towns, who were educated. The picture was much better for village boys, with some 63 percent receiving a government education, albeit limited, by the time the British administration came to an end.[152] Thus, those who did not benefit from the provision of government education were by and large women, especially village women, who faced double biases against them because of their geographical location and their gender.

When comparing the available statistics on government education from the end of the Ottoman rule, there is no doubt, however, that the British expanded the provision of state education for girls. If we accept Tibawi's figure of 1,480 girls enrolled in Ottoman government schools in 1914 as accurate, within eleven years, the British had doubled the number of girls who attended government schools. By the end of the Mandate, the number of girls enrolled in the government schools had increased tenfold since 1914, reaching 15,303 female students, including over 2,000 Christians, in 1944/1945.[153] Taking into consideration that the total Arab population had more than doubled, from 737,089 Arab inhabitants in 1914 to 1,864,108 in 1946, this expansion of girls' education was considerable.[154]

Yet, despite the growth in girls' education beyond what it had been at the end of the Ottoman period, the British still clung to the belief that Palestinians did not care about their daughters' education. The chief secretary stated that government efforts to extend girls' education had been discouraged because of "the traditional disfavour" toward educating girls as regarded "by the majority of the population of Palestine."[155] Indeed, the British regularly claimed that Palestinian obstinacy prevented any changes to the status quo, while brushing aside socioeconomic factors within the villages that prevented girls from attending school. The 1929 world collapse of the economic market, the subsequent impoverishment of the Palestinian villagers, followed by the migration of some 30 percent of the villagers to the cities in search of work surely did not contribute to the advancement of girls' education in the villages.

The absence of government schools in the villages and the inability of the urban schools to accommodate all those who demanded an education led to a growing disillusion among the Arab public towards the Department of Education. While many Muslim girls were unable to study at all or could not continue their studies, others turned to the private schools, both the Christian missionary schools and the nationalist schools, the subjects of the next two chapters.

Reading the Bible and Wearing the Veil

Chapter 3

MUSLIM GIRLS IN CHRISTIAN SCHOOLS

As the British administration focused mainly on providing educational services to the Muslim population, Catholic and Protestant missionary schools, in addition to a few confessional schools attached to local Arab churches, became the main source of education for the various Christian communities within Palestine. A small, but significant number of Muslim girls also studied in these schools.[1] The experiences of these girls, however, were undoubtedly different from those who attended the government and the locally initiated private schools. Moreover, even though the missionary schools never succeeded at attracting a large number of Muslim pupils, the impact of the missionaries on the Muslim population and on Palestine's educational development still was strongly felt, and became an intense cause of concern for Arab nationalists, whose pertinacious voices dominated the Palestinian Arabic press.

Most of the Catholic and Protestant schools had a relatively long legacy of educating several generations of Palestinians by the time the British had set up their administration in Palestine. In the early years of the British Mandate, the percentage of Muslim girls in the Catholic and Protestant schools hovered around 20 percent, because of the limited provision of government schools, while by the 1940s the percentage had declined to only 9 percent, as both government and locally founded private schools increased.[2] In specific areas, however, the number and percentage of Muslim girls attending Christian schools remained relatively high even as attendance dropped on a national level in the 1940s.

In Jerusalem, 13 percent of Muslim girls attended Christian schools, about 50 percent more than the national average, and somewhat less in Jaffa and

TABLE 2. DISTRIBUTION OF MUSLIM GIRLS BY TYPE OF SCHOOL AND
LOCATION, 1944–1945

Type of School	Christian	Government	Muslim	Total
Jerusalem	430	1,561	323	2,310
Jaffa	307	1,701	794	2,802
Haifa	149	514	627	1,290
Nablus	151	1,311	177	1,639
Jerusalem District Villages	65	654	60	779
Villages Southern District	—	796	108	904
Villages Samaria District	14	611	38	663
Villages Galilee District	112	646	99	857

Source: Department of Education, *Statistical Tables and Diagrams for the Scholastic Year, 1944–1945*, Table III, "Arab Public System. Teachers and Pupils Classified by Locality, Religion and Sex"; Table XVI, "Moslem Schools (Non-Public). Teachers and Pupils Classified by Locality and Sex"; Table XVII, "Christian Schools (Non-Public). Teachers and Pupils Classified by Locality, Religion and Sex."

Haifa. As Table 2 shows, in the villages of the Galilee, for example, the percentage of Muslim girls who attended missionary schools was like that of Jerusalem, given the many Catholic and Protestant schools in Nazareth. In contrast, only 2 percent of the Muslim girls who lived in the Samaria district, that is, the villages around Nablus, Tul Karim, and Jenin, attended Christian schools because few Christian schools operated in this district, which was predominantly Muslim. By the end of the Mandate period, Catholic schools continued to be the most popular of all the Christian schools. Figures from 1944–1945 indicate that the Catholic schools educated four times as many girls of all denominations as did the Protestant ones. Within the Muslim community, the Catholic schools were favored over the Protestant ones, with 1,077 Muslim girls enrolled in Catholic schools throughout the country, compared to only 454 Muslim girls in Protestant schools.[3]

A small number of Christian schools in Palestine developed ties with the British administration, which may have added to their popularity. Despite claims of an insufficient budget for government schools, the Department of Education annually provided grants-in-aid to a limited number of foreign schools, as was characteristic of the British administration in Egypt and India as well. Financial assistance was given according to the number of pupils per school, as long as the schools taught basic reading and writing skills, allowed yearly inspections by the Department of Education, and complied with sanitary regulations. Schools that offered only religious instruction or were below an elementary level were not eligible for assistance. Both the schools and the Department of Education benefited from this arrangement. Private schools were eager to receive financial assistance, especially when some barely had enough resources to stay open. While the grants relieved the Department of Education of having to educate several hundred Palestinian Arab children, at the same time, the department maintained some degree of control of these schools, especially vis-à-vis the curriculum.

Throughout the Mandate period, the majority of schools that received government financial aid were English-speaking Protestant schools. From the beginning of the British Mandate until the end, the Department of Education gave yearly grants to the Jerusalem Girls' College because its provision of teacher training was considered a "very valuable service" given "the dearth of female teachers and the desirability of expanding female education."[4] Other English-speaking Protestant institutions, such as the Friends' School in Ramallah and the Tabeetha Mission School in Jaffa, also received grants. The private Arab schools yearly submitted requests for government grants, but never received grants, even though one petitioner claimed that "these schools have assited [sic] greatly in struggling against ignorance and illiteracy [and] have collaborated with Government schools in spreading education in the country."[5] The Department of Education, however, deprecated the private Arab schools, believing that they were really "of the Moslem *kuttab*,"[6] and not deserving of government aid.

The British administration believed that English-language schools and the teaching of English in general would create support and a strong rapport between the British colonial administration and the Arab population.[7] Jerome Farrell, who succeeded Bowman as director of education, also supported English language instruction as a means of bettering relations between Arab and Jewish youth, and to enable them to communicate with one another in after-school activities.[8] It was these English-speaking Christian schools, especially those that provided secondary education to the upper-class elite, which corresponded to the vision of the colonial administration. Their graduates, who were a select few, were selected to serve the British administration; young men entered low-level administrative positions, as Sharkey has shown in the case of Sudan,[9] and young women took up teaching. The French Catholic Sisters of St. Joseph School in Bethlehem may have understood the favoring of English-language schools when in 1935 it announced that "because of the demand of the people" it decided to open a "special class to teach English and to prepare pupils to obtain the Cambridge Junior Diploma."[10] Such a move would enable the school not only to accommodate the demands of the public for English language education, but also to potentially please British interests as well.

Schools that taught in English undoubtedly became attractive institutions to the Palestinian elite, who clung to the notion that the education of the elite should be conducted in a language not understood by the masses, whereas Arabic as the language of instruction would imply, to use Hobsbawm's claim, a "homogenization and standardization of its inhabitants."[11] Instruction in foreign languages, especially in English, enabled members of the elite to maintain their distinction from others. In addition, an English language education was seen as opening the doors to British colonial circles, whether political or social, as well as to employment within the ruling administration. Foreign language skills not only identified Palestinians as belonging to a certain social class, but also provided them with a more cosmopolitan identity. As Hobsbawm writes, "to be monolingual is to be shackled, unless your local language happens to be a *de facto* world language."[12] In contrast, knowledge of other languages gave the elite access to the outside world, especially to western literature and the press, in addition to manifesting a "modern" identity, as foreign language fluency was a testimony to having received a new, western-style education.

The British favoring of the mainly English-speaking Christian private schools over others, together with their higher academic level, also helped to reinforce the image of the private Christian schools as being the elite (and better) schools. Forced by the Ottomans to close during World War I, the Catholic and Protestant schools had to reconsider their curricular aims if they wanted to reopen and compete with the small, but expanding government system supported by the British colonial administration. While in the past, the Catholic and Protestant schools were portrayed as being better schools merely because they were Christian and not "Ottoman" schools, this was no longer the case during the British Mandate. Rather, during this period many of the Catholic and Protestant schools adopted the use of entrance exams and comprehensive final exams, including those used for acceptance into the British universities, creating an atmosphere of heightened academic competition. The limited number of grants-in-aid also compelled the private schools to become increasingly competitive, as the administration would only give them to schools that met their criteria.[13] Considering the economic difficulties during the Mandate period, the governmental monetary grants became particularly coveted, especially when many schools accepted a significant percentage of pupils free of charge.

THE APPEAL OF THE ANGLICAN SCHOOLS

Two schools that enjoyed some popularity among Muslim families were the Jerusalem Girls' College and the English High School in Haifa, both founded by the J&EM. The Jerusalem Girls' College was established after World War I, on the foundations of St. Mary's Home and the day school, both of which had closed during World War I. Initially called the British High School and Training College, by 1919 it already had 250 pupils, the majority of them Greek Orthodox, while one-fifth included Jewish and Muslim pupils.[14] By 1923, competition from other schools, many of which provided free education, led to a declining enrollment, although the number of girls entering the secondary level of the school grew. In the same year, the school was renamed the Jerusalem Girls' College, reflecting the school's ambitious academic goal of providing secondary education to girls (hence the "College" in the school's title), as well as its attempt to become the main female educational institution in Jerusalem. In the words of the school's first headmistress, Mabel Warburton, "We do not want them to feel that Beyrout is the only possibility for further education and England is very undesirable."[15] In addition to a preparatory kindergarten class, and six primary classes, the school provided four years of secondary education, culminating in the Oxford and Cambridge School certificate exam; this exam was replaced by the Palestine Matriculation exam in the early 1930s. The school also offered a special diploma class in preparation for the Palestine Matriculation exam, which kept older girls in the school.

The English High School in Haifa was founded in 1919, with the J&EM having been involved in educating primarily Muslim girls in Haifa since the turn of the century.[16] The English High School was much smaller than its sister institution in Jerusalem, with only 140 pupils by the mid-1930s, or about half the number of girls who attended the Jerusalem Girls' College. The language of instruction in the younger grades was Arabic, with English the language of instruction from the sixth grade onward, and in the subsequent four secondary classes. Like the Jerusalem Girls' College, the English High School also prepared its pupils to take the Oxford and Cambridge certificates. Unlike the Jerusalem Girls' College, however, the English High School tried to present itself as a local Arab school, by having a mixed English and Palestinian staff. A 1934 report on the school praised the English teachers, writing that "the teaching at the secondary school is good and there is marked effort on the part of the English staff to develop good mind and character, and induce thought on the part of their pupils," but it criticized the Palestinian teachers, stating that "the teaching in the Primary school suffers from the fact

Pupils at the Jerusalem Girls' College, with headmistress Mabel Warburton, 1919. From the private collection of Nadia and Teddy Theodorie.

that so many of the teachers have no training in modern methods."[17] Despite the criticisms, however, the practice of hiring local women teachers for the lower grades in the school may have helped to increase the number of girls in the school.

Both the Jerusalem Girls' College and the English High School emphasized in their published brochures that they were "Christian institutions," and that they had "well educated and cultured Christian staffs."[18] According to the headmistress of the English High School, the school's spirit was based upon the teachings of the "life and ideals of Jesus Christ," and would only succeed if the teachers and the majority of the pupils were Christian.[19] Although both schools limited the number of non-Christian pupils, the administration of both schools also justified the admission of non-Christian pupils by stating that the schools would become "meeting places" for Christians, Muslims, and Jews, where peaceful coexistence and tolerance for the other would be promoted.[20] The missionary teachers often referred to the Anglican schools as having the unique position of being a "miniature League of Nations," reflecting the encounter and friendship between girls of different nationalities and religious backgrounds.[21] As Maria Småberg argues, this attitude constituted a redefinition of missionary education during the British Mandate, at least within the Anglican schools, as promoting religious tolerance rather than the intolerance that had characterized the missionary schools in the late Ottoman period.[22]

The Christian character of the school inevitably reduced the enrollment of Muslim students in both schools, which never exceeded more than 10 percent of the total student body. In their writings, the missionary teachers were

Girls from the English High School in Haifa on a picnic, 1933. From the Dorothy Morgan Collection, GB 165–0208, MECA.

particularly pleased when Muslim girls joined the school, although they were never satisfied with the numbers, with headmistress Warburton writing in 1922 that she was "sorry to say that the Moslem element is very lacking."[23] Three years later, in the fall of 1925, teacher Anna Irvine commented that the enrollment of Muslim students in the Jerusalem Girls' College was still low, as she counted only eight Muslim girls out of 127 girls total in the secondary section.[24] In the fall of 1929, the number of Muslim girls in the Jerusalem Girls' College suddenly increased to 25, while in the 1930/1931 school year, it had reached 53.[25] Although Okkenhaug writes that "not even the serious nationalist riots in 1929 discouraged either Arabs or Jews when choosing a school for their sons and daughters," the increase in Muslim students can only be tied to the Wailing Wall/al-Buraq riots, which in their aftermath evidently led parents to seek what they considered to be the safest and most secure institutions. In the following year, the school created "harim conditions" in response to the growing presence of Muslim girls. "Complaints from Moslem parents" that the school was "not at all harem," and that "large Jewish youths from the school next door" peered into the playground and into the school building itself, compelled the school to construct a high, durable "wall of coursed masonry" to ensure the privacy of the Muslim pupils inside the school and outside on its playground.[26]

More important than the actual number of Muslim girls in both schools were the families that they represented. In reference to the Muslim girls at the Jerusalem Girls' College who began the school in 1930, the headmistress commented that they were "all of the leading Moslem families, including a niece of the Mufti and two granddaughters of Musa Kazmi [sic] Pasha, who led the Arab delegation to London recently."[27] Similarly, Susanna P. ("Espie") Emery, headmistress of the English High School in Haifa, noted that although the number of Muslims was few, the school still boasted upper-class Muslim families, such as "the Beydouns, the Husseinis, the Tamimis, the Sadiks, the Abdul Rahmans and the Hashems, and a few other less well-known people [who] are very well satisfied. Their children come young, and go steadily through the school course."[28] Being able to attract girls from elite Muslim families was evidently seen as an accomplishment, as it gave both schools status within Palestinian upper-class society. Woodsmall, however, noted in 1928 that the "most conservative families" would not send their daughters to the Anglican schools, and that one woman from a conservative family was "severely criticized for sending her daughter" to the Jerusalem Girls' College,[29] apparently because of its strong missionary character.

By requiring students to pay the tuition fees, both the Jerusalem Girls' College and the English High School appealed mainly to the upper classes as well as the rising middle classes. The headmistress of the English High School even acknowledged that the fee was a means of attracting only those families with "any standing." Charging of a fee also compelled some families to send only one child to the Anglican schools, especially during the late 1930s and 1940, with the headmistress of the English High School musing that the drop in the lower grades was related to the "rise in the cost of living . . . [which] led parents to send the younger children to cheaper schools."[30] In contrast, the government elementary schools were all free of charge; the only exception was the Mamuniyya Girls' School, which charged a pound and a half per year, although 25 percent of those admitted were indigent girls and daughters of government schoolteachers who attended free of charge.[31] Charging tuition fees at the Jerusalem Girls' College was seen as giving the school an exclusive socioeconomic edge over the Mamuniyya, as well as the WTC, which began to accept girls free of charge as long as they agreed to work as teachers upon completing their studies. By appealing to girls who were able and willing to pay for their education, the Anglican missionary schools believed they could maintain a monopoly on education among the elite.

Both the Jerusalem Girls' College and the English High School held academic entrance exams, which enabled the schools to be selective in whom
they accepted. In 1942, for example, the English High School accepted only
forty out of sixty to sixty-five new applicants, with some girls withdrawing
their applications given the difficulties of the exam.[32] Older girls, mostly
Muslim, who wanted to transfer into the Jerusalem Girls' College, usually
from government schools or from private Arab schools in order to continue
their studies past the sixth or seventh grade, found this task nearly impossible,
as the Anglican schools claimed that their previous training was inadequate.
The four-year secondary course at the Jerusalem Girls' College also required
competency in English, which only girls from other English speaking missionary schools would have acquired.[33] Some young girls did manage to transfer into the Jerusalem Girls' College, such as Nadiyya, who, after one year at
the WTC, left for the Jerusalem Girls' College because it did not require local
pupils to reside in the school.[34]

One way in which both the Protestant and Catholic schools impressed
their teachings upon students was by providing a boarding section. Line
Nyhagen Predelli has argued that the purpose of boarding in a school was
twofold: to teach girls how to become "Christian housewives and establish
Christian homes, and to provide a marriage pool" for men educated in mission schools. She further argues that the missionary teachers hoped that by
residing in the boarding school the girls "would change their behavior and
that their Christian training would become so ingrained that they would be
able to withstand pressures" from their own culture after completing their stay
at the boarding school.[35] That is, the boarding school was seen as being the
best way of removing girls from their own culture and of immersing them in
a Christian one. The boarding section also reinforced what was learned in the
classroom and provided additional domestic instruction that the girls did not
necessarily receive at home.

Girls who boarded in the school participated in round-the-clock activities
that took place within the school. Anna Irvine, who served as the housemother of the boarding section at the Jerusalem Girls' College, noted that
all of the pupils "join[ed] in our House prayers night and morning," while
Emery relayed that she met with the older boarders each Sunday afternoon,
and taught them "Early Church History."[36] The boarding students were described as being particularly enthusiastic about their school, clearly reinforced
by their residency within the school. On "Diploma Day," for example, Irvine
wrote that the boarders were "busy ironing the folds into their pretty green
school tunics, and out of their white Sunday dresses," while she boasted that
they "are naturally well to the fore in teams for drill, choir, etc. in helping with

tea at such festivities."[37] Boarders also acquired new skills by living with the teachers and other girls. The headmistress noted that one Muslim boarding student from al-Salt in Transjordan, who had never left her hometown, was "amused and appalled at the new life, and had to be taught how to hold her fork and spoon at table, as well as many other little domestic lessons," while another Muslim boarder, described as being "rich and pampered," "had never made a bed or held a duster in her hand,"[38] a situation that was presumably rectified. Given the aims of the boarding school in transforming the girls, the housemother Irvine complained about visits of relatives, describing them as "too frequent or untimely,"[39] implying that they could potentially undermine their teachings.

The reluctance of families, however, to send their daughters to schools far from home affected the success of the boarding section in both Anglican schools. The English High School in Haifa closed its boarding section after a few years, as it could barely attract any boarders.[40] Similarly, the Jerusalem Girls' College never had more than two dozen boarders, and perhaps would have closed its doors if not for the Muslim boarders. In 1924, Warburton wrote that "for the first time, due to our move to the new building, we have three big Moslem girls (15–18) from two of the highest Moslem families (the Nashashibis and the 'Abd al-Hadi) as boarders," while housemother Irvine added that the three Muslim girls were "closely veiled."[41] The ability to attract girls from conservative, Muslim upper-class families was seen as a measure of success for the Jerusalem Girls' College, as girls from these families became models of example for others. Just as the number of pupils increased between 1929 and 1930, so did the number of boarders,[42] as families sought safe accommodations for their daughters following the Wailing Wall/al-Buraq riots. Although the three Muslim girls who boarded at the school in 1930 were not from Palestine, but from Transjordan, where girls' education was limited, by 1933–1934, the number of boarders had increased to a total of twenty-two, including eight Muslims.[43]

While the Jerusalem Girls' College sought upper-class girls, the English High School educated some lower-class Muslim girls at the expense of different dioceses, church societies, and individuals abroad. Among them were Lydia Hassun, who was described as being "a poor little misery," and whose mother left her father because of abuse.[44] Similarly, the New Zealand Board of Missions contributed twenty-four Egyptian pounds for the "upkeep of a Moslem girl, Sarah Timur."[45] A few letters about these girls tell about their educational progress, but also emphasize their exposure to Christianity, revealing the real intent behind financing the education of specifically Muslim girls. For example, Miss Gardner, who was the headmistress at the English

High School in the mid-1920s, wrote that "Nazmia is a Moslem girl. She always took the scripture lessons and was most devout at school prayers. Her mother was a pupil in this mission before the war. The mother assures me that she prays daily that God will bless this school."[46]

Supporting the education of Muslim girls in missionary schools was one of the main reasons why foreign women donated to the various missions. As Joan Jacobs Brumberg writes, women's missionary journals, which circulated among the various women's groups throughout the United States and England, were "preoccupied with the heathen practice of child marriage and infant marriage," with "the awful fate that awaited girls in non-Christian lands [being] a popular justification for the missionary school program overseas."[47] Common were reports of "girlless villages" in the Middle East and Far East, referring to villages where girls had been married young and thus deprived of girlhood. It was sensational stories like these that motivated middle-class British and American women to contribute funds toward the advancement of girls' missionary education in the two regions. As K. Pelin Başcı writes, by the turn of the century, this image of a terrible fate awaiting Muslim girls had begun to shift into more positive images of Muslim girls attending school and becoming educated, reflecting what was perceived to be the efforts of the western missionaries.[48]

The two schools also relied on contributions made by current and former students, indicating the degree of respect that they had for their school. While graduates of the two missionary schools occasionally contributed funds to the schools, current students held annual bazaars, usually around the Christmas and Easter holidays, where they sold their own hand-made embroidery and lace. Miss Gardner at the English High School relayed that students were most eager to help their school, even those pupils who were unable to pay the tuition fees. She wrote that, "At school prayers one day I told the girls how much our friends were helping us by giving us things for the bazaar, & said all kinds of gifts would be appreciated. After prayers, Lydia took her little bracelets off her arm, gave them to her mistress Miss Katreena Harameh & said, 'Please give these to Miss Gardner for the bazaar because I too want to help with my school,'" even though "these bracelets were the only little possession of value that the child had."[49] The story of Lydia, the same girl who was supported by a patron of the J&EM, was meant to illustrate that despite her poverty, she wanted to hand over her single valuable possession for the sake of her school, not unlike stories of village women who abetted the rebels during the Arab revolt by selling their jewelry and donating its proceeds.[50] The message was that Lydia, the impoverished Muslim girl, was slowly being transformed into a modern girl who cared about her school and her education.

This notion that students should contribute to their schools had become ingrained in the many women who had attended missionary schools, with the bazaar becoming a feature of the local Christian Arab women's associations; the majority of members had attended missionary schools, and by the 1930s, the bazaar had been adopted by Muslim women's associations and private Arab schools as well.[51]

THE SCHOOLS' CHRISTIAN CHARACTER, MUSLIM PUPILS, AND ATTEMPTS AT CONVERSION

Despite the belief that the two Anglican schools were a meeting grounds for different religions, religious instruction remained a contentious issue. Both schools insisted that all non-Christian pupils, including Muslims, participate with their Christian peers in the same religious instruction, thus ensuring that all students have the same foundation. Warburton, the first headmistress of the Jerusalem Girls' College, explained that although "the school promised to keep controversy out of [its] religious teaching . . . the Bible itself, Old and New Testament, is taught as part of [its] curriculum." Some parents evidently protested, with Warburton writing that, "I have had difficulty on this point, but the parents have now accepted my standpoint that this is a Christian school and those who come [to the school] must accept Bible teaching."[52] Warburton's attitude was that the non-Christian families had to realize that their daughters' exposure to Christian teachings in the Jerusalem Girls' College was the price of being educated in that school.

While both Muslims and Jews were required to attend scripture readings at the Jerusalem Girls' College, the first headmistress insisted that they not be compelled to attend daily prayers, stating that, "as regards attendance at Opening Prayers, I have found it best not to make this compulsory for others than Christians, and I feel sure myself this is the right thing to do, one cannot force Jews and Moslems to join in Christian Prayers, and yet we must be free to make the prayers definitely Christian."[53] Thus, the school drew a line between involuntary religious instruction and voluntary Christian prayer. The decision to not compel non-Christian students to participate in the morning prayers may have been a tactical one. While on one hand, it would have pleased parents to know that their daughters were exempt from worship in a religion other than their own, on the other hand, by exposing pupils to sufficient Christian religious instruction, the non-Christian pupils might voluntarily choose to partake in the prayers, thus relieving the school of any blame.

The attitude was slightly different at the English High School in Haifa, where headmistress Emery stated that "all pupils attend school prayers every morning, and though most of the non-Christians take no active part in the worship, they follow the Bible reading and hymns in their books."[54] Non-Christian pupils also participated in the scripture lesson given at the first hour of the day, with Emery noting, perhaps rather wistfully, that the students showed "interest, which grows more active as they get more accustomed to the school."[55] There is some evidence, however, that the obligatory prayer attendance at the English High School was a source of conflict between some of the parents and the school. Emery reported that "a Moslem father of a small girl in the Arabic KG [Kindergarten] wrote to ask that his daughter should be excused from attendance at prayer & scripture." She continued, writing that she had explained that "the goodness of the school depended on its Christian character," and offered to refund the school fees if he "still felt strongly on the matter." The father explained his position, fearful that his daughter would follow in the footsteps of his wife, who "had been educated at a convent school in Egypt, and was now Moslem only in name." Both Emery and the father refused to compromise, however, with Emery finally returning the school fees and the father withdrawing his daughter.[56]

Muslim families at the Jerusalem Girls' College also were not always supportive that their daughters should comply with the religious instruction. Winifred Coate, who served as headmistress of the Jerusalem Girls' College from 1929 onward after Warburton, complained, "One of these new Moslem girls sent two brothers and a cousin in here to intercede with me to allow exemption from religious instruction, as her uncle was a very important sheikh." Not moved by the fact that the girl's uncle had religious knowledge and a degree of social and political power, Coate suggested that it was the girl's being "new" to the school and her lack of familiarity with it that led her to evidently complain about the religious instruction. Coate proudly acknowledged that she did "not allow [her]self to be importuned, & the girl has come in spite of all & seems very much interested in the scripture lesson."[57] Fleischmann noted similar instances of girls and fathers who "contested the compulsory attendance" in church services and religious instruction at an American missionary school in Lebanon, with the missionaries considering the concession of one disgruntled father a real "victory,"[58] much the way that Warburton and Coate presented their stand. These requests for exemption suggest that parents did not fully comprehend the Christian character of the religious instruction when they enrolled their daughters, or that they rather naively believed that the teachers would not compel their Muslim daughters to learn about Christianity. The reassurance of the headmistress that the girl was "very much interested" in learning the scripture was one means of justifying why

Muslim girls attended the religious instruction, as it placed the student and her "interest" rather than the school as guiding her religious instruction. The implication was that even if the parents objected, the girls were eager to learn about Christianity, and this was a process that could not be stopped.

Although the correspondence of the teachers at the two Anglican schools provides little indication that the pupils resisted the Christian teachings, the lack of record does not mean that resistance did not take place, especially given that students did protest missionary teachings in other schools. Fleischmann notes that Muslim and Jewish students at the American Junior College in Beirut engaged in a strike, refusing to attend compulsory worship.[59] Similarly, a number of letters written by Zainat Nur al-Din of Safad, who was sent to the American missionary school in Sidon at the expense of the Supreme Muslim Council, detailed the pain and anger that she felt by her school's "treatment of pupils, especially the Muslim ones." She claimed that the school had debased her religion and had affected her "religious state and educational study." She requested to return home, where she would enroll in another school. She wrote to the inspector of education in the Supreme Muslim Council that "I had informed you last year that I refused to go to church, and I also refused to study the holy book . . . I was the only girl among the Muslim girls who took this action, and then this year there were five Muslim girls who refused to go to church. When they did that, the school's administration began to appoint a teacher to spend Sundays in the school to give us Christian training."[60] Nur al-Din's testimony sheds light on the ways that the schools used to weaken the religious convictions of the pupils, such as hiring special teachers to work closely with obstinate students in their religious studies. In another letter, Nur al-Din wrote that the school's English teacher degraded Islam and the Prophet Muhammad by teaching pupils to write sentences such as "Mohammad, he was an evel [sic] man."[61] Nur al-Din was contesting not only the missionary message, but also, in the words of Fleischmann, "the fundamental relations of power inherent in the message."[62]

What is interesting in the case of Zainat Nur al-Din is that Ishaq Darwish, the inspector of education for the Supreme Muslim Council, with whom she corresponded, did not immediately take her side, but insisted on hearing "an official version of this matter" from the school's headmistress,[63] suggesting that there were two sides to the story. Indeed, the headmistress of the school wrote to the inspector that she was disappointed by Nur al-Din's "low standard in schooling" and her "lack of interest in her studies,"[64] suggesting that the pupil had fabricated all the charges in order to be removed from the school because of a lack of inclination and ability. While we may never know whether the charges alleged by Zainat Nur al-Din against her school were accurate, she nonetheless was removed and admitted to the Quaker Friends School in Ramallah.[65] Ishaq Darwish, the inspector, it seems, was not fully convinced that the Christian schools sought to convert Muslim children until several years later following a trip to Nazareth, when he wrote that "I saw myself Christian crosses and rosaries and angels in the hands of Muslim children just as the headmistress took them into the school,"[66] as if these accoutrements confirmed that the Christian schools had designs on converting Muslim children.

Animosity toward Islam and attempts at conversion did not remain concealed within the schools, but rather became public knowledge during the Mandate period, in part due to the active campaign of the Supreme Muslim Council against the missionary schools done in tandem with the Arabic press. As early as 1922, the SMC had begun to accuse missionary schools of having caused young Muslim youth to abandon their morals and question their faith. An unseen circular was reportedly issued on June 28, 1922, and again in early 1923, calling upon the "people of religion to cooperate in repelling these [missionary] movements in a legal and cultural manner."[67] The SMC ordered qadis, judges in the religious courts, to collect names of Muslim children attending missionary schools, and then sent religious officials and sometimes muftis to persuade the families to remove their children from these institutions and instead admit them into private Arab schools or government ones, with the SMC at times helping to defray the tuition costs.[68]

Although it is not clear from the archives whether clerics from other parts of Palestine responded or not to the SMC's campaign, the qadi of Hebron did, pledging that he "would take precautions to repel that which is feared," even though he admitted that "the ignorance is a blow against us in the village," and recommended the "appointment of a traveling preacher" to "spread beneficial advice, and make the religious obligations understood . . . and to stop the spread of the missionaries."[69] In a later letter, he acknowledged that he had contacted the parents of boys attending an American missionary school in Hebron, and told them that "there is danger in sending your boys to the American school, and the result is not good for our religion, and we feel ashamed." Realizing that these youth could neither read nor write, he recommended that the SMC fund a "room and a teacher to teach them religion and Arabic" in order to provide an alternative to the missionary school and to take these youth "from darkness to lightness."[70]

The actions of the Supreme Muslim Council against the missionary schools were not out of the ordinary; rather, they were one of the multifaceted responses among Muslims throughout the Middle East to the Protestant and Catholic schools, which ranged from their acceptance to complete rejection. The modernist Islamic *salafiyya* movement called for social and spiritual reform and a return to a more pure form of Islam. Prominent among them were the Egyptian Muhammad 'Abduh, considered to be the intellectual leader of the Islamic reform movement; the Syrian religious scholar Rashid Rida, who published the influential newspaper *al-Manar* in Egypt; and Muhammad Kurd 'Ali of Damascus, a scholar and owner of the newspaper *al-Muqtabas*. Some Islamic reformers accepted the right of Muslims to pursue modern knowledge within the missionary schools, on the condition that they would be able to maintain their religious identity. Others perceived missionary education as endangering the Muslim religious identity and/or the Arab nationalist identity and called upon Muslims to establish their own schools.[71] The anti-missionary stance within the Muslim community in Palestine was buttressed by similar attitudes within the Jewish community, although there is no evidence that the two communities were unified in any way against their common enemy.[72]

The holding of an international missionary conference in Jerusalem in March and April of 1928 further fuelled the SMC's anti-missionary campaign. While the missionary conference called for the expansion of missions and Christian education, as well as an appeal to non-Christians to heed its call,[73] *al-Jami'a al-'arabiyya*, the SMC's official newspaper, carried full-page reports for several days denouncing the conference, the speeches given, and the decisions taken. Through its reporting, the newspaper created fear in the hearts of the readers, with the intention that the newspaper reports would lead parents to remove their children from the missionary schools. It also portrayed the missionaries as sowing the seeds of tensions between Muslims and Christians as well as among the Christian denominations in Palestine, at a time when unity among the different religious communities was seen as essential for maintaining a strong front against Zionism and the British.[74] A year later, the Supreme Muslim Council claimed that its campaign against the missionaries had been a success, and cited the closure of missionary schools in the districts of Jenin, Nazareth, and Hebron. In places where schools did not close, the Supreme Muslim Council asserted that it had successfully caused Muslim students to leave missionary schools for other institutions, such as in the case of male students in villages around Nazareth, and female students in the Haifa district.[75] Although the connection between the SMC's campaign and the closure of schools or the removal of pupils is not easily verified, the SMC wanted the public to see it as being the main force in weakening the missionary presence in Palestine, while ignoring other factors, such as the economic depression in 1929, which contributed to both the withdrawal of some pupils from their schools as they could no longer afford the tuition fees, as well as the closure of some schools.

NATIONALIST POLITICS AND LOCAL STRUGGLES

The Anglican schools survived the SMC's campaign against missionary education mainly because they were elite schools, and the ties of the two schools to the British administration provided additional protection. Nonetheless, neither school was completely insulated from the religious tensions that characterized Palestine from the late 1920s onward. While school was not in session during the Wailing Wall/al-Buraq riots of August 1929, four weeks later, the headmistress of the Jerusalem Girls' College began to express concern that the riots would affect the enrollment and atmosphere of the school. She wrote that "there is a 'curfew' law still in operation & special patrols are out every night to see that the streets are cleaned and all people in their houses before 9 p.m. The shops are open again, but very little business appears to be being done, as Jews are afraid to enter Moslem quarters and vice versa" (a reference to the fears that Arabs expressed at entering Jewish quarters). Coate expressed concerns that many families had "lost a good deal of money owing to the riots," and was particularly worried that they would "economise on their girls and refuse to pay fees for them," noting that "the education of the girls is usually the first thing to suffer in this country at any time of loss."[76] This especially was the case among girls from the middle classes, whose education in private schools was dependent upon the ability of their parents to pay tuition fees. Coate's anxieties about the effects of the riots on girls' education were justified, given that the numbers at the Jerusalem Girls' College dropped at the beginning of the school year in the fall of 1929 to about 150 students, about 50 less than the school was used to having.[77]

In addition to economic loss, fear of the other also played a determining factor in the diminishing number of students following the 1929 riots. Headmistress Coate noted that "people are still very much afraid of each other. Jews are still boycotting Arab goods & Arabs are spreading tales that the Jews sell poisoned goods & vice versa." According to Coate, parents had become reluctant to send their children to a mixed denominational school, as they are "all boiling over with enmity and full of suspicion."[78] A letter written by a Muslim student apologizing for no longer being able to attend the Jerusalem Girls' School is telling of the fears that some pupils and their parents must have felt after the Wailing Wall/al-Buraq attacks. She wrote, "My mother is afraid to send me to school . . . she thinks that it is not safe for me to go to school because the Jews are very hypocrites [*sic*] & can by many ways kill or poison or do any harm to Moslems." She herself added that she had heard from a Christian pupil that a Jewish classmate had threatened to kill some of her Muslim peers in retaliation for the murdered Jews, causing her to fear for her safety, which she justified by writing that "each day we heard of small attacks made by the Jews against the Arabs. It is not safe at all for Moslems to pass near or be with Jews."[79]

The school's location in Rehavia, a Jewish neighborhood in the new part of the city, also caused difficulties for the Arab students, and especially the Muslim ones. While the headmistress expressed hope that "the girls may gradually straggle back," she also had heard "that in many cases, the girls have been already put into other [schools] in what are considered safer districts." In order to "allay the fears of the parents" that their daughters studied in a Jewish neighborhood, the school hired police to patrol the school outside; "word soon went out" that the school was "well protected" as a result of the "British policemen with rifles," and according to the headmistress, this protection was the reason for the "increase of numbers [of pupils] [the] next day."[80] Although Muslim families "would not dare to send their own cars," fearful about the consequences if they did, they did agree to allow their daughters to ride the school's buses "if a teacher would bring them right to their door." With the introduction of escorted busing, Coate proudly stated that the school had "lost very few of the Moslem girls. We have now got back representatives of all our best Moslem families," referring to daughters of the Husayni, Khalidi, 'Abd al-Hadi, and Dajani families.[81] While busing may have relieved parents of the worries of traveling between the Arab neighborhoods of Jerusalem and the Jewish ones, it did not, however, solve the hostilities that took place between the Jewish children who lived or studied in Rehavia and the Arab pupils who arrived daily at the Jerusalem Girls' College. Nadiyya, who attended the school for nine years, related that she traveled "by bus from Shaykh Jarrah to Rehavia . . . [when] the students would get off in Rehavia. . . . the [Jewish] children would yell '*arab jarib, arab jarib*' (mangy Arabs)."[82]

The period that followed the 1929 Wailing Wall/al-Buraq riots was not an easy one for the Anglican schools. In the wake of continued religious tensions, the SMC convened a Pan-Islamic congress in Jerusalem in 1931, which was attended by ulama and other religious figures from around the Muslim world. Delegates called for increased teaching of religion in the government schools, and the creation of Islamic schools in order to quell the enrollment of Muslim children in missionary schools. One report presented to the congress gave a full overview of the missionary scope in Palestine and its results. Reiterating claims that missionary schools belittled Islam and its teachings, the report stated that "the faith of the youth has been shaken." Women in particular were singled out in the report. It posited that the "influence of this decay [i.e. the missionary schools]" was "in the development of the position of women especially in the cities," which was characterized by a "feminist revolution (*al-inqilab al-nisa'i*)," and "refusal of early marriage, expansion of women's freedom in which they have begun to attend parties, lectures, and places of entertainment, the creation of women's clubs, the way of acting freely with [wearing] the hijab, and demanding knowledge and education."[83] This report directly linked missionary education with the increased westernization, while negatively connecting it to the "women's awakening" of the late nineteenth and early twentieth century. Despite the strong accusations against missionary education, especially as it affected gender norms, the published resolutions of the conference were rather conciliatory toward missionary education. While the resolutions called for the creation of schools, they did not specifically declare their opposition to the missionary schools. The resolutions did not even specify that schools should be religious and nationalist, although they did call for the establishment of a higher Islamic university, where the "language of the Qur'an" would be the official language of instruction.[84]

The SMC intensified their attack on missionary schools in January 1935 when the mufti of Palestine and head of the SMC, Hajj Amin al-Husayni, convened a conference of ulama to demand an end to Jewish immigration as well as the cessation of land sales to non-Arabs. In his Friday sermon (*khutba*), not only did al-Husayni warn his audience about the Jewish immigrants' spreading "a spirit of promiscuity and infidelity," but he also added that "the missionary schools . . . work to destroy Muslim beliefs and Arabic culture, and our sons and daughters who finish studying in them denigrate the religion and make fun of the tradition and culture."[85] The following September, the SMC's Department of Religious Institutions (*da'irat al-ma'ahid al-diniyya*) issued a pamphlet appealing to parents to remove their children from missionary institutions and to admit them instead into the many private Arab schools that were being created, suggesting that the SMC had still not yet won their battle as they had claimed. The pamphlet read that the missionaries "hang their hopes upon your children who study in their schools. With their money, they [the children] turn into the enemy of you and your religion, and with picks, they will destroy your city and your home. Indeed, you will see with your own eyes many of our youth who make fun of our fathers and who are proud of belittling the principles of Islam . . . and this is the fruit of the foreign schools which are the most harmful missionary means among us."[86] The SMC also warned Muslims about dubious attempts at coeducation within the missionary schools,[87] most likely in reference to the small number of schools that accepted young boys into the lowest grades. Most likely, the SMC used the idea of coeducation, the mixing of Muslim girls with non-related boys, to suggest that the missionary schools posed a challenge to local norms of non-socializing between the sexes.

As a means of discouraging families from admitting their daughters into missionary schools, newspapers underlined the significance of girls' education to nationalist identity and the transmission of that identity to the next generation. A young Arab Christian woman writer from Jerusalem, Suʿad Khuri, asked rhetorically in *al-Difaʿ* if it was not "a shame that the Arab boys and girls are brought up without any knowledge of the great Arab history and the Arab customs and their literature after the conquests," and placed the blame on the foreign schools that "teach improper knowledge." According to Khuri, and many others who wrote in the press, girls particularly needed to know their nationalist history, as they, as future mothers, would become their children's "first schools."[88] In another article in *al-Difaʿ*, Khuri repeated that the "foreign and missionary schools," and even "some government schools," made girls ignorant of the "history of their country, their heroes, or their language," and keenly observed that the girls from these schools "are like a tomato salad. Some are English, others French, others German," in reference to the languages, histories, and cultures to which they were exposed. Rhetorically asking her readers "where are the Arab women," Khuri implied that Arab girls who attended the Protestant and Catholic schools had lost their identity. Her solution was directed to her peers in the missionary schools, calling upon them to "demand your rights for education; force your schools to teach Arabic and Arabic culture," in the realization that for some segments of the population, the missionary schools would remain central to their education.[89]

Concerns about girls being taught foreign languages were commonplace. Fatima Fahmi, an Egyptian woman residing in Palestine, complained that the lives of young girls "were lost and their time wasted" in learning foreign languages (as well as sports). According to Fahmi, girls needed to be trained only in reading and writing Arabic, and in religious knowledge, as "religion teaches the girl how to treat her husband, and children . . . and how to live with people."[90] The journalist Sadhij Nassar chided women for speaking in French instead of Arabic, and for adopting French names, or for pronouncing Arabic names with a western twist. Language was linked to the nation, she argued, and she could not understand why Palestinian women did not "mimic [western women] in their nationalism and feel the strength of their nationalism and in raising their children and serving their homes and loving their language?" She concluded by rhetorically asking whether or not the readers "see that the Jews will defeat us by actively encouraging their language Hebrew," suggesting that the learning of Arabic was essential if the Palestinians wanted to strengthen their position vis-à-vis the Jewish immigrants to Palestine.[91]

While Nassar believed that language was the key to the survival and strength of the nation, and that girls, as future mothers of the next generation, needed to be trained in Arabic rather than in other languages, others opposed the teaching of foreign languages to girls because the ability to speak another language was seen as potentially subverting the patriarchal order. Fadwa Tuqan, the Palestinian poetess from Nablus, recalled that in 1939, at the age of twenty-one, her father allowed her and a sister to take private English lessons from a Christian girl who had graduated from the Friends School in Ramallah. She writes, "We had the first lesson, then the order to stop was issued. Some of the heads of the family had raised objections to this freakish behaviour when they learned about it. . . . Father was eager to please." Although it was permissible for the men in the Tuqan family to become educated in foreign languages, they still lay "jealously in wait whenever one of us girls aspired to better things or tried to assert herself in quite natural ways."[92] Similarly, in the late 1940s, when the girls in the Abu Rish family of 'Izariyya, a village near Jerusalem, began to attend school, one of the older women in the family did not approve that they spoke among themselves in languages other than Arabic, as doing so was seen as lending to naughty and suspicious behavior.[93]

Missionary schools (as well as British officials) were also at the center of dubious press reports about girls and women who engaged in activities deemed as borderline immoral (such as dancing and even gambling).[94] A writer in the Muslim-owned newspaper al-Sirat al-mustaqim claimed that he had seen some of these women sitting in a seaside café, appearing "unveiled, made up, arms bare, breasts and neck visible," and accused them of being "mothers of lustful and contemptible daughters," rather than being the more praiseworthy "mothers of the future."[95] The implication was that their missionary education and constant exposure to western influences had caused these women not only to unveil, but also to wear makeup and expose themselves. They were portrayed as being narcissistic and hedonistic. Their behavior was contemptible in the eyes of the press, and their morality questionable. A song that was popular during the Mandate period compared the westernized Arab women to prostitutes, deploring their being "decorated up until their fingernails," and their "dress till the knees," as they lay in the sand at "Khayat beach" in Haifa, wearing "only underwear," as they entertained one another.[96] Although young women tended to be the main target of these criticisms, similar arguments were used to criticize the government boys' schools, namely that they failed to produce productive and politicized young men. Instead, they created young men who were "idle, sitting in coffee shops, habituating entertainment places and becoming patrons of the cinema, asking for nice clothes and perfumes and foreign (afranjiyya) drinks [alcohol] . . . while the nationalism in him becomes outdated or in passing."[97]

It was not only the western-style education within the Protestant and Catholic schools that was seen as endangering Muslim girls, but also the presence of non-Muslims in these institutions. The newspaper al-Sirat al-mustaqim believed that the mixing of Muslim girls with non-Muslims within the missionary schools would lead Muslim girls to unveil, writing that "the Muslim girl goes to visit her non-Muslim friend and some non-Muslim male relatives will be there . . . when the non-Muslim men see the Muslim woman in his home, he will not respect her nor will he avoid her . . . Then the visits will increase . . . [making it] easy for the Muslim woman to raise the piece of cloth from her life and her customs."[98] E. Fallet, the headmistress of a school in Jaffa that had a dominant Jewish presence and which belonged to the Church Missionary Society, commented that a girl from "a good Moslem family," and the only Muslim in the highest grade, "wore her veil most conscientiously, but soon discarded it in order to go to Tel Aviv to visit them [her Jewish friends] there." The girl's willingness to emulate her Jewish friends whenever she could was suggestive not only of the influence that the Jewish girls could have on their Muslim friends, but also of the degree of peer pressure encountered within school.[99] According to Yosef Vashitz, a contemporary journalist and student of Arab culture, the association between the unveiling of Muslim women with secular Jewish women was so apparent that when a group of Muslim women held a meeting to publicly declare the removal of their veils, a group of men taunted them by calling them "Jews," which quickly brought an end to the matter.[100]

These fears of Muslim and Jewish girls mixing in the missionary schools were closely associated with stereotypes that had developed about young secular Zionist Jews. Anna Irvine, who served as housemother in the Jerusalem Girls' College, claimed that at least two pupils, one a Jewish girl from the United States, and another a half Greek, half-British girl, were admitted to the school's boarding school because their parents were "becoming a little alarmed by the extent of their acquaintance among the youth of Tel Aviv."[101] Reference to the "youth of Tel Aviv" suggests images of young men and women flouting sexual norms, associated with the independence and self-reliance of many Jewish men and women who immigrated to Palestine often alone and without families, and who had flocked to the cities in the late 1920s in search of work, with women taking jobs as cooks, nannies, cleaners, and even prostitutes.[102] Even though Oz Almog claims that sex and sexual relations were still quite taboo in pre-1948 Zionist culture,[103] Ghada Karmi relates in her memoirs that Palestinian men would go to Jaffa Road in Jerusalem to look at Jewish girls because it was believed "they were all easy. They were anybody's."[104]

The stereotypes of Jewish women influenced the decision of the English High School in the mid-1930s to limit the number of non-Christians to only one-third of the whole school, and to one-half of any one class.[105] This "meant refusing 12–29 Jewish applicants,"[106] the majority of whom were refugees from Hitler's Germany. Many came from non-Zionist families, and had a difficult time integrating into the prevailing culture, hence their decision to enroll in schools outside of their community. In order to further limit enrollment, the schools also began applying age limitations, with the headmistress writing that "young pupils . . . are likely to stay longer, and therefore to be more strongly influenced by what they learn." She added that "a year or two in school" was not seen as being "of very much value to non-Christian girls if they come when they are fourteen or older, with their outlook strongly formed by their previous school; so we give an increasingly strong preference to pupils joining before they are fourteen."[107] Despite the quota policy, the headmistress Emery still complained in 1941 that "there are too many Jews, especially in the highest classes," and that the school "was trying to stem the influence . . . but it is difficult to refuse promising children."[108] A letter written in 1944 by parents of some Christian girls at the school continued to show concern about the attendance of Jewish girls, and conjured up the prevailing stereotypes about Jewish women and their "secular influences."[109]

The Muslim-owned newspapers also ran occasional sensationalized stories about Muslim girls who left their families and their religion after having attended missionary schools. *Al-Jamiʿa al-ʿarabiyya* warned readers about sending their daughters to the Italian Salesian School (known as Don Bosco) in Jerusalem, where reportedly a group of Muslim and Greek Orthodox girls had been taught about Catholicism without the knowledge or against the wishes of the girls' families. This exposure to Catholicism reportedly had led to the conversion of both a Muslim and a Greek Orthodox pupil. As in the story of the daughter of the mayor of Nablus prior to World War I as told in Chapter 1, the newspaper emphasized that the Muslim girl, like the Greek Orthodox one, had converted to Catholicism, and then fled to Damascus. According to *al-Jamiʿa al-ʿarabiyya*, the headmistress "played with the mind of a girl from *our* family and converted her, even though she is a minor and all this is done without her parents' knowledge. Our girl has been a prisoner in the convent for three weeks."[110] By referring to the girl as being from "our family," the author negated both the idea of the school being equivalent to a family, and the authority of the headmistress over the students. The use of the terms "our" girl and "our family" also emphasized that the education and re-ported conversion of a Muslim girl was not a private family matter, but rather was the concern of the entire Muslim community. Moreover, by stating that this girl had been converted quietly without her family even knowing, the newspaper suggested that parents were ignorant of what took place behind the doors of the missionary schools.

The press obsession about girls' education in missionary schools, the fears of their socializing with Jews, and their increasing westernization all need to be understood within the context of Palestinian nationalism. As Partha Chatterjee has argued, women within nationalist discourses came to be the preservers of culture against western colonialism; their westernization was tantamount to the destruction of national culture.[111] The concerns expressed here manifested what was understood as one of the weaknesses of the nation-alist movement: that it was unable to educate its own children, especially its daughters. The obsession with girls reflected their position as the guardians of Palestinian culture, but also the paucity of educational alternatives available for young Muslim girls compared to the much wider choice in boys' educa-tion. The notion that girls could not distinguish between local and foreign customs, or rather between right and wrong, also echoed throughout this discourse. By attacking female attendance in missionary schools, the press suggested that girls especially lacked the intellectual abilities necessary to discern between the academic benefits proffered by the schools and the Chris-tian, western ideologies that they tried to instill. By construing girls as the "weaker sex" (al-jins al-daʿif), the press also indicated that girls would not be able to refuse the religious teachings in their schools, and would be targeted for conversion, echoing the missionary discourse that girls and women were more susceptible to religious teachings. The notion that girls did not know any better also was a reflection of the patriarchal system that characterized Palestinian society, in which women's behavior, choices, and decisions were carefully monitored and controlled by their fathers, brothers, and other male family members.

The well-known newspapers al-Karmil and Filastin, both owned by Chris-tian Arabs, found themselves in a more difficult position in terms of the at-tacks by the press on the missionary schools, given the popularity of these schools among the Christian population. Seeking a middle ground, these two newspapers tended to be both supportive of specific schools and critical of missionary education, especially as it affected the unity of the community. For example, both praised the English High School because of its perceived "role in helping to advance the future of Palestine, the future of the home, in every means through learning and by arming its ladies [with knowledge]," but *al-Karmil* was careful to justify its support for this school by noting that it preserved "their [Arabic] customs, morals, and traditions," and respected "Muslim feelings."[112] Despite this backing, Najib Nassar, the owner of *al-Karmil*, believed that the missionary schools contributed to the division of the Christian community and asked rhetorically whether a country with multiple denominational schools could "become a nationalist community and raise the banner of true nationalism?"[113] Another article appearing in *Filastin* warned about the "dangers" of the missionary work in Palestine, noting that "the work of the missionaries does not only corrupt the relations between the Muslims of this country and its Christians, but it also creates fissures between the Christians themselves of the various denominations."[114] Thus, the struggle specifically of the Christian community against the missionary schools was not about conversion or cultural imperialism, but rather about Christian unity and strength vis-à-vis the larger Muslim community.

Christian newspapers also waged a battle with missionary education as a means of maintaining and preserving their indigenous Christian culture. The need to disavow themselves from the missionaries became especially urgent following the 1928 missionary conference in Jerusalem, when one newspaper began to accuse the local indigenous Christians and the foreign missionaries of being one and the same.[115] Failure to distinguish between the local, indigenous Arab Christians and the foreign missionaries clearly placed the local Arab Christian population in a precarious position. It made them equally foreign and labeled them as outsiders who were more Western than Palestinian. Thus, attacks on missionary education by the owners of the *al-Karmil* and *Filastin* were a means of emphasizing the local Palestinian identity of the indigenous Christians in the face of criticism from their Muslim counterparts, while they also asserted their difference from the western Protestant and Catholic missions.

The attack waged by both the SMC and the press against missionary education began to simmer by 1936, however, as the Arab population embarked on its nation-wide strike. The strike and the revolt that was to follow had their origins among impoverished Palestinian villagers who had migrated to the urban areas of Haifa and Jaffa in search of employment in the 1930s, as a result of debts and loss of agricultural lands.[116] It was in the shantytowns of Haifa and the surrounding villages where the charismatic Syrian-born and al-Azhar-trained religious scholar and roving marriage registrar for the Haifa shari'a court, Shaykh 'Izz al-Din al-Qassam, found a receptive audience. Preaching at Haifa's al-Istiqlal mosque, he called for people to mobilize against the

British and against the Zionists, mixing both religious and nationalist discourses. By this time, al-Qassam had already begun to organize military cells around the Haifa area, composed of destitute villagers and young men who were disenchanted with the traditional leadership.[117] In November 1935, after one of his followers killed a policeman, al-Qassam fled to Jenin with some of his men, where he died in a clash with British police and soldiers. His funeral procession was reported to be the largest one that Palestine had ever seen, and immediately he was evoked as a symbol of Palestinian nationalism and resistance.[118]

Al-Qassam's death was believed to be the catalyst for the tensions and violence that followed for the next three years, beginning with a series of intercommunal killings of both Jews and Arabs in April 1936. On the evening of April 19, 1936, following the murder of a group of Jews in Jaffa, a curfew was imposed and a state of emergency declared. Arabs in Nablus and Jerusalem called for a general strike of Arab businesses and Arab workers, in hopes that their refusal to work would cause the British to denounce their policy of allowing Jewish immigration into Palestine and the transfer of Arab lands to Jews. Five days later, Hajj Amin al-Husayni, the mufti of Jerusalem and the head of the Supreme Muslim Council, formed the Arab Higher Committee to coordinate the strike. According to Yehoshua Porath, "the strike looked all embracing, steadfast and vigorous, with Arab commerce and transportation almost completely at a standstill,"[119] with Fleischmann noting that "the adherence to the strike was surprisingly cohesive throughout its six month duration, revealing the depth of Arab feeling against the Zionist project."[120]

The repercussions of the strike, however, were not carefully taken into consideration by the Arab leadership. The strike especially affected the lower classes; having lost their livelihoods, they were compelled to seek donations and food relief collected by the Arab Women's Association.[121] The strike also inadvertently forced the Jewish economy to become increasingly self-sufficient and less dependent upon Arab labor, and thus fulfilled the Zionist ambition of employing only "Hebrew labor."[122] In mid May, in addition to the boycott, armed groups began attacking and sabotaging railroads, telephone lines, and British installations. By October 1936 the strike was called off, primarily as a result of the serious economic repercussions on the Arab economy. Although the armed rebellion also ceased in November 1936, it resumed again in July 1937. The British, however, began to more strategically counter the rebels by "utilizing measures such as collective punishment, deportations, mass arrests, house demolitions, night raids on villages, air strikes, restrictions on movement and martial law."[123] They also deported members of the Arab Higher Committee, with Hajj Amin al-Husayni fleeing to Lebanon in October 1937. In the summer of 1938, after the rebels took over the old city of Jerusalem, the British, with some 20,000 troops, began to strike back militarily against the rebels. Conservative British estimates placed the death toll among the Palestinians at over 3,000, with 110 rebels executed and some 6,000 imprisoned during 1939 alone, although in reality the numbers may have been higher.[124]

The events of 1936 to 1939 affected schools throughout the country. The press reported on the closure of government schools, with schoolboys and girls urging schools to shut down "until the immigration stops and the ranks are unified."[125] Government pupils were visible at a demonstration held after the Muslim Friday prayers during which several girls spoke about the need for unity, sacrifice, and the role of Arab women and young girls in "joining the jihad."[126] A former pupil in the government girls' school in Acre remembered girls joining student demonstrations and learning patriotic poems, which they wrote on their school desks.[127] In Qalqiliyya, at a meeting of "more than 200 women and young ladies," pupils from the local government school gave speeches and recited nationalist slogans.[128] Not everyone joined the strike because they wanted to, but rather, some were forced to strike under pressure from nationalist organizations and individuals. A graduate of the Jerusalem Girls' College who was working as a teacher in a government girls' school claimed that schoolboys had picketed near the door of the school, waiting for "any girls who were brave enough to go [to school]." While they allowed the teacher to enter the school building, they "drove the girls away," so she had nobody to teach.[129]

Unlike the government schools, many of the missionary schools tried to remain open, on the pretext that they were above the local politics. The teachers in the Jerusalem Girls' College did everything they could to keep the doors opened during the strike, in the belief that an "open school was also a symbol of normality and stability."[130] Letters written by the teachers to their families in England, however, reveal that the school had difficulties functioning. Headmistress Coate wrote in the early days of the strike that "the Strike Committee told the Moslem parents that they send their children to school at their own risk, and that they are now definitely beginning to interfere with girls' schools as well as boys',"[131] with the strike committees organizing a "good deal of picketing" of schools that remained open during the strike.[132] Although some girls from the Anglican schools did not attend school during the strike, it is not entirely clear if they were involved in picketing their own schools. Emery noted that during the strike "a number of little boys in the uniform of the Government school, clustered about the [English High School's] gate,"[133] indicating that it was not her students who were picketing their own school, but rather young boys, who were taking advantage of their celebrated position as males in Palestinian society, to either taunt the girls who sought to break the strike and attend school or to forcibly prevent them from entering the building. Coate later reported that the "13% who absented themselves [from school] were Moslems or Christians living in the Moslem Quarters," indicating that the social and political pressure to abide by the strike was particularly strong in these neighborhoods.[134]

Rather than admit that some of her pupils may have been conscientiously striking out of solidarity with the rest of the country, the headmistress at the Jerusalem Girls' College tried to blame their absence on the picketing of schools, as well as on the transportation difficulties that arose as a result of the strike. In her correspondence, the headmistress noted that she feared the buses would be stoned, and that "the Strike Committees [were] encouraging small boys to interfere with girls' school buses," just as they had tried to inter-fere with students trying to enter schools. The Jewish-owned bus company used by the Jerusalem Girls' College to transport girls to and from school was afraid for the safety of its drivers, and "absolutely refused to send a bus to Herod's Gate or to the Sheikh Jerah [sic] Quarter," just outside the Old City, even with a police escort.[135] The ability of the students to attend the school was clearly dependent upon the running of the buses; when the buses ceased to run, the school had "rather few girls." Teacher Dorothy Norman wrote that she even "walked down our bus route to collect such girls as were wait-ing and bring them to school on foot,"[136] indicating the determination and perseverance of both the teachers and the students to ensure that the school continued to function. By mid May, Norman wrote that "all the school buses were running, and most day-girls came back with the exception of a contin-gent of Moslems who were obviously on strike."[137] That a group of Muslim girls continued to strike while the Christian girls returned to school evinced much wider socio-political tensions between Muslims and Christians that began to develop during the strike, as noted by Yehoshua Porath, and which as Ted Swedenburg has argued, have been obscured by "the current rhetoric (and practice) of sectarian unity."[138]

In early 1937, the headmistress acknowledged that "some of the older girls definitely joined the strike and took part in the activities of the Girl Stu-dents' Strike Committee,"[139] presumably in reference to the *Ittihad al-talibat al-'arabiyya* (Union of Arab female pupils). Despite her acknowledgement, western women educators in Palestine seem to have been reluctant to ac-knowledge that their female pupils were politicized and influenced by the politics around them. H. M. Wilson, a British woman who taught at Bir Zeit National School near Ramallah during the height of the Arab rebellion in 1938–1939, recalled that on Balfour Day, which marked the British recognition of a Jewish national home in Palestine, the rebels told the school that it was a "strike day." While the male pupils spent the morning "marching round the village waving sticks and singing patriotic songs," Wilson affirmed that "none of the girls particularly wanted to go on strike. They were not politically-minded as the boys were."[140] Later, however, she admitted that some did express political affinities, noting that "an admiring crowd of girls" had gathered around a former pupil who displayed a home-made Arab flag, adorned with pictures of political figures including the Mufti Hajj Amin al-Husayni, King Faisal of Iraq, and Salah al-Din al-Ayyubi, the medieval liberator of Jerusalem.[141] It appears that Wilson was describing her personal beliefs about women's politicization, that they should remain indifferent to politics and outside of the public eye. While the girls may not have visibly wanted to demonstrate their political affinities with the Arab rebellion by striking or marching, their veneration of the flag suggests that they too identified, albeit quietly, with the rebels.

The Anglican schools, as well as other foreign Christian schools, inadvertently benefitted from the strike as well. The closure of government schools during both the strike and the Arab revolt made the non-government schools all the more attractive in the eyes of some, as they remained opened and functioned more or less as usual. In addition to a long list of boys' schools, the girls' schools that closed during the strike included the Rural Teachers' Training Center with fourteen pupils, and government girls' schools in Bethlehem, Bayt Jala, Ramla, Hebron, 'Ajami, Manshiyya (both in the Jaffa area), and Gaza.[142] While most of the schools quickly resumed functioning, the girls' schools in Ramla and Gaza were both suspended for longer periods of time.[143]

While the end of the strike meant that all the pupils would return to school, the Arab revolt that followed perhaps disrupted the normalcy of the Anglican schools even further, especially as students were expected to visibly show their support for the revolt. In the summer and fall of 1938, the rebellion began to spread from Palestine's rural areas to urban ones, with the rebels taking refuge from the British in the towns of Jaffa, the old city of Jerusalem, Haifa, and Nablus. Given the difference in dress between the rebels and the urban residents, the rebels ordered male residents to remove their Ottoman *tarbush* (fez) and replace it with the white *kufiya*, held in place with a black cord or *'iqal* so the British could not distinguish between the rebels and the urban residents.[144] Ted Swedenburg also claimed that urban Palestinian men agreed to wear the *kufiya* and the *'iqal* as a means of identifying with the

Arab revolt and the peasant rebel fighters, whose *kufiya* had become their insignia.[145]

Rebel communiqués also urged urban, upper- and middle-class girls and women to wear black veils over their hair, and to stop imitating the western styles of dress, in order to show their support for the uprising. Fleischmann points out that Christian women were also expected to remove their European hats and to wear the black *mandil* or head scarf, with the *Times* of London emphasizing the degree of coercion that reportedly was involved, as "church-going women had their hats torn off by boys and destroyed."[146] Yet it was not just western hats that became forbidden; other markers of modernity, such as women's wearing of short sleeves and lipstick, were also targeted, suggesting that this sartorial campaign was more than just an attempt to camouflage the rebels, but rather an attack against the westernized, upper- and middle-class educated women, who were seen as "symbols of, or guilty by association, with the enemy, the British."[147] Swedenburg also contends that these sartorial orders were directed primarily "at urban women and not at their rural sisters, who did not wear Western dress or go to hairdressers, who normally covered their heads with scarves, and for whom veiling would have been impractical."[148] As Fleischmann suggests, these decrees need to be contextualized as one of the outcomes of the internal power struggles within the nationalist movement itself, increasingly marked by conflict between the urban notable leadership and the rural peasant rebels who bore the brunt of the revolt, as both combatants and victims.[149]

These edicts also need to be understood as having been issued after nearly two decades of popular press depictions of urban girls who were educated in the Protestant and Catholic schools as being "overly westernized." It was not just that women were removing their veils, but rather, as an article in *Filastin* read, urban girls and women were being accusing of "spend[ing] too much time on idle gossip, dances and fashion, and it is due to the failure of Palestinian women's education," referring specifically to girls' education in the Christian schools.[150] Similarly, the Muslim-owned newspaper *al-Sirat al-mustaqim* declared the "westernized" women in Palestine as products of missionary schools and denounced them as those who "like to go to Tel Aviv, walk in the markets, and go to the cinema,"[151] at a time when other women throughout the rest of the country were expressing concern for Palestine's future.

In many ways, it could be argued that the edicts issued by the rebels as they related to women were also implicit critiques of western education, especially the missionary schools and the role that they had played in transforming women. It was also expected that the rebel edicts would target women's veiling as a symbolic and contested marker of Arabic and Muslim culture that had been subjected to scorn by the West and by some Arabs themselves. In her work on Norwegian Protestant missions to Madagascar in the late nineteenth century, Line Nyhagen Predelli notes that clothing "figured in creating moral boundaries between Christian behavior and Malagasy traditions."[152] The same can be said within the context of Palestinian girls within the Christian schools, as their western-style clothing became the marker of their Christian education and of their physical and moral separation from their own traditions and culture.

Missionary schools, however, did not work in a vacuum, but were aided by writers in the local Arabic press and the women's press, where, as Fleischmann points out, a lively debate took place between veilers and unveilers, ultimately examining much wider issues of gender, culture, and society.[153] A trend toward unveiling was set by Huda Sha'arawi, the leader of the Egyptian feminist movement, who removed her face veil upon her return to Cairo from an international feminist conference in 1923. By the end of the decade a trend toward unveiling could be discerned in Egypt, Syria, Lebanon, and Palestine buttressed by the publication of *Unveiling and Veiling* (*al-Sufur wa-l-hijab*) in Damascus in 1928 by Nazira Zayn al-Din, a young Muslim woman well versed in Islamic law who condemned the practice of covering a woman's face.[154] Photographs of upper-class women show their heads covered with black opaque scarves resembling turbans that descended down their necks, while still other women wore black scarves wrapped around their heads, as well as either opaque or diaphanous face covers, some that came down to the chin and others to the neck.[155] In the urban areas where the rebels issued orders to veil, a visible number of girls and women evidently did not veil, while in some cases the veil's fabric had become lighter and less concealing. In Nablus, for example, women were ordered to "cover themselves heavily and not to travel about with light or transparent veils,"[156] suggesting that even there, a town known for its conservatism, women were more inclined to "downveil."[157] Vashitz, writing in the 1940s, claimed that most of the urban women then covered their faces, while "only a few hundreds of educated women are contemptuous of tradition and show their faces,"[158] indicating that pressure to veil continued and may have even intensified in the years after the revolt.

During the revolt, the Anglican schools realized that they had to accommodate the sartorial orders of the rebels, and allow pupils to wear the veil. As the English High School had a diverse population, the school decided that "girls whose parents wish them to do so may wear a blue veil instead of a uniform hat," acknowledging that wearing the veil was a "concession to the times."[159] It did not want to enforce veiling itself, nor allow girls to decide for themselves, but rather left this decision up to the girls' parents. The school understood that the veil would ensure the safety of its pupils, as it identified them as Arabs and as supporters of the rebellion. By allowing girls to wear the veil, the Anglican schools also challenged the anti-missionary school campaign, by asserting that the pupils in the Anglican schools at least identified with the local nationalist politics, despite their seemingly foreign education.

The decision to allow girls to wear the veil during the revolt must not have been an easy one. On one hand, the veil was "a naturalized, unifying, and transcendent representation of the nation,"[160] and created a sense of greater unity between Christian and Muslim pupils. On the other, the veil became a kind of cultural barrier between Arabs and Jews within the school as it distinguished Arab girls from Jewish ones, which had not been previously the case. Headmistress Emery wrote that she had "a stream of anxious parents, asking if it was safe for their children to come [to school]" adding that "the Jews are especially afraid, because the Arab girls have to wear veils, & the Jewish parents are afraid that their children will be marked in hats, & they dare not wear veils."[161] Allowing the Arab girls to wear the veil instead of the hat worked against the "Christian character" and "League of Nations" vision that the Anglican schools had tried to promote.

Much to the relief of the headmistress, the girls at the English High School did not exactly wear the veils as they were supposed to. Rather, the headmistress noted, "they mostly wear neither veil nor hat, but carry a wisp of veil round their necks."[162] By wearing the veil around their necks, the pupils transformed the veil from a religious practice to a symbol of identification. By wearing the headscarf in a creative, fashionable, and even western way around their necks, they essentially disregarded the edicts of the rebels to veil. At the same time, placing the headscarf around their necks rather than over their hair reveals the degree to which these girls had internalized the missionary message of removing the veil. Their scarves around their necks also showed how different they were from their mothers' generation. Wearing a scarf around their necks also may have been a compromise for the Christian Arab schoolgirls who for obvious reasons did not want to veil. It is not clear, however, whether the pupils also ventured out in public with scarves around their necks or if they adjusted their veils into neck scarves only upon entering the school. Outside of the school, however, reports and photographic evidence from the time indicate that there were Christian Arab women and girls who did cover their heads as the rebels instructed, so that they would avoid looking like Jews, and appear indistinguishable from their Muslim peers.[163]

The way that the Muslim and Christian girls in the Anglican schools wore the veil was a clear manipulation of the traditions expected of them in terms of their religion, education, and national identification. Fleischmann identified the use of traditional norms and their subsequent manipulation as a common tactic of the Arab Women's Association. It used the upholding of these norms as a kind of weapon against the British, and regularly petitioned the British against various transgressions of local norms, especially those having to do with Islam and women's seclusion "in an effort both to affect British policies and measures to enforce them (particularly during the revolt) and to shame and alarm the British."[164] At the same time, we see Palestinian schoolgirls in the Anglican schools also playing with traditional norms and religious identity in order to make their own political statements. In fact, the wearing of the veil, however innovative, as a neck scarf among both Muslims and Christians was somewhat reminiscent of the way in which the Arab Women's Association manipulated both religious and gender norms when Matiel Mogannam, a Protestant Christian woman, delivered a speech at the Mosque of 'Umar on *al-haram al-sharif,* while Tarab 'Abd al-Hadi, a Muslim woman, spoke at the Church of the Holy Sepulchre.[165]

Despite the apparent tensions and the attempts to unify the Arab pupils, reports submitted to the Royal Commission investigating the disturbances, as well as correspondence of the missionary teachers throughout the 1930s, emphasized friendships between Muslims and Jewish girls, especially during the years of the revolt. In January 1937, headmistress Coate wrote that "the pupils continued to mix with one another freely in the play ground, during play times and dinner hours," and added that "at no time were the pupils forbidden to discuss politics or to read the newspapers."[166] That is, despite access to current events and perhaps even heated discussions, pupils interacted with one another. Similarly, the headmistress at the English High School noted in November 1938 that a "Turkish Moslem" pupil who had taken ill was escorted home by a Jewish girl, while a Jewish girl "who was taken ill during School Prayers . . . was escorted out and cared for by an Arab and a Greek."[167] Inter-communal relations between students, however, were not just limited to the school premises itself; according to Coate, "a considerable number" of girls from the Jerusalem Girls' College continued "to meet and visit one another's homes after they had left school" as well as correspond with one another. The headmistress of the Jerusalem Girls' College acknowledged that "if no distinction of race or religion were made, a habit of friendliness and mutual trust could be formed." Coate believed that "teaching all pupils a common language" helped to unify the students, while the promoting of common interests such as "team games of various kinds, Girls Guide and Ranger

Companies, picnics and expeditions" connected the students, despite differences in religious and national identities.[168] Moreover, the Jewish and Muslim students were a minority in both schools, and in some classes, only numbered a few students; being few in number, it was difficult for them not to interact with students who shared neither the same religious nor nationalist identity.

The education of Muslim girls in the two Anglican missionary schools did not always meet the cultural demands placed upon young Arab women, particularly young Muslims. These two schools exposed Muslim girls to teachings about Christianity, which at times caused tensions between the schools, the pupils, and their families. Moreover, the emphasis on the "League of Nations" within the Anglican schools and the supposed tolerance of other religions brought Muslim girls into contact with non-Muslim pupils, including Jewish ones. During times of national and religious unrest, namely during 1929 and again in 1936 to 1938, aspects of missionary education, namely the exposure to Christianity and to the "other," became points of criticism.

In many ways, the criticism of the missionary schools reflected the lack of Palestinian control over their own education. When the press came out against the missionary schools, it was not only criticizing the missionary schools and their agendas, but also the Palestinian political elite, which continued to send their children to these schools even after nationalist schools began to flourish in the late 1930s and 1940s. While the comparison was not always voiced, the concern for the domination of the missionary cultures also disclosed fears of the growing Zionist presence in Palestine. Like the missionaries, the creation of the "new Jew" and the Zionist Jewish culture was seen by many Palestinians as not only a political threat to the future of Palestine, but also as a kind of cultural imperialism that stood to undermine the Palestinians, their customs and traditions, livelihood, and culture, similar to that of the Catholic and Protestant missionary schools.

It was these paradoxes in part that caused the Muslim community to open its own schools. In particular, the Supreme Muslim Council very early on realized the problems of educating girls, as well as boys, in the missionary schools. In order to provide them with an education that was consistent with Arab culture and with their religion, the SMC chose to open several schools throughout Palestine, the subject of the next chapter.

Chapter 4

"The Love of the Nation Is from Faith"

THE ISLAMIC GIRLS' SCHOOL IN JERUSALEM

In September 1935, Salih Fathi al-Shirk requested help from Hajj Amin al-Husayni, the mufti of Jerusalem and the head of the Supreme Muslim Council, in admitting his two daughters into the Islamic Girls' School in Jerusalem. Salih Fathi al-Shirk noted that his youngest daughter was ready to enter kindergarten, while the older daughter was eager to learn "sewing and the Qur'an." Al-Shirk explained that the older daughter had been accepted into the Islamic Girls' School the previous year, but was unable to attend because she could not afford the required school uniform and textbook. The mufti, who rarely intervened in such petty matters, agreed to the request, and ordered the school to accept the two girls free of charge.[1]

Although the petition of Salih Fathi al-Shirk is terse, it can be read in several ways. Rather than expect his daughters to remain at home in the care of either their mother or another female relative, Salih Fathi al-Shirk's petition suggests that his daughters would benefit more from being in school, where they would acquire knowledge and skills that they could not learn from being at home. That he turned to the Islamic Girls' School, rather than a nearby government school, reflects the ongoing struggle of Palestinians to control their own education, as well as the ongoing inability of the government schools to accommodate all those who wanted to learn, particularly the urban poor. That a relatively impoverished man acknowledged his older daughter's ambitions to learn to sew and to read the Qur'an also underlines the importance that girls' education, however rudimentary, had acquired for even the most impoverished segments of Palestinian society. By learning to read and to sew, the daughters of Salih Fathi al-Shirk could become modern, educated mothers of the future. And even though Hajj Amin al-Husayni may have had political reasons for accepting the two girls into the school, as his intervention would have translated into political support, he too may have recognized that training young women in domestic skills and religious principles would be beneficial to building the nation.

The Islamic Girls' School was one of many private, locally founded schools established throughout the Mandate period, and seen by some Palestinians as the best solution to their children's education. These schools were initially called *al-madaris al-ahliyya*, meaning that they were founded by local initiative, and differed from the governmental, public schools (*al-madaris al-amiriyya*) and the foreign schools (*al-madaris al-ajnabiyya*). In Palestine, the *ahliyya* schools included those created and funded by the Muslim religious endowments, the various Arab Christian denominations, as well as those schools supported by the local municipality rather than by the Department of Education.² Around the 1930s, the press began to refer to *al-madaris al-ahliyya* as *al-madaris al-wataniyya*, just as the Protestant and Catholic schools fell under the rubric of *al-madaris al-ajnabiyya al-tabshiriyya* (the foreign, missionary schools). This shift from *ahliyya* to *wataniyya*, as well as the use of the emphatic *al-tabshiriyya*, reflected growing nationalist sentiments in Palestine. The change here also signified the increasing opposition toward the missionary schools, seen as being representatives of colonialism and as not nurturing any nationalist identity. While the *ahliyya* schools were emblematic of the fruits of local educators, the *wataniyya* schools became politicized sites for disseminating the Arabic language and culture, and represented the growing polarization between the education that the Palestinians envisioned for themselves and that which others envisioned for them.

Although Anderson has claimed that a Europeanized, colonial education was crucial to spreading nationalism among youth within the context of colonial Dakar,³ the creation of nationalist schools in Palestine was a local response to the existing colonial schools that sought to circumscribe nationalist identities among schoolchildren rather than promote them. The establishment of private local schools was not unique to Palestine, however, but was part of a much larger trend that took place throughout parts of the Ottoman Empire beginning in the mid to late nineteenth century.⁴ As Rashid Khalidi writes, the establishment of these schools "represented an important phenomenon in terms of the unmediated response not of the state, but of civil society, to the challenge of the West and of the modernity with which it was identified."⁵ Thus, the nationalist schools must be understood not only as an expression of dissatisfaction with the existing schools, but also as a means with which the Arab population could control their own destiny, by determining the future of their children's education.

As in colonial North Africa, where the elementary-level *kuttab* schools

played a role in confronting the colonizers and in shaping local Muslim identity,[6] elementary education contributed to the early formation of competing
nationalist identities and nationalisms within Palestine, particularly among
lower-class girls whose socioeconomic status prevented them from attending
missionary schools. While several scholars have acknowledged secondary education as crucial to cultivating nationalist male leaders,[7] gender and socioeconomic strata also were significant, as they determined the kind of education
one might receive, and particularly filtered out those who could continue onto
secondary education. Gender norms dictated that as girls approached puberty,
there was a greater tendency for them to be kept at home or to marry early,
which in turn limited their access to primarily a lower level of education. This
was not the case in the education of young boys, whose socioeconomic status
was the limiting factor. Socioeconomic standing often determined the level
of education of both girls and boys, with those from the lower classes being
less likely to acquire much beyond a few years of a rudimentary education, as
secondary education required tuition fees. Thus, the histories of elementary
schools and elementary education can reveal what secondary education does
not: the role that elementary schools had in shaping the identities of both
girls and pupils from the lower classes.

EDUCATIONAL ALTERNATIVES

This chapter focuses on the history of a single nationalist school, the Islamic
Girls' School (*al-Madrasa al-islamiyya lil-banat*) in Jerusalem. This school
was one of several local nationalist schools established for girls in Palestine
during the Mandate period, reflecting the growing concern for girls' education within nationalist circles as well as disillusionment with private and government education. Sectarian divisions, however, overrode nationalist unity,
and implicitly dictated that schools be established along confessional lines.
The Islamic Society of Haifa opened its girls' school in 1921, offering a diverse curriculum including religion, Qur'an, Arabic language, history, geography, mathematics, domestic science, singing, and sports.[8] One of the earliest
women's charitable associations, the Jaffa Orthodox Ladies Society, established its National Orthodox Girls' School in Jaffa in 1923, with three teachers and one hundred pupils; despite the religious orientation of the school, it
reportedly had both Muslim and Christian pupils.[9] A number of women also
established their own nationalist schools, paralleling similar actions by women
in Syria and Lebanon.[10] In 1924, Nabiha Nasser established *al-Madrasa al-
wataniyya al-ʿaliyya* (the National High School) in Bir Zeit for children from
the Protestant community. A year later, a teacher from this school, Ratiba

Khalil Shuqair, who originally hailed from al-Khiyyam village in southern Lebanon, opened *al-Madrasa al-wataniyya* (the National School) in Bir Zeit, later moving to Bethlehem in 1932.[11] In July 1928, Amina Shufani, a former teacher from the Department of Education, opened the al-Najah Nationalist School for Girls in Haifa.[12] *Al-Karmil* praised her school as a place where girls could acquire "a proper education, that preserves the honorable Arab traditions and customs," in contrast to the missionary schools where girls acquired foreign traditions and customs.[13]

The number of local and national schools in Palestine and their impact is difficult to determine as many were ephemeral, short-lived ventures with a small number of pupils. The Department of Education also required official registration of all schools, which included a health inspection; schools that did not meet their standards were closed by the Department of Health. Schools also changed their names, locations, and owners, making their histories even more elusive. We do know, however, that at least through the late 1930s, these schools were primarily an urban phenomenon, nourished by a city's politicization, although by the 1940s, nationalist schools were found also in villages, such as in Kafr Qaraʿ, Sabbarin, and Balad al-Shaykh, all close to Haifa.[14] The success of these schools also depended upon the already existent educational infrastructure or lack thereof, and thrived both in places where the government did not provide adequate schooling or none at all, and where Protestant and Catholic schools prevailed.

Mandate statistics for 1935–1936 reveal that Jaffa had the largest number of nationalist schools, followed by Haifa, Hebron, Jerusalem, and Gaza respectively.[15] These schools continued to flourish through the 1940s, encouraged by the Arab revolt, as well as the downsizing and even closure of some missionary schools during World War II.[16] The inability of the government schools to accommodate enrolling students also helped the nationalist schools to flourish. According to a report written by A. L. Tibawi, Jaffa had thirty national schools by 1945, attended by 4,000 pupils, which was roughly equivalent to the number of pupils in Jaffa's government schools.[17] Assuming that some children in Jaffa attended missionary schools, the government schools could not accommodate even half the school-aged children in that town. Even in towns where the government had well-established girls' schools, such as in Acre, nationalist schools emerged by the 1940s, attended by 31 percent of the schoolgirls in that town.[18]

The Islamic Girls' School in Jerusalem opened in September 1925 as part of an ambitious project of the Supreme Muslim Council to provide both religious and nationalist education to Muslim youth throughout Palestine. The SMC was influenced by the Islamic reform movement that emerged in the late nineteenth century, led by influential ulama such as Muhammad ʿAbduh and Rashid Rida. Made possible by its control over the *awqaf* funds, the SMC managed, administered, and financed a number of schools, which fluctuated over the years from nearly twenty in 1924 to only eleven in the 1940s.[19] Its educational institutions included several former *madaris*, whose reputations for teaching religious exegesis, Islamic jurisprudence, and classical Arabic once had attracted pupils from all over the region during the Ottoman period.[20] It also assumed the administration of Rawdat al-Maʿarif School, as well as al-Najah School (*Madrasat al-najah al-wataniyya*), which had been privately established in Nablus in 1918.[21] Of the several schools for girls that the SMC administered, the Islamic Girls' School in Jerusalem was considered its showcase institution.

The Islamic Girls' School offered the same westernized subjects as did the better missionary schools, while it also emphasized the religious and national-ist identities of its pupils by devoting more hours to the study of Arabic, Arabic history and geography, and the principles of Islam. Located on the northern edge of *al-haram al-sharif,* the institution was placed within close proximity to the SMC's other educational and cultural projects, namely the library of al-Aqsa Mosque, the Islamic Museum, and Rawdat al-Maʿarif School. By opening the Islamic Girls' School in the very same building that had once been the Ottoman government girls' school, the SMC implicitly stated that Muslim girls' education already had a long history in Jerusalem, with the building ingrained in people's consciousness as a site of girls' education.

The creation of the Islamic Girls' School in Jerusalem took place within the context of the SMC's campaign against the missionary schools. In 1923, and again in 1925, six months before the school's opening, the SMC had requested all *qadis* to gather information on missionary activities through-out the country. Based on their reports, the SMC was able to determine the number of Muslim children who attended missionary schools, and assess the community's educational needs. Estimates of the Department of Education placed the number of Muslim girls in missionary schools throughout Pales-tine in 1925–1926 at 1,024, or 25 percent of all Muslim girls being educated at that time,[22] a significant number that was cause for concern among members of the SMC and the Muslim community in general. Jerusalem was a natural place for the SMC to open a high-level girls' school, given the city's wide range of missionary activity, as well as its political and religious significance. The school's initial appeal to girls from the Muslim elite, many of whom were attending Protestant and Catholic schools, only strengthens the notion that the school was opened to counterbalance the influence of the Christian schools. A year after the school opened, the head of the city's local educational committee praised the SMC for trying to "remove Muslim girls from missionary and colonial schools," and stressed that the school's location in the heart of Muslim Jerusalem was the best choice,[23] implying that girls from elite families who lived around the old city might be attracted to the school because it was close by. A register of pupils reveals that the Islamic Girls' School did have some success at "rescuing" pupils from missionary schools, especially those from wealthy families who could afford to pay the school's tuition fees.[24] Nonetheless, the missionary schools, especially the Jerusalem Girls' College and the German Catholic Schmidt's College, proved difficult competition, particularly during the school's first few years.

The SMC also saw the Islamic Girls' School, together with other nationalist schools, as a new model of the indigenous school, replacing the *kuttab*, which was deemed inadequate and unable to maintain the pace of modernity, and emblematic of the so-called decline of Islamic society. Educational officials in the colonial government saw the *kuttab* as having low standards and being staffed by "old fashioned Shaikhs with limited qualifications."[25] Similarly, Arab residents in 'Ajami, a neighborhood of Jaffa, complained that their local school had gradually "retreated backwards to the level of the local *kuttab*" because the SMC had failed to fund it.[26] A report written by a school inspector in Nazareth is telling about the way in which the SMC sought to eradicate the *kuttab*, but with little success in the eyes of the local residents. The inspector remarked that when he asked a driver to take him to the local girls' school run by the SMC, the driver responded that he did not know of any such *madrasa*, but that he could take him to "*kuttab bint al-Banna*'" (the *kuttab* of the daughter of al-Banna'), without realizing that he was referring to the very same *madrasa* whose head teacher at that time was Tharwa al-Banna'.[27] In doing so, the driver associated girls' education with the fundamental teachings of the *kuttab*, and nothing more; however, in the opinion of the inspector, the driver had belittled the school's stature, degrading it from a modern, academic school, as the term *madrasa* had come to mean, to a *kuttab*, by then considered a disorderly, non-modern institution of a low academic standard.

The presence of a parallel Jewish Zionist school system in Palestine also may have motivated the SMC to create its schools for girls. Although the records of the SMC are silent on this development, Ruth Woodsmall claims it was one of the driving forces. She met with Ishaq Darwish, an official within the SMC, and quoted him as saying, "Zionism brought an awakening of National Consciousness and the sense of necessity for social uplift which must affect women. To oppose Zionism we realized the necessity for the same weapon. The Jews have a high educational level both for men and women.

Hence to bring up the Arab level we must educate Moslem women."[28] At the same time, however, Woodsmall argues that "the presence of an entirely different civilization — nothing could be more different than the conservative Moslem and the modern Jew — has aroused a fear of contamination and absorption, and has therefore produced a defense psychology of protecting tenaciously Arab and Islamic culture."[29] Thus, the Islamic Girls' School in Jerusalem could be understood as an attempt to challenge the Jewish Zionist presence in Palestine, while at the same time, it also served to protect and promote Muslim traditions and culture out of fear of the westernized, European "other."

THE TEACHERS AND THEIR STUDENTS

In its early years, the Islamic Girls' School hired a number of non-local Arab women teachers, the majority whom had been trained in missionary schools outside of Palestine. The first headmistress and head teacher, Hadiya and Maryam Lutfi, sisters from Sidon, were specifically brought to administer the school, which they did for about one year.[30] Matilde Saʿad, a thirty-seven-year-old Christian woman from Beirut, who had been educated in an American Missionary School, served as headmistress from 1926 to 1929.[31] She was succeeded by Munira Saffuri, a Christian woman from Nazareth, who had graduated from the American University in Beirut. Resigning in 1931, Saffuri later became a teacher in a girls' school in Mosul, Iraq.[32] Widad al-Muhmasani, a Muslim woman from Beirut, who later became a writer, served briefly as headmistress,[33] until the appointment of Suʿad al-Asir al-Husayni in 1932. A Muslim from Beirut who had been educated at the Ottoman Teachers' College in Istanbul, Suʿad al-Asir al-Husayni remained the school's headmistress until the school's closure in 1948.[34]

The employment of women from outside of Palestine evidently gave the school prestige. Nuzha, a former pupil, remembered that the school built its reputation upon having a foreign Arab teaching staff, while Serene Husseini Shahid wrote in her memoirs that the foreign teachers contributed to the school's high academic standards.[35] Foreign teachers were apparently appealing in other cultural contexts as well; Muslim, Hindu, and Sikh parents in the Punjab sent their daughters to Kinnaird College, a missionary institution, specifically because of the chance to study with British and American teachers.[36] Although the teachers of the Islamic Girls' School became increasingly local over time, the headmistress was nearly always a non-local, Arab woman; the only exception was when Raqiyya Khalil Hidaya of Jerusalem held the position for no more than three months in 1938 and then again in 1947. Although the school's documents do not reveal why the school hired foreign headmistresses over local ones, the administration may have perceived Arab women from outside of Palestine as having a higher level of education, primarily because they were not educated locally, and therefore were perceived as being more "modern," and more capable of administering the school. By having an outsider as headmistress, a kind of pyramidal hierarchy was created within the school, with the foreign headmistress at the top of the pyramid and the local teachers at the bottom. Moreover, imported teachers may have commanded more respect from parents and students alike than local women did, with foreign headmistresses especially being subjected less to local factionalism and favoritism.

The school also hired a number of local Christian women teachers. Nastas al-Shammas and Olga Tleel, both graduates of the Jerusalem Girls' College, taught briefly in the school in the late 1920s, while Olga Harami, a graduate of Schmidt's College, worked in the school from 1927 until 1934. In addition, Melia al-Sakakini, the sister of the educator Khalil al-Sakakini, who had attended the Russian Teachers' College in Bayt Jala, taught in the school from 1928 to 1938.[37] The marked presence of Christian women teachers in a Muslim girls' school was typical of other schools both in and outside Palestine. Not only did it reflect the predominance of Christian women teachers throughout the 1930s, but also the preference of primarily urban schools, both private and government ones, to hire Christian women, in the belief that they would be better role models for pupils than Muslim women. The SMC also may have been following the precedent made by the Islamic al-Maqasid Society in Beirut, which hired Julia Dimashqiyya, a Christian woman educator and writer, to work as headmistress in its girls' school before World War I.[38] The hirings of Christian women teachers during this time also were conspicuous attempts to project Muslim-Christian unity and to deemphasize religious differences. Although nationalism was seen as transcending religious differences, occasional problems did arise. On at least one occasion, a Christian Arab woman hired to serve as the headmistress in the SMC's Islamic Orphanage was dismissed because she was deemed not capable of teaching Islam to Muslim girls, and because of the public anger that prevailed over hiring a Christian woman to work in a Muslim institution.[39] Notably, this took place not long after the Department of Education had decided to fire the Christian women teachers who worked in the government girls' school in Nablus because they had wanted to observe Christian holidays, following protests of the Muslim community.[40]

Throughout the 1920s, the Islamic Girls' School attracted pupils from prominent Muslim families; of the nine girls in the sixth grade class in 1926–

1927, all were from the upper echelons of Jerusalem's Muslim community. Nuzha's family was close to the mufti; her father had worked for the Ottomans and then for the British.[41] Na'amati al-'Alami's father, Amin al-'Alami, was a religious scholar and marriage registrar, whose family had been for generations the custodian of *al-Khanqa al-salahiyya*, a religious endowment founded during the time of Salah al-Din al-Ayyubi to house Sufis in Jerusalem. Raqiyya and Jihan Hidaya's father, Khalil, was a textile merchant and owned several shops. Shaykh Yahi Hidaya, the father of Fatima Hidaya, was also a merchant. The fathers of Safa Sa'id al-Khatib, 'Adawiyya Tawfiq Rif'at al-Husayni, and Fatima Sa'id al-Husayni were all shaykhs, and presumably held positions within the SMC, while the father of Wafiqa al-Husayni was the shaykh of *al-haram al-sharif*.[42]

School records indicate that the pupils in the higher grades all had studied elsewhere before entering the Islamic Girls' School. Most had been educated in government schools in the early years of the Mandate. Nuzha had previously attended the Mamuniyya School in Jerusalem. In 1925, at age twelve, she entered the sixth grade of the Islamic Girls' School, then the highest class, and remained in that same class for four years until age sixteen.[43] Similarly, twelve-year old Na'amati al-'Alami also had studied in a government school, most likely the Mamuniyya, before joining the highest class at the Islamic Girls' School, where she remained for two years.[44] Sixteen-year-old Ruwaida 'Uthman al-Shihabi joined the class in 1927, having previously attended the 'Alawiyya and Mamuniyya schools, as did Su'ad al-Kazami, who was admitted to the seventh-grade class in 1928.[45] Records showed that some pupils also came from the Protestant and Catholic schools. Jihan and Raqiyya Hidaya, Widad Bamiyya, 'Adawiyya Tawfiq al-Husayni, Fatima Sa'id al-Husayni, and Fatima Qulaibu all previously had attended an Italian Catholic school, most likely the Salesian school,[46] which the SMC had led a public campaign against because of its missionary activities.

On average, girls remained in the Islamic Girls' School for about three or four years. Of the forty-three girls registered in the first-grade class of 1930–1931, some twenty-two girls, or 51 percent, returned the following year, with 9 percent remaining in the school through the fifth grade and beyond. Overall, those who acquired the majority of their elementary school education in the Islamic Girls' School never exceeded 10 percent. This progressive decline in pupils corresponded to the findings of a committee formed to investigate the finances of the British administration in Palestine in 1931, which found that it was common for many parents to withdraw their daughters from school after they had learned the basics of sewing, reading, and writing.[47] The same committee enumerated that only 20 percent of schoolgirls continued to the higher elementary classes, that is, past the fourth grade. Not all girls left the Islamic Girls' School, however, because their parents felt they had learned enough. Girls also left the school as a result of transferring to other schools, marriage, or illness.

Early marriage was one of the main reasons why girls left the Islamic Girls' School before finishing, which the headmistress duly noted in the school's registration book. While the records do not disclose if the teachers tried to prevent parents from removing their daughters for early betrothal, the SMC did have some control over the girls who resided in the Islamic Orphanage. In the few cases found, while the medical doctor determined that the girls had reached puberty and thus were eligible to marry, following closely the Hanafi legal doctrine, the inspector of Islamic schools often thwarted this decision. In one case, the inspector asked that a group of girls from the Islamic Orphanage who had already reached puberty and were going to be returned to their guardians, be allowed to continue studying free of charge at the Islamic Girls' School, implicitly understood as a means of preventing them from marrying early.[48]

In another case, a Palestinian man, who resided in Chile, sent via a notable of Bethlehem his request to marry "an educated Muslim girl, educated in the principles of knowledge and manners in the Islamic schools, especially from the Islamic orphanage."[49] Rather than offer a young girl who had just reached puberty, the inspector of Islamic schools suggested Faride Ahmad, who resided in the orphanage and had attended the Islamic Girls' School, and was at the time studying nursing at the SMC's expense. Although her age is never given, her educational experience suggests that she was older than the other girls who had been declared to be of marriageable age and whose ages ranged from twelve to seventeen.[50] In his letter proposing Faride Ahmad for marriage, the inspector stated that "the customs and Islamic law do not permit us to be lax in regard to one of our Muslim girls,"[51] indicating that he would do everything in his power to prevent girls from marrying too early.

The Islamic Girls' School created two ways for girls to remain in school after having finished the school's curriculum, all tactics for delaying marriage. One was to remain in the same class for more than a year. Nuzha, for example, attended the highest class for four years. Given that most of the pupils who reached the highest class tended to be from elite families, we may assume that money was not a factor preventing their move to other schools, but rather it was a solution to the lack of higher classes for girls in the nationalist schools. The creation of a special sewing class in the fall of 1927 also enabled girls to remain in school after completing their studies. Open specifically to graduates of the school, the sewing class may have been a means of delaying the common tendency among parents "to remove their girls [from school] with a view to early marriage as soon as they can read, write, and sew."[52] In the first year of operation, some twenty girls had registered, with a number remaining in this class for several years after having completed the highest academic grade at the Islamic Girls' School. Hikmat Daʾudi attended for four years until age seventeen,[53] while Khadija, the sister of Suʿad, studied in the sewing section for at least two years in her late teens after the SMC had told her she was too young to become a teacher.[54] In 1936, financial difficulties forced the school to temporarily close the sewing class, although it reopened three years later. The Islamic Girls' School, however, could not force girls to remain in the class, although given the ages of the girls, it appears that parents were willing to allow their daughters to continue their studies until reaching their late teens, whether in the academic classes or in the sewing class.

The pupils' register reveals that between 1925 to 1934, at least 55 percent of the students lived within the old city of Jerusalem, 29 percent of the pupils resided in the Arab neighborhoods outside of the old city, 6 percent came from outside of Jerusalem altogether, and 10 percent gave no indication at all as to where they lived. That the majority of pupils came from within the old city reflects its Muslim character, as well as the presence of elite families still within the city walls. The six girls in Suʿad's family attended the Islamic Girls' School mainly because of its proximity to their home, and continued to attend it even after the family moved to Jerusalem's western neighborhoods outside the old city.[55] In order to attract pupils from outside of Jerusalem, the SMC decided to open a boarding school in the summer of 1929, as if they were anticipating the 1929 riots and parental concerns for their daughters' safety. The boarding house was located in the wealthy Bab al-Zahre neighborhood outside the city walls, in a large mansion that had belonged to Saʿid Bek al-Husayni, a former member of the Ottoman parliament. It housed several teachers and two dozen girls who came from Jaffa, Haifa, Gaza, and Ramla, and from Jerusalem as well, with Nuzha recalling that the teachers strictly "guarded" the boarding school girls.[56] The cost of boarding was £27, which was thirteen times as much as the school's tuition, which meant that only daughters of the elite could afford to board in the school. Creating a relatively exclusive boarding school echoed practices in France, where boarding schools served as finishing schools for middle-class girls.[57]

The boarding school did not last long, the result of the SMC having to decrease the funding that it gave to the school during the years 1929 to 1931. In particular, the construction of the Palace Hotel, an impressive, moorish-style hotel which closed not long after it opened, caused the SMC to go into considerable debt. In addition, the decline in the revenues from *waqf* tithes, based upon agricultural yields and profits in 1930, also did not improve the financial state of the SMC.[58] As a result, the SMC was compelled to make cutbacks in various projects, including the Islamic Girls' School. It reduced teachers' salaries, cancelled teaching positions, closed the boarding school, and abolished the school's secondary classes where the number of pupils was minimal. In 1931, inevitably fuelled by rumors that the SMC was going to close the Islamic Girls' School altogether, a dozen young boarders wrote in protest to the SMC:

> We heard the news to abolish our dear school and we, the pupils of the boarding section and the higher classes, ask you to not deprive us in attaining that [knowledge] which guides us in this life, which demands action and resistance towards those who wish to exterminate our nation and humiliate our religion. If you decide to abolish this higher school dear to us, many of us will be forced to move. Do you permit indifference and ignorance to be instilled us, and for us to be deprived of skills and the benefits . . . We will never accept ignorance and we are half the builders of the Muslim nation [*umma*]. We will never accept being deprived and we have the right to breathe life into our intelligence and our aptitude . . . and [our education] will be returned with goodwill to the *umma* by the revival of this singular Islamic School . . . We are devoted to you, as you have pushed us to work for the nationalist zeal and the defense of the right of the Palestinian Muslim girl, and we hope that you will show concern.[59]

Although the Islamic Girls' School did not close, the level of the school evidently plummeted, as the SMC's poor financial situation began to tarnish the school's reputation. Many girls left the school during this time, including some who had attended the school since its opening and whose families had been supporters of the SMC. Serene Husseini Shahid, the daughter of Jamal al-Husayni, who was Secretary of the Supreme Muslim Council, left the school in 1930 when the boarding section was closed temporarily, and entered the Friends' School in Ramallah,[60] while several girls from the al-Taji family of Wadi Hanin, near Ramla, who boarded in the school, had little choice but to leave once the boarding section was closed.[61]

The deficit of the Supreme Muslim Council also affected the school's teaching staff, as the non-local teachers all resigned about the time of the school's financial crisis, ostensibly because of the cuts made to their salaries.[62] As a result of the financial setbacks, the school began to hire local Palestinian women at lower salaries. For example, in 1933, Na'amati al-'Alami and

Raqiyya Hidaya, two local young women who had been sent by the SMC to undergo teachers' training in Cairo, agreed to salaries of £6 each, instead of the usual £8, so that the school could hire yet an additional teacher.[63] While the SMC's decision to hire local women enabled the school to continue functioning, the replacement of the non-local Arab teachers with local women in the early 1930s may have spoiled the reputation of the Islamic Girls' School, particularly when many local Palestinians were still ambivalent about teaching as a suitable occupation for Palestinian Muslim women. The fact that the other private schools in Jerusalem continued to maintain teaching staffs that were primarily foreign, such as the Jerusalem Girls' College with a staff of 70 percent British and 30 percent Arab,[64] may have further weakened the image of the Islamic Girls' School by reinforcing the idea that it could not possibly provide a strong, academic education the more it became increasingly "local."

By 1938, the school's staff was composed almost entirely of local and Muslim women, mainly from well-known, notable Jerusalemite families, among them some of the first graduates of the school. Although the financial setbacks caused the non-local teachers to leave, the Islamic Girls' School did not exert much effort at keeping the local Christian teachers in their positions; it dismissed them with expired contracts and other claims (such as old age in the case of the Melia al-Sakakini), and replaced them with local Muslim women who increasingly sought employment through the 1930s, perhaps reflecting a kind of favoritism of the SMC toward girls from notable local families. This transformation, however, was only possible as a result of the slowly changing attitudes toward teaching as a proper female profession among middle- and upper-class, urban Muslim families, as evidenced by the growing number of Muslim girls accepted into the WTC. Undoubtedly, the nationalist context contributed to this shift. Women increasingly saw teaching, alongside education, as part of their nationalist duty. A young Muslim girl from Jerusalem, for example, wrote to the administration of the Islamic Girls' School that she had completed the seventh grade at the Mamuniyya Girls' School, and even though she ranked only 13 out of 28 pupils, and admitted "it's not a high ranking," she wanted to teach at the Islamic Girls' School. She wrote that, "I am in favor of serving girls . . . and teaching them a true nationalist education. I would like to be appointed as a teacher to one of the elementary schools under your administration. I am able to teach the following: Qur'an, Islamic religion, math, geography, history, Arabic reading, Arabic letters, English, sport games, and all that is requested."[65] Throughout the 1930s, Muslim women from outside of Palestine also sought employment in the Islamic

Girls' School, as did a number of non-Muslim girls, reflecting not only the growing demand for teaching positions but also the regional-wide recognition of the SMC as leading the nationalist battle within Palestine.

Despite promoting local and Muslim character and despite its recognition outside of Palestine, the school had a difficult time attracting students throughout the 1930s. In the mid-1930s, the school's administration began to worry that the tuition fees of £2, which students had to pay, were the reason for "the small number of pupils in the school" at the time.[66] Although on one hand the fees may have prevented a large number of potential students from enrolling in the school, on the other hand, the low tuition fees at the Islamic Girls' School may have been less appealing to wealthier Muslim families, giving the school an unfavorable image in comparison to the more expensive missionary schools. A year later, the inspector of Islamic schools argued that the school should drop the fees altogether, given that "the government schools have abolished the school fees for elementary sections, as have many foreign schools, like the Frères school, and as the Christian denominational schools have . . . because they were founded to fill a vacuum in teaching the sons of its confession." The fees, he argued, in reality were insignificant, and did not even cover the salary of a single teacher.[67]

In 1938, the Islamic Girls' School finally reduced its tuition fees to 750 mils, attracting students who had previously attended the government schools, or who could not get into the government schools for lack of room. At the same time, it had lost much of its financial resources, some of which were derived from the tuition fees, needed to maintain all of its classes, as well as any potential of reclaiming the upper- and middle-class Muslims whom they had lost in the early 1930s. Acknowledging that not everyone could afford the tuition fees, the schools belonging to the SMC had followed a rule of exempting between 10 to 15 percent of the pupils from the tuition fee, which reached 20 percent by 1938, but on condition that they could "prove" their poverty before a local *mukhtar* or *qadi*.[68]

It was not easy to exempt only 20 percent of the pupils from the tuition fees, however, especially as the school increasingly began to cater to girls from poor, lower-class families. The poverty of the students was apparent by 1939–1940, when 90 percent of them reportedly were unable to pay the tuition fees.[69] According to the school's register from the same year, the fathers of many of these girls were described as shoemakers, peddlers, and unskilled laborers, who most likely could not make ends meet, but still nonetheless sent their daughters to school. The headmistress who admitted the students at the beginning of the school year was aware of their impoverishment when they registered, as their socioeconomic status was noted in the margins, next to their names and addresses. "Poor" (*faqira*) and "very poor" (*faqira jidan*) described seven out of twelve girls enrolled in the fifth-grade class, then the school's highest class, while another four were noted as being orphaned (*yatima*), most likely housed in the Islamic Orphanage, and one was listed as the daughter of the school's servant. Likewise, in the fourth-grade class, only two out of the sixteen pupils, from the families of al-Shaykh and Hidaya, were able to pay the school fee.[70]

The headmistress, in particular, found herself in a difficult situation, confronted with having to demand tuition fees from pupils who were unable to pay them. She complained to the inspector of schools,

> The poor pupils in the school have abstained from paying the school fee and there are many in the school and it is not possible to adhere to the 20 percent exempt only. All the poor pupils brought signed documents from their local *makhatir* attesting to their severe poverty, and many of them take their necessary strength from the *Jam'iyat al-sayyidat* (Arab women's association) although the alms are very small, while some of them take charity from the government and it does not fatten them up and does not eradicate their hunger. Some of them are orphans who do not have any family except an uncle or a brother, and who are either imprisoned or do not know a place to live [i.e., homeless] because of the current circumstances. How do you expect me to request these poor [children] to pay the fee, when the mothers of some of them came and said that the only thing which they are able to do is withdraw them from the school.[71]

The poverty that the headmistress described characterized Jerusalem's old city by this time. Upper-class and aspiring middle-class Muslim families who had once populated the old city had left for new spacious neighborhoods in Jerusalem's new city during the first half of the twentieth century.[72] The urban poor who were left behind were joined by new families, who had migrated from towns and villages, especially from Hebron and its hinterland, looking for economic opportunity and, in some cases, better education for their children. The Arab revolt had also affected the school's student body, as it had opened its doors to children whose fathers had died or had been imprisoned because of their involvement in the revolt.

Throughout its history, the Islamic Girls' School had accepted a small number of orphaned girls who resided at the nearby *Dar al-aytam*. By Islamic law, an orphan is a child who has not yet reached puberty and whose father or both parents have died. Although Islamic law stipulates that relatives are supposed to look after minor orphans, this is not always possible.[73] The inability of relatives to care for orphaned minors was particularly acute follow-ing World War I, given the poverty, famine, and predominance of infectious diseases. The SMC's decision in 1922 to create an Islamic orphanage was seen as a solution to two problems: it addressed the immediate need for shelter-ing Muslim children, left orphaned and impoverished by the war, while it also offered a religious and national alternative to the many foreign mission-ary orphanages throughout the region.[74] Within two years after opening its doors, *Dar al-aytam* became home to 180 boys and girls, reaching nearly 260 children by 1932.[75] Although the sources are fragmentary, it appears that the SMC had hoped to acquire a building near the orphanage in order to create a school for the orphaned girls. When this did not materialize, it was suggested that the girls attend a government school, a move that would save the SMC the salaries of two women teachers and a headmistress who specifically had been hired to educate the orphaned girls.[76] After two years, however, the De-partment of Education informed the SMC "that this school year the [govern-ment] Madrasa al-Rasasiyya for girls cannot accept pupils from the Islamic Orphanage School who were accepted before in the school, as the school has left its old home and was forced to take a much smaller building."[77] Although space was given as an excuse, the admission of orphans was evidently seen by the Department of Education as a special favor to the SMC that could easily be reneged upon. By this time, however, the SMC had already established the Islamic Girls' School, which accepted pupils from the Islamic Orphanage.

By the 1930s, and especially during the Arab revolt, aiding orphans had be-come a "nationalist" act, with the inter-denominational Arab Women's Asso-ciation, for example, collecting funds for children who lost parents during the revolt, several of whom were admitted into the Islamic Orphanage.[78] The SMC also expressed concern about its ability to accommodate the "great number of orphans admitted to the Islamic Orphanage," yet were fearful that "they'll find refuge in foreign shelters if we don't place them in the Islamic Orphan-age and this will create disorder and dangers."[79] Despite the national sympa-thy expressed toward orphaned children and the concern that they would find themselves in missionary institutions, the headmistress of the Islamic Girls' School, Su'ad al-Asir al-Husayni, did not show much compassion for them. She reportedly insulted the orphaned pupils in front of other teachers on a regular basis, calling them "mentally deranged girls," and claiming that they were "suitable only for paring eggplants and tomatoes."[80] Although her words were clearly derogatory, the headmistress also was expressing a kind of upper-class antagonism toward these children, whose extended families could not care for them because of their lower-class backgrounds. The director of the Islamic Orphanage recognized that the conflict between the headmistress and the orphans was class-based, and in his defense of the rights of the orphaned and other misfortunate girls to be present in the Islamic Girls' School and to obtain an education, he wrote that "the girl who masters the art of washing clothes and paring eggplants and tomatoes will master the management of her home and her children, and benefit her husband in his days of misfortune more than the girl who only masters poetry and piano playing."[81]

Impoverished students continued to enroll in the Islamic Girls' School throughout the 1940s. In 1942, the inspector of Islamic schools wrote to the school's administration that the "girls of our school are among the most poor in Jerusalem, and the headmistress tells stories, sad in their essence, that many of the girls pass the day without food."[82] Malnutrition coupled with poverty was a pressing problem in Palestine of the 1940s. According to one medical officer, "food staffs [sic] and other commodities are dearer than ever." The same medical officer "was struck by the poor and anemic appearance of a big majority of the students" in the government schools in Hebron, and recommended that schools be supplied "with enough tins of canned milk" for the teachers to pass out, "thus giving a glass or two of milk a day for the week [sic] ones," in addition to providing cod liver oil, also to be distributed by the teachers.[83] In order to combat malnutrition, the Department of Health urged the formation of "local welfare committees" to address the urgency of feeding malnourished children.[84] In Jaffa, for example, A. L. Tibawi, then an inspector of schools, along with teachers and other officials, launched a municipality-supported school luncheon program for some 2,500 schoolchildren in early 1942.[85] The Department of Social Welfare, created in 1944, subsequently became responsible for feeding nearly 10,000 Arab schoolchildren in school luncheon programs, the majority of them in Jaffa, Jerusalem, and Haifa.[86]

Encouraged by the creation of feeding programs elsewhere, the inspector urged the Islamic Girls' School to do the same. The inspector understood that if the Islamic Girls' School did not feed its pupils, they would ultimately leave the school, writing that "feeding the poor in the government schools and in others, while not feeding the poor in our school demands attention. The parents of the girls have begun to think of entering their daughters into the government schools, which give free books and feed the children for free, and this situation will lead to a decrease in the number of girls in our school without delay, and perhaps will lead to the closure of some classes."[87] Despite the concern and goodwill of the inspector, some ninety pupils at the Islamic Girls' School began receiving food only in the middle of the following school year, when they joined a feeding program sponsored by the Department of Education.[88]

CULTIVATING NATIONALIST AND
MUSLIM IDENTITIES

The Islamic Girls' School prided itself on its emphasis on both Islam and nationalism, which distinguished it from the government and missionary schools. These overlapping identities are evident in the early curriculum of the Islamic Girls' School. In its first few years, the Islamic Girls' School followed the curriculum of Palestine's government schools, with some input from the teachers. In 1928 the SMC introduced its own curriculum for all of its schools, using the curricula of the government schools of Iraq, Turkey, and Palestine as its basis. In creating its own curriculum, the SMC acknowledged the claims of the headmaster of al-Najah School, who stated that "the adherence of the local (*ahliyya*) schools to teaching the curriculum of the government schools is a clear mistake and it is essential that they have a curriculum that agrees with the spirit of the nation (*umma*) and its needs."[89] According to the SMC, a curriculum for all its schools would meet the needs of the people and would "create courageous, honorable, active, nationalist working youth cultured in Islamic, Arabic culture." Pupils would develop "a love for the nation through the study of the Arabic language, history and geography." Local Palestinian nationalism, however, was not mentioned. The curriculum also emphasized an Islamic identity and "love for religion" through the study of the Qur'an and Islam. Training pupils "to adhere to the loftiest manners and highest morals, including ideas of order, cleanliness, and discipline, through scouting, sports, and educational outings" was also among the curricular aims.[90] Although these were all Muslim religious values, the vehicle of instruction through scouting, sport competitions, and school trips was explicitly secular and grounded in the curriculum's nationalist orientation.[91]

As part of its commitment to promote an Islamic identity, pupils in the Islamic Girls' School studied between one and two hours weekly of religion, two to four hours of Qur'an, and eight to fourteen hours of Arabic.[92] Although the school prided itself on being the only Muslim school for girls, the government schools did not entirely ignore religious training. The government syllabus for town schools issued in 1925 reveals that all elementary classes spent between three and five hours weekly on religious instruction, and between eight and twelve hours on Arabic language,[93] only slightly less than in the Islamic Girls' School. From the preparatory class through the second grade, religious instruction included reading "simple but authentic stories adapted to the understanding of the children," learning the five pillars of Islam, and practical instruction in prayers. From the third grade on, pupils acquired religious textbooks, presumably after they had mastered the principles of reading; pupils were also expected to commit the Qur'an to memory. In the fourth grade, they began to study *hadith*. The teaching of *tahdhib* (moral instruction) appeared only in the 1940s in the government schools, which included topics such as caring for the orphan, conversational manners, choosing proper friends, and the rights of parents and children.[94]

Unlike the urban schools, the government girls' schools in the villages provided fewer hours of religious instruction. While the officially published elementary curriculum for the rural boys' schools shows between six and nine hours weekly of religion, a handwritten syllabus specifically for village girls' schools that was circulated among the teachers indicates that the pupils spent only two hours a week on religious instruction.[95] The limited religious instruction for village girls embodied rural attitudes toward gender and religious knowledge. Although Rema Hammami has argued that village women participated in practices of popular religion, such as worshipping at the tombs of saints, they did not visit the mosque, which was considered a male domain. As Hammami points out, women were "marginalized from the textual tradition because of a taboo on women reading."[96] That is, the belief that girls should not learn to read (or to write) was prevalent throughout the villages, a belief that prevented them also from acquiring religious knowledge. In contrast, the village boys' schools gave more weight to religious knowledge than to math, geography, history, and agriculture. As Hammami argues, the growing importance of the religious knowledge among village males was reinforced by the increasing interactions between villagers and urban populations, and particularly by religious leaders such as 'Izz al-Din al-Qassam, who spoke out against popular religious practices and called for a return to pure Islamic practices while preaching among rural migrants in the Haifa area.[97] Despite the emphasis on religion within village schools, the extent of the knowledge taught still differed from that in the urban ones. Pupils in the rural schools learned only eight *hadith*, instead of the fifteen that schoolchildren in the urban schools were asked to do, suggesting that the educational officials did not perceive village youth as having the same intellectual capacity as their urban peers.

As part of its emphasis on Islam, the Islamic Girls' School also demanded that both pupils and teachers alike wear the veil, in and outside of school. According to Woodsmall, the SMC saw veiling as part of its safeguarding of Muslim traditions; according to one person whom she interviewed, "the awakening of the Arab interest has led us to re-examine the Arab religious source and to keep the true idea of the veil."[98] While girls in the missionary schools were wearing hats in the late 1920s, Nuzha recalled that "the girls would come to school with their heads covered. The teachers too, including those from Beirut and from here. They would all cover."[99] Suʿad remembered that her older sisters, the teachers Raqiyya and Jihan, wore face veils made of "crepe georgette," a thin, transparent material, and wore dark, long silk overcoats below their knees, which were covered with silk stockings.[100] The school instructed boarding pupils to bring a *mandil* (scarf) for covering their heads, presumably when walking to and from school.[101] The veiling, however, was not uniform and varied among teachers and pupils; as Nuzha relayed, "those (teachers) from Beirut did not cover like those from Jerusalem. They wore a coat with a hood and they put the hood on their head."[102]

In addition to stressing Islam, the Islamic Girls' School underlined Palestinian nationalism. The school became increasingly politicized by the end of the 1920s and into the 1930s, shaped by both national and local factors. Given that the school was administered by the SMC, the leadership role of the SMC in the Palestinian national struggle was reflected in the school and its curriculum as well. The growing involvement of elite and urban middle-class Palestinian women in the nationalist movement also gave impetus to teaching female pupils that they too had a role in determining Palestine's political future. At the local level, the transformation of the teaching staff undoubtedly affected what the pupils were taught. Local teachers Melia al-Sakakini, Raqiyya Hidaya, and Jihan Hidaya were involved in the Arab Women's Association, revealing overlap between teaching and women's politicization. Although the relationship between the school and the Arab Women's Association is fragmentary, the Islamic Girls' School served as a meeting place for the association either at the request of the teachers or at the order of the SMC. Demonstrators at the first congress of Arab women held in Jerusalem in October 1929, during which they announced their participation in the nationalist movement, stopped at the boarding house of the Islamic Girls' School, where teachers and pupils hosted them and served them food.[103]

The Arab Women's Association gathered again at the school in 1936 to mobilize women in support of the general strike,[104] reflecting the continued relationship between the school and women's nationalist activities. At the request of the AWA, some pupils joined the female branch of the Union of Arab pupils (*Ittihad al-talibat al-ʿarabiyya*), composed of girls from missionary, government, and national schools in Jerusalem. In May 1936, *al-Difaʿ* reported that members of this association met in the Islamic Girls' School to express their support for the Arab general strike and to refrain from attending school until Arab nationalist demands against Jewish immigration were met. They also declared a boycott of foreign goods, including Jewish-made products, and called for the promotion of local Arab goods.[105] Throughout the next few years, the headmistress occasionally reported that she had to close the school because many pupils and teachers did not attend, either in support of the strikes or out of pressure to respect strike days in the city and in the rest of Palestine.[106]

The school's administration also encouraged the politicization of the Islamic Girls' School. The inspector of Islamic schools donated copies of books and pamphlets on land sales and political figures, which presumably were used by the teachers in their lessons or were placed within the school's small library collection.[107] In 1935, for example, the SMC ordered the school to wave what became the prototype of the Palestinian flag above its building.[108] The school also closed its doors for a one-day strike in solidarity with French actions against Syria in February 1936.[109] Students were told to buy locally made Arab products from a "national store," as supporting nationalist merchants and their products was seen as integral to the "future of the country."[110] Although the school correspondence from 1936 is minimal, it appears that all the SMC schools, including the Islamic Girls' School, joined the nation-wide strikes.

Even the school decorations had a political appeal. Among the items inventoried in the school's possession were banners that read, "O women, you are sisters of the nations," reminding the pupils that they too as women were part of the nation and could shape its future, while yet another one proclaimed "The love of the nation is from faith," stressing the connection between nationalism and religion. Another banner was inscribed with the *hadith* "Take half your religion from this *humayra*," in reference to the reddish hair of 'A'isha, the wife of the Prophet, who was known not only for her religious knowledge, but also for her involvement in military battles and political decisions of the early Islamic community. The *hadith* "Work in this life as if you will live forever; prepare for the next world as if you will die tomorrow"[111] that also adorned the school walls encouraged girls to work hard and be high achievers, as life was short.

The nationalist and Islamic identities cultivated by the Islamic Girls' School were complicated, however, by the school's relationship with missionary schools and organizations. The number of teachers, both Muslim and Christian, resident and non-resident, who had attended missionary institutions was particularly striking for a school that prided itself on being both nationalist and Islamic. Of the thirty-one teachers whose educational backgrounds could be determined, 74 percent were missionary school graduates. Teacher Olga Harami had studied at the German Catholic Schmidt's College, while Zulaikha 'Arif al-Dajani and Hind al-Husayni had attended the Jerusalem Girls' College. Art teachers Amna Sha'th and her cousin Husniyya

Sha'th had spent eight years at the Protestant English Orphanage in Nazareth.[112] The hiring of graduates of missionary schools over those from the
WTC, for example, suggests that the administration of the Islamic Girls'
School had also internalized the prevalent view that missionary schools by far
provided better training.

A number of pupils from the Islamic Girls' School continued their education at local missionary schools. Zainat Mustafa Nur al-Din, whose trials
and tribulations were discussed earlier, was sent by the SMC to study at the
American Presbyterian Girls' School in Sidon in its specialized program in
home economics. Evidently, the SMC had hoped that she would not only become a trained teacher of home economics, but could also set up a similar field
of study at the Islamic Girls' School. Although Nur al-Din did not complete
her studies there because of the school's extensive proselytizing, the inspector
of Islamic schools discouraged her from writing complaint letters to the local
newspapers about her experience as a Muslim girl in a Christian missionary
school, telling Nur al-Din that her "Eastern feelings" which "preserved her
Muslim faith" were enough and did not require her to publicize her experiences.[113] It appears that the inspector of Islamic schools did not want Nur
al-Din to complain for tactical reasons; not only would a complaint lodged
against the school reflect poorly on the headmistress of the Islamic Girls'
School at the time, Matilde Sa'ad, who also had been trained in an American
missionary school in Beirut, but it also would have jeopardized future relations between the Islamic Girls' School and the Presbyterian Girls' School.
Indeed, two years after the fiasco with Zainat Nur al-Din, the inspector of
Islamic schools turned to the same institution again and requested teachers
to apply for a position in home economics at the Islamic Girls' School. The
headmistress, Lois Wilson, responded that "no girl who has graduated from
the Sidon Girls' School has had the full course in home economics because it
has only been in operation for three years, and it is a six year course. In order
to organize a course in another school, a girl should be very well trained."[114]
The social and political dynamics that gave specific missionary schools authority over other schools not only rendered the Islamic Girls' School unable
to complain against the Presbyterian Girls' School, but also left it somewhat
ineffective in negotiating with this particular school for a teacher.

In addition to the missionary schools, during the years 1928 and 1929, the
Islamic Girls' School tried to develop a scouting troop affiliated with the
British Girl Guides.[115] Although the sources are limited, it appears that
the scout troop may have been the influence of the headmistress Sa'ad, who
tried to pattern the Islamic Girls' School after Protestant missionary schools
and may have seen the scout troop as a means of bettering the school's repu-

tation among upper-class families, and of demonstrating to potential pupils that the school offered the same extracurricular activities as did the missionary schools. The headmistress turned to Miss Talbott-Rice, the district commissioner for the Jerusalem Girl Guides, which was closely linked to the YMCA, to help create a branch of the scouts in the Islamic Girls' School. At the suggestion of Talbott-Rice, Olga Tleel was appointed scout instructor for an unknown period of time, but resigned due to being "very busy with her work and [finding] she has no time for Girl Guides as well." Talbott-Rice suggested that Julia Lubbat, "a very good senior guide," take over the position.[116] Before the school agreed to appoint Lubbat, headmistress Saʿad ensured that she had "morals and intelligence."[117] Lubbat, like Tleel, was a graduate of the Jerusalem Girls' School,[118] and both were from Protestant Jerusalemite families.

Although little is known about the activities of the scout troop, the newspaper *al-Jamiʿa al-ʿarabiyya* reported that the scouting troop collected money to support the education of a poor girl in the school, with the paper writing, "On this occasion, we thank the Headmistress of the school, the lady Matilde Saʿad on the importance that she has made in promoting this matter . . . and we thank the leader of this young group and we hope that it will achieve all progress and success."[119] The girl guides appear to have come to an end, however, by 1929 when Saʿad left her position as headmistress. It is not clear from the sources why the school did not continue with its scouting troop, but its lack of continuation suggests that the troop may have been a personal project of the headmistress, which was supported neither by her successor nor by the school's administration. The school's growing nationalist orientation, shaped by the events of late 1929, also may have caused it to neglect rather than develop ties with colonial and Christian organizations such as the Girl Guides.

The ties of the Islamic Girls' School to missionary schools and other western organizations underscore that the school's administration and its teachers were not always sure of the identities that they wanted to nurture among the pupils. This confusion is also apparent from the correspondence between the school's administration and teachers. For example, in a visit to the school in 1928, the inspector of Islamic schools objected that the history teacher of the first-grade class "exchanged a text" about Harun al-Rashid, the ʿAbbasid Caliph of Baghdad, with one about Salah al-Din al-Ayyubi, the Muslim commander who liberated Jerusalem from the Crusaders.[120] That this teacher adapted the curriculum to her own liking is very telling, as it showed that women teachers had some leverage in teaching according to their own preferences, although it placed them in conflict with the male school inspectors.

Moreover, exchanging of the text of Harun al-Rashid with Salah al-Din al-Ayyubi also illuminated the growing Palestinian nationalist consciousness of the local women teachers, who, like others, sought a figure who could liberate the Palestinians from both British and Zionist hegemony. Tibawi concurs that the teachers in Palestine "were so fired by the claims of nationalism that they found no difficulty in circumventing the restrictions in the classroom," and "lost no chance to give [the syllabus] a national spirit of their own."[121] Two years later, the inspector complained that "the pupils studied the geography of Palestine and Syria, while it is necessary to teach the pupils that Palestine is an integral part of Syria," suggesting that the teacher had taught separately the geography of Palestine and Syria, without emphasizing the connection between the two.[122] That is, by teaching Palestine and Syria as separate geographical units, the teacher highlighted the idea of Palestine as a distinct territorial entity with its own nationalist aspirations. Although the inspector regularly visited the school and lodged complaints, the teachers continued to adapt the school's curriculum to reflect their own political identities and that of the student body.

The school's manner of teaching about Islam also was far more relaxed than the SMC might have liked. Suʿad, who attended the school in the late 1930s, recalled that daily prayers were not part of the school day, despite the religious obligation of Muslims, both male and female, to pray five times a day. Instead, once or twice a year, teachers guided pupils in performing the ablutions, the correct postures, and the recitation of the prayer in a special room within the school. As Suʿad said, "The prayers were a big event. We did not do them every day. It was like a field trip."[123] As the teacher queried the pupils about the prayer exercise, performing the prayers became more like an educational experience rather than a religious one. Despite the close proximity of al-Aqsa Mosque, praying in the mosque would have countered local gender norms that did not encourage women to engage in public prayer. By engaging in communal prayers within the confines of the school once or twice yearly, the Islamic Girls' School provided its pupils with at least a basic knowledge of worship, while the irregularity of the exercise emphasized that women's prayer was really to be performed within the privacy of one's home.

In the early months of the Arab revolt, the relaxed attitude of the teachers toward Islam became a concern of the SMC. A letter written by the inspector of Islamic schools in September 1937, only days before the British dismissed Hajj Amin al-Husayni from the presidency of the SMC, encouraged the Islamic schools to adhere to a more conservative Muslim lifestyle.[124] Although this letter was written months before the targeting of urban women's dress during the revolt, it highlighted the way in which the SMC used Islam as a defense against what was seen as a western attack on Islam, whether through dress, missionary schools, or even Jewish immigration. The letter also implied that the schools of the SMC were not living up to the curricular aims envisioned in 1928, especially of cultivating youth who loved their religion. Discussing "religious instruction for teachers and pupils in the Islamic schools," the letter declared that the pupils of the Islamic schools administered by the SMC should serve as an example to other schools. It called upon all pupils, age seven and up, to participate in prayers either at home or in the mosque, and from age ten onward, to demonstrate that they had mastered their prayers by performing them in school before their teachers. It also called for the establishment of mosques in the schools, so that teachers and pupils could hold Friday prayers.

The same letter urged pupils to dress more modestly and according to Muslim religious norms. While male pupils were to refrain from covering their heads with the western-style hats, the inspector wrote that "women teachers and pupils are forbidden from adorning themselves, from removing the face veil (*al-sufur*), from wearing western-style hats (*al-barnita*), and from wearing any clothing incompatible with modesty and Islamic morals." This preferred dress code was to be reinforced in the girls' school from the fourth class onward by teaching the interpretation of religious scholars (*tafsir*) of Qur'anic verses (*sura*), especially *surat al-ahzab* and *surat al-nur*, which stressed women's seclusion, modesty, and veiling.[125] These demands placed upon the teachers and their pupils reflected Su'ad's description of how she and her younger sisters did not wear any kind of veil when they attended the school in the late 1930s, while the girls who resided in the Islamic Orphanage came to school wearing the *kufiya* and *'iqal*, marking their rural background as well as their support for the revolt. By covering their heads with what was considered to be traditionally the dress of village males, these pupils challenged gendered conceptions of what girls should wear, in addition to ignoring the school's request that all the pupils wear the face veil even though it was not a custom with which they were all familiar, given their different backgrounds.[126]

By the 1940s, the Islamic Girls' Girl was nothing like the school that it had been when it opened in 1925. Gone were the Christian Arab teachers and those teachers who had come from outside of Palestine. Gone also were the elite families whose daughters had once attended the school. Instead, the school was a mere shadow of what it had once been, staffed by local, Muslim women teachers who presided over a school of primarily impoverished girls. The school's Islamic and nationalist curriculum had also been replaced by a modified version of the 1927 government school curriculum,[127] bringing an end to the school's reputation as being both nationalist and Islamic. The only difference between the Islamic Girls' School of the 1940s and the government girls' schools was that the curriculum of the Islamic Girls' School placed more emphasis on Islam; whether the teachers followed the curriculum, however, is questionable. While some of the changes to the school can be attributed to the transformation of the population living around the old city as well as the increasing acceptance of Muslim women teachers, the school's reputation and character was undoubtedly affected by the transformations within the SMC itself. The government's dismissal of Hajj Amin al-Husayni from the SMC in 1937 because of his role in inciting the revolt, the subsequent firing of other members of the SMC for "subversive activities," in 1938, and the British appointment of the Awqaf Committee to oversee the affairs of the SMC and the endowed properties of the Muslim community surely took its toll on the school.

Following the establishment of the Islamic Girls' School in Jerusalem, the SMC founded similar schools in Jaffa and Nazareth, while it irregularly funded already established girls' schools in Hebron and Nablus. Whereas the Islamic Girls' School in Jaffa evolved from a kindergarten into a four-year elementary school by the 1940s, the school in Nazareth never exceeded the second-grade class. Neither school could really develop, as the SMC did not allocate enough funding to these schools. From the years 1942 to 1944, the SMC, under the supervision of the Awqaf Committee, gave the schools in Jaffa and Nazareth only an average of 615 and 238 pounds respectively, in contrast to the average of 1,233 Palestinian pounds awarded to the Islamic Girls' School in Jerusalem.[128] The support given by the SMC to the school in Nazareth was especially paltry; the headmistress complained that the SMC did not even provide prayer rugs for students to learn how to pray, forcing the headmistress to "borrow" rugs, which inevitably was an embarrassment.[129]

Although some prominent Muslim families initially sent their daughters to the school in Jaffa, both schools found themselves unable to compete with the existing missionary and government schools, especially given the lack of finances and poor resources of the two schools. As a result, both schools catered to girls from the lower classes. For the 1937/1938 school year, the headmistress in Jaffa reported that nineteen of the seventy-nine pupils, or 15 percent, were unable to pay tuition fees.[130] By the 1943/1944 school year, the number of pupils who could not afford the tuition had grown to 59 percent,[131] with the headmistress reporting that same year that the pupils were so impoverished that fifty of them "eat in the school under the supervision of the teaching staff," with food from a local feeding program, and that "the school is built basically in an area of mostly poor inhabitants," the majority of whom were in need of assistance.[132] The school in Nazareth also did not charge tuition fees mainly because the girls simply were not able to pay.[133] Although the school attracted a number of poor students away from missionary schools, its location in the *qasba*, the town's traditional center, surrounded by dilapidated houses and open playgrounds, discouraged many families from enrolling their daughters.[134]

The opening of the Islamic Girls' School in Jerusalem, and its sister schools in Jaffa and Nazareth, underlines the importance that members of the Palestinian nationalist and religious leadership attributed to girls' education. In order to attract pupils, however, the Islamic Girls' School in Jerusalem had to bill itself as an alternative to the foreign-run and government schools on the one hand, and as different from the traditional *kuttab* on the other. The combining of religious instruction with a modern, western curriculum, and the employment of Arab women teachers from outside of Palestine, gave the Islamic Girls' School a reputation of being a serious academic institution that catered to the needs of Muslim girls. Although the financial difficulties of the SMC and the gradual replacement of the teaching staff with local Palestinian women affected the school's reputation among the upper classes, it also contributed to the strengthening of a Palestinian identity within the school and the school's relationship to local nationalist politics.

The narrative of the Islamic Girls' School reveals that education, and more specifically an education touted as being both nationalist and Islamic, did not just appeal to the privileged elite, but also to Jerusalem's lower classes, as is also evident from our limited knowledge of the two sister schools in Jaffa and Nazareth. The fact that the Islamic Girls' School was a local school, created by members of Jerusalem's Muslim community, may have made the school more attractive to the urban poor. It was not a missionary school, after all, and it did not seek to convert Muslim girls, as many of the missionary schools were accused of doing. Like the missionary schools, the Islamic Girls' School in Jerusalem tried to accommodate the poverty of its students by admitting them free of charge and feeding them, although the sources do not significantly address the kinds of relations that developed between the impoverished pupils and the educated teachers from notable families.

The Islamic Girls' School sought to inculcate its pupils with both overlapping and at times conflicting nationalist and religious identities by providing an education that was different from that in the government and missionary schools as well as in the *kuttab*. The Islamic Girls' School is one example of how elementary education was significant in shaping the ways in which young girls thought and acted at this time. In many ways, the school sought to paint a different picture of Muslim womanhood than commonly understood, that of socially and politically involved girls who were both modern and Muslim at the same time. Although the Islamic Girls' School was distinguished from other schools by the political and religious identities that it cultivated among its pupils, the school's underlying aim was to transform girls into the "mothers of tomorrow," a goal that was shared by the majority of girls' schools in Palestine, as discussed next.

| *Chapter 5* | Learning to Be "The Mothers of Tomorrow" |

In the summer of 1932, the Arabic newspaper *Filastin* announced that Widad al-Khuri, a Palestinian girl originally from Kafr Yasif, had received her BA in Arabic language from the American University of Beirut. A month later, the same newspaper reported that twelve female students at the Tabeetha Mission School in Jaffa had passed the University of London exam.[1] Both announcements were entitled "The mothers of tomorrow." The use of the descriptive phrase "the mothers of tomorrow" for Palestinian girls who succeeded academically underlines the aims of girls' education at the time: to prepare young girls for a new type of motherhood, which had been redefined as requiring a specific kind of education, instead of motherhood being an experience in which women learn by trial and error, as well as from the experiences and knowledge of previous generations of mothers. Yet the emphasis on the "tomorrow" suggested a "modern" motherhood that was different from that of previous generations. The use of "tomorrow" also indicated that motherhood could wait for the future, as women first had to acquire an education before they could marry and raise children. When exactly "tomorrow" would arrive was never raised.

The emphasis on educating girls for their future as mothers reflected both modernist and nationalist aims. Girls had to be educated so that they could become modern mothers who would raise nationalist sons. As one male reader of *Filastin* wrote, "Every creature must work for what he is created [for]. The judge in the court, the teacher in the school . . . the mother in the home. The woman must raise children well and guide them in their duty and raise them with the sentiment of love for the nation, just as the French woman who gives her child two types of sweets: one good, inscribed France, the other bad, inscribed Germany."[2] This rhetoric had been heard elsewhere, notably in British-ruled Egypt at the turn of the century, where the reform of the family became the symbol of a modernizing Egypt, with the domicile and especially the role of the mother at the center of this discourse. "The home," according to Pollard, "was situated at the bedrock of modernity, upon which the nationalist project would be built."[3] By teaching girls how to be future mothers, homemakers, and wives, schools in Palestine were preparing for their own modern nation.

This idea of training girls and women for motherhood has also been referred to by some historians as "maternalism," in which officials, medical experts, social reformers, and educators alike promoted the role of mothers within the private sphere of the family as well as within the public (nationalist) sphere. As Seth Koven and Sonya Michel have argued, "Late nineteenth and early twentieth-century maternalists envisioned a state in which women displayed motherly qualities and also played active roles as electors, policy makers, bureaucrats, and workers, within and outside the home."[4] Developed in response to high infant mortality rates in the West, which threatened the stability of the colonial empires, maternalism targeted mothers and future mothers as the cause of, as well as the solution to, lowering infant mortality rates, and improving the health of young children, rather than seeking to eradicate the real causes of infant mortality—namely, diseases, poor maternal care, and poverty.[5] The national solution was to educate girls and women so that they would be well versed in rules of cleanliness, hygiene, and childcare, in order to effectively decrease the infant mortality rates. As Anna Davin has posited in the context of Britain, it was easy to blame mothers and to provide training for present and future mothers, rather than to focus on the real causes of infant deaths and the inadequacies of social and medical services.[6]

Palestine at the end of World War I suffered from hunger, disease, poor sanitary conditions, and high infant mortality rates.[7] As in the West, women and girls in Palestine were blamed and targeted for their country's ailments. Private organizations were organized with women and motherhood at the center of their agendas. Erica B. Simmons has shown how American Jewish women exported maternalism to the Jewish community in Palestine, through Hadassah, the Women's Zionist Organization of America. Hadassah opened some twenty-one infant welfare centers throughout Palestine, providing pasteurized milk, medical examinations for infants, and home visits to observe mothers and their babies. Attributing high infant mortality rates to parental ignorance, Hadassah targeted Jewish and Arab women alike, presenting them with a "new version of motherhood based on science rather than superstition, and modeled on American values rather than traditional folk customs. Scientific knowledge delivered by American (and American-trained) professionals, would substitute for shared female and communal knowledge."[8] Although Hadassah's leadership saw its work as advancing the Zionist project in Palestine, both Simmons and Mary McCune point out that the leaders of Hadassah and its American supporters also saw their work as a means of creating mutual respect and goodwill between Arabs and Jews, using medical work as a means of reconciling the two populations, which McCune refers to as a kind of "gendered Zionism."[9] At the same time, as Dafna Hirsch has argued, Hadassah's projects saw both Jews of Middle Eastern origin and Arabs in Palestine as being the antithesis of the "new man," with the "Easterner being a code for all that is not hygienic," who was characterized by a "primitiveness," with no interest in adopting the rational rules of health that doctors and nurses of Hadassah promoted.[10]

Parallel to the work of Hadassah was that of the American Colony, which had founded the Anna Spafford Baby Home and two child welfare centers serving the Arab population in Jerusalem. According to publications of the American Colony, the Anna Spafford Baby Home came into fruition "on Christmas Eve," in 1925 when a sick mother, "carrying a bundle of filthy rags" containing a brand new infant, travelled for "six hours on donkey-back to hospital only to find that it was closed to out-patients." As the American Colony publications wrote, "The picture was striking: a rustic Madonna and child . . . seeking shelter and finding none. Right methods opened hospital doors, but the poor sufferer was beyond help, and died in two days, leaving a beautiful baby boy."[11] Beginning with that one orphaned infant, the Anna Spafford Baby Home cared for a number of orphaned or abandoned babies. By 1929, "Mothercraft Training Center" had been added to its name, reflecting its new role of training young Arab mothers in "up-to-date methods" of mothering. Although based in Jerusalem, the women were reportedly sent to the home from all over Palestine by "nurses, doctors, and missionaries" who evidently believed they needed training in mothercraft.[12] In addition to the home, the American Colony administered a child welfare station in the impoverished Harat al-sa'adiyya quarter of the old city of Jerusalem and a weekly station in the village of Sharafat, south of the old city, which attracted women from neighboring villages as well. The two child welfare stations provided medical attention for hundreds of babies, while the one in the old city also provided cooking lessons, lessons in hygiene, and "sewing classes for expectant mothers."[13]

Palestinian women internalized this notion that they needed to adopt a more "modern" version of motherhood, contextualizing it as part of their nationalist duties. In the women's column of *al-Karmil*, journalist Sadhij Nassar remarked that "the home is the beginning of the foundation of the nation," and in order to achieve "independence, freedom and happiness," Palestinians had to "begin by teaching the girl home management, child care, economics, and relations with the husband."[14] An article in *Filastin*, criticizing the state of girls' education in Palestine, read that "the future of Palestine and other countries depends greatly on family life, just as it depends on its schools. It is not possible to improve the life of the family and the majority of [the nation's] people without teaching the mother. If teaching the girl has some influence on the future of the country, then it is the duty to educate girls to understand the value of the good home, where cleanliness, health, and raising the children must be the goals of the woman in the home."[15] Another article in *al-Difaʿ* stated that girls had to be educated in order to be good mothers, as "there is no better school than the woman. She is the one whom the child first encounters. The woman is the child's mother, teacher, and friend, while the schoolteacher's duties are a continuation of her efforts."[16]

Part of the maternalist ideology meant teaching women to become "modern" mothers and eradicating beliefs that were contradictory to constructions of modernity. Yusuf Haikal, who served as inspector of Islamic schools and later as mayor of Jaffa, wrote in favor of girls' education, arguing that education transformed women:

> If she were educated and free she would be a sophisticated woman who does not believe in nonsense and superstition, and she would train her son's mind, regulate his emotions, correct his disposition and educate him for a progressive life, and for the welfare and interests of his homeland . . . Our country today is different than yesterday; we need to adapt the woman in a new way that corresponds to the modern spirit of the present time, so that she will keep pace with the western girls of her age. Otherwise she will be a ghost of the past in the present.[17]

It is clear from Haikal's statement that he believed Palestine's struggle for independence would be lost if girls did not receive a modern education. He blamed Palestine's weakness on women and their lack of education, which had caused them to believe in "nonsense and superstition," clearly in reference to indigenous practices such as the use of charms and plants for curing and warding off illnesses.[18] By educating girls, Palestine would not only eradicate what Haikal saw as causing its degeneration, but the nation would become increasingly "modern."

TEACHING GOOD HYGIENE AND BETTER HEALTH

Teaching maternalism involved eradicating bad hygienic habits and replacing them with a quasi-scientific, modern, if not western, knowledge of hygiene. As Dafna Hirsh has argued, "'Hygiene' signified a much broader domain of knowledge, technologies and practices. The hygienic repertoire provided models of conduct designed to achieve a 'rational' and 'scientific' regulation of daily behavior in order to maintain good health. Within the framework of the hygienic knowledge almost everything could be considered a potential cause of disease or poor health."[19] Schools immediately became sites where young children would learn better hygienic habits, and would then become emissaries of good hygiene in their homes and neighborhoods. This idea was reiterated by one senior medical officer with the Department of Health, who stated that "the foundation of all public health activities should be laid in the schools which are most suitable nuclei for disseminating modern ideas of sanitation. Any hygienic reform or innovation can be obtained only by educating the people to the value of it, and it is obvious that hygienic education should commence early in life . . . The school itself and its surroundings should serve to the children as a model of what is considered perfection."[20] In order to reinforce this idea of the school as a site of modern hygiene, the Department of Education also began in 1925 to require all new schools, both government and private, to pass health inspections before the Department of Education would give permission to the school to operate. Despite the good intentions, the health inspections often curtailed the opening of many schools each year, which exacerbated the problems of not having enough educational institutions to meet the demand.

The school principals saw the instruction of hygiene within schools as a means of transforming the population. When Bertha Spafford Vester accepted the position of headmistress of the Ottoman girls' school in Jerusalem at the turn of the century, she believed that she had found an opportunity to eradicate what she considered to be bad habits among the pupils. She wrote that "the children had been accustomed to come to school or not as their fancy took them. There had never been any criticism of tangled hair or dirty faces. Under the new regime, not only had they to be clean and tidy, but their eyes were attended to and the gratitude of the parents was sincere."[21] Vester saw herself as radically transforming the public display of her pupils, which, according to her narrative, had not been a concern of the previous administration. Noting cases of having "found clothes sewn onto the girls which meant that they were not removed until they dropped off," Vester recognized that the poverty of her pupils would impede any attempts at teaching them about hygienic knowledge and cleanliness. As an immediate solution and reminiscent of how many of the Palestinian women's charitable organizations came into being, Vester turned to the wealthier families whose daughters were enrolled in the school and asked that they provide clothing for some of the more impoverished schoolgirls.[22]

Although we know little about how schools during the late Ottoman period instructed girls in hygienic practices, the provision of "school medical services" was one of the main ways in which the British instructed Palestinian youth in basic hygiene. According to instructions issued for health inspection of schools and their pupils, a medical officer from the Department of Health was to inspect both male and female pupils three times during the course of their education: upon admission to school, again between the ages of eight and eleven, and finally during their last year of school. This was similar to medical inspections that had been made compulsory in England and Scotland in 1908, in the wake of the poor physical condition of army recruits during the Boer War.[23] The medical officers, usually nurses, also vaccinated all pupils against smallpox, and disinfected children infested with lice and other parasitic infections, and closed schools if there were threats of health epidemics.[24] One of the earliest tasks of the school medical services was treating children for trachoma, an eye disease that if left untreated could lead to blindness. In 1921, the Department of Health reported that 74 percent of schoolchildren in Palestine were infected with trachoma, while it was particularly acute in the south, where 97 percent of the children were afflicted, the result of poverty and poor sanitary conditions. District nurses were sent on behalf of the school medical services to large, urban schools where they checked the eyes of each pupil.[25] Ruth Woodsmall, upon visiting a school in Jaffa, was impressed by "an attractive young nurse . . . in neat white uniform, deftly examining and treating a class of little girls one after one in her simply but adequately equipped school clinic, [who] made ophthalmic care real . . . in terms of children."[26]

The school medical services also lectured to teachers, instructing them in hygienic knowledge. The lectures covered subjects such as "the importance of personal cleanliness, bathing, use of soap and water," as well as the "formation of good habits," which included getting regular hours of sleep, waking up early, and maintaining good posture. Although the content of most of the lectures appears to have been gender neutral, one lecture about food and drink was clearly intended for girls or for young boys who then would instruct their female relatives about the "need for cleanliness in dealing with food, vessels, and cooking utensils," as well as "proper storage protection [of food and drink] from flies." Teachers were also instructed in how to keep the school clean and sanitary. Hygienic concerns within the classroom in-

An Arab nurse and schoolchildren, 1946. Photograph by Anna Riwkin-Brick,
CZA PHR/1173783.

cluded the dangers of the common drinking mug and towel, as well as the
best means of ventilating the school, cleaning the school equipment, and the
need for "daily sweeping, clean desks, clean windows, [and] weekly scrub-
bing of floors." Finally, teachers were taught to recognize "defective vision,"
and "early signs and symptoms" of common infectious diseases, under the
assumption that a nurse would not necessarily visit the school on a regular
basis.[27] Some four hundred teachers, including almost one hundred teachers
from village schools, attended these lectures yearly,[28] underlining the central
role that teachers were expected to assume as agents of hygienic knowledge.

In the government schools, at least, hygiene was not based on classroom
work from a textbook, but rather the teachers were expected to follow "the
English practice," in which the pupils gain hygienic knowledge "by example
and by remarks introduced by the teacher when giving instruction in other

subjects."[29] In a set of written guidelines, the Department of Health encouraged teachers to set an example for their pupils by ensuring that the classrooms and school building "are well ventilated, scrupulously clean and bright and cheerful," with "lavatories and latrines . . . kept in a proper state."[30] Teachers were also expected to ensure that pupils "pay attention to their personal hygiene, i.e. come to school with clean clothes and clean skin, hair brushed, teeth and nails clean, etc.,"[31] although as Fleischmann points out, there was little consideration of the poverty of many of the schoolchildren, together with limited access to water, making many of these requirements such as clean bodies and clothing "inappropriate, defeatist, and naïve."[32] Yet teachers still carried out these inspections, and in doing so, the teachers not only became agents of cleanliness, good hygiene, and modernity, but also were able to differentiate themselves from their pupils. The fact that a medical officer had the right to inspect any government school and any school supported by government funding also left teachers with little choice but to carry out the personal inspections of students.

Private schools adopted these measures as well. Teachers at the Islamic Girls' School had to arrive early in the morning to inspect the cleanliness and order of the classrooms.[33] The headmistress of the Islamic Girls' School ordered all teachers to start the school day with inspections of pupils' hygiene and cleanliness.[34] Su'ad recalled that the teachers checked that the pupils' shoes were polished and shined, fingernails cleaned and neatly trimmed, and that each pupil had a collapsible metallic drinking cup attached to her belt loop,[35] so that they would not all drink from the same communal cup, as was customary. These inspections may have been useful, particularly in controlling epidemics of lice in schools. According to a 1920 report, between one-quarter and three-fourths of the children in a given school were infected with lice. As lice spreads through close contact, children are particularly prone to it. By 1923, the percentage of lice-infested children was said to have decreased, especially in the girls' schools, because of the individual attention given by teachers to the personal cleanliness of their pupils.[36]

Teachers in the villages in particular had the sole responsibility of teaching about hygiene and dealing with common health problems. The medical officers supplied village schools with medicine, and taught teachers how to recognize the symptoms of malaria and other common diseases, and how to administer eye drops, among other things.[37] The responsibility given teachers in administering medical services in the villages, in contrast to the nurses in the urban schools, reflects the dual role that they were expected to fulfill as both educators and medical workers. It also underlines the discriminatory practices of the Department of Health together with the Department of

Education toward the village population, and the reluctance of the Department of Health to send nurses, the majority of whom were Arab Christian women, to primarily Muslim villages because of differences in social norms and fears of religious antagonism.

The different approach to urban and village schools inevitably led to better hygiene and health in the urban schools than in the rural ones. For example, in 1927, it was reported that "the anti-trachoma work in the schools continued to make favourable progress," although the rates were much lower in the urban areas than in the villages because "school nurses trained in ophthalmic work" carried out the daily treatment, in addition to being supervised by medical officers, while the village schools had to rely on the teachers, with less frequent medical supervision.[38] As Nira Reiss points out, health care provision in the village schools was "partial at best," owing to the limited number of schools, in addition to the low school attendance rates of village children. Village girls especially were among those who were "medically isolated," as they either did not attend school or left school early, and therefore received only minimal medical attention if any at all.[39]

Hygiene education was taken outside the classroom as well. From November 17 to November 30, 1924, the Departments of Education and Health devoted lectures and exhibitions in Arabic and Hebrew for children and adults under the rubric of "Health Week," covering subjects such as "maternity and child welfare," "school hygiene," "domestic hygiene," and "personal hygiene," among others. A "special Harem Day for Moslem ladies" was also arranged, so that Muslim women and girls could attend. Students wrote essays about what they had learned during health week. Overall, some 34,000 people, of whom 4,830 were schoolchildren, attended the events of health week, which, according to Sandra M. Sufian, was considered successful because of its "nonpolitical nature" and the ability of the different communities to cooperate over issues of hygiene and health.[40]

Recognizing the potential of schoolchildren as the harbingers of this knowledge, five different leaflets about health in Arabic were created and distributed during "Health Week." One of the pamphlets had originally been written in Hebrew by Dr. Mordechai Brachyahu, who headed the school hygiene department within the Hadassah Medical Organization,[41] and another by Dr. Joachim Caspari, a well-known children's doctor in Haifa who was also affiliated with the Hadassah Medical Organization, indicating how ideas and concepts originating within the Jewish Yishuv also reached the Arab community through British mediation. Overall, some 125,000 Arabic pamphlets were distributed in the schools, "five to each child in all Government and non-Government schools," to take home to their families, although not much thought was given to the literacy, or lack thereof, of the intended recipients.[42] The informal manner in which hygiene was instructed through pamphlets and informative fairs, as well as in the classroom, enabled schoolchildren to assume the role of informing others about hygiene and cleanliness; that is, it did not require one's presence within school. Nahid remembered as a young girl in Nablus that her mother would equip her with cotton and eye drops to pass out to children playing in the street, whose eyes were irritated and dirty, suggesting that she was expected to be the messenger about good hygiene for other children who did not necessarily attend school and may not have known about cleaning their eyes to prevent trachoma.[43] Similarly, Jasamin Rostam-Kolayi also found that girls who attended an American missionary school in Iran in the early twentieth century brought their learning about hygiene into their homes, criticizing their mothers for what they considered to be the "bad hygiene" of the older generations.[44]

In that hygiene knowledge was portrayed as quasi-scientific and "modern," any customs that pupils learned at home were castigated as inappropriate, foolish, and even superstitious. Schoolteachers, in particular, worked to eradicate these customs in favor of modern hygienic knowledge. For example, the headmistress of the government girls' school in Gaza expelled two daughters of a notable family because they had come to school with henna on their hands following a wedding celebration. Although the district inspector of education informed the headmistress that the use of henna dye for decorating the hands of young girls, especially at celebrations, "is an old custom of the country that cannot be avoided," indicating that the male inspector was willing to avert his glance from such matters, the headmistress, in contrast, apparently disagreed with him, and dismissed the girls, as the use of henna evidently did not meet her standards of cleanliness and modern appearance.[45] Putting henna on one's hands during a wedding also was considered very much an "Eastern tradition" that conflicted with the adoption and adaptation of western wedding traditions, such as the white bridal gown, among both Palestinian Christians and Muslims.[46]

Teaching pupils how to eat and what to eat was also linked directly to hygiene education as well as for preparing girls to be future mothers. Okkenhaug noted how pupils at the Jerusalem Girls' College sat at child-size tables as they ate and learned about "English manners,"[47] while pupils at the Islamic Girls' School in Jerusalem learned table manners as part of the "health" curriculum, introduced already in the first-grade class.[48] By teaching table manners, namely, learning to sit at a table and to use silverware, educators sought to eradicate dining habits that were perceived as unhygienic, namely the norm of sitting on the floor and eating from the same bowl, and using fingers and bread to scoop up servings of meat, rice, and so forth.[49] These attempts to inculcate pupils with western-style eating habits, deemed "modern," were reinforced by the Arabic press, both local and non-local, which carried articles about how people should eat at dining room tables, each with his or her own plate and silverware, while advertisements for "healthy" food products in the Palestinian press illustrated the same concepts.[50]

Not every school, however, managed to inculcate its pupils with this notion of eating at a dining table. During a visit to the CMS orphanage in Nazareth, Espie Emery, the headmistress of the English High School in Haifa, was dismayed that the pupils "eat with their hands, in village fashion," even though she claimed that "spoons and forks are so cheap now that people can get them in every village."[51] The implication was that the pupils were resistant to the idea, which Emery implicitly blamed on their rural "backwardness," and not poverty, since, as she noted, silverware was cheap and available everywhere. It was not always students, however, who were resistant to these ideas, but rather the failure of various schools to provide adequate accommodations for implementing these ideas of hygiene and modernity. The headmistress of the Islamic Girls' School in Nazareth, for example, wrote to the SMC, stating that "a group of girls eat lunch in the school although there is no table for them to sit at," noting that "it's necessary to purchase a table of two meters long."[52] Several months later, she again wrote that "the children need food in the afternoon as well as tables and chairs."[53] Without food, tables, or chairs, the headmistress recognized that she could not teach pupils about the proper means of dining, nor could she attract girls from higher class families without a dining room.

The teaching of physical education also became part of the hygienic repertoire in response to the poor physical state of many children throughout Palestine. Throughout the British-administered colonies, sports for girls were promoted by both missionary and British government schools. Missionaries introduced "light drills" and calisthenics into their schools at the end of the nineteenth century, copying the curricula in Britain, where educators and policy makers hailed physical education as a panacea for the poor physical state of Britain's youth and for inculcating citizenship.[54] In post–World War I Palestine, health officials noted in their inspections of schools that pupils were malnourished and weak.[55] Girls' schools specifically adopted sports as a tool for strengthening girls' bodies for future childbearing and motherhood. Hilda Ridler, the principal of the Women's Training College and inspector of girls' schools, even remarked that physical education in the girls' schools was essential given the "stunted growth and undevelopment" [sic] of the pupils,[56] implying that without it, they would not physically mature enough in order to have children, echoing the primary arguments used by women educators who had introduced physical education into girls' schools in London at the end of the nineteenth century.[57]

As scholars have shown, sports were also about developing nationalist consciousness as manifested by the emergence of nationalist sports clubs in Palestine in the 1920s and 1930s, and the regular columns within the Arabic press linking sports with strong, healthy, and nationalist youth.[58] A male student at the private nationalist Rawdat al-Ma'arif School hailed sports as "a microcosm of life," writing that sports is "defending and struggling," and "its victory is nourished by strength and power,"[59] a rhetoric that was also heard in the call to defend Palestine against Jewish immigration. Although the link between nationalism and sports was less apparent within the girls' schools, an undated sports curriculum found among the documents of the Islamic Girls' School in Jerusalem stressed the ability of sports to unify people. Acknowledging that sports was important for good health, building bones, and calming nervous disorders, the curriculum also justified the teaching of sports because "most of all, sports give the pupils a social life, and strengthen their human and social sympathies and their kindness. Each one thinks he is part of a group and needs to help everyone so they will work together."[60] That is, in the Islamic Girls' School, sports also may have been seen as promoting nationalist sentiments.

Despite the linking of sports to nationalism, at times sports were used to diminish nationalist and religious differences. As part of its goal of creating a kind of "League of Nations" within its walls, the Jerusalem Girls' College encouraged its pupils to engage in netball, as well as other activities requiring interaction, cooperation, and sportsmanship, despite differences in national and religious identities.[61] The pupils of this school took their sports seriously, with one issue of the school's magazine proclaiming that "the new tennis court has been fully appreciated this year. During the breaks and in the dinner hour girls are seen running with their racquets and balls, eager to play more games," noting that "many girls play well now," and that the school is "eager to produce champions."[62] The desire to produce successful athletes outweighed any religious or nationalist differences or tensions. It was not just private missionary schools, however, that tried to diminish conflict between pupils through sports, as the Department of Education also promoted competition between various schools, government and private, Jewish and Arab, and from 1923 onward, sponsored an annual school-wide sports competition for various boys' schools in the Jerusalem district.[63] In the early 1930s and through the 1940s, sport matches were also held between various girls' schools, including the Jewish Evelina de Rothschild School, the Women's Training College, the

Mamuniyya Government School, and the Islamic Girls' School.[64] Through basketball, for example, pupils could overcome temporarily their differences, fears, and animosity; Suʿad, for example, recalled that she felt only sportsmanship and goodwill when the Islamic Girls' School played a basketball match against a Jewish school sometime in the 1940s.[65]

The provision of sports in the girls' schools, however, was often limited both culturally and physically. As Tamir Sorek has argued, the Palestinian press presented sports as "rehabilitating images of masculinity"; that is, the press used sports as "a cure for Arab (male) inferiority."[66] As a result, while the press commended the role of European women in sports, it questioned the appropriateness of Palestinian girls' engaging in sports, which was seen as defying normative gender behavior.[67] Ruth Woodsmall confirmed that parents in Ramla were "still inclined to look askance at active games. 'Basket-ball must be just like foot-ball, a boy's game,' they say. But the 'peppy' teacher eliminates the basket-ball 'standards' and teaches the game modified for Ramleh requirements."[68] According to Woodsmall, the ability of the teacher to adapt what was seen as a boy's game into an easier version for girls gave this particular girls' school greater legitimacy in the eyes of the rather conservative parents. Some schools found a solution to the male gendering of sports by introducing so-called "feminine" sports, such as ballroom dancing and netball, the latter of which had been introduced into the WTC and then spread to girls' elementary schools by graduates of the WTC.[69] The attitude of local Palestinians toward sports and gender echoed British notions of what constituted appropriate sports for girls, suggesting that many of the ideas in Palestine regarding gender norms originated in the West. In Britain, educators considered certain sports too masculine and unsuitable for girls and women to play, while they saw other games, such as field hockey, lacrosse, and netball, neither as overtly masculine nor as posing a threat to women's femininity or physiology, and therefore fitting for women.[70] The accommodations of many of the girls' schools also limited the provision of sporting activities, as many of the schools were housed in urban, rental buildings with only small courtyards. The ʿAlawiyya Girls' School in Jerusalem, for example, had five different secluded courtyards, which it used as playgrounds, but which were not necessarily large enough for certain athletic games.[71]

The importance of physical education coupled with the lack of adequate school playgrounds and the low number of children who attended school compelled the American Colony to create a community playground in the old city. With the American Colony promoting the playground as a means of emphasizing "the development of a sound, vigourous body; the necessity for good living, for fresh air and for exercise," the playground attracted between seventy and one hundred children who would jump rope, play basketball and "rounders," and enjoy ping pong, among other activities. Although both boys and girls came to the playground, on Friday afternoons it was opened exclusively to girls and women. The playground had "a hard struggle at first with the men of the quarter who were determined to so persecute the older girls by standing on the opposite wall and in windows commanding a view of the playground and shouting sarcastic epithets and calling them horrid names that they would desist from coming."[72]

Although the protection of a policeman put an end to the harassment, the resistance to girls engaging in sports and games, regardless of its link to the future of the nation, was deeply ingrained in many quarters of Palestine. The American Colony was able to convince parents to allow their daughters to attend, by presenting the playground as an alternative to the dangers of the "smelly street" where children usually played.[73] In addition to providing a place to play and engage in sports, the playground also provided showers and lavatories,[74] indicative of the ties between hygiene and sports, as well as of the absence of washing facilities in the homes of many of the children in the old city.

As part of the emphasis on hygienic knowledge, schools also stressed a clean body and a neat appearance. Although it was difficult to require students to bathe on a regular basis, imposing uniforms gave the façade of cleanliness. By donning identical outfits, pupils essentially looked the same, appearing as "one honorable family," in the words of the inspector of the Islamic schools vis-à-vis pupils and teachers.[75] The uniform not only made the girls appear as a single family, but it provided them with "a symbol of distinction, of social inclusion in a different class of people, and in that respect it was more fiercely defended by those who have to rely on this acquired cultural capital for success than for those who took this success for granted."[76] Within Palestinian society, uniforms identified young girls not only as attending school, but also as belonging to a specific school, as each school had its own uniform. The pupils at the Jerusalem Girls' College and at the English High School had to wear uniforms, because the headmistresses wanted the pupils to feel part of elite society, with Okkenhaug noting that they consciously copied the practice of the Cheltenham Ladies' College in England, a prestigious school only for the daughters of "Noblemen and Gentlemen."[77] Moreover, the uniforms lent a sense of unity and camaraderie among the pupils themselves, while enabling them to distinguish themselves from pupils from other schools.

Wearing a uniform became a solution to the complexities of dress and especially class during the Mandate period, particularly as the press vociferously criticized women's consumerism and changing fashions. By imposing a dress code, educators dictated their dress codes to the young girls, and not the other way around. The uniforms enabled schools to curb tacky or ostentatious displays of modernity and wealth through appearance. By imposing their notion of modernity and their ideas of how young girls should dress, schools attempted to camoflauge class differences, which determined dress and styles worn.[78] While everyday clothes would reveal socioeconomic status, the uniform enabled poor pupils to hide behind a pinafore as in the case of the Islamic Girls' School, where the uniforms were provided free of charge to orphaned or destitute pupils, enabling them to hide their class background. When the SMC suggested that the provision of uniforms come to an end in the early 1940s, the inspector of Islamic schools scoffed at the idea, remarking that the school had to outfit its needy pupils because the pupils were poor and "it is not possible to benefit from being in the girls' school without having uniforms."[79] Although he did not elaborate what he meant by his statement, it can be inferred that he saw the school uniforms as transforming, albeit superficially, the poor pupils into "modern" and presentable girls.

Although many schools demanded that pupils don uniforms, the wearing of shoes was more difficult to impose. As Davin points out within the context of educating London's urban poor in the early twentieth century, teachers were required to admit students who came to school barefoot, although "a school trying to establish or defend a reputation would no doubt discourage barefoot children; while at one already 'known as rough' they would hardly matter."[80] Adela Goodrich-Freer, who had resided in Jerusalem for twenty-four years in the late Ottoman period, noted that schools often had to provide shoes to their pupils,[81] suggesting that despite the attempt to impose dress codes, schools may have recognized that shoes were prohibitively expensive for many families. While the headmistress of the Islamic Girls' School in Nazareth was willing to admit students into the school without shoes or while wearing wooden clogs, the inspector, in contrast, insisted that the pupils wear leather shoes at all times. Education went hand in hand with "concern for dressing and neatness," which, according to the inspector, "cultivates good taste and social progress within the nation."[82] That is, the student who cared about her school and her nation would never come barefoot, as it negated the desired modernity to which school officials aspired.

Unveiling was another issue that girls' schools addressed. With the exception of the WTC, the schools run by the SMC, and presumably also those by the Islamic Society in Haifa, most schools encouraged unveiling, as it came to be associated with modernity and progress, while veiling was yoked to the uneducated women from the past. Dorothy Norman, a teacher at the Jerusalem Girls' College, who wrote home in the 1930s about how she had to greet the boarding students as they arrived for the start of a new school year, recognized the considerable influence that the school had upon the girls' appearance. She was awed by their "quaint costumes," and women who were heavily veiled, writing that the Muslim girls who arrived at the school in black veils "soon changed into ordinary summer dresses."[83] The implication of the girls' removing their veils as soon as they came into the school was that the school itself was a bastion of modernity, where the Muslim girls were transformed into "modern" women in both dress and thoughts. As soon as the girls had to go outside the school building, however, even to play on the playground, the headmistress "had to arrange that the Moslem girls veil in the playground, which they hate,"[84] a situation that was remedied by the building of a wall that provided privacy for the Muslim pupils. A decade later Norman remarked that her students in the highest class "are extremely grown up ladies with pointed nails and cinema star hair dressing,"[85] indicating that by the time they reached the highest class, the pupils had been transformed from wearing quaint costumes and veils to looking like movie stars, reflecting the decline of the veil and the western influence of the school.

Much in the way Qasim Amin evoked the veil as being a barrier to women's education and knowledge, teachers expressed similar sentiments. The headmistress of the Jerusalem Girls' Day School in the old city of Jerusalem related that the "Moslem girls usually leave this school when they begin to veil. They grow self-conscious among so many girls who are under no compulsion to veil. Frequently too, they are engaged to be married quite soon after they veil, if not before. All this tends to make a break between them and a school where they are in such a minority."[86] According to Småberg, this particular school, which was administered by the Church Mission to the Jews, initially had been made up of predominantly poor Jewish girls who left the school following threats made by the Jewish community in the mid-1920s. The school opened its doors to non-Jewish pupils. The numbers of Muslim girls in this school remained minimal, however.[87] The headmistress's statement indicates that both school and local pressures worked together to convince the veiled girls that they could not benefit from an education if they remained veiled, which as a result led to their early departure.

Although the veil was contentious in some missionary schools, in others it served to distinguish the Muslim pupils from the non-Muslims. A group of Muslim pupils at Schmidt's College were photographed in the late 1920s sitting together outside, dressed identically in black uniforms, and with their hair covered in black scarves. Although they did not wear face veils, their black scarf identified them as "the Muslim students," and as progressively "modern," as their faces were visible, yet while still maintaining an element

Muslim girls wearing veils at Schmidt's College, Jerusalem, 1928. Sitting on the right side is Samiha Taji, and standing on the left side is Suʿad Faruki, both born in 1912. From the private collection of Saʿid al-Husseini.

of modesty by covering their heads. This was in contrast to the Islamic Girls' School, for example, where the only photographs of the pupils were of the small children.[88]

Neither unveiling nor imposing school uniforms completely camouflaged a student's socioeconomic background. Suʿad bought hair buckles in Tel Aviv, white socks with colored threads, boots, and gloves,[89] and in doing so, she was able to distinguish herself from other pupils at the Islamic Girls' School who could not afford such accessories. Thus, the dresses worn underneath the pinafores, the shoes, accessories, and habits of cleanliness, or lack thereof, became a means of reading class and social strata. The inspector of Islamic schools, for example, was aware of these practices and urged the headmistress to ensure that pupils did not deviate from their uniform appearance, writing that "the girl who wears a coat over her pinafore distorts this image [of uniformity], just as the one who cuts her hair and the one who does not cut it."[90] Class differences, however, made it difficult for schools to maintain complete and total uniformity.

COMBATING EARLY MARRIAGE

Along with hygienic knowledge, girls' schools helped to shape new ideas about women and marriage, especially regarding the age of marriage. Until 1917, the Hanafi doctrine of Islamic jurisprudence, followed in Palestine and throughout the rest of the Ottoman Empire, delineated that a person was eligible to marry at the onset of puberty, with puberty beginning as early as age twelve for boys and nine for girls, and no later than age fifteen.[91] As Mahmoud Yazbak points out, however, there was a difference between drawing up a marriage contract between minors and the actual consummation of the marriage, which often took place years later.[92] Although we do not have absolute data about the numbers, research indicates that minor marriages were not uncommon, and traversed Palestine's religious communities as well as socioeconomic strata. Judith Tucker found that of the 107 Muslim marriage contracts examined in the Nablus Islamic court and dating from the late eighteenth to the mid-nineteenth century, less than 20 percent involved minors, with the upper and more affluent middle classes most likely to engage in this practice, as they were able to ask for high dowries for their young daughters.[93] Margalit Shilo has argued that marrying minor girls at least within Palestine's Jewish community was common and may have become increasingly popular during the late Ottoman period as it relieved families from having to support their daughters past their teen years, while it also allayed fears of young girls' asserting and acting upon their sexuality.[94]

As Beth Baron's work on marital practices in Egypt shows, by the beginning of the twentieth century child marriage increasingly had come under attack, attributed to the spread of girls' schools and the rising marriage age in Europe.[95] Perhaps in response to some of these criticisms of early marriage, the Ottoman state issued the Ottoman Law of Family Rights of 1917, which legislated a minimum marriage age of eighteen for boys and seventeen for girls. Those who were younger than the minimum age could petition the court to marry as long as they had consent from their legal guardian, although the law also gave the *qadi* the power to refuse the issuing of marriage licenses, including for cases in which the girl was too young. By raising the marriage age, the Ottoman state sought to represent itself as "modern" and similar to Western Europe, where medical professionals had argued that marriage should only take place when both men and women reached physical, economic, and social maturity, with many believing that a couple should be in their twenties when they married; marriage laws throughout Western Europe revealed these concerns.[96]

When the British arrived in Palestine, they had already been shaped by experiences in India where they had successfully criminalized sexual relations with married and unmarried girls under the age of twelve, made punishable by ten years' imprisonment.[97] The tendency to compare Palestine to India, especially regarding education and social issues, made child marriage a significant concern for the British in Palestine. In 1934, British parliament member Eleanor Rathbone arrived in Palestine to investigate the custom and to stir the attention of government officials.[98] A memo sent to the high commissioner, presumably written by Rathbone, read that "the Ottoman Family Law, as appears, provides safeguards against [child marriage]," noting that the Christian and Jewish communities especially prohibited the practice. The memo noted a decrease in the number of minor marriages, which it attributed to "contact with European culture and the ways of conduct and the spread of education [which] generally are beginning to make themselves felt," in addition to the work of the government and private welfare centers. The memo warned, however, that child marriage was still practiced among Muslims, particularly "in rural areas or in some backwards towns."[99] Within two years of Rathbone's investigative trip to Palestine, the British criminalized child marriage under the Criminal Code Ordinance of 1936. Although this ordinance defined the legal age of majority for both men and women as eighteen, it allowed a minimum marriage age of fifteen with permission of parent or guardian, and contingent upon proof of sexual maturity assessed by a doctor, departing from the Ottoman Family Law that gave the *qadi* the final decision. Those who violated this code were liable to spend six months in prison if found guilty.[100] At the same time that the Criminal Code Ordinance was passed, the high commissioner for Palestine reported that child marriage already had begun to decline, at least among the urban population, crediting himself with having "made an appreciable advance," in Palestine, by having legislated the Criminal Code Ordinance.[101] According to an unnamed study conducted by a member of the Dajani family in 1943, 12 percent of girls ages thirteen to seventeen and 89 percent of young women between the ages of eighteen and twenty-one were already married,[102] indicating that the majority of women married as soon as they reached the legal age of majority, while only a minority of girls continued to marry young.

Within the Muslim community, the SMC tried to discourage early marriages by setting a minimum marriage age of eighteen for Muslim women and twenty for men,[103] although research shows that men and women both lied about their ages in order to get around these age restrictions. Understanding that families lied about their daughters' ages, the SMC attacked the practice of giving expensive dowries, which often corresponded to the age of the bride, as the younger the bride, the more expensive the dowry. A pamphlet issued by the SMC on this matter contended that "the honor of the girls is dependent upon morals and manners and not upon the price of the dowry and the ostentatious dress. She should adorn herself with good character, while a proper upbringing maintains her honor and makes her happy."[104] Although the pamphlet did not directly attack the practice of marrying minor girls, the implication was that the girl's training, that is, her education, was far more important than her age and the wealth fetched with her dowry.

Schools in particular had different means of preventing early marriage. Some of the Protestant and Catholic schools required families to enroll their daughters in their boarding schools until they reached the age of sixteen or seventeen, or else face pecuniary charges for leaving school early.[105] The threat of being fined prevented many poor and even middle-class families from taking their daughters out of school prematurely, while the high tuition costs of the elite schools most likely deterred elite families from removing their daughters in the middle of the year to marry. The creation of orphanages, especially those belonging to the Protestant missions and Catholic orders, also protected girls from early marriages. Khadigie Ersas, an eight-year-old Muslim girl who came to live in the Christian Herald Orphanage, was "advertised" to donors in the following way:

> Her father, Ruside Ersas, is dead. Her mother, Rabaa, came from Hebron, and was left absolutely destitute by the death of her husband, with two younger boys to care for. She is quite helpless, like the majority of Moslem women of her class, and relies entirely on charity for support. This tiny child of eight, Khadigie, was to be dragged away and married when the Orphanage rescued her.[106]

While early marriages were clearly one solution to destitution, particularly in the case of widowed women who likely had little chance of finding employment, reports such as this one, together with already existing colonial discussions of child marriage, helped to sensationalize and transform the practice into a far greater problem than it may have really been.

The plethora of trade schools that opened for girls at the end of World War I and throughout the Mandate period were also intended to combat child marriage. A report of the American Colony, which had established a school of handicrafts and dressmaking in the wake of World War I, read that it enabled "these unfortunate girls" to be "self-supporting or even to swell the family budget," and as a result "shifted the danger of early marriage a few years."[107] The idea was that girls were married early out of economic necessity, but if they could earn some money, the likelihood of marrying early would diminish. The school reportedly educated between forty and fifty girls of various religious denominations, including an unknown number of Muslim girls from elite Jerusalem families. In addition to teaching girls plain sewing, dressmaking, lace making, and "home industries," the school also provided lessons in Arabic and English.[108] While the American Colony saw the school as "creating wise public opinion about the age of marriage,"[109] it also played a role in educating and transforming its pupils, with one report of the American Colony reading that "the girls that are reached by this School are those who cannot afford an education elsewhere. When they first come to us, they looked uncivilized and unattractive . . . but after they have been to School for a time, they change, and it is difficult to believe that they are the same girls. . . . Their dress and personal appearance becomes tidy and they are respected and happy, for they have been given an object to live for."[110] That is, learning handicraft skills not only kept these girls from early marriages, but by saving them from early marriages the school could transform them into "modern" and productive citizens.

Educators believed strongly in the connection between education and later marriage. A government schoolteacher in Hebron was quoted as saying, "Hitherto due to the very early marriage custom it has been difficult to keep girls in school for the whole course (two years of kindergarten and three years of primary) but this year eight girls are finishing."[111] That eight girls were completing the three year primary cycle was seen by this teacher as an achievement in Hebron, given that town's conservative character. Similarly, in the Mamuniyya Government School in Jerusalem, enrollment in the sixth-grade class had nearly tripled between the years 1922 and 1929; according to the headmistress, the increase was indicative of the "steadily advancing marriage age in the better classes."[112] Rather than decrease their chances of marrying, Fleischmann has argued, girls' education actually "improved chances in the marriage market," with "young educated Palestinian men of the upper classes" wanting "educated wives, and vice versa."[113] The local and non-local Arabic press also extolled educated wives and mothers as better than uneducated ones.

Schools also used the perceived link between education and marriage to their advantage. In the early 1920s, British feminist Millicent Fawcett, having visited the Jerusalem Girls' College, wrote that the school and its headmistress, Miss Warburton, had earned a certain level of respect within Palestinian Muslim society, to the degree that "young Moslem men [were] beginning to tell their parents, when arranging marriages for them that they would prefer it if they could have as their future wife a girl trained in Miss Warburton's school."[114] The linking of education to marriage, and suggesting that girls educated at the Jerusalem Girls' College or at any other school would graduate as skilled homemakers, may have been a clever ploy to encourage Muslim families to educate their daughters in specific schools. It was a way of ensuring parents that their daughters' education would not harm their chances of getting married, but rather would transform them into desirable marriage partners.

The declaration that young men wanted to marry educated girls also foreshadowed the "marriage crisis" of the late 1920s and 1930s, the real or perceived crisis that prevented or delayed Palestinian young men and women from marrying. While unemployment and poverty made it difficult for men to afford the high cost of dowries asked by the parents of marriageable women, women were also charged as being responsible for the crisis. As Fleischmann writes, men were reluctant to marry women who had been educated in the Protestant and Catholic schools. Depicted in the press as only caring about "fashion and luxuries and interested in new forms of entertainment,"[115] these women, it was implied, would not make "good wives" because they were overly materialistic and westernized. Although Fleischmann identifies discussions about the marriage crisis within the Arabic press in late 1927, the actual marriage crisis may have been tangible already a few years earlier as the first young women began to complete their studies; many were then employed as teachers and not allowed to marry as long as they remained employed.

The marriage crisis itself was not only a criticism of increasing materialism and westernization palpable within the urban areas of Palestine, but it also contained an underlying criticism of women's education, seen in some circles as the reason why some women did not marry at all. As Fleischmann has shown in her work, many educated Palestinian women, particularly those from elite families, either married late or did not marry at all as they pursued careers rather than families. According to some of her interviewees, educated women were "special," meaning that they did not want to marry by the traditional arranged marriage, while others were "too old" to marry after completing their education. Arguably, it was primarily girls from elite families who could delay marriage, as they had access to better education, especially the private schools that offered full secondary programs.

Young women who became teachers upon completing their studies may have really been at the center of the "marriage crisis." As Fleischmann has pointed out, the decision of many women teachers to marry later or remain single can be attributed to government regulations restricting the employment of married women. In the late 1920s, the British raised concerns about employing married women in its service, as a significant number of Arab women were in its employ, particularly as teachers. Fearing the possibility of married women employees becoming pregnant, taking sick leave, and causing overall embarrassment, as well as concerns that they would work long enough to obtain a pension, it was decided that married women could not carry out both a career in government service and the "normal duties of married life," and therefore should not be employed in government service. In 1933, the government issued regulations that "required a woman to resign her position upon marriage, at which time [she] would be paid a gratuity," as long as she had worked five years beyond the age of twenty.[116]

Although these regulations placed educated women in a difficult position, compelling them to choose between careers and marriage when it was expected of them, it was not only the employment regulations that forced women to marry later or not at all. The economic situation also helped to determine whether or not educated girls would marry. Girls from lower- and middle-class urban families saw the chance of delaying matrimony in order to work as a means of supporting their families. This was the case of Wasfiyya Khalifa, the daughter of a cobbler from Safad, who had trained at the Rural Teachers' Training Center in the late 1930s, and then worked to support her ailing father and ten siblings, until she married at age twenty-six.[117]

Undoubtedly, some schools realized that they were preparing girls for lives as unmarried women. Warburton, the first headmistress of the Jerusalem Girls' College, understood that the girls who attended her school were not the same girls that they had been when they entered the school. Writing about the first Muslim girl who had received a teachers' diploma at the school, the headmistress noted that this student had been "nearly taken away once to be married at Constantinople," but added that "there is not much Moslem about her now."[118] The time spent at the JGC had changed this girl to the point that she could refuse her family's wishes to marry and tenaciously pursue her decision to train as a teacher. The implication was that this woman also had the support of the school's headmistress and teachers, who may have also convinced her family to allow her to finish her education before marrying. Warburton's comment was also typical of how missionary women perceived marriage as defining Muslim women. By refusing marriage, this young woman challenged the customs and social expectations of her society, while her education, at least according to Warburton, had exposed her to another way of living, which was implicitly more "Christian" and less restrictive in the eyes of the teachers of the JGC.

IMPROVING "HOME LIFE" THROUGH DOMESTIC SCIENCE AND INFANT WELFARE

While some schools challenged the marriage norm, other schools saw their job as preparing girls to become future mothers and homemakers under the assumption that they would marry and set up households upon completing school. Head of the WTC and inspector of girls' education Hilda Ridler strongly believed that "the future of Palestine depends, like that of other countries, as much upon its home life as upon its schools," arguing that the "home life" could be improved by changing the way women understood their roles as wives, mothers, and homemakers. According to Ridler, "if female education is to have any direct effect upon the future of the country, girls must be brought up to understand the value of a good home, where cleanliness, sanitation and above all care of children, are to be regarded as the aim of every woman."[119] The first director of education also believed that girls' schools would save the "Moslem woman of the future from the fate of her predecessors," and that through education, "she would no longer be a chattel and a drudge, but a wife capable of bringing up her children in clean and healthy surroundings."[120] Both officials saw girls' education as instrumental in modernizing and reforming the future mothers of Palestine. Yet, despite the pronounced importance of educating Palestinian girls for domesticity and motherhood, the curriculum was bifurcated and shaped by class, religious, and urban-rural differences.

While the government schools in the villages emphasized the necessity of teaching practical household and sewing skills,[121] all in accordance with the "needs and environment of the village girl,"[122] the urban government schools in contrast taught "domestic science," a quasi-scientific body of knowledge developed in the late nineteenth and early twentieth century.[123] The urban bias of this subject is evident from the "domestic science centers" that were built in the urban government girls' schools between 1931 and 1933,[124] which also physically manifested the commitment of the Department of Education to modern domesticity. Despite the intention to teach a quasi-scientific domesticity, one former pupil of the New Mamuniyya School in Jerusalem recalled learning very practical skills, from how to "iron aprons, handkerchiefs, and how to cook pancakes, *katayif* (an Arabic dessert served during the month of Ramadan), and simple cookies," while another woman who attended the school in the 1940s remembered learning how to cook and having to wear all-white pinafores and carry white handkerchiefs,[125] which evoked a kind of antiseptic modernity. The implication was that the domestic science teaching and the centers may have really been just a means of marketing the government schools to the urban middle classes.

Girls who attended the WTC also continued to study domestic science as part of the curriculum for training teachers. Throughout the early 1930s, all pupils studied two hours each of cookery, household management, and laundry during the first three years, as well as weekly lessons on hygiene, while those studying to become primary schoolteachers had additional lessons in cookery in their fourth year.[126] In conjunction with the classroom instruction, pupils at the WTC also had to regularly clean the school and its dormitories.[127] In order to underline the importance of teaching "proper" domestic science, the WTC employed English women specialists in the subject.[128] By doing so, the WTC indicated that knowledge of domestic science should be entirely shaped by British worldviews. Employing British domestic science specialists also was a way of marketing the school to upper- and middle-class Muslim families who wanted their daughters to learn "westernized" domestic skills.

Domestic science could only appeal to the Palestinian middle classes, as its incorporation into the curriculum of the urban government schools reflected both the middle-class ideology of self-sufficiency and the technological changes that this segment of the population was experiencing. Middle-class domesticity that was emanating from the West posited the woman as the center of the home, and called upon women to fulfill their duties as (future) mothers and homemakers themselves rather than depend upon household help, as many of the middle- and upper-class Palestinian families did.[129] As Baron has argued within the context of Egypt, female (and male) intellectuals tried to discourage women from relying upon servants, because they tended to be lower class, uneducated, and with reputations for having corrupting effects on the household. Teaching domestic science thus was intended to make girls feel that running the household was a kind of scientific art that they could easily do themselves, without the need to depend on household help.

The incorporation of domestic science into the girls' schools in Palestine was shaped by the introduction of gas, water, electricity, and modern household appliances into urban middle-class homes in the early 1930s, and the need to master the new gadgets.[130] These were changes that were accompanied by the growth of suburbs and the building of new spacious homes, especially in the case of Jerusalem, but also noticeable in other cities of Palestine as well. Advertisements within the Palestinian press at this time both promoted and capitalized upon this middle-class domestic ideology, with the newspaper *al-Karmil* advertising the British baby carriages, which proclaimed that mothers (and not servants) could carry out their household work because their babies would sleep soundly in "Tan-Sad" carriages, with their "patented curve."[131]

While the British saw domestic science for girls as being an apolitical and practical field,[132] domestic science was incorporated into the nationalist discourse regarding women's roles and their participation in the nationalist struggle and in contributing to Palestine's independence.[133] Women who undertook their domestic duties were portrayed within the Palestinian press as being "noble," "independent," and "responsible."[134] While domestic science provided girls with the skills for being self-sufficient and independent, these skills also could be read as a metaphor for Palestine to free itself from the grip of colonialism as well as Zionism, and to determine its own fate, rather than to allow others to do it for her.[135] Fleischmann similarly argues that domestic education was intended to create "the ultimate helpmates," that is, wives who were "sympathetic, intelligent—not merely domestic—assistants to their husbands," and who would convey the "best in Arab culture to their children in order to make them brave, strong, and intelligent enough to provide for the future of the nation."[136] That is, domestic education trained young girls so that they would be capable of nurturing the next generation, who would ensure the freedom and stability of the nation.

Despite the linkage between domestic science, nationalism, and the middle class, many of the elite missionary schools downplayed domestic science within their curricula, reflecting a different approach to upper-class girls. Both the Jerusalem Girls' College and the English Girls' School in Haifa taught domestic science with a very theoretical and scientific approach and did not instruct pupils in practical domestic skills.[137] The Quaker Friends' School in Ramallah, with a majority of Christian pupils, also found it difficult to incorporate domestic skills into its curriculum, as the school's population considered it inappropriate for an educated girl, particularly from the elite, to cook or to sew. In 1930, the school opened a specialized, separate track for domestic science, in hopes of advancing its study,[138] very much like the urban government schools had done. Despite the creation of this educational track, domestic science was not incorporated into the school's curriculum; pupils in the elementary classes did not study domestic science at all, while in the secondary classes, it was offered only as an elective subject. Secondary school pupils who sought to graduate with the lower-level General Certificate instead of the more prestigious College Preparatory Certificate could choose to study domestic science instead of mathematics.[139] The offering of domestic science as a low-level course and as a replacement for mathematics indicated the way that the school felt about domestic science: that it was inappropriate for girls from elite families who wanted to continue their studies at the university level, a growing option especially for those educated in the missionary schools.

The matriculation exams also reveal changes in the kinds of domestic knowledge that girls were expected to have upon completing their secondary education. Overseen by the Board of Higher Studies, the matriculation exams were administered to the select number of male and female pupils who had completed their secondary education in government schools and in most private ones by the mid-1930s.[140] In 1925, the domestic science component consisted of a written paper on hygiene and practical tests in needlework, cookery, and in either laundry or "housewifery," showing how domestic science at that time was treated as practical knowledge. Pupils had to demonstrate cooking of various vegetables, their knowledge of removing stains, and washing linens, handkerchiefs, and silk. The housewifery test determined whether one had learned sufficiently to polish furniture, clean brass and copper, wash windows, and make beds. The test in needlework examined girls for their finesse in cutting garments, creating buttonholes, mending, and sewing special garments, including clothes for babies. In the written exam on hygiene, pupils had to articulate the basic requirements needed for healthy living (light, fresh air, and pure water), as well as knowledge of infant welfare, common illnesses, and personal hygiene. Girls sitting the matriculation exams, however, were not required to be tested in domestic science, as it was not one of the six subjects required for matriculating.[141]

By 1934, however, the domestic science component of the Palestine Matriculation Exam had changed drastically as the Board of Higher Studies categorized domestic science as a real science, alongside physics, chemistry, botany, and geography, although only girls were to be examined in it. Indeed, instead of the practical exams given in 1925, pupils now had to write three-hour-long exams. The subject material had become increasingly grounded in scientific principles and tested one's knowledge of heat, acids, soap, foodstuffs, weights, mass, and measures. In addition, the test examined pupils in basic physiology and hygiene.[142] The shift away from practical skills to a more theoretical and scientific approach clearly reflected the adoption of the matriculation exams by the elite private missionary schools, where practical domestic skills were simply not taught.

By the 1930s, domestic knowledge had become dichotomized into teaching practical household skills to elementary school girls and offering the more theoretical, reading and writing based "domestic science" to girls in the secondary classes. The fact that the Department of Education emphasized practical domestic skills at the elementary school level underlines the limited career expectations that the Department of Education accorded to the government elementary school pupils, the majority of whom were Muslim. The implication was that these pupils would not continue their education past the sixth or seventh grade level, and therefore the schools had to provide domestic skills already in the elementary classes in order to prepare these girls for their futures as wives and homemakers. This is also evident from the curriculum of the Islamic Girls' School from the late 1930s onward; as the school became increasingly impoverished, it placed greater emphasis on teaching practical household skills.[143] In contrast, the provision of "domestic science" rather than domestic skills to pupils in secondary classes underlines the social expectations of these young women. The absence of domestic skills in the secondary classes, dominated mainly by girls from the elite, signaled a different set of social expectations for these young women; their education was intended to open doors to careers and not necessarily to marriage and motherhood. Moreover, their social position in Palestinian society meant that they did not need to learn domestic skills, as most likely they would have household help.

Part of the domestic training in the elementary schools included teaching girls about infant care, emphasizing the public perception that motherhood played a central role in the lives of Muslim women.[144] Schools commonly organized field trips to local infant welfare clinics and hospitals; the Islamic Girls' School, for example, took its two highest classes to visit both the English and German hospitals, while the senior girls in the government school in Hebron attended weekly lessons at the English Hospital where they learned about the washing, dressing, and feeding of infants, as well as simple home nursing.[145] Government nurses, as well as one of the first Palestinian Arab women doctors, Salwa Khuri, gave lectures in the girls' schools in Jerusalem on hygiene and baby care.[146] The Haifa Social Service and Infant Welfare Association, established by wives of British officials and upper-class Arab women in 1924 to monitor the well-being of infants and to fill a gap in the government provision of social welfare, gave prizes to girls who excelled in the exams on infant welfare, in order to "encourage teaching" the subject and to demonstrate the seriousness of the topic.[147]

Motherhood and girls' education was so intrinsically bound together that government officials proposed that infant welfare centers share the same space as the girls' schools in both Bethlehem and Jericho.[148] While the reasons behind this decision may have been related to lack of other rental spaces, this convergence of educational and medical work among babies and women seems to have been common elsewhere, such as the Northern Sudan, where it was promoted by CMS missionaries.[149] The sharing of space between schools and infant welfare clinics was obviously a practical choice, as the girls' schools, which usually were established first, were locations already known within the community, and thus made the infant welfare clinic all the more familiar. Moreover, the location and even design of the girls' schools, as spaces ideally kept secluded from male onlookers, also would have served the needs of mothers who came to the infant welfare centers. Yet this sharing of space also revealed an ongoing collaboration between schools and health associations, as well as the Department of Education and the Department of Health to promote hygiene, health, and infant welfare among young girls especially.

The book *Infant Welfare for Women and Girls in Palestine* by Eva Cotching illustrates the overlap between health associations and girls' schools, while also revealing the type of instruction given to pupils in the upper classes of the government schools. Cotching was a medical doctor who worked closely with the Social Service and Infant Welfare Association in Haifa. Cotching's book, which was translated into Arabic and first used in the 1931–1932 school year,[150] was based on her experiences working among the mainly impoverished Muslim women who attended the two branches of the association. The book itself was directed at young urban middle- and lower-class schoolgirls, written with the intention of distancing them from the practices of their poor sisters.

In the introduction Cotching wrote that "many babies die in Palestine and many more suffer from ill health, simply because their mothers do not know the art of rearing them."[151] According to Cotching, mothers could raise healthy babies if they followed her instructions properly. Cotching informed her readers how they should hold, dress, feed, bathe, and put to sleep their babies, while negating common practices such as swaddling or overdressing as being bad for the baby's health. Cotching also believed that social class did not prevent women from raising healthy babies, and, for example, urged readers that "the best nursery is a place outside in the open air where there is no dust. The poorest woman can have this kind of nursery if she wishes."[152] While Cotching urged mothers to breast-feed their babies for health reasons, she also recognized the need for wet nurses and justified their employ, particularly when mothers could not nurse their babies themselves. This was in sharp contrast to the Palestinian press, which deemed wet nursing archaic, associated with lower-class women who lacked an education. The newspaper al-Hayat had even stated that "the educated mother would not even consider it appropriate to use a wet nurse."[153] Although she may not have been aware of what she was doing, Cotching clawed at the stigma associated with the use of wet nurses among the upper classes by suggesting that both upper- and lower-class mothers shared the same goals of maintaining healthy babies.

Good mothers were also expected to know how to use a needle and thread. As Baron has written, the ability of women to sew their own clothing for themselves and their children was a means of "economizing,"[154] a skill especially desirable in Palestine in the wake of the poverty and misery of World War I. Although most of the schools taught their pupils how to sew, greater emphasis was placed upon embroidery (*tatriz*); for example, girls attending the government schools, both urban and rural, spent a few hours a week learning to embroider. Embroidery was not introduced by the girls' schools, however. Rather, throughout Palestine, young girls had learned to do *tatriz* as soon as they were old enough to hold a needle, receiving instruction from their mothers, grandmothers, or other older women. Around puberty, but sometimes even as early as age seven, girls began to work on their trousseaus for their future married lives, which included lavishly embroidered wedding dresses, pillow covers, and other functional items. An aspect of this exclusively female undertaking was women's use of colors and motifs in the embroidery to reveal information about their wealth, marital status, the region of their village, and even their hopes and aspirations.[155]

Even though girls learned embroidery at home, schools still incorporated the craft into their curricula. The inclusion of embroidery in the curricula of girls' schools across the country was seen as a tactical move, to reassure parents that their daughters were being educated according to the local cultural dictates. Within the government and missionary schools, however, this was not necessarily the case. They were fueled by western beliefs that the embroidered dresses of Palestinian women, as well as their accoutrements, were "proof" of the biblical narrative, believing that this embroidery had remained static since biblical times.[156] The appropriation of embroidery by the girls' schools may have also been shaped by aspirations of British officials and missionaries to transform embroidery into a craft for sale and exportation, especially as many western women became obsessed with collecting Palestinian embroidered dresses.[157] H. M. Wilson, a teacher at the Friends' School in Ramallah, wrote in her memoirs that British soldiers looted Arab homes when searching for rebels during the Arab Revolt, taking embroidered cloths, among other things,[158] indicative of their value among the British.

By teaching embroidery within the schools, the schools assumed control over the skill, ensuring its continuation, while at the same time controlling the styles and kinds of embroidery that the girls did. Having influence over the embroidery was seen as imperative, with the inspector of girls' education stating that if allowed, the Palestinian girls would "imitate the tasteless machine made designs of the West." The purpose of teaching embroidery, according to the inspector, was to eradicate "these perverted designs," and to teach girls according to "design based on the golden age of Arabic art . . . by reviving the old stitches and patterns of the traditional dress of the women."[159] Similarly, the teacher Sabine Shalfun, who later became headmistress of the Mamuniyya Government Girls' School in Jerusalem, insisted to the readers of the Beiruti women's magazine *al-Mar'a al-jadida* that girls should be educated "with good taste for simple, plain handwork, despite its having paltry value," evidently in response to the intricacy and variety of embroidery that girls were beginning to do, and argued "that real beauty is in simplicity rather than in variety."[160]

Despite the intentions of teachers and inspectors of girls' education, schools often were responsible for introducing changes, however small and seemingly trivial, into Palestinian embroidery. Although Leila El Khalidi argues that education improved the quality of embroidery in the villages, the missionary

Doing embroidery at the Rural Teachers' Training Center, al-Bireh, 1946. Photograph by Anna Riwkin-Brick, CZA PHR/1174724.

schools in particular introduced new materials, patterns, and stitches, and innovative uses. The French schools acquainted pupils with "fine arts designs and cotton thread," while the British missions taught girls to use the simple cross stitch. Similarly, the American missionary schools urged girls to embroider items that could then be sold to tourists,[161] thus transforming the normative way in which embroidery had been used. Social class and education also determined the materials used; only girls whose parents could afford the expensive threads and Irish linens were taught the more labor-intensive cross-stitch, while poor girls tended to do the plain embroidery (*tij*), using lesser quality threads and fabrics.[162] The patterns taught within the missionary schools were unusual too, depicting compact roses and flowers departing from the traditional geometric patterns of Palestinian embroidery.[163] A school teacher in the village of Bayt Dajan in the mid-1930s reportedly introduced girls to imported French pattern books and to new, western-influenced designs, including the *kanabat* (sofas) pattern, reflecting the economic and social changes taking place in urban upper- and middle-class Palestinian homes that village girls could only dream about.[164]

Teaching embroidery in girls' schools also overlapped with Palestinian perceptions of embroidery as an expression of nationalist tradition, which girls and women were expected to safeguard. Palestinian nationalist discourse appropriated the image of the peasant and folkloric customs, including embroidery, as representative of national culture and its "timeless character."[165] Learning to embroider may have assuaged male fears that Muslim girls would discard their embroidered dress and veil in favor of western fashion, as they became increasingly exposed to western culture, particularly through the Jewish Zionist presence. By learning embroidery, young girls were entrusted with the formidable task of preserving national identity. Teachers in particular also were entrusted with its preservation; not only did they teach embroidery but they also wrote about it, as in the case of Nabiha Hannush and Hannie J. Iranie, who published a book on the subject in 1920, followed by ʿAzize Daoud in 1930.[166]

Transforming Muslim schoolgirls into the "mothers of tomorrow" was at the center of girls' education throughout Palestine. Shaped by ideas of maternalism that were imported from the West, girls' schools placed emphasis on simple hygiene, cleanliness, caring for infants, and cooking, all deemed essential skills for becoming future mothers and homemakers. Although the aims may have been the same, the manner of instruction differed between village and urban schools. While village girls learned simple household tasks, urban girls were exposed to the more academic "domestic science," shaped by a middle-class ideology that promoted a kind of domestic emancipation, while freeing women from being dependent upon servants and household help. The "mothers of tomorrow" were also seen as the "preservers" of national culture, and entrusted with the important duty of continuing and maintaining the art of embroidery, which became part of the curriculum in girls' schools at this time.

Although girls were expected to aspire to be future mothers and to maintain their nation's culture, the schools also exposed them to female role models such as teachers and nurses, working women who had not (yet) fulfilled the social expectations of marriage and motherhood. It was exposure to these role models, together with the need for such women to professionally serve female members of their society, and the growing realization and acceptance of the women's awakening in Palestine, that led a small number of Muslim women who had been educated in Palestine's schools to tread in the public sphere and delay or forego motherhood altogether.

Chapter 6

The Mothers of Tomorrow in the Public Sphere

In 1925, when Augustine Tleel reportedly told the graduating class at the Greek Orthodox Girls' School in Jerusalem to move "forward, my sisters, forward, and whoever shakes the cradle with her right hand rocks the world with her left,"[1] she understood that girls' education was not just about creating mothers of the future, but that it was also about the entrance of women into the public spheres. Undoubtedly, the spread of girls' education from the end of Ottoman rule and through the British Mandate was one of the most important social changes to take place in Palestine during that period. Although slow to develop and not evenly distributed throughout the different segments of the population, the growth of girls' education still had important consequences. It created a new generation of literate women, albeit a small percentage of the population, who were very different from previous generations. Although their education emphasized their roles as future mothers and wives, it also challenged the normative gendered roles, as it was their education that enabled them to slowly enter spheres from which women had been excluded, namely the workforce, higher education, and associations. Both maintaining and challenging gender roles through girls' education echoes Afsaneh Najmabadi's argument that modern education within the context of nineteenth-century Iran was crucial to the formation of two seemingly conflicting notions of "woman." While education shaped the companionate wife, educated mother, and manager of the home, at the same time, it also molded the female citizen, whose education provided her with the tools for entering the public sphere.[2]

The education of Palestinian Muslim girls, even at the most basic and elementary level, should be understood as providing some access to public spaces; by the 1930s and 1940s, there were Muslim women in Palestine whose education might seem minimal compared to that of men or to that of their Christian peers who had assumed public roles mainly through government employment, but also by writing in the press and participating in charitable, political, and social associations. Frances Newton, who had resided in both Nazareth and Haifa from the late Ottoman period onward, wrote at the end of the Mandate that girls whom she "remembered as cradled babies in swaddling clothes who, in their early schooldays, had excused themselves for arriving late by saying that they had to fetch water from the village spring or sweep the dung for fuel from under the cattle in their homes had blossomed out into well-dressed young women employed in Government [to] serve as postal clerks, nurses, and teachers, and as secretaries to administrative officials."[3] Access to education transformed the lives of many women, as it provided them with the tools and skills necessary, which gave them an opportunity to be part of the growing Palestinian civil society.

Educated girls believed that they were far more liberated than previous generations. In written essays dating to 1929, students at the Jerusalem Girls' College, both Muslim and Christian, argued that they were a different generation, having received a better education than their mothers had. Most girls traced this change in education to the arrival of the British in Palestine. According to these pupils, the British Mandate also liberated women from being "prisoners" in their own home, by encouraging educated girls to seek employment. Yet not only did this generation of girls argue that they could go out to work, but they also argued that they could choose their own spouses, while their parents' generation could not. Most, however, believed that they would marry only after being able to work or volunteer for a specific period of time.[4]

ENTERING THE PUBLIC SPHERE VIA THE PRESS AND RADIO

Even before women began to enter the workforce, educated women used their literacy to take small steps within the public sphere, particularly by writing in the local and non-local Arabic press and delivering talks on the radio. Both served as a vehicle for transmitting ideas, and in the cases of women, for making their voices heard. For Muslim women, both the radio and the press provided a degree of modesty, as women writers and radio announcers were not seen, while also enabling women to maintain a degree of anonymity if desired.

The Palestinian Arabic press started later and developed on a much smaller scale than the neighboring presses of Egypt, Lebanon, and Istanbul, mainly because of its relatively limited readership and fierce competition. The local press was complemented by dozens of newspapers and journals from outside of Palestine that began to circulate in Palestine at the turn of the century. Over thirty different agents operated in Palestine before World War I, selling newspapers to consumers, who came from both urban and rural settings, while those who could, purchased subscriptions.[5] The press became very much ingrained in Palestinian educational culture. Social and cultural clubs, many of which also created reading rooms, provided newspapers to their members,[6] while many of the urban schools also had small libraries available to students. The Islamic Girls' School, for example, subscribed to *al-Hilal, al-Kishaf,* and *Majallat al-tarbiyya al-haditha,* all from Egypt.[7] Nuzha remembered reading Egyptian newspapers while a student there in the 1920s, as did a friend of hers who had attended the Jerusalem Girls' College.[8] Mustafa Kabha claims that the number of schoolchildren who read the Arabic press was quite high, with teachers encouraging pupils to read and purchase specific newspapers.[9] Teachers may have encouraged reading newspapers and journals because the level of language was easier and more accessible to pupils than that of the classical Arabic used in other texts. The press also remained the main source of news and information, at least until the introduction of the radio in 1936.

Educated women (and men) became the potential audience for the expanding market of printed literature, which, as Anderson argued, was tied to the emergence of national communities. As a result, women were often given journal subscriptions as gifts, underlining the significance of their literacy as well as of the press in the eyes of the reading public. The press noted when readers gave subscription gifts to others, indicating that the editors too understood the potential role that the press could play in the lives of people and the marketing role that publishing people's names and their beneficence may have filled. The Egyptian journal *al-'Arusa* (The Bride), for example, noted that "the notable lady, the princess (*al-wajiha al-amira*) Hasiba Shihab, wife of Dr. Fu'ad Abu Ghazala, gave the magazine *al-'Arusa* as a present . . . to Miss Zakiyya, headmistress of the girls' school in Nablus."[10] While in this case a notable woman gave a subscription to a woman teacher, male teachers also gave journals to their fiancées or relatives, as in the case of a subscription to *al-Mar'a al-jadida* from the "teacher Muhammad effendi Sabah to his fiancée Miss Fawziyya Sabakh in Safad," or from "the teacher Sa'di effendi Badran to his sister Miss Bahira Badran in Safad."[11] Although these announcements do not give many details about the women themselves, the giving of journal subscriptions indicates the value attached to reading and to owning publications among both men and women alike. That men gave journal subscriptions to women, namely their fiancées or sisters, also highlights their approval and appreciation of the education that these women had acquired, and supports the notion expressed by the headmistress of the Jerusalem Girls' College that educated men wanted educated wives. That teachers were the recipients of journals also underlines their role not only as consumers of literary culture, but also as its patrons.

While educated girls and women read the press, they also contributed to it. Schoolgirls and their teachers alike sent articles and letters to various periodicals, using them as a platform to promote issues related to the mothers of tomorrow. Several pupils at the Islamic Girls' School published articles in *Majallat rawdat al-maʿarif,* a journal published by the male teachers and pupils of Rawdat al-Maʿarif School. Although this journal was intended to serve those affiliated with that particular school, the fact that girls were among the contributors indicates that this journal served a much wider audience. With the possible exception of the Jerusalem Girls' College, most Arab girls' schools did not produce their own journals, leaving girls little choice but to publish articles in the local press and in the journals published by boys' schools, although the latter may have been the exception rather than the rule. Pupil Rabiha al-Dajani, for example, used the journal of *Majallat rawdat al-maʿarif* to remind readers that girls, like boys, also should be able to serve their country, but had to be educated, as "knowledge is one of the pillars of independence."[12] By choosing specifically to write in this journal, she sent a direct message to educated male readers that their sisters, wives, and daughters had a right to be educated. Naʿamat Kamil of Tul Karim, "one of the educated girls and ladies," used the daily newspaper *al-Difaʿ* to call upon "the female readers" to uplift the level of the family and to "spread the ways of God and of the nation and of good moral behavior."[13] Some women published outside of the local press, such as Sabine Shalfun, the future headmistress at the Mamuniyya School in Jerusalem, who wrote in the Beiruti women's journal *al-Marʾa al-jadida* about the importance of mothers and daughters doing handicrafts together during the summer months, thus reinforcing the domestic ideal.[14] Mothers even sent in photographs of their "beautiful babies" to the journal *al-ʿArusa,* manifesting their devotion to being "good mothers" as well as their modernity, exposed through the photograph itself.[15]

Schoolgirls in particular began writing in the pages of *al-Ghad,* the monthly journal created in the late 1930s by the Arab Students' Union, which organized during the revolt. Maisar al-Shawwa, a pupil at the government girls' school in Gaza, complained that the women of her generation would have "no influence on the morals" of their children as long as they were not trained in "home education." Her article stressed the importance of educating girls, implicitly suggesting that there were still families who did not understand the merits of female education. According to reports, only 26 percent of the girls aged six to eleven attended school in Gaza in the late 1930s.[16] She went on rhetorically to ask what was the purpose of the schools, answering that "schools are a door to the education of virtue. They are a door to the education of the youth who in the future will become one of the sons of the nation and the *umma*. Schools are the homes in which families live, each one of them a single family composed of pupils as sisters and the teacher as the mother and the headmistress as the father."[17] The school as a family was a commonly used metaphor at the time, underlining the elevated position attributed to schools, as well as their role in "nurturing" young children. Another article implied that the school as fostering good mothers and homemakers was merely just a metaphor for germinating the seeds of a feminist revolution. Tawaddud ʿAbd al-Hadi, a pupil at the Rural Teachers' Training Center in al-Bireh, proudly declared that "the woman has broken the shackles that man placed around her neck thousands of years ago, and she competes with him shoulder to shoulder and she has met with progress and equality." She ended her piece by writing that despite resistance from men, she did "not know to which degree the revolution of the Eastern woman will reach, but perhaps they will get the throne and return the golden period."[18]

Introduced in 1936, the Palestine Broadcasting Service (PBS) became another arena in which educated women found a space for employing their knowledge and voicing their views, similar to the press. Like the press, the radio cloaked their identity, familiarizing listeners with only names and voices. Comparable to the press, radio ownership was coveted among the middle classes, as it represented "affluence, sophistication, [and] urbanity linked to a cosmopolitan modern life."[19] Although radio ownership was limited because of the purchasing costs, by 1945, some 10,000 radio sets had been sold to the Arab population in Palestine. Given that numerous people could listen to a single radio, and that radios became fixtures in public places such as coffee shops and the village *madafeh* (guest house), the listenership was conceivably much greater than the number of radios purchased.[20]

As Andrea L. Stanton notes, the PBS created special programming for the different segments of society who tuned into the radio, including shows specifically for schoolchildren and women.[21] Educated women were recruited to serve as broadcasters, and to promote the idea of the educated, modern woman, as illustrated by a radio program entitled "New Arab House," delivered by a Mrs. Salwa Saʿid from December 1940 through February 1941. The program included nine fifteen-minute talks on various aspects of household management, all of which were transcribed in full on the pages of the newspaper *Filastin*, pointing to an interesting interaction between the two mediums. According to Stanton, this particular radio program emphasized the importance of girls' education, and linked the ability to manage the household with a woman's knowledge.[22] The British understood well the contribution that broadcasting could make to advancing education, and especially girls' education.

By the mid to late 1940s, the director of the PBS understood that a "company of Arab actors" and an increase in the number of wireless transmitters installed in government schools were essential for transmitting messages of modernity to schoolchildren, especially those in the villages.[23] Nuzha Khalidi, from one of the well-known Muslim families in Jerusalem, was recruited as a program assistant for developing the Arabic school broadcasts, having been trained at the WTC and having worked as a teacher. Qudsiyya Khurshid of Jaffa and Fatima al-Budayri of Jerusalem also were employed in broadcasting radio programs to the schools.[24] Qudsiyya Khurshid, for example, gave talks about Islam, including one on the late nineteenth-century Muslim woman writer 'Aisha Taymur,[25] subjects which were seen as having appeal to young schoolgirls.

Transcripts and even details about content of the radio shows are not readily available, making it difficult to evaluate what women broadcast over the radio and what the listeners heard. The published talks of Hadiya 'Abd al-Hadi do give some indication of the content of her radio talks. 'Abd al-Hadi, from a landowning Muslim family in Jenin, was a regular broadcaster on the Near Eastern Broadcasting Station. Initially established in Jaffa during World War II for broadcasting pro-British propaganda in Arabic, by the end of the war the station, also known as *al-Sharq al-'adna'*, had become a regular Arabic radio station, and reportedly had an even larger percentage of Muslim listeners than Christians.[26]

'Abd al-Hadi's talks focused on women and gender roles. In one broadcast that aired in February 1942, she refuted the idea of women as the "weaker sex" (*al-jins al-da'if*), noting that history was full of strong, independent women. 'Abd al-Hadi, however, did not support the idea of equality between men and women, nor the domination of men over women; rather, she believed that men and women complemented one another "like a piece of music that includes the oud and the violin, and the music is only beautiful as long as the two are together as two eternal partners." She then warned her listeners of "the new [women's] awakening," and more specifically of the "trend of pomp and circumstance and the love of imitation that has swept away many women." Cautioning her listeners to avoid mimicking the consumerism of the West, she urged women to show more concern for their children, as "children were more valuable than material wealth," mentioning Queen Nazli of Egypt as an exemplar.

Although 'Abd al-Hadi's talk was typical of the middle-class domestic ideology, her discussion of limiting the number of children, clearly directed at young mothers, was intriguing and reflected some of the contemporary concerns of the 1940s. Economic crises apparently were causing men and women to consider having only one child. 'Abd al-Hadi warned her listeners against this idea, as the only child tended to be "spoiled, weak of character, and would not be able to deal with difficulties." Children who grow up with sisters and brothers, in contrast, were considered tougher and more self-reliant. There were only two cases in which 'Abd al-Hadi recommended limiting births: in case of danger to the mother and if one parent had a hereditary disease. 'Abd al-Hadi's recommendation also reflected both nationalist and modern concerns. Couples should not limit births, as it was better for the children to grow up with siblings, whereas more births also contributed to the growth of the nation. Yet 'Abd al-Hadi also showed concern for the health of the mother and the unborn child, while also alluding to the ability to actually limit births. Vashitz relays in his writings that birth control devices were sold in public in the markets of the larger cities, indicating that there may have been pressure toward having smaller families by the 1930s and 1940s, especially as smaller families corresponded to the norm of the "modern" nuclear family.[27]

WORKING WOMEN

The right of educated upper- and middle-class women to work and pursue careers had been an ongoing struggle throughout the region since the late nineteenth and early twentieth centuries. The spread of girls' education, the publication of the press, especially the women's press—which, as Marilyn Booth has shown, published biographies of exemplary women engaged in various professions—led to a growing struggle for women's employment.[28] The real catalyst, however, was World War I; as Elizabeth Thompson has argued within the context of Syria, the war compelled the middle and upper classes to accept women's employment as it "had left so many women without means of support."[29] Essays written in 1929 by young female students at the Jerusalem Girls' College acknowledged that women's entry into the workforce was one of the changes that they had noticed since World War I, equating it with growing access to education, greater freedoms for women, and increased westernization. One student wrote that the women in Palestine after the war "think higher and they are more free than what they were from before. . . . They also go and work and earn some money to help their families. Before the war they would not do it."[30] Another girl noted that before the war "woman had all kinds of indoor employment, but they were practically prisoners" in their homes, while since the war "they train girls as teachers, nurses to help the needy person."[31] The poverty, disease, and loss of wage earners during and in the aftermath of the war left many women with no choice but to seek employment.

During the Mandate period, against the backdrop of the struggles of Egyptian women to increasingly enter the workforce in the 1930s,[32] women in Palestine, especially Muslim women, waged their own struggles to enter the teaching profession, the most accessible and most popular profession for women at this time. The special teacher training that women had to acquire gave them a degree of respect and social prestige. Booth has shown that teachers were regular subjects of biography in the Egyptian women's press, as a way of celebrating their social position within society and inspiring girls to follow in their footsteps.[33] Women interviewed remembered wanting to become teachers, or being encouraged to emulate their teachers, as teachers were considered to be *qawiyye* (strong) and *shakhsiyye*, meaning they had personality.[34] Teachers also earned a social position equivalent to that of the mother, as both were responsible for the future generations, with the press referring to the mothers as the "child's first school," before the teacher assumed responsibility. Unlike some of the other professions, however, the teaching profession adhered strictly to gender segregation; as a result, women teachers could maintain an air of modesty, and even righteousness. Among their students, they commanded nothing but respect and at times even fear.[35]

Although during the late Ottoman period and the first few years of the Mandate, Christian women outnumbered Muslim women teachers within the government schools, this was not the case by the 1930s and 1940s. Over 230 Muslim women worked as schoolteachers in government schools in the 1943–1944 school year, compared to only 123 Palestinian Christian women.[36] That is, 65 percent of the women working in the government schools were Muslim, compared to 35 percent Christian. Although Arab Christian women were more likely to procure employment in the Protestant and Catholic schools, the predominance of Muslim women teachers in the government schools inevitably was significant for young Muslim schoolgirls. It exposed them to Muslim women who were not only educated, but who also worked and led relatively independent lives.

Several interwoven factors contributed to the increase of Muslim women working as school teachers. First, the demands of the local population that Muslim women teachers be hired to teach in the government schools forced the British administration to increasingly allow Muslim girls to train and work as teachers. The case of Nablus illustrates this well, in which clashes between the Muslim population and the Department of Education over Christian women teachers in a government girls' school led to the school's temporary closure and eventual removal of the teachers in 1923.[37] In his history of Nablus, Ihsan al-Nimr suggested that the school had little choice but to hire Christian women because local families had refused to allow their daughters to study at the Ottoman teachers' college in Beirut and then at the WTC in Jerusalem.[38] Situations such the one in Nablus undoubtedly influenced the decision of the WTC to admit more Muslim girls than Christian ones by the mid-1920s. Secondly, Muslim women from elite families paved the way for girls from non-elite families by entering the WTC and by taking up teaching jobs. The fact that elite Muslim women in Egypt had already waged a similar battle during and after the British administration in Egypt for the right to train and work as teachers and headmistresses may have also helped local Palestinian women to achieve their goals.[39] Finally, the Department of Education was compelled to train Muslim women as teachers, especially as the number of Christian women studying at the WTC began to drop in the mid-1920s, as opportunities for higher studies became increasingly available to them.

The nature of the teaching profession in Palestine was difficult, and only a small percentage of women made it into a lifelong career. The forced retirement of women teachers upon marriage meant that the majority of women left teaching after just a few years, preferring marriage over their careers. The appointment of teachers to schools that were outside of their home towns, so that pupils would be less likely to buy favors from familiar teachers, was another obstacle that women teachers faced. As women, they were expected to live with relatives or with other women teachers, but they could not live alone as male teachers could. Gendered norms also restricted women teachers in their movement, especially in rural villages, where local residents, school officials, and other teachers closely monitored them. In the routine reports written by the educational inspectors, who were all Palestinian men, whether or not the woman exhibited "proper behavior" and had "good standing" within the community was always noted. Female teachers were usually transferred if they caused friction with local residents, if they were suspected of immoral behavior, or if their teaching skills were deemed insufficient by the school inspector.[40]

The censuring of teachers' behavior reflected primarily male criticisms directed at working women, especially Muslim women. The newspaper al-Jami'a al-'arabiyya, for example, expressed anger at a number of women employed at the WTC and their graduating pupils, who would soon be working as teachers, for allegedly having behaved inappropriately at the home of the Director of Education, Humphrey Bowman. The newspaper claimed that

Bowman had asked the women to dance and sing for him, which they did, with gender and power relations dictating their actions. The paper wrote:

> After the eminent teachers finished dancing *dabke* [a traditional Levantine line dance] and singing, two pupils, one Muslim and one Christian, stood up and danced *baladi* [belly dancing] knowing that this kind of dancing is not part of our customs . . . Is there anyone among the supporters of the awakening of Muslim youth in this country who can keep from protesting . . . upon seeing Muslim girls dance, adorned in beauty, before a foreigner? . . . just as we believe that the customs and practice among our Christian sisters do not permit this kind of outward dancing. What do the readers say about this kind of activity of the educated mothers of the future?[41]

Although *al-Jami'a al-'arabiyya* expressed concern that Muslim women had danced in front of a man, and a foreign one at that, the implication was that both the teachers and the graduating pupils, who soon would become teachers as well as future mothers, were being taught to engage in immoral activities such as belly dancing[42] as a result of their training in the WTC, a foreign-administered institution. This criticism was similar to that noted by Marilyn Booth in the context of the Egyptian women's press, which occasionally yoked girls' education with leisurely pursuits, indolence, and decadence.[43] This criticism of the teachers, the WTC, and the girls who studied there was meant to cast a dark shadow over the teaching profession and raise questions about the morality of those women who trained to become teachers.

Many women, especially those educated at the WTC, encountered antagonisms from the residents in the places where they taught. It was particularly difficult for urban women to work in the villages or in some of the more isolated and conservative towns where the teachers encountered differences between their standards and expectations versus those of the village residents. Upon completing her studies at the WTC, Nadiyya took a job as the headmistress of the government girls' school in Hebron in the 1940s. There she received numerous complaints from parents who questioned her motives as a teacher for holding school parties and taking the pupils on field trips, activities typical of urban girls' schools. These families saw Nadiyya as disregarding the socially and religiously conservative gendered norms of Hebron, affirming Woodsmall's observation that even though "Moslem communities that are especially reactionary such as Hebron and Nablus" demand Muslim women teachers, the "social conditions make it difficult for a Moslem woman from outside to live there."[44] At the same time, they rejected what they saw as her use of her authority as a teacher to introduce the students to activities that may have been considered "foreign" and inappropriate in Hebron. Nadiyya did not defer to the demands of the local parents, however, and eventually won their trust by increasing the number of grades in the school.[45]

While the best students were urged to take up teaching, some girls were guided toward other occupations, such as sewing. Although women already sewed clothing by hand at home for their families, the appearance of the sewing machine in the region as early as 1860 facilitated the opening of sewing workshops and tailoring businesses operated by both men and women. As "a craft-based industry, with clothing mainly produced on demand in small artisanal workshops, where high skilled tailors worked with a number of apprentices," garment production was gender segregated, thus requiring a number of women dressmakers and seamstresses to work with female clientele.[46] The advertising of sewing machines from the 1880s onward in the early Arabic press paved the way for private consumption while the introduction of payment plans, the first of their kind in the Middle East, enabled people of all socioeconomic backgrounds to be able to purchase them. By the turn of the century, advertisements for sewing machines also appeared in the Arabic women's journals, reflecting the growing upper- and middle-class discourse on the "new women" and modern domesticity,[47] in sharp contrast to the portrayal of the seamstress in Victorian iconography as often being orphaned.[48] The attempts to market this product to different clientele correspond with Judith G. Coffin's research, which shows that in nineteenth-century France, the Singer sewing company ran ads portraying the "sewing machine girl," who was simply dressed, and while she easily could have passed as "working class," Coffin argues that she also was portrayed as being "a paragon of domestic industry and womanly virtue who transcended her social class,"[49] suggesting that women who worked on sewing machines represented certain values and were not to be associated with a specific socioeconomic background.

The marketing of the sewing machine as a modern accoutrement for all classes together with the gendering of tailoring may have facilitated the incorporation of sewing into girls' schools and the acceptance of dressmaking and sewing as respectable careers among middle-class, educated girls. The American Colony, which saw its school of handicrafts and dressmaking as delaying early marriages among Muslim girls, also recognized that sewing and dressmaking could serve them in their future. In its publications it encouraged "all girls to go to Government or Mission Schools," and "after their graduation," to join its training program. Nonetheless, it still admitted girls who had not completed school, but required them to attend Arabic and English classes, again linking sewing to some academic instruction.[50]

Throughout the 1930s, the Arabic press was replete with advertisements for sewing machines, seamstresses, and sewing workshops. While an advertisement for a Singer sewing machine promised to make girls into "proper mothers,"[51] appealing to middle-class sensibilities, a sewing workshop in Jerusalem linked the skill to the advancement of the nation. This particular workshop was founded by an Estella Jadallah al-Daboub, and advertised a year-long training in sewing or typewriting for "young girls and ladies," with the latter track reflecting the small number of mainly Christian girls who began to work as typists in government offices. The ad associated the efforts to train girls for careers with the state of the nation, reading that its aim was "raising the condition of the nation without any distinction" between Muslim or Christian, and that this work was "not for material profit," implying that other sewing workshops were intended to benefit the owners. Rather, this workshop stressed that it was founded for "uplifting the Eastern woman," as "the nation will not progress without advancing its women."[52] Young women, who could sew either for themselves or for profit, were seen as advancing the nation in that they contributed to the local garment industry, instead of purchasing their clothes from "foreign" tailors, in reference to the Jewish tailors and clothing manufacturers that had begun to predominate throughout the country.[53]

Socioeconomic difficulties and the lack of academic skills needed to use a sewing machine, however, meant that despite all efforts to appeal to educated, upper-class girls, the sewing profession shifted toward appealing primarily to lower-class women so that they could earn a livelihood. The Arab Women's Association in Jerusalem opened a workshop in the Musrara neighborhood, advertising that its establishment was essential "since it will employ, upon [their] learning, many of our girls who do not have work, so that they will be able to undertake their burden."[54] Similarly, the sewing workshop at the Islamic Girls' School in 1939 was primarily attended by poor girls whose poverty prevented them from finishing their elementary education.[55] In a few cases, however, girls attended this particular sewing workshop for reasons other than poverty. Suʿad al-Khalidi reportedly entered the sewing workshop for a lack of a better alternative, as she was unable to enter the government secondary classes, having exceeded the maximum age for admission.[56] Widad attended the workshop in preparation for married life, so that she could learn to mend and make clothing for herself and her children,[57] reflecting the nationalist ideology that women should be self-sufficient. The newspaper *Filastin,* in praise of a sewing workshop in Jaffa, wrote that "what is most important for the woman in her married life, after getting an education and culture, is cutting and sewing,"[58] implying that households could be more thrifty if women would learn to sew their families' clothing.

While educated as well as non-educated girls were willing to take up sewing, this was not the case for nursing. Nursing as a woman's profession was first introduced in Palestine in the late nineteenth and early twentieth century by the employment of foreign women as hospital matrons and nurses in the various missionary hospitals and medical clinics. As scholarship has shown, a strong connection had been forged between various missions, science, and medicine. In particular, the medical missions reached out to diverse populations by ridiculing folk remedies and offering "cures" to people's ailments by applying western-based medicine.[59] By the early twentieth century, the missionary schools began to encourage local Christian girls upon completing their studies to work as nurses[60] in the hospitals and clinics associated with the missions. Malakeh and Margaret Melkon, young Armenian sisters from Jerusalem who had been educated at a German Protestant school in Jerusalem, both trained as nurses, with one at the German Hospital in Jerusalem and the other at a hospital in Hebron administered by the United Free Church of Scotland. At the recommendation of the wife of Dr. Paterson, the missionary doctor stationed in Hebron, the two sisters applied around 1909–1910 to the nursing program at the Syrian Protestant College in Beirut, later to become AUB.[61] Established in 1905, this program required that the students be between the ages of eighteen and thirty, in good health, and able to speak and read English, with the language requirements essentially restricting enrollment to those who had studied in missionary schools. Despite the Balkan wars (1912–1913), which were used to mobilize women to take up nursing,[62] the nursing program at AUB never exceeded more than twenty pupils.[63]

Poverty and dire health conditions caused by World War I became a catalyst for recruiting women nurses during the Mandate period. In 1918, the American Zionist Medical Unit established a nurses' training school for Jewish women, with twenty-two graduating with the first class in 1921.[64] In 1919, the Department of Health also issued regulations for training nurses, requiring the completion of elementary school and three years of training in one of the eighteen municipal and private hospitals.[65] Although the elementary school requirement was intended to prevent impoverished and illiterate women from training as nurses, so that the nursing profession could acquire a rather elevated status, the educational requirement also excluded the majority of Muslim women in Palestine from applying.

Between 1919 and 1925, some one hundred girls trained as nurses, although the Department of Health acknowledged that "only Jewish and Christian women have offered themselves for service."[66] Deciding that the lack of interest in nursing among Muslim women was related to the custom of gender segregation, the government announced a special program to train Muslim nurses in "harim conditions" in the government hospital in Nablus.[67] The concern of the Department of Health that a separate nursing program for Muslim women would be of "considerable cost" to maintain, and that Muslim girls would "not be forthcoming for training,"[68] was not unsubstantiated, as the program attracted only two Muslim women in 1926,[69] in contrast to the thirty-five young Muslim women enrolled that same year in the teachers' training program at the WTC.[70] The reluctance of Muslim women to take up nursing was much more complex than merely an issue of gender segregation.

The Department of Health, however, was eager to recruit Muslim women nurses, as they were seen as integral to the successful promotion of better health throughout Palestine's villages. It was anticipated that the nurses would live in the larger villages, and visit "a large number of villages, each village on only two or three occasions a month, giving such medical relief as a nurse is capable of." The nurses were expected to "get to know personally all the women and children in each village," and to care for the health of the children, reflecting the maternalist aims of British rule toward the local population. These village nurses were to be responsible also for giving vaccinations and reporting "serious cases of illness."[71] The difficulties of convincing Muslim women to serve as nurses, however, as well as the reluctance of Christian women nurses to work in Muslim villages, meant that nursing duties, such as providing eye drops to pupils, fell upon the teachers, the next most maternal figures within the villages.

Despite the attempts, albeit minimal, of the government to accommodate gendered norms of segregation, nursing remained stigmatized among Muslim women. In her study of Egyptian upper-class women from the 1920s to the 1940s, Margot Badran noted that "of all the categories of work in medicine, the most difficult to open up for women was nursing."[72] While Badran blamed the difficulties of recruiting Egyptian women into nursing because of its association with the male *tamarji*, or orderly, this was not necessarily the case in Palestine. According to a questionnaire sent to the headmistresses of unnamed schools about why Arab girls were reluctant to become nurses, the main reason cited was the "undesirability of nursing men," that is, the fear of potential social contact with male patients, and the potential scandals that could arise if unmarried Muslim women and unrelated men came into contact with one another. While nursing was seen as calling gendered norms into question, many also regarded it as "menial work and therefore dishonorable."[73] As one student at the Friends' School in Ramallah wrote in a school essay, "Nurses are nothing more than servants."[74] The "explicitly inferior status in hospital hierarchy," with the Palestinian nurses at the bottom and British matrons at the top,[75] was illustrated in 1927 by an incident in which a British matron at the Government Mental Hospital in Bethlehem locked an Arab nurse in a cell reserved for maniacal patients following a disagreement. As the director of the Department of Health was quoted as saying, this particular incident had "severely shaken the confidence of the Palestinian nurses of the service in the attitude of the British members of the Department of Health towards them."[76] This incident, which was said to be reported widely throughout Palestine, undoubtedly compiled with other reports of the poor treatment meted out to nurses, lent little appeal to the profession, particularly among upper- and even middle-class girls. The reluctance of going into nursing may have also been related to the socioeconomic class of the women themselves, who may have been hesitant to have to physically help others from the lower classes. Why Christian women were not deterred by nursing's poor reputation is not entirely clear, although as products of missionary education, they may have been taught to think differently about nursing than women who did not graduate from missionary schools. Oddly, the relationship between nursing and Christian missions was not mentioned as a reason why Muslim women shunned nursing. The stigma that Muslim women attached to nursing meant that the profession consequently became dominated by Christian women. Out of eighty-five Arab women who began training in both government and missionary hospitals in Palestine between the years 1921 and 1943, 94 percent were Christian.[77] A significant number were Armenian Christians who may have been convinced that nursing careers would improve their position as an ethnic, linguistic, and religious minority in Palestine.[78]

The stigmatizing of nursing among Muslim women and the inability to recruit Muslim women as nurses caused Palestine to suffer from an overall "dearth of Arab nurses."[79] During World War II, the Department of Education embarked on a vigorous campaign to encourage primarily Muslim pupils within the government girls' schools to (re)consider the nursing profession. The Department of Education's campaign included giving lectures to pupils in the higher grades about the merits of the profession, and requiring headmistresses to actively identify potential candidates, in addition to regular visits to infant welfare clinics and hospitals, as a means of exposing girls to the benefits of modern medicine and medical careers.[80] Photographs of local nurses tending to patients, placing emphasis on the human face of nursing and its importance, even appeared in *Huna al-quds,* the Arabic journal belonging to the Palestine Broadcasting Service, which had regular broadcasts for the government schools.[81] The attempts to recruit local girls into nursing fit into a much larger campaign that linked nursing with the agenda of the Colonial Office, and which sought to increase the number of nurses, both local and

British, throughout the British domains.[82] It also paralleled the entry of large numbers of Arab women into the workforce, whose employment was fuelled by expanding industries and opportunities during World War II.[83]

Despite efforts to improve the image of nursing, Muslim girls and their families continued to show little enthusiasm in the profession until the mid-1940s, when, against the backdrop of escalating tensions and violence between Arabs and Jews, upper-class Palestinian women began to take an interest in nursing and "imbued it with patriotic meaning."[84] At a gathering of elite women in Haifa in 1946, participants cited the poor education of Muslim girls as one of the obstacles in the way of training them as nurses. The gathering acknowledged that "girls' schools in Haifa Rural [district] are being expanded but not sufficiently enough yet to favour a good educational standard for training." The absence of higher grades within the villages also meant that village girls tended to finish their studies at the latest by age fourteen, which was too young for nurses' training. The women in Haifa concluded that in order to engage more Muslim girls in nursing, the local population, and not the British officials, had to play a more substantial role. It was suggested that village leaders publicize the need for Arab women nurses, that headmistresses in the local girls' schools select candidates, while "the leading ladies of Haifa" would make personal contacts with the mothers of young Muslim girls to try to convince them of the merits of nursing. The only way to elevate the profession was by enlisting "girls of good family social standing" and "by organizing parties for recruits where ladies of a reputed social position should participate."[85] The goodwill of the Haifa ladies, however, went unheard, as less than a year later, in July 1947, some one hundred Arab women in Nazareth met and expressed concern that the disinterest of Arab (read Muslim) women in the nursing profession had led to the closure of hospitals and had prevented the establishment of new national (*watani*) hospitals.[86]

Equally unpopular as nursing was midwifery. From the late nineteenth century, the native midwives had been depicted with contempt by British colonial officials, western missionaries, and tourists throughout the region. Described as "ignorant, old, often blind or half-blind, always filthy and always of the lowest class," the midwife, according to Woodsmall, was "the greatest hazard" to women and children,[87] and throughout the British colonies, she was blamed for high mortality rates for both mothers and babies.[88] The real issue at stake, however, was not the high mortality rates, but a struggle to eradicate an indigenous female profession led by male doctors from the West. As Elise G. Young has written, "Midwives in Palestine had a different orientation to their work from that of 'imported' male physicians. The highly evolved skills of midwives were acquired through experience and through knowledge based on oral traditions . . . that knowledge and practices of midwives were denigrated as superstition and as untrustworthy was part of the colonial struggle for control of validation of knowledge."[89] In the case of colonial Egypt, Hibba Abugideiri has argued that the introduction of the modern, western-trained (local male) doctor, based on the British model, intentionally compelled indigenous midwives to give up their roles as independent medical practitioners, forcing them into positions of dependency upon the male medical establishment.[90]

Seeking to supervise and limit the role of midwives, the British colonial government issued Public Health Ordinance No. 1 of 1918, requiring midwives, as well as doctors, dentists, and pharmacists, to be officially licensed. Later the British passed Midwives Ordinance No. 20 of 1929, obligating midwives to undergo at least six months' training and certification in a recognized institution. In addition, the law also circumscribed the practice of midwifery to childbirth only, and forbade practicing gynecology or any other branch of medicine,[91] clearly an attack on the older generations of midwives who historically had worked in these fields. The result of this ordinance was the creation of two types of midwives: a trained, modern and urban nurse-midwife (*qabila*), versus the untrained midwife (*daya*), who was still allowed to practice her profession within the limits of the law, and as long as she did not work in the same (mainly urban) areas delineated for the certified midwives.[92] As Fleischmann argues, the British campaign to reform the midwives created conflicts between the midwives themselves, leading to a "confrontation between two competing, gendered hierarchies of medicine, representing (male) 'science' and 'modernity' on the one side, and indigenous (female) authority, folk wisdom, and experience on the other."[93]

The British campaign to reform midwives had supporters within the Muslim community as well. In 1924, a number of elite Muslim men and women formed a committee to supervise and encourage the training of Muslim midwives. The ideal candidates were to be over the age of twenty, be of "good moral behavior," and literate in Arabic,[94] with the literacy prerequisite typical of midwifery training throughout the British colonies.[95] These requirements created a younger and somewhat more educated midwife, unlike the previous generations. Marital status also was not taken into consideration. This contrasted with the British-ruled Sudan, where only married women were recruited into midwifery, as unmarried midwives were perceived as being too independent and as women attracted to other women.[96] In contrast in Palestine, as Hilma Granqvist was told in the mid-1920s, it had become acceptable for unmarried women to be present at births, whereas in the past it would have caused them shame.[97]

The SMC agreed to find a number of pupil midwives, presumably from among graduates of its girls' schools and orphanage, and fund their training. It assisted about eight pupil midwives per year from 1925 to circa 1930. At the same time, the SMC financed several beds for pregnant Muslim women within Jerusalem's government hospital, where the women were kept in "harim conditions."[98] The provision of beds both encouraged Muslim women to give birth in the hospital, which at this time numbered only 170 births per year, and also provided patients for the midwives to train upon. While the imposition of "harim conditions" on the midwives and the birthing mothers may have been a means of attracting women from the elite to the hospital and to the midwifery profession, it also kept midwives out of the public eye, essentially restricting them to a corner of the hospital. It may have also been a way of differentiating between midwives and nurses, with Woodsmall noting rather ironically that although "the girls in training were kept in the small maternity ward and re-tained the veil," Muslim girls in the nurses' training "serve in the whole hos-pital and move about freely unveiled," wearing uniform nurses' caps.[99] While the motives of the SMC in supporting this program may have been to present itself as pioneering both a maternalist and modernist policy in Palestine, the SMC recognized that midwifery could provide a future for some of the female graduates of its schools, without threatening gender norms. Although finan-cial difficulties forced the SMC to withdraw its funding for training Muslim midwives, it continued to finance the maternity beds.[100]

Despite attempts to transform midwifery into a career for young educated, Muslim women, midwifery remained a profession dominated by older, un-educated women. According to an official of the Department of Health, of the 1,277 women registered as untrained midwives by 1928, only fifty were under the age of forty, and only five were literate. Part of the problem, accord-ing to this official, was the poor salary. If the salary was higher, then "a better type of woman should, in time, be attracted to the work and many of the larger villages may be able to support licensed midwives."[101] In the late 1930s, Freda Ghaith received only six Palestinian pounds a month for her work as a licensed and trained midwife and nurse in Bayt Jibrin near Hebron.[102] In the 1940s, the same woman was accused of violating Midwife Ordinance No. 20 of 1929, as she ran a private (and illegal) clinic for general medical and gyne-cological problems,[103] in order to supplement her paltry income.

The movement of Muslim women into the workplace was paralleled by small numbers of young Muslim women who embarked on higher education mainly in Beirut, joining an already small number of Christian Palestinian women. The access that Christian girls had to higher education, together with that of Muslim males, as well as the growing independence exhibited by some educated Muslim women, particularly those who became teachers, paved the way for Muslim girls to continue their education outside of Palestine. Although women had attended AUB before World War I, enrolling in its professional schools or attending as auditors, the 1920s witnessed a greater demand from women to attend the university. Their demand for higher education, coupled with fears of coeducation, was resolved in 1927 with the opening of the American Junior College for Women.[104] It offered two years of college study in an all-female environment, after which students could then transfer to AUB. From 1926 to 1940, Palestinian women constituted 13 percent or 39 out of 300 graduates of the American Junior College for Women.[105] In addition to regular academic studies, the school offered courses deemed suitable for young women, household management and hygiene, while also encouraging pupils to engage in social work, from working in infant welfare clinics to supervising playgrounds,[106] all very reminiscent of girls' education available in Palestine.

Financial and moral support provided by the government and other bodies enabled families to agree to their daughters' education outside of Palestine. Nuzha recalled that Hajj Amin al-Husayni, the head of the Supreme Muslim Council, and Hilmi Pasha, president of the Arab Bank, convinced her father to let her attend a teachers' college in Helwan, outside of Cairo. As was customary, Nuzha's father accompanied her to Helwan, where the school's headmistress reassured him that Nuzha would not leave the school without the escort of a teacher; it should be noted that she was only a teenager at the time.[107] Sa'ida relayed that her father, who was a judge in the Muslim religious court, strongly supported women's education and agreed to her learning in England, despite criticism from Muslim circles.[108] Some families also permitted their daughters to go away to college because they had brothers or male cousins studying nearby, thus ensuring a degree of supervision and safety.[109] This more permissive attitude of women traveling to other countries to continue their education was not just a Palestinian phenomenon; of the forty-three women who had graduated from AUB between 1925 and 1933, five of them hailed from Iraq, two from Syria, and one each from Turkey and Egypt, respectively, with the rest coming from Beirut itself.[110]

The number of Muslim women who were able to continue their studies in institutions of higher education was limited, however, as they had to fulfill and overcome certain social and cultural expectations. All of the women who attended the American Junior College in Beirut had to have excellent English skills in order to gain admission, meaning that they were almost all graduates of the high-level, English-language missionary schools. Yusra Salah, the daughter of a shaykh from Nablus, entered the American Junior College in

1942 after completing her studies at the Friends' School in Ramallah.[111] Competence in English also was a factor in receiving government scholarships for study in England, with the reports of the Department of Education revealing that the majority of the female grantees were Christian, and almost all graduates of the Jerusalem Girls' College.

THE ATTRACTION OF ASSOCIATIONS

During the Mandate period, a number of young educated women, Muslims and Christians alike, became active members of various charitable, social, and later political associations. Charity has a long history in the Arab Muslim world, from the religious obligations of giving alms (*zakat*) to the poor to the endowment of property as *waqf*, with the revenues of a given property earmarked for educational, religious purposes, and charitable purposes. Randi Deguilhem has argued that women in late Ottoman Damascus endowed *waqf* property as markers of their wealth and in order to associate their names with public properties and with acts of goodwill, as a kind of "local networking."[112] The beginning of the twentieth century saw a shift away from this older, more established form of charity and toward the creation of charitable associations, the result of growing state attempts to challenge the power of the ulama by controlling the *awqaf* property and the income generated by these properties. The lack of state-provided services, in the late Ottoman period and during the British Mandate, created a need for "indigenous welfare societies," especially as the challenges of the new century demanded new ways of alleviating poverty and distress.[113]

According to Fleischmann, Palestinian women first created charitable societies in the early twentieth century, paralleling the activities of women throughout the world.[114] The early organizations in Palestine were dominated by graduates of the Protestant and Catholic missionary schools, as Asma Tubi's biographical dictionary of well-known Palestinian women shows. Tubi wrote that the Protestant and Catholic schools promoted the idea of benevolence among their pupils by providing funding for poor and orphaned girls, in addition to creating separate sections for them.[115] Some of the early women's groups may have originated within the schools themselves, as Baron indicates was the case with a learned society of young girls in Cairo.[116] The creation of sewing circles also may have served as the basis of some of the early women's organizations, such as the "afternoon sewing party" held at the Anglican missionary school in Haifa in 1911 for girls who had already finished their studies.[117] Yet not all of these organizations were necessarily born out of the foreign schools. Barbara Reeves-Ellington has shown how a Russian-educated Bulgarian woman in Stara Zagora, Bulgaria, in order to counter the influence of the American Protestant missionaries, also informally gathered local women for reading scriptures, which eventually was transformed into a women's association for promoting girls' education.[118]

As Fleischmann claims, educated women were at the heart of these organizations because schools taught them about benevolence, and because "doing voluntary work in these associations . . . provided an outlet for them to use many of the skills they had acquired through education."[119] It would be a mistake, however, to see these associations as imitations of western associations and as the contribution solely of the Protestant and Catholic schools. The history of benevolence, as well as that of mainly male collective associations, such as guilds and sufi orders, had been a central component of Arab, Muslim society before the western penetration of the region.[120] Rather, the new charitable associations should be understood as incorporating both the familiar religious tradition of giving *zakat* to the poor[121] with elements of western-based associations, namely the creation of committees, paying dues for membership, fundraising, and the issuing of reports and newsletters to members.

The early women's associations in Palestine were organized along confessional and communal lines, despite the fact that the founders had mostly attended schools with mixed student bodies. While religion was still the main framework within which women organized, the confessional character of the early women's associations emphasized the continuing presence of religious divisions within Palestinian society. This was also the case in Egypt, as Baron has shown.[122] Although a few token Christian and Muslim women participated in some of the British-led charitable organizations, namely the Palestine Women's Association and the Social Service Association,[123] women only began to cross religious and communal lines and work together in interdenominational and intercommunal organizations after 1929, as the nationalist struggle intensified.

According to Tubi, the first women's association in Palestine, *Jam'iyat ighatha al-miskin al-urthudhuksiyya* (the Orthodox society for aiding the poor), was founded in 1903 by Christian women in Acre, to help poor girls acquire a trousseau.[124] In the period following the 1908 Young Turk Revolution, the dashed anticipations of educational provision as promised by the revolution compelled women to shift their focus away from only alleviating poverty to also helping girls gain an education. *Jam'iyat 'add al-yatimat al-urthudhuksiyya* (the Orthodox society for helping the orphans), founded in 1910 by Christian women in Jaffa, was created with this purpose in mind; it took the most promising girls in Jaffa's schools and paid for their education at the higher level *Zahrat al-ihsan* (Flower of charity) school and the American Girls' School, both in Beirut, with a similar society established in Jerusalem in 1918.[125]

Muslim women also formed their own charitable-educational associations, several years after Orthodox Christian women began to organize, with the creation of *Nahda al-fatat al-ʿarabiyya* (Awakening of the Arab girl) in Jerusalem in 1919. All that could be found about this organization was its statute, which expressed the concern of upper-class, educated Muslim women and their willingness to take action on behalf of educating less fortunate girls in their community. The organization was overseen by a seven-member executive committee, including a cashier who had to "keep the minute books in proper order," and a private secretary whose role was to "introduce the good spirit in the hearts of the lady members," and fill in for the society's director when absent. Women who wanted to join the society as members were allowed to do so, as long as they were willing to pay the regular dues, making the association exclusively upper and upper middle class. The founding members did not pay dues, but rather were expected to "donate at their will," which may have been a reflection upon the ability to own and endow property as they wished.[126]

According to the statutes of *Nahda al-fatat al-ʿarabiyya*, its aims were "to educate the young women and to teach them the art of sewing, embroidery and all handwork." The association appealed to girls between the ages of twelve and twenty, that is, girls who had not attended school at all, or who had ceased to study. While the involvement of women in charitable associations may have been influenced by their own education, and was seen as an extension of their femininity and maternalism, Fleischmann also links this "sense of social and civic responsibility" to protonationalist stirrings among upper- and middle-class women, quoting the writer and journalist Asma Tubi, who connected the "welfare of the community" to the "welfare of the homeland."[127] Throughout the region, nationalist struggles motivated women to work on behalf of their communities, in part because charitable organizations and the provision of charity did not challenge the work of male nationalists, whose primary concern was political. They also refrained from challenging patriarchal authority, by showing at least initially no interest in politics. That is, women's charitable organizations "worked within a framework of appropriate female behavior that did not deviate from cultural norms,"[128] although as Baron contends, the women's charitable associations served not only as "paths to professions," but also as "an entry into the world of politics."[129]

A student at the Jerusalem Girls' College acknowledged the responsibility that educated women felt toward educating others, writing that "we, edu-- cated and happy women, ought to give more thought than we do to those unfortunate members of our own sex who in the midst of civilization and surrounded by the light of education are living more like beasts of burden than anything else." Her reasoning was that "this same ignorant woman has her share in molding society as you and I have."[130] The emphasis on women's education manifested in many women's organizations and the linkage between education and serving the nation clearly lent to the legitimacy of women's organizing, and may have provided them with a camouflage for what Badran and Fleischmann have described as "discreet public activism."[131] Even though these educational-oriented associations may have led women, at least some, to more overt political expression, we should not underestimate the personal commitment of educated women in advancing the training and knowledge of others.

As Fleischmann has argued, by establishing charitable associations women manifested "their awareness of socioeconomic disparities or, at the least, problems caused by them in Palestinian society and desires to alleviate distress."[132] Although these organizations did seek to uplift impoverished girls and improve their lives to some degree, they did not truly challenge the social inequalities within Palestinian society, as they were hampered by limited funding and their own personal prejudices against the lower classes. Although upper- and middle-class Palestinian women demanded the right to learn in formal academic settings, instruction in sewing was sufficient for many of the lower-class girls whom they assisted. The religious separation, isolation, and tensions between the different religious communities were also reinforced by these associations, as they all organized along confessional lines.

Women's education as both a means and an end also characterized the women's political organizations that developed during the Mandate period, especially in the 1930s and 1940s. Fleischmann has carefully documented the establishment of the Arab Women's Association (AWA) in Jerusalem in 1929, and chronicled its development and activities, as they reflected both nationalist and feminist agendas. While Fleischmann emphasized the association's often consanguine and overlapping ties with male nationalist leaders, as well as the elite background of the members, she argues that the members recognized the significance of their own education to formulating strategies of action within the AWA. Alongside staging demonstrations, the members of the AWA used the written word, which was seen as a less controversial form of protest, as it was less likely to disrupt the prevailing patriarchal order. Thus, the AWA relied heavily upon their own literacy to write what Fleischmann estimated to be "virtually hundreds of telegrams, letters, and memoranda," sending them to whomever they believed would listen to their demands, from the British government to women's organizations around the world.[133]

In 1938 the Jerusalem branch of the AWA split into two different groups: the AWA, and the AWU, or the Arab Women's Union, sometimes appearing also as the Arab Women's League. The reason for the split was competition between leading members, the ongoing rivalry between Jerusalem's elite families, as well as competing visions of the group's aims and actions. The AWU, which according to Fleischmann became the more influential of the two groups, was dominated by members of the Husayni family, and emphasized the significance of education to the nationalist struggle. According to the AWU's statutes, its work included "charity work, such as putting orphans in schools, giving food and clothing to those very needy families in Jerusalem." In addition, the group established a clinic and a child welfare center. By the 1940s, they also ran a school in the Musrara neighborhood of Jerusalem, which is where their office was located; unfortunately we do not have any more knowledge about this school beyond its existence. The charity of the Arab Women's Union, however, could not be divorced from the nationalist struggle, with the association expressing concern especially for those who had been "affected in any political way," which translated into visiting prisoners and providing assistance to their families.[134] In 1939, a woman's association called *al-Ittihad al-nisa'i al-'arabi lil-is'af al-yatim* (Arab women's union for helping the orphan)[135] appeared with the aim of educating children orphaned by the revolt. According to one report, they had arranged for the admission of fifteen orphans into the Islamic Orphanage, and hoped to assist an additional fifteen.[136] It is possible that this organization was an offshoot of the AWU.

By the 1940s, some twenty women's associations were existent, according to one contemporary source, most of which focused on educational and other reform endeavors, and many of them confessional, similar to the organizations that had formed before and around World War I. The shift away from politics and toward educational reform was a reflection of changing attitudes and aims in the wake of the Arab revolt.[137] The prioritizing of education also evoked growing feminist agendas of Arab women's organizations elsewhere that also began to demand legal and social change for women. Specifically in the Palestinian context, this shift also may have been in reaction to the criticisms of urban women's conduct and dress that emerged during the revolt.

The Women's Social Endeavour Society (*al-Jam'iyat al-tadamun al-nisa'i*) was another organization that promoted girls' education. According to Fleischmann, the organization was founded by Luli Abu al-Huda, the daughter of the former prime minister of Transjordan, who had been educated

A girls' school administered by the Arab Women's Union in Musrara neighborhood, Jerusalem, 1940s. From the G. Eric and Edith Matson Photograph Collection, Prints & Photographs Division, Library of Congress, LC–DIG–matpc–04562.

at Oxford. Originally part of a "secret British public relations scheme," the organization had been founded with the intent of creating Palestinian loyalty to Britain. Anti-British sentiments in Palestine had been growing since the 1930s, culminating with the Arab Revolt, which struck at British as well as Jewish targets. British officials discussed various ways of using "combative propaganda," such as through advertising British goods in the Arabic press and through programs favorable to Britain on the Palestine Broadcasting Service. The teaching of English in schools, as well as the kinds of books provided to school libraries, all were intended to combat anti-British feelings.[138]

At the recommendation of Abu al-Huda, the Women's Social Endeavour Society targeted women through social work and "home building," based upon the nationalist rhetoric that the mother is the child's first school, and she would raise children who would look favorably to Britain. The focus on women and social work led to significant financial support from the Department of Social Welfare,[139] which reportedly gave a grant-in-aid of £500 every three months, in addition to the funds generated by membership fees and annual bazaars.[140] The society reportedly had a total of nine hundred members in both Palestine and Transjordan together, overseen by an executive committee and a council of members representing the organization's different branches.[141] As Fleischmann points out, most likely those who joined the society did not know about its connections with the British, especially given that it attracted women from prominent nationalist families. By the 1940s, the society tried to downplay its association with the British administration,[142] with Ya'acov Shim'oni claiming that the society completely denied any relations with the British.[143] Its significant membership enabled the society to focus on Jerusalem, Hebron, and Tul Karim, as well as Lifta and Abu-Ghosh, two villages outside of Jerusalem, where it opened schools for girls who either did not have financial means to attend school or who had been denied admission to government schools because of age restrictions. In all, the Women's Social Endeavour Society educated some five hundred girls, the majority of whom were poor, with the society paying tuition and providing them with clothing.[144]

Despite the fact that a significant number of educated Muslim women became visible within the public sphere during the Mandate period, they were very careful to maintain the local Palestinian customs with which they had been raised, and believed it was important to receive their families' approval of their education and life choices. Wafi'a, originally from Ramla and educated at Schmidt's College, related that "even when we worked we took our traditions into consideration. We just did not do anything wrong, nothing out of the ordinary."[145] The mother of Sa'ida, who had received a government scholarship to study in England, reportedly feared that her daughter would talk to strange men while abroad and ruin her chances of marrying, as well as those of her six unmarried sisters who remained in Palestine, the implication being that living in the West could lead Palestinian girls astray. As a result, Sa'ida was very cautious with whom she spoke and with whom she visited.[146] Similarly, Nuzha feared that she would overstep her father's boundaries while she was studying at the Primary Teachers' College in Helwan, after having completed her studies at the Islamic Girls' School. Even though she shared the same religion and language as the Egyptian women whom she encountered, her Palestinian upbringing, and specifically the expectations about gender that she brought with her from Jerusalem to Helwan, differentiated her from her fellow Egyptian students. She relayed that the Palestinian pupils did not have the same cultural "freedoms" as the Egyptian pupils had. The Egyptian girls "would talk about having boyfriends, but that was not for us . . . They always asked us why we kept to ourselves, and did not join them."[147] Nuzha refrained from even attending lectures outside her college because they were composed of mixed audiences. In most cases, young women who left their homes, whether to study or to work, were carefully watched by older brothers, cousins, or other relatives, and were aware that they had to uphold their local traditions and maintain their gendered norms in order to pursue their educational and career opportunities.

Local traditions and gendered norms were not always enough to bind women together, however, especially as education did create difference, particularly toward peers who were uneducated or who had received an inferior education. Su'ad related that her sister Khadija was disappointed when she visited the Islamic Girls' School in the 1950s, and found it full of pupils, whom she described as "from Hebron, fallahin, refugees, and orphans." As Su'ad pointed out, the school once had the top class of families, whereas the "others [had gone] to public school."[148] Although Khadija may have been shocked to see her former school no longer as it had been, the idea that those who went to "public school," that is, the government schools, would now attend her school may have been difficult for her to comprehend.

The Muslim girls who were educated in Palestine from the turn of the century until 1948 should be seen as "pioneers," as they were often the first girls in their families to obtain an education, however minimal it may have been. They were also harbingers in the sense that they used their education not only to become "mothers of tomorrow," but also to pursue professions, establish various organizations for women, and even to continue on to higher education. By obtaining a "modern" education, which previously had been limited to men only, this stratum of the population challenged gendered social norms and broke down barriers for subsequent generations.

Class, religion, and national affiliation helped to shape these women as well as divide them. A stereotypical view of the "Orient" mixed with preconceived notions of gender and class especially influenced the development of girls' education. Through education, Muslim girls would be rescued from being "shackled and fettered" by the veil and early marriage. Instead of extending education to Muslim girls en masse, however, education became the purview of a select few. Although shifts occurred by the mid-1920s to include more Muslim women in the Women's Training College, for example, Christian women continued to benefit more from post-primary education, which the British left to the missionary and foreign schools. This favoring of a minority of Christian women over the Muslim majority had its consequences. It meant that the education of Muslim girls in villages was delayed until a sufficient number of Muslim women could be trained in teaching. It also meant that the education of Muslim girls became primarily urban-based, even though Muslim village girls throughout the Mandate period petitioned the Department of Education for schools.

The inability and unwillingness of the British to provide universal education, coupled with fears of growing missionary encroachment and of overt westernization, led some Arabs to create their own schools, such as the Islamic Girls' School in Jerusalem and others like it throughout Palestine. The establishment of local schools was also motivated by the desire of some Palestinians to control their daughters' education, influenced by successful precedents primarily in boys' education during the late Ottoman period. In particular, the appearance of these schools is tangible proof that some Palestinians did indeed support the idea of educating their daughters, despite the claims of British officials to the contrary. As the case of the Islamic Girls' School shows, this support was evident among all strata of the population, from the urban elite to the rural and lower classes. In addition, contrary to the common belief that only male intellectuals advanced girls' education, Palestinian men and women alike worked to realize girls' education and improve its accessibility.

Although the British Mandate symbolized the introduction of the West into Palestinian society, girls' education was not a foreign and western concept; rather, it was a blend of indigenous and imported, Muslim and western. The case study of the Islamic Girls' School, for example, reveals how local Muslim educators combined the teaching of the Qur'an, the staple of the *kuttab* school, together with the introduction of new modern subjects, reflecting the agenda of Muslim reformers throughout the region. This fits nicely with the overall thread running through the essays in Lila Abu-Lughod's important book *Remaking Women*, which posit that to become "modern" at the beginning of the twentieth century meant, in effect, the combining of western and indigenous beliefs and traditions.[149] This mixing of western imports with Arab culture, however, did not always work. Some Palestinians were, in fact, suspicious of their daughters' adoption and adaptation of western customs and their being educated in a westernized framework, while others were critical of their own indigenous educational systems, such as the *kuttab* school.

In addition to being able to dismantle barriers between different religious communities, education had the potential of narrowing the gaps between the classes as well as bridging different social strata. One of the most important facets of education at this time was that both government and the locally founded schools increasingly began to cater to the urban lower classes. The extension of education to these strata was perceived by educators and teachers alike as part of their nationalist and modernist duty, although class tensions were apparent. Planting the seeds of education among Palestinians from lower socioeconomic backgrounds would have important ramifications for Palestinian society in general, especially in the decades after 1948. The expansion of education to include segments of the lower classes as well as some villages by the 1940s facilitated the acceptance of education among Palestinians in their post-1948 exile, with Rosemary Sayigh referring to the enthusiasm for education in the refugee camps of Lebanon in the early 1950s as an "educational revolution."[150]

Education, in fact, shaped girls and women to the extent that they differed from previous generations. Although on a smaller scale, they were not unlike the educated girls and women of Egypt, Lebanon, and Turkey who were represented as "modern," and "new," by means of their education, employment, dress, mannerisms, and even motherhood. Girls' education did not develop in Palestine the same way as it did in other countries, however, because the 1948 war and the establishment of the state of Israel inevitably forced unknown numbers of girls and young women in the process of obtaining their education in the 1940s to leave school altogether, or to put their education on hold as they adjusted to their new lives as refugees or as living under Israeli rule. The post-1948 period, however, witnessed the still untold story of the increasing visibility of educated Palestinian Muslim women throughout the region who used their skills and knowledge acquired at the end of Ottoman rule and throughout the British Mandate to educate others and to hold together their communities despite the ongoing tragedy of having lost Palestine.

NOTES

INTRODUCTION

1. Najib al-Hakim, "The Woman, the Nationalist Upbringing and the Foreign Schools," *Filastin*, February 9, 1930.

2. Lisa Pollard, *Nurturing the Nation: The Family Politics of Modernizing, Colonizing, and Liberating Egypt, 1805–1923* (Berkeley and Los Angeles: University of California Press, 2005).

3. Albert Hourani, *Arabic Thought in the Liberal Age, 1798–1939* (1962; repr., Cambridge: Cambridge University Press, 1983), 130–192.

4. Beth Baron, *Egypt as a Woman: Nationalism, Gender, and Politics* (Berkeley and Los Angeles: University of California Press, 2005).

5. Afsaneh Najmabadi, "Crafting an Educated Housewife in Iran," in *Remaking Women: Feminism and Modernity in the Middle East*, ed. Lila Abu-Lughod (Princeton: Princeton University Press, 1998), 91–95.

6. Butrus al-Bustani, *Ta'lim al-nisa'*, 1849, reprinted by Fu'ad Afram al-Bustani (Beirut: Al-matba'at al-kathulikiyya, 1929).

7. William Boyd, *The History of Western Education*, 5th ed. (London: Adam and Charles Black, 1950), 300.

8. Hourani, *Arabic Thought*, 72, 77–78.

9. Boyd, *History of Western Education*, 334–335.

10. Beth Baron, *The Women's Awakening in Egypt: Culture, Society, and the Press* (New Haven and London: Yale University Press, 1994).

11. About Amin, see Leila Ahmed, *Women and Gender in Islam: Historical Roots of a Modern Debate* (New Haven and London: Yale University Press, 1992), 159–160; Baron, *Women's Awakening*, 4–6; Hourani, *Arabic Thought*, 164–170.

12. Baron, *Egypt as a Woman*, 5.

13. Ibid., 36.

14. Ellen L. Fleischmann, *The Nation and Its "New" Women: The Palestinian*

Women's Movement 1920–1948 (Berkeley and Los Angeles: University of California Press, 2003).

15. Rashid Khalidi, *Palestinian Identity: The Construction of Modern National Consciousness* (New York: Columbia University Press, 1997), 41.

16. Ruth Kark and Michal Oren-Nordheim, *Jerusalem and Its Environs: Quarters, Neighborhoods, Villages 1800–1948* (Detroit: Wayne State University Press and Jerusalem: Magnes Press, 2001); Mark LeVine, *Overthrowing Geography: Jaffa, Tel Aviv, and the Struggle for Palestine 1880–1948* (Berkeley and Los Angeles: University of California Press, 2005); May Seikaly, "Haifa at the Crossroads: An Outpost of the New World Order," in *Modernity and Culture: From the Mediterranean to the Indian Ocean,* ed. Leila Tarazi Fawaz and C. A. Bayly (New York: Columbia University Press, 2002), 99–100.

17. LeVine, *Overthrowing Geography,* 174. See also Diala Khasawneh, *Memoirs Engraved in Stone: Palestinian Urban Mansions* (Ramallah: Riwaq-Centre for Architectural Conservation and Jerusalem: Institute of Jerusalem Studies, 2001).

18. Salim Tamari and 'Issam Nassar, *Al-quds al-'uthmaniyya fi al-mudhakkirat al-Jawhariyya: al-kitab al-awwal min mudhakkirat al-musiqi Wasif Jawhariyya 1904–1917* (Jerusalem: Mu'assasat al-dirasat al-muqaddasiyya, 2003), 50–51, 169.

19. Ami Ayalon, *The Press in the Arab Middle East: A History* (New York: Oxford University Press, 1995), 65.

20. Ibid., 145–154.

21. Ibid., 96–100. See also Khalidi, *Palestinian Identity,* ch. 6, and Mustafa Kabha, *The Palestinian Press as Shaper of Public Opinion 1929–39: Writing Up a Storm* (London: Vallentine Mitchell, 2007).

22. Mark LeVine, "The Palestinian Press in Mandatory Jaffa: Advertising, Nationalism, and the Public Sphere," in *Palestine, Israel and the Politics of Popular Culture,* ed. Rebecca L. Stein and Ted Swedenburg (Durham: Duke University Press, 2005), 51–76.

23. Ami Ayalon, *Reading Palestine: Printing and Literacy, 1900–1948* (Austin: University of Texas Press, 2004).

24. See, for example, Salma al-Nasr, "About Our Syrian Girls," *al-Nafa'is al-'asriyya* (December 1909): 97; Khalil al-Sakakini, "The Eastern Girl and the Western Girl," *al-Nafa'is al-'asriyya* (February 1911): 87–88.

25. Fleischmann, *Nation and Its "New" Women,* 67.

26. See, for example, "The women's awakening in Turkey," *Filastin,* April 6, 1930; "Turkey: At the women's conference," *al-Difa',* May 1, 1935; "French women demand their rights," *al-Difa',* June 17, 1936.

27. "Freedom of woman," *Filastin,* May 31, 1927.

28. See, for example, "Celebration at Schmidt's College for Girls," *Filastin,* July 17, 1931; "Graduates of the Women's Training College in Jerusalem and the Rural Training Center in Ramallah," *al-Difa',* July 21, 1940.

29. About the congress and the Arab Women's Association, see Fleischmann, *Nation and Its "New" Women.*

30. Ibid., 164.

31. See, for example, "Feeding the children," *al-Nafir*, December 10, 1926; Kamil Samu'il Masiha, "To the nursing mothers," *al-Hayat*, July 20, 1931; Dr. Hafiz Afifi, "Methods of breast feeding," *al-Karmil*, September 20, 1930.

32. Nelly Za'arib, "Speech about women," *al-Karmil*, March 22, 1928; Sadhij Nassar, "A girl's diaries," *al-Karmil*, July 29, 1928.

33. "Sadhij Nassar, "The child and his customs," *al-Karmil*, July 3, 1927; "Ten instructions for the nursing mother," *al-Nafir*, November 25, 1926; "Organization of times for nursing the baby," *al-Nafir*, May 27, 1927.

34. "Ten instructions for the nursing mother," *al-Nafir*, November 25, 1926; Kamil Samu'il Masiha, "Raising a child," *al-Hayat*, July 23, 1931.

35. See, for example, "Contest of the babies," *Filastin*, December 15, 1935.

36. Pollard, *Nurturing the Nation*, 101.

37. Ibid., 122.

38. *Encyclopedia of Islam*, 2nd ed. (Leiden: Brill, 1960), s.v. *kuttab;* S. D. Goitein, *A Mediterranean Society: The Jewish Communities of the Arab World as Portrayed in the Documents of the Cairo Geniza*, vol. 2, *The Community* (Berkeley: University of California Press, 1971), 173-183.

39. Ayalon, *Reading Palestine*, 27-29.

40. Edward W. Lane, *An Account of the Manners and Customs of the Modern Egyptians* (London, 1842; repr., 1890), 51, note 2.

41. Virginia Danielson, *The Voice of Egypt: Umm Kulthum, Arabic Song, and Egyptian Society in the Twentieth Century* (Chicago and London: University of Chicago Press, 1997), 22.

42. Ian C. Dengler, "Turkish Women in the Ottoman Empire, the Classical Age," in *Women in the Muslim World*, ed. Lois Beck and Nikki Keddie (Cambridge: Harvard University Press, 1978), 229-244; Emel Dogramacı, "Education of Women in Ottoman and Republican Turkey: A Comparative Perspective," in *IIIrd Congress on the Social and Economic History of Turkey, 1983*, ed. Heath W. Lowry and Ralph S. Hattox (Istanbul: ISIS Press, 1990), 214-215.

43. 'Abd al-Razzaq al-Hilali, *Ta'rikh al-ta'lim fi al-'iraq fi al-'ahd al-'uthmani* (Baghdad: Ahliyya Press, 1959), 60. See also Eleanor Abdella Doumato, *Getting God's Ear: Women, Islam, and Healing in Saudi Arabia and the Gulf* (New York: Columbia University Press, 2000), 117.

44. Jonathan P. Berkey, "Women and Islamic Education in the Mamluk Period," in *Women in Middle Eastern History*, ed. Nikki R. Keddie and Beth Baron (New Haven and London: Yale University Press, 1991), 145-147.

45. Ibid., 147-148.

46. Huda Shaarawi, *Harem Years: The Memoirs of an Egyptian Feminist*, trans. Margot Badran (New York: Feminist Press, 1987), 15-17, 39-41.

47. About western tutors, see Sarah Graham-Brown, *Images of Women: The Portrayal of Women in Photography of the Middle East, 1860-1950* (New York: Columbia University Press, 1988), 192-193; Saphinaz-Amal Naguib, "Modelling a Cosmopolitan

Womanhood in Egypt (1850-1950): The Role of Nannies and French Catholic Girls Schools," *Acta Orientalia* 62 (2001): 92-106.

48. J. Heyworth-Dunne, *An Introduction to the History of Education in Modern Egypt* (London: Luzac, 1938), 15; Lane, *Manners and Customs,* 51; Elizabeth Brown Frierson, "Unimagined Communities: State, Press, and Gender in the Hamidian Era" (Ph.D. diss., Princeton University, 1996), 98-99.

49. John H. Melkon Rose, *Armenians of Jerusalem: Memories of Life in Palestine* (London: Radcliffe Press, 1993), 77-78.

50. Selim Deringil, *The Well-Protected Domains: Ideology and Legitimation of Power in the Ottoman Empire, 1876-1909* (London: I. B. Tauris, 1999), ch. 4.

51. Khalidi, *Palestinian Identity,* esp. ch. 7.

52. Benedict Anderson, *Imagined Communities,* rev. ed. (London and New York: Verso, 1991).

53. Eric Hobsbawm, "Mass-Producing Traditions: Europe, 1870-1914," in *The Invention of Tradition,* ed. Eric Hobsbawm and Terence Ranger (1983; repr., Cambridge: Cambridge University Press, 1992), 293-300. See also Ian Grosvenor, "'There's No Place Like Home': Education and the Making of National Identity," *History of Education* 28, no. 3 (1999): 235-250.

54. Benjamin C. Fortna, *Imperial Classroom: Islam, the State, and Education in the Late Ottoman Empire* (Oxford: Oxford University Press, 2002). For similar arguments in Egypt, see Gregory Starrett, *Putting Islam to Work: Education, Politics, and Religious Transformation in Egypt* (Berkeley and Los Angeles: University of California Press, 1998).

55. See, for example, Ellen L. Fleischmann, "The Impact of American Protestant Missions in Lebanon on the Construction of Female Identity, c. 1860-1950," *Islam and Christian-Muslim Relations* 13, no. 4 (2002): 411-426; Inger Marie Okkenhaug, *The Quality of Heroic Living, of High Endeavour and Adventure: Anglican Mission, Women and Education in Palestine, 1888-1948* (Leiden: Brill, 2002); Heleen Murre-van den Berg, "Nineteenth-Century Protestant Missions and Middle Eastern Women: An Overview," in *Gender, Religion, and Change in the Middle East: Two Hundred Years of History,* ed. Inger Marie Okkenhaug and Ingvild Flaskerud (Oxford and New York: Berg Publishers, 2005).

56. See, for example, Orit Ichilov and André Elias Mazawi, *Between State and Church: Life-History of a French-Catholic School in Jaffa* (Frankfurt am Main: Peter Lang, 1996); Mona Hajjar Halaby, "School Days in Mandate Jerusalem at Dames de Sion," *Jerusalem Quarterly* 31 (Summer 2007): 40-71; Naguib, "Modelling a Cosmopolitan Womanhood."

57. Heather J. Sharkey, "Empire and Muslim Conversion: Historical Reflections on Christian Missions in Egypt," *Islam and Christian-Muslim Relations* 16, no. 1 (January 2005): 45.

58. Heather J. Sharkey, "Christians among Muslims: The Church Missionary Society in Northern Sudan," *Journal of African History* 43, no. 1 (January 2002): 51-75.

59. Sharkey, "Empire and Muslim Conversion"; Heather J. Sharkey, *American Evangelicals in Egypt: Missionary Encounters in an Age of Empire* (Princeton: Princeton University Press, 2008); Mahmoud Haddad, "Syrian Muslims' Attitudes toward Foreign Missionaries in the late Nineteenth and Twentieth Centuries," Columbia International Affairs Online, http://www.ciaonet.org/conf/mei01/ham01.html (accessed September 1, 2008).

60. A. L. Tibawi, *Arab Education in Mandatory Palestine: A Study of Three Decades of British Administration* (London: Luzac, 1956). For a comparison of nationalist struggles in education in Egypt, see Donald M. Reid, *Cairo University and the Making of Modern Egypt* (Cambridge: Cambridge University Press, 1990), and Haggai Erlich, *Students and University in 20th Century Egyptian Politics* (London: Frank Cass, 1998).

61. See, for example, Rochelle Davis, "Commemorating Education: Recollections of the Arab College in Jerusalem, 1918–1948," *Comparative Studies of South Asia, Africa and the Middle East* 23, nos. 1–2 (2003): 1–17; Mahmoud Abidi, "The Arab College, Jerusalem," in *Arabic and Islamic Garland: Historical, Educational and Literary Papers Presented to A. L. Tibawi* (London: Islamic Cultural Center, 1977), 28–35; Sadiq Ibrahim ʿAwda, "Al-kulliya al-ʿarabiyya fi al-quds 1918–1948: maʿlumat wa-dhikrayat," *Majallat dirasat al-filastiniyya* 40 (Winter 1999): 170–188; Walid Raghib al-Khalidi, "Al-kulliya al-ʿarabiyya fi al-quds: khalfiya taʾrikhiyya wa-nathra mustaqbaliyya," *Majallat dirasat al-filastiniyya* 44 (Winter 2000): 136–144.

62. Julia Clancy-Smith, "Envisioning Knowledge: Educating the Muslim Woman in Colonial North Africa, c. 1850–1918," in *Iran and Beyond: Essays in Middle Eastern History in Honor of Nikki R. Keddie*, ed. Rudi Matthee and Beth Baron (Costa Mesa: Mazda, 2000), 101.

63. About the *millet* system, see Benjamin Braude, "Foundation Myths of the Millet System," in *Christians and Jews in the Ottoman Empire*, vol. 1, *The Central Lands*, ed. Benjamin Braude and Bernard Lewis (New York: Holmes and Meier, 1982), 69–88.

64. Nancy L. Stockdale, *Colonial Encounters among English and Palestinian Women, 1800–1948* (Gainesville: University of Florida Press, 2007); Pollard, *Nurturing the Nation*, ch. 2.

65. Avi Rubin, "Ha-mizraḥ davar aḥad ve-ha-maʿarav davar aḥer: Muhammad Bahjat ve-Rafiq al-Tamimi be-wilayet bayrut," *Jamaʿa* 7 (2001): 54–81. See also Ussama Makdisi, "Ottoman Orientalism," *American Historical Review* 107, no. 3 (June 2002): 768–796.

66. Muhammad Rafiq al-Tamimi and Muhammad Bahjat, *Wilayet bayrut* (Beirut: Matbaʿat al-iqbal, 1333–1335), 355.

67. See, for example, the *Annual Report* of the Department of Education.

68. See, for example, Helen N. Boyle, *Quranic Schools: Agents of Preservation and Change* (London: Routledge, 2004).

69. Donald J. Cioeta, "Islamic Benevolent Societies and Public Education in Ottoman Syria, 1875–1882," *Islamic Quarterly* 26, no. 1 (1982): 40–55; Martin Stroh-

meier, "Muslim Education in the Vilayet of Beirut, 1880–1918," in *Decision Making and Change in the Ottoman Empire*, ed. Caesar E. Farah (Kirksville, MO: Thomas Jefferson University Press at Northeast Missouri State University, 1993), 215–241.

70. Khalidi, *Palestinian Identity*, 49–50.

71. Uri M. Kupferschmidt, *The Supreme Muslim Council: Islam under the British Mandate for Palestine* (Leiden: Brill, 1987); Weldon C. Matthews, "Pan-Islam or Arab Nationalism? The Meaning of the 1931 Jerusalem Islamic Congress Reconsidered," *International Journal of Middle East Studies* 35, no. 1 (February 2003): 1–22.

72. See, for example, S. Abdallah Schleifer, "The Life and Thought of 'Izz id-din al-Qassam," *Islamic Quarterly* 22, no. 2 (1979): 61–81.

73. About this school, see Khalidi, *Palestinian Identity*, 49, and Ela Greenberg, "Majallat Rawdat al-maʿarif: Constructing Identities within a Boys' School Journal in Mandatory Palestine," *British Journal of Middle Eastern Studies* 35, no. 1 (April 2008): 79–95.

74. Ayalon, *Reading Palestine*, 38.

75. Rashid Khalidi, "Society and Ideology in Late Ottoman Syria: Class, Education, Profession and Confession," in *Problems of the Middle East in Historical Perspective: Essays in Honour of Albert Hourani*, ed. John P. Spagnolo (Reading, UK: Ithaca Press, 1992), 126.

CHAPTER I

1. About *al-Nafaʾis al-ʿasriyya*, see Yusuf Q. Khuri, *Al-sihafa al-ʿarabiyya fi filastin 1876–1948* (Beirut: Muʾassasat al-dirasat al-filastiniyya, 1976), 16.

2. Kh. S., "Juhaina and Servant," *al-Nafaʾis al-ʿasriyya* 3, no. 4 (April 1911): 176–179.

3. See, for example, Susan O'Brien, "French Nuns in Nineteenth Century England," *Past and Present* no. 154 (February 1997): 142–180.

4. Pierre Medebielle, *The Diocese of the Latin Patriarchate of Jerusalem* (Jerusalem, 1963), 28–32.

5. Sharkey, "Empire and Muslim Conversion," 45.

6. A. L. Tibawi, *British Interests in Palestine 1800–1901: A Study of Religious and Educational Enterprise* (London: Oxford University Press, 1961), 166.

7. P. J. Vatikiotis, "The Greek Orthodox Patriarchate of Jerusalem between Hellenism and Arabism," *Middle Eastern Studies* 30, no. 4 (1994): 916–929.

8. Derek Hopwood, *Russian Presence in Syria and Palestine 1843–1914* (Oxford: Clarendon Press, 1969), 140.

9. Evgeniy Davydov, "Ha-peʿilut ha-hinukhit shel ha-aguda ha-imperialit ha-pravoslavit ha-falastinit be-erets yisrael ba-shanim 1882–1914" (master's thesis, University of Haifa, 2000), 13–14.

10. Ellen L. Fleischmann, "'Our Moslem Sisters': Women of Greater Syria in the Eyes of American Protestant Missionary Women," *Islam and Christian-Muslim Relations* 9, no. 3 (1998): 308–309.

11. Rosa E. Lee, *The Story of the Ram Allah Mission* (Board of Foreign Missions of the Yearly Meeting of Friends for New England, 1912), 14.

12. Fleischmann, "Our Moslem Sisters," 314. See also her "Impact of American Protestant Missions," 412–413.

13. Murre-van den Berg, "Nineteenth Century Protestant Missions," 105–106. See also Patricia R. Hill, *The World Their Household: The American Woman's Foreign Mission Movement and Cultural Transformation, 1870–1920* (Ann Arbor: University of Michigan Press, 1985); Leslie A. Flemming, ed., *Women's Work for Women: Missionaries and Social Change in Asia* (London: Westview Press, 1989).

14. Billie Melman, *Women's Orients: English Women and the Middle East, 1718–1918*, 2nd ed. (Basingstoke: Macmillan, 1995), 177.

15. Willy Jansen, "Arab Women with a Mission: The Sisters of the Rosary," in *Christian Witness between Continuity and New Beginnings*, ed. Martin Tamcke and Michael Marten (Berlin: LIT Verlag, 2006).

16. Joan Jacobs Brumberg, "Zenanas and Girlless Villages: The Ethnology of American Evangelical Women, 1870–1910," *Journal of American History* 69, no. 2 (September 1982): 351–352.

17. Constantia Kiskira, "'Evangelising' the Orient: New England Womanhood in the Ottoman Empire, 1830–1930," *Archivum Ottomanicum* 16 (1998): 279–294.

18. Melman, *Women's Orients*, 10–13; Roberta Wollons, "Travelling for God and Adventure: Women Missionaries in the Late 19th Century," *Asian Journal of Social Science* 31, no. 1 (2003): 55–71.

19. Ann White, "Counting the Cost of Faith: America's Early Female Missionaries," *Church History* 57, no. 1 (March 1988): 23–24.

20. Frances E. Newton, *Fifty Years in Palestine* (London: Coldharbor Press, 1948), 59–60, 65–66.

21. Pierre Duvignau, *Une Vie au Service de l'Église: S. B. Mgr. Joseph Valerga* (Jerusalem, 1972), 101.

22. About the different Catholic orders, see ibid.; Victor Guérin, *Jérusalem: son histoire, sa description—ses établissements religieux* (Paris, 1889); Claude Langlois, "Les congrégations françaises en Terre Sainte au XIXe siècle," in *De Bonaparte à Balfour: La France, l'Europe Occidentale et la Palestine 1799–1917*, ed. Dominique Trimbur and Ran Aaronsohn (Jérusalem: Centre de Recherche français, 2000); Vital Cuinet, *Syrie Liban et Palestine Géographie Administrative Statistique, Descriptive et Raisonnée* (Paris: Ernest Leroux, 1896).

23. Fleischmann, "Impact of American Protestant Missions," 413. See also Samir Khalaf, "On Doing Much with Little Noise: Early Encounters of Protestant Missionaries in Lebanon," Columbia International Affairs Online, http://www.ciaonet .org/conf/mei01/khs01.html (accessed September 1, 2008).

24. Henry Harris Jessup, *Women of the Arabs* (New York, 1873), 54–55, 58–60.

25. Jeremy Salt, "Trouble Wherever They Went: American Missionaries in Anatolia and Ottoman Syria in the Nineteenth Century," *Muslim World* 92, nos. 3–4 (Fall 2002): 292–293.

26. Jessup, *Women of the Arabs*, 54, 59.

27. About the SPFEE, see Newton, *Fifty Years in Palestine*, 29–31; As'ad Mansur, *Ta'rikh al-nasira min aqdam azmaniha ila ayamina al-hadira* (Cairo: Matba'at al-hilal, 1924), 182–183; Rafiq Farah, *Ta'rikh al-kanisa al-usqufiyya fi matraniyyat al-quds 1841–1991* (Beirut: N.p., 1995), 1:239; Margaret Donaldson, "'The Cultivation of the Heart and the Moulding of the Will . . .' The Missionary Contribution of the Society for Promoting Female Education in China, India, and the East," *Studies in Church History* 27 (1990): 429–442.

28. Tibawi, *British Interests*, 90–110.

29. See Graham-Brown, *Images of Women*, 208.

30. Murre-van den Berg, "Nineteenth Century Protestant Missions," 112.

31. Newton, *Fifty Years in Palestine*, 31.

32. See, for example, Ghada Karmi, *In Search of Fatima: A Palestinian Story* (London and New York: Verso, 2002), 15–18.

33. Newton, *Fifty Years in Palestine*, 41. See also Graham-Brown, *Images of Women*, 205.

34. Tibawi, *British Interests*, 158–159.

35. Dr. Reinicke, "Die evangelische Mission in Palästina," *Zeitschrift des Deutschen Palästina-Vereins* 6 (1883): 20, 23.

36. Frederic John Scrimgeour, *Nazareth of To-day* (Edinburgh and London: William Green and Sons, 1913), 86.

37. About these schools, see Ellen Clare Miller, *Eastern Sketches: Notes of Scenery, Schools, and Tent Life in Syria and Palestine* (Edinburgh, 1871), 164; Anisa Ma'luf, *Mu'assasat jam'iyat al-asdiqa' al-amirkiyya fi filastin min sana 1869–1939* (N.p.: al-Matba'at al-'asriyya, n.d.); Jamal 'Adawi, "Pe'ilut ha-quakerim ha-Amerikanim ba-Palestina, 1869–1948" (Ph.D. diss., University of Haifa, 2000), 126–133; Lee, *Story of the Ram Allah Mission*.

38. Lee, *Story of the Ram Allah Mission*, 40.

39. Ibid.

40. Ibid., 12.

41. Ibid., 31.

42. Halaby, "School Days," 45.

43. Shahin Makariyus, "Education in Syria," *al-Muqtataf* 7, part 9 (1883): 537; Guérin, *Jérusalem*, 466.

44. Yael Ilan, "Ha-pe'ilut ha-tsarfatit be-sanjaq yerushalayim be-thum ha-hinukh ve-ha-si'ud be-shalhe ha-tequfa ha-'otmanit" (master's thesis, University of Haifa, 1987), 81.

45. Ibid., 92, 96.

46. Guérin, *Jérusalem*, 467.

47. Asma Tubi, *'Abir wa-majd* (N.p., 1966), 29–30.

48. Ya'qub al-'Ansari and Ibrahim al-Husayni, *Jam'iyat al-sayyidat al-'arabiyyat bil-quds* (Jerusalem: N.p., 1985).

49. Guérin, *Jérusalem*, 467.

50. Hajjar, "School Days," 45.

51. Guérin, *Jérusalem*, 467.

52. Naguib, "Modelling a Cosmopolitan Womanhood," 104.

53. Phyllis Stock, *Better Than Rubies: A History of Women's Education* (New York: G. P. Putnam and Sons, 1978).

54. Miller, *Eastern Sketches*, 127.

55. Isobel Goodwin, *May You Live to Be 120! The Story of Tabeetha School, Jaffa 1863-1983* (Edinburgh: St. Andrew Press, 2000), 17-19, 24-26. See also Ruth Kark, "The Impact of Early Missionary Enterprises in Palestine on Landscape and Identity in Palestine, 1820-1914," *Islam and Christian-Muslim Relations* 15, no. 2 (2004): 225; Ruth Kark, *Jaffa: A City in Evolution, 1799-1917* (Jerusalem: Yad Ben Zvi, 1990), 176.

56. Goodwin, *May You Live to be 120!* 26, 37-40, 52.

57. "St. Mary's Home, Jerusalem," *Bible Lands* 2, no. 21 (July 1904): 63.

58. See Okkenhaug, *Quality of Heroic Living,* 28; Tibawi, *British Interests,* 258-261.

59. Okkenhaug, *Quality of Heroic Living,* 23.

60. "St. Mary's Home, Jerusalem," *Bible Lands* 2, no. 21 (July 1904): 63.

61. "Annual Meeting," *Bible Lands* 4, no. 50 (October 1911): 25-32.

62. Okkenhaug, *Quality of Heroic Living,* 21, 28.

63. "Free Day School at St. Mary's Home," *Bible Lands* 3, no. 35 (January 1908): 35.

64. Okkenhaug, *Quality of Heroic Living,* 29.

65. A. L. Tibawi, "Russian Cultural Penetration of Syria-Palestine in the Nineteenth Century—Part One," *Journal of the Royal Central Asian Society* 53, no. 2 (1966): 166-182; Hopwood, *Russian Presence,* 137; Hanna Abu Hanna, *Dar al-mu'alimin al-russiyya fi al-nasira "al-seminar" (1886-1914) wa-athariha 'ala al-nahda al-adabiyya fi filastin* (Nazareth: Department of Arab Culture, Ministry of Education and Culture, 1994), 21-22.

66. Tibawi, "Russian Cultural Penetration," 175.

67. Davydov, "Ha-pe'ilut ha-ḥinukhit," 51-52; Hopwood, *Russian Presence,* 141; 'Umar Mahamid, *Safahat min ta'rikh madaris al-jam'iya al-russiyya-al-filastiniyya fi filastin bayn a'wam 1882-1914* (Taybe: Markaz ihya' al-turath al-'arabi, 1988), 80-82.

68. Davydov, "Ha-pe'ilut ha-ḥinukhit," 98-109; Hopwood, *Russian Presence,* 146-150.

69. Mathew Burrows, "'Mission Civilisatrice': French Cultural Policy in the Middle East, 1860-1914," *Historical Journal* 29, no. 1 (March 1986): 116, 121. See also Cuinet, *Syrie Liban et Palestine,* 522.

70. Ichilov and Mazawi, *Between State and Church,* 9-10.

71. University of St. Joseph report cited in al-Tamimi and Bahjat, *Wilayat bayrut,* 24.

72. "Association for helping the orphans," *Filastin,* February 19, 1913.

73. Mustafa 'Asim al-Turk, "The future of the nation depends on educating the children," *Filastin,* August 20, 1913.

74. O. Eberhard, "Die Arabischen Volksschulen Jerusalem," *Palästinajahrbuch des deutschen evangelischen Instituts für Altertumswissenschaft des heiligen Landes zu Jerusalem* (1906): 86.

75. Ibid., 107.

76. Bahjat and Tamimi, *Wilayat bayrut,* 385.

77. See, for example, Shaarawi, *Harem Years,* 39–41.

78. About ideas of courtship and romance circulating in turn-of-the-century Egypt, see Beth Baron, "The Making and Breaking of Marital Bonds in Modern Egypt," in *Women in Middle Eastern History,* ed. Nikki R. Keddie and Beth Baron (New Haven and London: Yale University Press, 1991).

79. Eric J. Hobsbawm, *Nations and Nationalism since 1780* (Cambridge: Cambridge University Press, 1990), 115.

80. Stockdale, *Colonial Encounters,* ch. 5.

81. Willy Jansen, "Visions of Mary in the Middle East: Gender and the Power of a Symbol," in Okkenhaug and Flaskerud, eds., *Gender, Religion and Change in the Middle East,* 138–140, 146–147.

82. About Mary in Islam, see Jane I. Smith, "The Virgin Mary in Islamic Tradition and Commentary," *Muslim World* 79, no. 3 (1989): 161–187.

83. David Kushner, "Zealous Towns in Nineteenth Century Palestine," *Middle Eastern Studies* 33, no. 3 (July 1997): 597–612.

83. Heather J. Sharkey, "Arabic Antimissionary Treatises: Muslim Responses to Christian Evangelism in the Modern Middle East," *International Bulletin of Missionary Research* 28, no. 3 (July 2004): 98–104.

85. Le Père J. A. Jaussen, *Coutumes Palestiniennes: Nablouse et son district* (Paris: Librarie Orientaliste Paul Geuthner, 1927), 48–49n.

86. Julius Richter, *History of the Protestant Missions in the Near East* (1910; reprint, New York: AMS Press, 1970), 266.

87. 'Abd al-Ra'uf Sannu, *Al-masalih al-almaniyya fi suriya wa-filastin 1841–1901* (Beirut: Ma'had al-inma' al-'arabi, 1987), 98–100.

88. Richter, *History of the Protestant Missions,* 421.

89. Sharkey, "Empire and Muslim Conversion," 47.

90. Jeremy Salt, "A Precarious Symbiosis: Ottoman Christians and Foreign Missionaries in the Nineteenth Century," *International Journal of Turkish Studies* 3, no. 1 (Winter 1984–1985): 56. See also Cagri Erhan, "Ottoman Official Attitudes towards American Missionaries," http://128.36.236.77/workpaper/pdfs/MESV5-11.pdf. (Accessed September 16, 2008.)

91. Stanford J. Shaw and Ezel Kural Shaw, *History of the Ottoman Empire and Modern Turkey,* vol. 2, *Reform, Revolution, and Republic: The Rise of Modern Turkey, 1808–1975* (Cambridge: Cambridge University Press, 1977), 125.

92. Saul P. Colbi, *A History of the Christian Presence in the Holy Land* (Lanham, MD: University Press of America, 1988), 104.

93. Tubi, *'Abir wa-majd,* 125; "Association for helping the orphans," *Filastin,* February 19, 1913. For a discussion of the Jaffa Orthodox Ladies Society, which may

have been related to the Association for Helping Orthodox Orphans, see Fleischmann, *Nation and Its "New" Women*, 104-105.

94. 'Abd al-'Aziz Muhammad 'Awad, *Al-idara al-'uthmaniyya fi wilayat suriya 1864-1914* (Cairo: Dar al-ma'arif, 1969), 254-255; Shaw and Shaw, *History of the Ottoman Empire*, 108, 111.

95. Frierson, "Unimagined communities," 100, 104.

96. Ahmad Samih al-Khalidi, "The System of Turkish Education," *Majallat dar al-mu'allimin* no. 1 (November 1925): 15.

97. Yucel Gelişli, "Education of Women from the Ottoman Empire to Modern Turkey," *South-East Europe Review* no. 4 (2004): 122-124.

98. Tevfik Temelkuran, "The First Teacher Training College for Girls in Turkey," *Journal of the Regional Cultural Institute* (Tehran) 5, no. 1 (Winter 1972): 37-44. See also Fanny Davis, *The Ottoman Lady: A Social History from 1718 to 1918* (New York: Greenwood Press, 1986), 50-52; Frierson, "Unimagined Communities," 104-106.

99. Selçuk Akşin Somel, *The Modernization of Public Education in the Ottoman Empire 1839-1908: Islamization, Autocracy and Discipline* (Leiden: Brill, 2001), 132.

100. "Women's Teachers' College," *Filastin*, July 2, 1911.

101. "Registration of Employees in the School, Su'ad al-Asir al-Husayni," IIRHR, 13/39/1,20/1/75.

102. About *Maktab Jamal Pasha*, see Halide Edib Adıvar, *Memoirs of Halide Edib* (1926; repr., New York: Arno Press, 1972), 391, 402, 439-440. About Afifa Malhas, see Marie Aziz Sabri, *Pioneering Profiles: Beirut College for Women* (Beirut: Khayat Book and Publishing, 1967), 243.

103. Fortna, *Imperial Classroom*, 50-60; Benjamin C. Fortna, "Islamic Morality in Late Ottoman 'Secular' Schools," *International Journal of Middle East Studies* 32, no. 3 (August 2000): 369-393; Deringil, *Well-Protected Domains*, chs. 4 and 5.

104. Deringil, *Well-Protected Domains*, 105.

105. Ibid., 117.

106. Tibawi, *British Interests*, 96-97, 109, 181.

107. About the imperial photographs, see Carney E. S. Gavin and the Harvard Semitic Museum, eds., "Imperial Self-Portrait: The Ottoman Empire as Revealed in the Sultan Abdul Hamid II's Photographic Albums," special issue, *Journal of Turkish Studies* 12 (1988).

108. Palmira Brummett, "Gender and Empire in Late Ottoman Istanbul: Caricature, Models of Empire, and the Case for Ottoman Exceptionalism," *Comparative Studies of South Asia, Africa and the Middle East* 27, no. 2 (2007): 287, 301.

109. Mahmoud Yazbak, "Nabulsi Ulama in the Late Ottoman Period, 1864-1914," *International Journal of Middle East Studies* 29, no. 1 (1997): 79; Makariyus, "Education in Syria"; Zuhayr Ghanayim 'Abd al-Latif Ghanayim, *Liwa' 'akka fi al-'ahd al-tanzimat al-'uthmaniyya 1864-1918* (Beirut: Institute of Palestine Studies, 1999), 270-274.

110. See Cuinet, *Syrie Liban et Palestine*, 564; Yazbak, *Haifa in the Late Ottoman Period 1864-1914: A Muslim Town in Transition* (Leiden: Brill, 1998), 74, 187; Ghana-

yim, *Liwa' 'akka*, 273; Tamimi and Bahjat, *Wilayat bayrut*, 237; *Salname-i nezaret-i ma'arif-i 'umumiye 1318* (Yearbook of the Ministry of Education, 1900), 1201, 1229, and *Salname-i nezaret-i ma'arif-i 'umumiye 1321* (Yearbook of the Ministry of Education, 1903), 421.

111. See charts for the distribution of elementary education throughout the Empire, in Somel, *Modernization of Public Education*, Appendix 12, 341.

112. Yazbak, "Nabulsi Ulama," 78–79.

113. About the development of the soap industry in Ottoman Nablus, see Beshara B. Doumani, *Rediscovering Palestine: Merchants and Peasants in Jabal Nablus, 1700–1900* (Berkeley and Los Angeles: University of California Press, 1995).

114. Yazbak, "Nabulsi Ulama," 79–80.

115. Kushner, "Zealous Towns," 604–605.

116. Rev. John Mills, *Three Months' Residence at Nablus* (London, 1864), 100–103; Tibawi, *British Interests*, 95–96, 115–116.

117. Kushner, "Zealous Towns," 607–608.

118. Cuinet, *Syrie Liban et Palestine*, 185.

119. Sannu, *Al-masalih al-almaniyya*, 102.

120. Bertha Spafford Vester, *Our Jerusalem: An American Family in the Holy City 1881–1949* (Beirut: Middle East Export Press, 1950), 192. On the American Colony, see Yaacov Ariel and Ruth Kark, "Messianism, Holiness, Charisma and Community: The American-Swedish Colony in Jerusalem, 1881–1933," *Church History* 65, no. 4 (December 1996): 641–657; Ruth Kark, "Sweden and the Holy Land: Pietistic and Communal Settlement," *Journal of Historical Geography* 22, no. 1 (1996): 46–67, and her "Post Civil War American Communes: A Millenarian Utopian Community Linking Chicago and Nås, Sweden to Jerusalem," *Communal Societies* 15 (1995): 75–113.

121. Bertha Vester, "Moslem Girls' School, Draft of Chap. 26 of Our Jerusalem," 4, Container II, American Colony in Jerusalem Collection, Manuscript Division, Library of Congress, Washington, D.C.

122. Michael Hamilton Burgoyne, *Mamluk Jerusalem: An Architectural Study* (World of Islam Festival Trust on Behalf of British School of Archaeology in Jerusalem, 1987), 154.

123. Vester, "Moslem Girls' School, Draft of Chap. 26 of Our Jerusalem," 2.

124. Tubi, *'Abir wa-majd*, 20.

125. Vester, "Moslem Girls' School, Draft of Chap. 26 of Our Jerusalem," 5.

126. Ibid., 5–6.

127. Rozsika Parker, *The Subversive Stitch: Embroidery and the Making of the Feminine*, rev. ed. (London: Women's Press, 1996), 74.

128. Vester, "Moslem Girls' School, Draft of Chap. 26 of Our Jerusalem," 10–11.

129. Ibid., p. 4.

130. Eberhard, "Die Arabischen Volksschulen Jerusalem," 100.

131. Diary entry, September 28, 1914, *Yawmiyat Khalil al-Sakakini*, vol. 2, *al-nahda al-urthudhuksiyya, al-harb al-'uthma, al-nafi ila dimashq, 1914–1918*, ed. Akram Musal-

lam (Ramallah: Markaz Khalil al-Sakakini al-thaqafi, al-Quds: Mu'assasat al-dirasat al-muqaddasiyya, 2004), 104.

132. Diary entry, January 1, 1911, *Yawmiyat Khalil al-Sakakini,* vol. 1, *New York, Sultana, al-Quds 1908–1912,* ed. Akram Musallam (Ramallah: Markaz Khalil al-Sakakini al-thaqafi, al-Quds: Mu'assasat al-dirasat al-muqaddasiyya, 2003), 347–348; Khalidi, *Palestinian Identity,* 50. About the school's activities, see *Filastin,* July 13, 1911; April 15, 1912; June 29, 1912.

133. Feroz Ahmad, *The Young Turks: The Committee of Union and Progress in Turkish Politics 1908–1914* (London: Oxford University Press, 1969), 136; Masami Arai, *Turkish Nationalism in the Young Turk Era* (Leiden: Brill, 1992), 45–46; Hasan Kayalı, *Arabs and Young Turks: Ottomanism, Arabism, and Islamism in the Ottoman Empire, 1908–1918* (Berkeley and Los Angeles: University of California Press, 1997), 76, 91–93.

134. Butrus effendi Shihada, "The schools in Palestine," *Filastin,* July 2, 1911.

135. Muhammad Taha Dawla, "Jaffa and progress," *Filastin,* October 23, 1912.

136. About this law, see al-Khalidi, "The System of Turkish Education"; Shaw and Shaw, *History of the Ottoman Empire,* 300; Kayalı, *Arabs and Young Turks,* 135; *Encyclopedia of Islam,* 2nd ed., s.v. "Ma'arif," 902–915; Joseph S. Syzliowicz, *Education and Modernization in the Middle East* (Ithaca: Cornell University Press, 1973), 167–169.

137. al-Tamimi and Bahjat, *Wilayat bayrut,* 174.

138. Ibid., 368.

139. Ibid., 175.

140. Ibid., 88–89.

CHAPTER 2

1. Petition to the high commissioner for Palestine from residents of Safad, September 23, 1935, ISA, RG 27, 2682M, file S.271/1.

2. Petition, not dated, circa 1936–1937, ISA, RG 27, 2682M, file S.271/1.

3. Gordon Hewitt, *The Problems of Success: A History of the Church Missionary Society, 1910–1942* (London: SCM Press, 1971), 1:359; A. L. Tibawi, "Russian Cultural Penetration of Syria-Palestine in the Nineteenth Century—Part Two," *Journal of the Royal Central Asian Society* 53, no. 3 (1966): 321; Abigail Jacobson, "From Empire to Empire: Jerusalem in the Transition between Ottoman and British Rule, 1912–1920" (Ph.D. diss., University of Chicago, 2006), ch. 1.

4. Tibawi, *Arab Education,* 23.

5. Jacobson, "From Empire to Empire," 36.

6. Linda Schatkowski Schilcher, "The Famine of 1915–1918 in Greater Syria," in *Problems of the Modern Middle East in Historical Perspective: Essays in Honour of Albert Hourani,* ed. John P. Spagnolo (Reading, UK: Ithaca Press, 1992), 229–258.

7. Elizabeth Thompson, *Colonial Citizens: Republican Rights, Paternal Privilege, and Gender in French Syria and Lebanon* (New York: Columbia University Press, 2000), 20–22.

8. Diary entry, March 1, 1928, *Yawmiyat Khalil al-Sakakini*, 2:247.

9. Norman and Helen Bentwich, *Mandate Memories 1918–1948* (New York: Schocken Books, 1965), 43.

10. Margalit Shilo, "Women as Victims of War: The British Conquest (1917) and the Blight of Prostitution in the Holy City," *Nashim: A Journal of Jewish Women's Studies and Gender Issues* 6 (Fall 2003): 72.

11. Newton, *Fifty Years in Palestine*, 147.

12. "No. 8 Erfat Ersas," in "Christian Herald Orphans Conducted by the American Colony, List of Children," Container I:2, American Colony in Jerusalem Collection, Manuscript Division, Library of Congress, Washington, D.C. See also "Little Orphans of Jerusalem," *Christian Herald*, n.d, circa 1919, same collection.

13. "No. 24 Faruze Saallah," in "Christian Herald Orphans Conducted by the American Colony, List of Children," Container I:2, American Colony in Jerusalem Collection, Manuscript Division, Library of Congress, Washington, D.C.

14. Fleischmann, *Nation and Its "New" Women*, 104.

15. Social Service Association, *Social Service Association Report, 1923–1924*, 1.

16. Ibid., 4.

17. "Active in the woman's awakening: the lady Katinko Deeb," *al-Mar'a al-jadida* 5, no. 2 (1925): 55–56.

18. "Moslem Women's Association," Ottoman Societies Register, ISA, RG 23, 833M, file 3939/92.

19. Great Britain, Colonial Office, *Report by His Britannic Majesty's Government on the Administration under Mandate of Palestine and Transjordan for the Year 1924* (London: HMSO, 1925), 27.

20. Tibawi, *Arab Education*, 24; Great Britain, Colonial Office, *Report on Palestine Administration, July 1920–December 1921* (London: HMSO, 1922), 50.

21. Government of Palestine, Department of Education, *Annual Report 1933–1934*, 4.

22. Tibawi, *Arab Education*, 34; Great Britain, Colonial Office, *Report on Palestine Administration, July 1920–December 1921*, 50.

23. Diary entry, March 13, 1919, *Yawmiyat Khalil al-Sakakini*, vol. 3, *ikhtibar al-intidab wa-as'ila al-huwiya, 1919–1922*, ed. Akram Musallam (Ramallah: Markaz Khalil al-Sakakini al-thaqafi; al-Quds: Mu'assasat al-dirasat al-muqaddasiyya, 2004), 98.

24. "Education," in Palestine Sessional Papers: Advisory Council Minutes, December 7, 1920, National Archives, PRO, CO 814/6.

25. "Education," in Palestine Sessional Papers: Advisory Council Minutes, October 6, 1920, National Archives, PRO, CO 814/6.

26. Jacobson, "From Empire to Empire," 221–223.

27. Tibawi, *Arab Education*, 79.

28. Heather J. Sharkey, *Living with Colonialism: Nationalism and Culture in the Anglo-Egyptian Sudan* (Berkeley and Los Angeles: University of California Press, 2003), 22.

29. Bishop George Francis to director of education, June 22, 1934, and director of education to Bishop George Francis, July 7, 1934, CO 733/267/36580.

30. Inspector of Islamic schools to general director of awqaf, February 23, 1935, IIRHR, 15/44/1,6/1/75.

31. Government of Palestine, Department of Education, *Statistical Tables and Diagrams for the Scholastic Year 1943–1944*, table III, "Arab Public System, Teachers and Pupils Classified by Locality, Religion and Sex"; A. L. Tibawi, "Religion and Educational Administration in Palestine of the British Mandate," *Die Welt des Islams*, n.s., 3, no. 1 (1953): 9–10.

32. Government of Palestine, Department of Education, *Annual Report 1924*, 5. About Iraq and Egypt, see Humphrey Bowman, *Middle-East Window* (London: Longmans, Green, 1942), 68, 193. In 1934, the nomenclature changed, so that the kindergarten (also known as the preparatory class) became the first grade, while the sixth grade and top elementary class became the seventh grade. See Great Britain, Colonial Office, *Report by His Majesty's Government in the United Kingdom of Great Britain and Northern Ireland to the Council of the League of Nations on the Administration of Palestine and Transjordan for the Year 1934* (London: HMSO, 1935), 124.

33. Tibawi, *Arab Education*, 162.

34. According to a petition submitted by residents of Hebron, ISA, RG 23, July 18, 1934, 854/3M, file 19/44.

35. Government of Palestine, Department of Education, *Annual Report 1931–1932*, 17.

36. Director of education to district commissioner, Jerusalem, June 20, 1933, ISA, RG 23, M854/3, file 19/44 (original petition not found); Petition from Hebron notables to high commissioner, July 18, 1934, ISA, RG 2, 135/22M, file E/53/34.

37. Director of education to treasurer, November 26, 1935, ISA, RG 2, microfilm G 92-123, file E/8/36.

38. Report of sitting board, January 27, 1938, ISA, RG 10, 1537M, file 18/4.

39. District commissioner to chief secretary, December 3, 1935, ISA, RG 2, microfilm G 92-123, file E/8/36; Petition of Hebron residents to high commissioner for Palestine, November 10, 1936, ISA, RG 23, 854/3M, file 19/44.

40. Government of Palestine, Department of Education, *Annual Report 1931–1932*, 17; Treasurer to director of education, November 26, 1935, ISA, RG 2, microfilm G 92-123, file E/8/36.

41. 'Aref Abu-Rabi'a, *Bedouin Century: Education and Development among the Negev Tribes in the Twentieth Century* (New York: Berghahn Books, 2001), 78.

42. About the opening of the school, see director of education to district commissioner, Northern district, June 9, 1933, ISA, RG 25, 884M, file 581/212/-1.

43. Kupferschmidt, *Supreme Muslim Council*, 121.

44. See file "Education Properties," ISA, RG 8, 1012M, file 663/8.

45. About educational properties in Tiberias, see, for example, president, Supreme Muslim Council, to chief secretary, August 7, 1929, and December 15, 1929, ISA, RG 2, 293M, file K/29/31.

46. See Government of Palestine, Department of Education, *Annual Report, 1941–1942.*

47. Great Britain, Colonial Office, *Report by His Majesty's Government in the United Kingdom of Great Britain and Northern Ireland to the Council of the League of Nations on the Administration of Palestine and Transjordan for the Year 1930* (London: HMSO, 1931), 119.

48. Ruth Woodsmall, Bound reports, 317, Box 25, Ruth Woodsmall Papers, Sophia Smith Collection, Smith College, Northampton, Mass. See also Ruth Frances Woodsmall, *Moslem Women Enter a New World* (London: George Allen and Unwin, 1936), 190.

49. Adawiyya al-ʿAlami, "Taʿlim al-banat fi al-quds," in *Al-quds madinat al-ʿilm: yawm al-quds: abhath al-nadwa al-khamisa yawm al-quds,* ed. Lajnat yawm al-quds (Amman: N.p., 1995), 48–49.

50. Miss H. Ridler, "Special Problems in the Training of Women Teachers in the Near East," in Government of Palestine, Department of Education, *Annual Report 1926–1927,* 28.

51. See, for example, Eliza F. Kent, "Tamil Bible Women and the Zenana Missions of Colonial South India," *History of Religions* 39, no. 2 (November 1999): 117–149.

52. Woodsmall, Bound reports, 317v.

53. Woodsmall, Bound reports, 319–320.

54. Woodsmall, *Moslem Women,* 192.

55. Najwa Kawar Farah, *A Continent Called Palestine: One Woman's Story* (London: Triangle, 1996), 22–23.

56. Woodsmall, Bound Reports, 317.

57. Fleischmann, *Nation and Its "New" Women,* 41.

58. Mohammad Kassim El Hussein, Acre, to chief secretary, August 25, 1947, ISA, RG 2, 128/20M file E/12/45; Muzim bint Husain al-Masri petition, November 23, 1928, CO 733/162/13.

59. Government of Palestine, Department of Education, *Annual Report 1924,* 3; Government of Palestine, Department of Education, *Annual Report, 1930–1931,* 28.

60. Evelyn Barin Cromer, *Modern Egypt* (London: MacMillan, 1908), 2:531.

61. Fleischmann, *Nation and Its "New" Women,* 40.

62. Great Britain, Colonial Office, *Report on Palestine Administration 1922–1923,* 28; Government of Palestine, Department of Education, *Annual Report, 1923,* 2; Government of Palestine, *Annual Report of the Department of Education for the Year 1924,* 3.

63. Department of Education, *Annual Report for the Scholastic Year 1927–1928,* 7.

64. Department of Education, *Annual Report 1930–1931,* 28; Saʿida, interview by Ellen Fleischmann, Jerusalem, April 19, 1994.

65. About Nasser, see Government of Palestine, Department of Education, *Annual Report 1929–1930,* 28; Government of Palestine, Department of Education, *Annual Report 1930–1931,* 28. About other women attending school in England, see high

commissioner for Palestine to J. H. Thomas, principal secretary of state for the colonies, Colonial Office, October 21, 1931, CO 733/211/87408. See also the annual reports of the Department of Education from 1929–1930 to 1933–1934.

66. "Return of an educated lady from England," *Filastin*, September 18, 1940; *Jerusalem Girls' College Magazine* (June 1938); Saʿida, interview.

67. Bowman, *Middle-East Window*, 89; Tibawi, *Arab Education*, 26–35; Cromer, *Modern Egypt*, 2:534.

68. Fleischmann, *Nation and Its "New" Women*, 38–39.

69. See, for example, Government of Palestine, Department of Education, *Annual Report 1929–1930*, 29. About Iraq, see Bowman, *Middle-East Window*, 193.

70. A. L. Tibawi, "Report on Education in the Southern District, February 1941–October 1945," 9, ISA, 4490M, file 10/9; Tibawi, *Arab Education*, 47.

71. Jerome Farrell, acting director of education to chief secretary, October 3, 1928, CO 733/161/57559.

72. Government of Palestine, Department of Education, *Statistical Tables and Diagrams for the Scholastic Year 1944–1945*, table IV, "Arab Public System. Pupils distributed by classes, ages, locality, and sex."

73. Ibid., table XXII, "All Schools classified as public, assisted and non-assisted with detailed lists of secondary, agricultural, technical, and vocational schools."

74. Government of Palestine, Department of Education, *Annual Report 1926–1927*, table XXIV.

75. Government of Palestine, Department of Education, *Statistical Tables 1944–1945*, table XXII.

76. See, for example, Government of Palestine, Department of Education, *Statistical Tables 1943–1944*, table XXII, "All Schools classified as public, assisted and non-assisted with detailed lists of secondary, agricultural, technical, and vocational schools."

77. Annelies Moors, *Women, Property and Islam: Palestinian Experiences 1920–1990* (Cambridge: Cambridge University Press, 1995), 214–215, 225–226.

78. A. Kafah ʿAwda, *Yusra Salah 1923–1993* (Nablus: n.p., 1995). See also Jaussen, *Coutumes Palestiniennes*, 46.

79. "Nationalist College, Shweifat, Lebanon," advertisement, *Filastin*, September 17, 1940; "Brummana School," advertisement, *Filastin*, September 26, 1940.

80. See, for example, Salwa Khayat, "Our School," *British Syrian Training College Magazine* 1 (1932): 10–11.

81. Ylana N. Miller, *Government and Society in Rural Palestine, 1920–1948* (Austin: University of Texas Press, 1985), 97.

82. Humphrey Bowman, "Rural Education in the Middle East," *Journal of the Royal Central Asian Society* 26, no. 3 (July 1939): 402–414. See also Miller, *Government and Society*, 109; Roza I. M. El-Eini, "British Agricultural-Educational Institutions in Mandate Palestine and Their Impress on the Rural Landscape," *Middle Eastern Studies* 35, no. 1 (January 1999): 98–99.

83. Cited in Starrett, *Putting Islam to Work*, 30.

84. El-Eini, "British Agricultural-Educational Institutions," 101.

85. Humphrey Bowman, "The Provision and Organisation of Schools in Rural Districts," Appendix C, in Government of Palestine, Department of Education, *Annual Report 1926–1927*, 25.

86. Cromer, *Modern Egypt*, 2:533–534.

87. Mona L. Russell, "Creating the New Woman: Consumerism, Education, and National Identity in Egypt, 1863–1922" (Ph.D. diss., Georgetown University, 1997), 238.

88. Moors, *Women, Property and Islam*, 158–159.

89. Bowman, *Middle-East Window*, 277.

90. Government of Palestine, Department of Education, *Annual Report 1924*, 5; Tibawi, *Arab Education*, 156–157.

91. Petition from notables of al-Bireh to district commissioner, Jerusalem, August 12, 1934, ISA, RG 23, 853M, file 19/36. About the impoverishment of Palestinian villagers during the Mandate period, see Mahmoud Yazbak, "From Poverty to Revolt: Economic Factors in the Outbreak of the 1936 Rebellion in Palestine," *Middle Eastern Studies* 36, no. 3 (July 2000): 93–113; Issa Khalaf, "The Effect of Socioeconomic Change on Arab Societal Collapse in Mandate Palestine," *International Journal of Middle East Studies* 29, no. 1 (February 1997): 93–112.

92. Petition of mukhtars of al-Khadder, August 1, 1935, ISA, RG 23, 853M, file 19/27.

93. Miller, *Government and Society*, 153.

94. See "Mujeidil Village Girls' School," ISA, RG 27, 2663M, file N.665.

95. Acting director of Department of Education to district commissioner, Nazareth District, December 17, 1945, ISA, RG 27, 2663M, file N.665.

96. Maryam, interview by the author and Laila 'Abed Rabho, Silwan, January 16, 2001.

97. Gabriel Baer, "The Economic and Social Position of the Village-Mukhtar in Palestine," in *The Palestinians and the Middle East Conflict*, ed. Gabriel Ben-Dor (Ramat Gan: Turtlegrove Publishers, 1978).

98. Miller, *Government and Society*, 48–70.

99. Walid Khalidi, ed. *All That Remains: The Palestinian Villages Occupied and Depopulated by Israel in 1948* (Washington, D.C.: Institute for Palestine Studies, 1992), 35–37.

100. "Schedule of Government Schools Provided by Government School Medical Service, 1946," CZA, J17/8356.

101. Palestine Arab Workers' Society, March 30, 1947, ISA, RG 27, 2642M, file G.666/I. About PAWS, see Issa Khalaf, *Politics in Palestine: Arab Factionalism and Social Disintegration, 1939–1948* (Albany: SUNY Press, 1991), 38–40.

102. Wadi'a Bulus to inspector of education, Galilee district, July 8,1943, ISA, RG 8, 1037M, file 1391/3.

103. Mustafa al-Dabbagh, *Madrasat al-qarya* (Jerusalem: Matba'at al-'arab, 1935), 99.

104. Hilda Zeibak to director of education, March 3, 1935, ISA, RG 8, 1026M, file 1130/10.

105. See Ela Greenberg, "Between Hardships and Respect: A Collective Biography of Arab Women Teachers in British-ruled Palestine," *Hawwa* 6, no. 3 (2008): 284–314.

106. Memo to Colonial Office, June 6, 1934, CO 733/263/37454.

107. Clive Whitehead, "The Historiography of British Imperial Education Policy, Part I: India," *History of Education* 34, no. 3 (May 2005): 324.

108. Memo on continued expansion of rural schools, CO 733/282/75254.

109. Director of Education, "Observations upon the Report of the O'Donnell Commissioner, Chap. XII, Paragraphs 125–142," CO 733/208/83770.

110. Memo by director of education on rural education expansion, submitted in conjunction with financial estimates, 1934–1935, CO 733/263/37454.

111. High Commissioner for Palestine Wauchope to colonial secretary, January 3, 1935, CO 733/277/75132.

112. High Commissioner for Palestine Wauchope to Sir Philip Cunliffe-Lister, principal secretary of state for the colonies, March 30, 1935, CO 733/270/75029. See also Bowman, *Middle-East Window*, 277.

113. See their employment files: Balqis ash-Sheikh, ISA, RG 8, 1035M, file 1343/5; Khadija Kilani, ISA, RG 8, 1039M, file 1460/3; Nazmiya Muhammad Hassoun, ISA, RG 8, 1040M, file 1520/23.

114. Cromer, *Modern Egypt*, 2:528.

115. Tibawi, *Arab Education*, 157–159, 165–166.

116. Government of Palestine, Department of Education, *Annual Report 1944–1945*; Great Britain, Colonial Office, Palestine Royal Commission, *Minutes of Evidence Heard at Public Sessions* (London: HMSO, 1937), 354.

117. Government of Palestine, Department of Education, *Annual Report, 1929–1930*; "Schedule of Government Schools Provided by Government School Medical Service, Acre Town and Sub-district," CZA, J17/8356.

118. Petition from village educational committee, elders, and mukhtars of Malha village to director of education, September 1, 1942, ISA, RG 65, 367P, file 2355.

119. Al-Rabita al-shabiba al-ramiyya to director of education, March 30, 1946, ISA, RG 27, 2642M, file G666/I. See also Miller, *Government and Society*, 154.

120. See Fleischmann, *Nation and Its "New" Women*, 41.

121. Muhammad Sa'id Muslih Rumman, *Suba: qarya muqaddasiyya fi al-dhakira* (Jerusalem: Matba'at 'Ain Rafa, 2000), 162.

122. Said K. Abu Rish, *Children of Bethany: The Story of a Palestinian Family* (London: I. B. Tauris, 1988), 135.

123. Government of Palestine, Department of Education, *Annual Report 1931–1932*. Table XVII, "Moslem Schools classified by Their Governing Bodies."

124. Na'ame, interview by the author and Laila 'Abed Rabho, Bayt Safafa, January 30, 2001.

125. 'Aliyye, interview by Laila 'Abed Rabho, Bayt Safafa, Spring 2001.

126. Najib Nassar, "Education: A school for girls," *al-Karmil*, November 4, 1931.

127. Najib Nassar, "Girls' school," *al-Karmil*, October 7, 1933.

128. Najib Nassar, "Practical schools," *al-Karmil*, July 31, 1927.

129. Sadhij Nassar, "Education in Palestine," *al-Karmil*, January 30, 1927.

130. Bowman, *Middle-East Window*, 263–264.

131. See Karmi, *In Search of Fatima*, 18–20.

132. See, for example, Najib Nassar, "Education: The method of teaching in Palestine," *al-Karmil*, March 25, 1931.

133. About the Palestine Arab Party, see Weldon C. Matthews, *Confronting an Empire, Constructing a Nation: Arab Nationalists and Popular Politics in Mandate Palestine* (London: I. B. Tauris, 2006), 226.

134. Palestine Arab Party, "Report on Illiteracy in Palestine Submitted to the Members of the British Parliament," June 10, 1935, ISA, RG 65.02, 986P, file 113.

135. Palestine Royal Commission, *Minutes of Evidence*, 351–352.

136. Ibid., 355.

139. "Hebron: transfer of teachers and a word to the Department of Education," *al-Difaʿ*, August 24, 1937.

138. E. Mills, *Census of Palestine* (Alexandria, 1933), 1:207, 215.

139. Khalidi, *Palestinian Identity*, 40–41.

140. Graham-Brown, *Images of Women*, 192; Baron, *Egypt as a Woman*, 87; Frierson, "Unimagined Communities," 141.

141. Tibawi, *Arab Education*, 220.

142. Al-Dabbagh, *Madrasat al-qarya*, 70.

143. Government of Palestine, Department of Education, *Statistical Tables 1943–1944*, table IV, A; table IV, B.

144. Baron, *Egypt as a Woman*, especially chs. 3–4.

145. Fleischmann, *Nation and Its "New" Women*, 68.

146. Matthews, *Confronting an Empire*, 87–95.

147. Sharkey, *Living with Colonialism*, 102–111.

148. Subhiyya Maqdadi, "Education of women and their upbringing," *Filastin*, May 29, 1931.

149. Fatima Fahmi, "Voice of a girl: The girl is the teacher," *al-Jamiʿa al-ʿarabiyya*, July 11, 1927.

150. "The association for educating the girl," *al-Karmil*, November 30, 1920, and December 12, 1920.

151. Tibawi, *Arab Education*, Table I, 49.

152. The Anglo-American Committee of Inquiry, *A Survey of Palestine, Prepared in December 1945 and January 1946* (1946–1947; repr., Washington, D.C.: Institute for Palestine Studies, 1991), 2:638–639.

153. Government of Palestine, Department of Education, *Statistical Tables, 1944–1945*, table III.

154. Justin McCarthy, *The Population of Palestine* (New York: Columbia University

Press, 1990), table 2.18, 37. These population statistics did not include Druze, Shi'a, and Bedouins, who were counted as "other."

155. Chief secretary to Matiel Mogannam, August 15, 1935, as quoted in Matiel Mogannam, *The Arab Woman and the Palestine Problem* (London: Herbert Joseph, 1937), 253.

CHAPTER 3

1. A small percentage of Jewish girls also studied in the Catholic and Protestant schools, despite protests from within the Jewish community, and continued to do so at least into the 1950s and 1960s after the creation of the State of Israel.

2. Calculations based on Government of Palestine, Department of Education, *Annual Report*, 1924, table III, "Non-Government Schools, Distribution of Schools by Communities," and table V, "Government and Non-Government Schools: Distribution of Pupils by Communities"; Government of Palestine, Department of Education, *Annual Report for the Scholastic Year 1925–1926*, table III, "Government Schools: Distribution of Pupils by Religion," and table V, "Non-Government Schools: Distribution by Communities"; Department of Education, *Statistical Tables 1944–1945*, table XX, "Non Public Schools, Development since 1929–30."

3. Government of Palestine, Department of Education, *Statistical Tables*, table XVIII, "Christian Schools (Non-Public) Classified by Their Governing Bodies."

4. Deputy high commissioner to secretary of state for the colonies, April 12, 1935, ISA, RG 2, 125/15M, file E/39/33.

5. Mohammad Yacoub El Ghusein, president, Executive Committee of the Arab Youth Federation, Jaffa to high commissioner, July 31, 1935, ISA, RG 2, 125/15M, file E/39/33.

6. Jerome Farell, acting director of education to chief secretary, September 7, 1935, ISA, RG 2, 125/15M, file E/39/33.

7. Tibawi, *Arab Education*, 83–86.

8. Jerome Farrell, director of Department of Education to chief secretary, November 20, 1937, CZA, S25/22717.

9. Sharkey, *Living with Colonialism*, 65, 68–69.

10. "School of the Sisters of St. Joseph in Bethlehem," *Filastin*, November 17, 1935.

11. Hobsbawm, *Nations and Nationalism since 1780*, 93–94.

12. Ibid., 116.

13. Starrett, *Putting Islam to Work*, 46.

14. Excerpt of letter from Espie Emery to M. E. Emery, October 26, 1919, MECA, Emery Collection, GB 165-0099, box 1, file 1.

15. Mabel C. Warburton to Mr. Bickersteth, May 18, 1927, MECA, J&EM, GB 165-0161, box 42, file 1. For a more detailed history of these two schools, see Okkenhaug, *Quality of Heroic Living*, especially chs. 2–5.

16. Okkenhaug, *Quality of Heroic Living*, 28.

17. "Notes on Visits to Schools: English High School for Girls Haifa," December 6–11, 1934, MECA, J&EM, GB 165-0161, box 42, file 2.

18. English High School for Girls, *Prospectus of the English High School for Girls Haifa, 1931–1932*, 4; al-Kulliya al-inkliziyya lil-banat, *Barnamaj al-Kulliya al-inkliziyya lil-banat fi al-quds 'an sana 1931–1932*, 4.

19. "Concerning the Work of the English High School Haifa during the Recent Political Unhappiness," December 5, 1936, MECA, J&EM, GB 165-0161, box 63, file 3.

20. Okkenhaug, *Quality of Heroic Living*, ch. 5; Maria Småberg, "Ambivalent Friendship: Anglican Conflict Handling and Education for Peace in Jerusalem 1920–1948" (Ph.D. diss., Lund University, 2005).

21. See Okkenhaug, *Quality of Heroic Living*, esp. 149–172.

22. Småberg, "Ambivalent Friendship," 258–259.

23. Mabel C. Warburton to Mr. Bickersteth, October 17, 1922, MECA, J&EM, GB 165-0161, box 41, file 4.

24. Anna G. Irvine to Mr. Bickersteth, October 18, 1925, MECA, J&EM, GB 165-0161, box 43, file 4.

25. Okkenhaug, *Quality of Heroic Living*, 115.

26. Winifred A. Coate to Mr. Bickersteth, December 7, 1929, MECA, J&EM, GB 165-0161, box 42, file 3.

27. Winifred A. Coate to Mr. Bickersteth, October 24, 1930, MECA, J&EM, GB 165-0161, box 42, file 4.

28. S. P. Emery to Bishop, April 29, 1940, MECA, J&EM, GB 165-0161, box 55, file 2.

29. Woodsmall, Bound reports, 316v.

30. Espie Emery to her mother, October 13, 1940, MECA, Emery Collection, GB 165-0099, box 1, file 5.

31. Government of Palestine, Department of Education, *Annual Report of the Department of Education for the Year 1924*, 6, and Government of Palestine, Department of Education, *Annual Report for the Scholastic Year 1925–1926*, 6.

32. Espie Emery to her mother, September 27, 1942, MECA, Emery Collection, GB 165-0099, box 1, file 6.

33. Secretary [of the J&EM] to Miss Warburton, November 22, 1940, MECA, J&EM, GB 165-0161, box 42, file 2; Okkenhaug, *Quality of Heroic Living*, 70.

34. Nadiyya, interview by Khader Salameh, Bethlehem, October 6, 2001.

35. Line Nyhagen Predelli, "Sexual Control and the Remaking of Gender: The Attempt of Nineteenth Century Protestant Norwegian Women to Export Western Domesticity to Madagascar," *Journal of Women's History* 12, no. 2 (Summer 2000): 85.

36. Anna G. Irvine to Mr. Bickersteth, December 10, 1925, MECA, J&EM, GB 165-0161, box 43, file 4; Espie Emery to her mother, October 12, 1924, MECA, Emery Collection, GB 165-0099, box 1, file 1.

37. Anna G. Irvine to Mr. Bickersteth, November 3, 1932, MECA, J&EM, GB 165-0161, box 43, file 4.

38. Winifred A. Coate to Mr. Bickersteth, October 24, 1930, MECA, J&EM, GB 165-0161, box 42, file 4.

39. Anna G. Irvine to Mr. Bickersteth, November 3, 1932, MECA, J&EM, GB 165-0161, box 43, file 4.

40. "Note to the Bishop from J. G. M.," December 9, 1932, MECA, J&EM, GB 165-0161, box 55, file 1.

41. Mabel C. Warburton to Mr. Bickersteth, October 16, 1924, MECA, J&EM, GB 165-0161, box 41, file 4; Anna G. Irvine to Mr. Bickersteth, October 15, 1924, MECA, J&EM, GB 165-0161, box 43, file 4.

42. Anna G. Irvine to Mr. Bickersteth, October 9, 1930, MECA, J&EM, GB 165-0161, box 43, file 4.

43. "Jerusalem Girls' College," November 18, 1933, MECA, J&EM, GB 165-0161, box 41, file 2.

44. H. Gardner to Mr. Bickersteth, March 22, 1924, MECA, J&EM, GB 165-0161, box 55, file 3.

45. Secretary, Girls' High School, Haifa, to Miss Gardner, May 27, 1926, MECA, J&EM, GB 165-0161, box 55, file 3.

46. H. Gardner to Mr. Bickersteth, November 7, 1926, MECA, J&EM, GB 165-0161, box 55, file 1.

47. Brumberg, "Zenanas and Girlless Villages," 363.

48. K. Pelin Başcı, "Shadows in the Missionary Garden of Roses: Women of Turkey in American Missionary Texts," in *Deconstructing Images of "the Turkish Woman,"* ed. Zehra F. Arat (New York: Palgrave, 2000), 111–113.

49. Miss Gardner to Mr. Bickersteth, March 22, 1924, MECA, J&EM, GB 165-0161, box 55, file 3.

50. Fleischmann, *Nation and Its "New" Women*, 133.

51. See, for example, "Charitable bazaar of the Islamic girls' school," *Filastin*, June 14, 1932.

52. Mabel Warburton to Mr. Oldham, February 9, 1919, MECA, J&EM, GB 165-0161, box 41, file 3.

53. Ibid.

54. Espie Emery, "Annual Report, English High School, Haifa," April 12, 1938, MECA, J&EM, GB 165-0161, box 55, file 2.

55. Ibid.

56. Espie Emery to her mother, January 14, 1940, MECA, Emery Collection, GB 165-0099, box 1, file 5.

57. Winifred A. Coate to Mr. Bickersteth, October 24, 1930, MECA, J&EM, GB 165-0161, box 42, file 4.

58. Fleischmann, "Impact of American Protestant Missions," 418.

59. Ibid., 419.

60. Zainat Nur al-Din to inspector of ahliyya schools, November 23, 1928, IIRHR, 13/27/4,2/2/75.

61. Zainat Nur al-Din to Muhammad Bek al-Barda'i, circa 1927–1928, IIRHR, 13/27/4,2/2/75.

62. Fleischmann, "Impact of American Protestant Missions," 419.

63. Inspector of ahliyya schools to Rashid al-Khatib, Sidon, December 28, 1928, IIRHR, 13/27/4,2/2/75.

64. Lois C. Wilson to inspector of ahliyya schools, December 25, 1928, IIRHR, 13/27/4,2/2/75.

65. Inspector of Islamic schools to Zainat Nur al-Din, March 5, 1929, IIRHR, 13/27/4,2/2/75.

66. Inspector of Islamic schools to director of *awqaf*, February 21, 1935, IIRHR, 15/44/1,6/1/75.

67. Head of the SMC to the *qadi* of Hebron, October 8, 1923, IIRHR, 0/25/3,1/2/75.

68. Circular issued by the SMC on February 22, 1925, ISA, RG 65, file 3453; Hajj Amin al-Husayni to the treasurer of the awqaf, July 12, 1925, IIRHR, 0/25/3,1/2/75.

69. *Qadi* Abdallah Tahbub to the president of the SMC, February 23, 1923, IIRHR, 0/25/3,1/2/75.

70. *Qadi* Abdallah Tahbub to the president of the SMC, March 17, 1925, IIRHR, 0/25/3,1/2/75.

71. Haddad, "Syrian Muslims' Attitudes toward Foreign Missionaries."

72. Kelvin Crombie, *For the Love of Zion: Christian Witness and the Restoration of Israel* (London: Hodder and Stoughton, 1991), 142, 182.

73. The World Mission of Christianity, *Messages and Recommendations of the Enlarged Meeting of the International Missionary Council held at Jerusalem, March 24–April 8, 1928* (London: International Missionary Council, 1928).

74. "The general recommendation from the missionary conference in Palestine and the Islamic lands," *al-Jami'a al-'arabiyya*, April 9, 1928. See also *al-Jami'a al-'arabiyya*, March 22, 29; April 2, 5, 16, 19, 24, 26, and May 3, 1928.

75. Kupferschmidt, *Supreme Muslim Council*, 249; al-Majlis al-shar'i al-islami al-a'la, *Bayan al-majlis al-shar'i al-islami al-a'la le sane 1347–1348 (1928–1929)* (Matba'at dar al-aytam al-islamiyya al-sina'iyya bil-quds), 14–15.

76. Winifred A. Coate to Mr. Bickersteth, September 20, 1929, MECA, J&EM, GB 165-0161, box 42, file 3.

77. Winifred A. Coate to Mr. Bickersteth, October 8, 1929, MECA, J&EM, GB 165-0161, box 42, file 3.

78. Ibid.

79. Khaldiyya to Miss Coate, n.d. (circa 1929), MECA, J&EM, GB 165-0161, box 42, file 3.

80. Winifred A. Coate to Mr. Bickersteth, October 8, 1929, MECA, J&EM, GB 165-0161, box 42, file 3.

81. Ibid.

82. Nadiyya, interview.

83. Rushdi ʿAli, *Taqrir lil-muʾtamar al-islami al-ʿamm* (Jerusalem: Matbaʿat dar al-aytam al-islamiyya, 1350).

84. *Muqararrat al-muʾtamar al-islami al-ʿamm* (Jerusalem: Matbaʿat dar al-aytam al-islamiyya, 1931).

85. [Muhammad Amin al-Husayni,] *Khutbatan li-samaha al-mufti al-akbar wa-raʾis al-majlis al-islami al-alʿa al-sayyid Muhammad Amin al-Husayni fi muʾtammar al-ʿulamaʾ wa-fi ijtimaʿ wufud al-qura bi-shaʾn baiʿ al-aradi bi-filastin lil-sahyuniyyin waʾl-hath ʿala al-amr bi-l-maʿruf waʾl-nahy ʿan al-mufkar* (Jerusalem: Matbaʿat dar al-aytam al-islamiyya al-sinaʿiyya bil-quds, n.d).

86. Daʾirat al-maʿhad al-diniyya, *Nidaʾ ila al-muslimin ʿammatan bil-tahthir min al-madaris al-tabshiriyya* (Jerusalem: Matbaʿat dar al-aytam al-islamiyya, n.d.). The publication of this pamphlet was also announced in "Warning against the missionary schools," *al-Sirat al-mustaqim*, September 29, 1935.

87. Kupferschmidt, *Supreme Muslim Council*, 247–249.

88. Suʿad Khuri, "Nationalist education from the house until the age of maturity," *al-Difaʿ*, January 23, 1935.

89. Suʿad Khuri, "The schools and the woman," *al-Difaʿ*, July 21, 1935.

90. Fatima Fahmi, "Voice of a girl: The girl is the teacher," *al-Jamiʿa al-ʿarabiyya*, July 11, 1927.

91. Sadhij Nassar, "The home," *al-Karmil*, March 4, 1928, and "Do not mimic the western women," *al-Karmil*, June 24, 1928; "These are the foreign schools," *al-Difaʿ*, February 28, 1937.

92. Fadwa Tuqan, *A Mountainous Journey: A Poet's Autobiography* (St. Paul: Gray-wolf Press, 1990), 78.

93. Abu Rish, *Children of Bethany*, 141.

94. See, for example, "Gambling and the ladies," *al-Karmil*, March 6, 1927; "Female teachers dance and pupils sing," *al-Jamiʿa al-ʿarabiyya*, June 27, 1927.

95. "The indifference of the police," *al-Sirat al-mustaqim*, May 25, 1931.

96. Yosef Vashitz, *Ha-ʿaravim be-erets-yisrael* (Merchavia: Sifriat ha-poʿaalim, 1947), 268.

97. "The method of teaching in Palestine," *al-Karmil*, March 25, 1931.

98. "Oh for shame, Muslim women in Tel Aviv," *al-Sirat al-mustaqim*, March 21, 1932.

99. "Report" by E. Fallet, acting principal, English High School, Jaffa, n.d. (circa Fall 1936), MECA, J&EM, GB 165-0161, box 63, file 3.

100. Vashitz, *Ha-ʿaravim be-erets-yisrael*, 220.

101. Anna G. Irvine to Mr. Bickersteth, November 3, 1932, MECA, J&EM, GB 165-0161, box 43, file 4.

102. Gerald M. Berg, "Zionist Women of the 1920s: The Voice of Nation Building," *Journal of Israeli History* 25, no. 2 (September 2006): 313–333. About prostitution

in Tel Aviv and Jaffa during the British Mandate, see Deborah Bernstein, *Nashim be-shulayim: Migdar ve-leumiyut be-Tel Aviv ha-mandatorit* (Jerusalem: Yad Ben Zvi, 2008).

103. Oz Almog, *The Sabra: The Creation of the New Jew* (Berkeley and Los Angeles: University of California Press, 2000), 219–225.

104. Karmi, *In Search of Fatima*, 36.

105. Okkenhaug, *Quality of Heroic Living*, 117–118.

106. "Report to the Royal Commission," by Espie Emery, January 8, 1937, MECA, J&EM, GB 165-0161, box 63, file 3.

107. S. P. Emery, "Annual Report, English High School, Haifa," April 12, 1938, MECA, J&EM, GB 165-0161, box 55, file 2. See also "Principal's Report, English High School Speech Day," July 1, 1942, MECA, J&EM, GB 165-0161, box 55, file 2.

108. Espie Emery to her mother, October 12, 1941, MECA, Emery Collection, GB 165-0099, box 1, file 6.

109. Okkenhaug, *Quality of Heroic Living*, 118.

110. "The truth of what takes place in the Italian Salesian School in Jerusalem," *al-Jami'a al-'arabiyya*, February 22, 1935.

111. Partha Chatterjee, *The Nation and Its Fragments: Colonial and Postcolonial Histories* (Princeton: Princeton University Press, 1993), 121–122.

112. See, for example, "Successes of female pupils," *Filastin*, August 9, 1931; "Palestinian female pupils sit university exam," *Filastin*, September 23, 1931; "The English College for Girls in Haifa," *al-Karmil*, August 26, 1928.

113. "Education: Our social weakness: The confessional school," *al-Karmil*, July 3, 1929.

114. "The world missionary conference," *Filastin*, October 4, 1928.

115. Yehoshua Porath, *The Emergence of the Palestinian-Arab National Movement, 1918–1929* (London: Frank Cass, 1974), 300.

116. Yazbak, "From Poverty to Revolt."

117. Ibid.

118. Schleifer, "The Life and Thought of 'Izz-id-din al-Qassam." See also Yehoshua Porath, *The Palestinian Arab National Movement: From Riots to Rebellion*, vol. 2, *1929–1939* (London: Frank Cass, 1977), 132–139.

119. Porath, *Palestinian Arab National Movement*, 168.

120. Fleischmann, *Nation and Its "New" Women*, 124.

121. Porath, *Palestinian Arab Nationalist Movement*, 172–173. See also Fleischmann, *Nation and Its "New" Women*, 132–133.

122. Porath, *Palestinian Arab Nationalist Movement*, 175.

123. Fleischmann, *Nation and Its "New" Women*, 125.

124. Philip Matar, *The Mufti of Jerusalem: Al-Hajj Amin al-Husayni and the Palestinian National Movement* (New York: Columbia University Press, 1988), 82–85.

125. See, for example, "Committee of female students," *al-Difa'*, April 30, 1936. See also Fleischmann, *Nation and Its "New" Women*, 129–130.

126. "Nablus: Large demonstration after Friday prayers," *al-Difaʿ*, May 2, 1936.

127. Ibtihaj, interview by Ellen Fleischmann, Acre, May 20, 1993.

128. "Qalqiliyya: Great meeting of ladies," *al-Difaʿ*, May 21, 1936.

129. Dorothy Morgan to her family, Easter Day 1945, MECA, Norman Collection, GB 165-0219.

130. Okkenhaug, *Quality of Heroic Living*, 162–163, 179.

131. Winifred A. Coate to the archdeacon, April 29, 1936, MECA, J&EM, GB 165-0161, box 63, file 3.

132. "Report on Experiences of St. George's School, prepared for Palestine Royal Commission," MECA, J&EM, GB 165-0161, box 63, file 3.

133. S. P. Emery, "Concerning the Work of the English High School Haifa, during the Recent Political Unhappiness," December 5, 1936, MECA, J&EM, GB 165-0161, box 63, file 3.

134. Winifred A. Coate, "The System of Mixed Schools in Palestine with special reference to the Jerusalem Girls' College," January 6, 1937, MECA, J&EM, GB 165-0161, box 63, file 3.

135. Winifred A. Coate to the archdeacon, April 29, 1936, MECA, J&EM, GB 165-0161, box 63, file 3.

136. Dorothy Norman to her family, May 17, 1936, MECA, Norman Collection, GB 165-0219.

137. Ibid.

138. Porath, *Palestinian Arab National Movement*, 269–271; Ted Swedenburg, *Memories of Revolt: The 1936–1939 Rebellion and the Palestinian National Past* (Minneapolis: University of Minnesota Press, 1995), 90.

139. Coate, "The System of Mixed Schools in Palestine."

140. H. M. Wilson, "School Year in Palestine, 1938–1939," 19, MECA, GB 165-1302.

141. Ibid., 54.

142. Humphrey Bowman, director of Department of Education to district commissioners, October 13, 1936, ISA, RG 2, 126/4M file E/44/36; director of Department of Education to chief secretary, October 17, 1936, ISA, RG 2, 126/4M file E/44/36.

143. Rushdi Shawwa, mayor of Gaza, to chief secretary, September 20, 1939; Jerome Farrell, director of education to chief secretary, November 1, 1939, and March 27, 1940; M. Tomlinson for director of education to chief secretary, July 6, 1946, ISA, RG 2, box 126/6M file E/59/37.

144. Porath, *Palestinian Arab National Movement*, 268.

145. Swedenburg, *Memories of Revolt*, 30–32.

146. "20 Deaths in Palestine," *Times*, September 5, 1938.

147. Fleischmann, *Nation and Its "New" Women*, 134.

148. Swedenburg, *Memories of Revolt*, 183.

149. Fleischmann, *Nation and Its "New" Women*, 134.

150. "A Christian view of unveiling," *Filastin*, May 26, 1927.

151. "Oh for shame, Muslim women in Tel Aviv: Threat of chaos," *al-Sirat al-mustaqim*, March 21, 1932.

152. Predelli, "Sexual Control and the Remaking of Gender," 87.

153. Fleischmann, *Nation and Its "New" Women*, 73–80.

154. Thompson, *Colonial Citizens*, ch. 7; Margot Badran, *Feminists, Islam, and Nation: Gender and the Making of Modern Egypt* (Princeton: Princeton University Press, 1995), 67–69, 91–94; Baron, *Egypt as a Woman*, 36; Fleischmann, *Nation and Its "New" Women*, 30.

155. See Walid Khalidi, *Before Their Diaspora: A Photographic History of the Palestinians 1876–1948* (Washington, D.C.: Institute of Palestine Studies, 1991), 101, photograph 93, for a good illustration of the changing styles of veiling in Mandate Palestine.

156. Swedenburg, *Memories of Revolt*, 183.

157. I am borrowing the term *downveiling* from Linda Herrera, who has used it to refer to the (current) tendency of urban women and girls to wear less concealing and less conservative Islamic dress. See her "Downveiling: Gender and the Contest over Culture in Cairo," *Middle East Report*, no. 219 (Summer 2001): 16–19.

158. Vashitz, *Ha-ʿaravim be-erets-yisrael*, 219.

159. Espie Emery to Mr. Matthew, November 22, 1938, MECA, J&EM, GB 165-0161, box 55, file 2.

160. Swedenburg, *Memories of Revolt*, 30.

161. Espie Emery to her mother, October 8, 1938, MECA, GB 165-0099, Emery Collection, box 1, file 4.

162. Espie Emery to Mr. Matthew, November 22, 1938, MECA, J&EM, GB 165-0161, box 55, file 2.

163. Fleischmann, *Nation and Its "New" Women*, 133.

164. Ibid., 169.

165. Ibid., 121.

166. Coate, "The System of Mixed Schools in Palestine."

167. S. P. Emery to Mr. Matthew, November 22, 1938, MECA, J&EM, GB 165-0161, box 55, file 2.

168. Coate, "The System of Mixed Schools in Palestine."

CHAPTER 4

AUTHOR'S NOTE: Originally published in a slightly different form as "Educating Muslim Girls in Mandatory Jerusalem," *International Journal of Middle East Studies* 36, no. 1 (February 2004): 1–19. © 2004 Cambridge University Press. Reprinted with permission.

1. Hajj Amin al-Husayni to inspector of Islamic schools, September 22, 1935, IIRHR, 13/39/2,35/1/75.

2. Tibawi, *Arab Education*, 175.

3. Anderson, *Imagined Communities*, 120–122.

4. See, for example, Barbara Reeves-Ellington, "A Vision of Mount Holyoke in the Ottoman Balkans: American Cultural Transfer, Bulgarian Nation-Building and Women's Educational Reform, 1858–1870," *Gender and History* 16, no. 1 (2004): 146–171, and Strohmeier, "Muslim Education."

5. Khalidi, "Society and Ideology in Late Ottoman Syria," 124.

6. Alf Andrew Heggoy and Paul J. Zingg, "French Education in Revolutionary North Africa," *International Journal of Middle East Studies* 7, no. 4 (October 1976): 575–576.

7. See, for example, Anderson, *Imagined Communities*, 123–124; Reeva S. Simon, "The Education of an Iraqi Ottoman Army Officer," in *The Origins of Arab Nationalism*, ed. Rashid Khalidi et al. (New York: Columbia University Press, 1991), 163; Sharkey, *Living with Colonialism*, ch. 4.

8. About the Islamic Girls' School in Haifa, see Head of Education Committee Yahi al-Shihabi to Headmistress Sabiha al-Tanir, Haifa, December 8, 1925, IIRHR, 13/25/2,66/1/75; Headmistress Sabiha al-Tanir to president of the SMC, July 20, 1926, IIRHR, 5/26/2,1/75.

9. Fleischmann, *Nation and Its "New" Women*, 104.

10. Thompson, *Colonial Citizens*, 96.

11. About the schools founded by Nasser and Shuqair, see Farah, *Ta'rikh al-kanisa al-usqufiyya*, 1:210, 354–355; Mogannam, *Arab Woman*, 254; Mary Shihada, "Our national schools," *Mir'at al-sharq*, July 12, 1935; "The National high school in Bethlehem," *Mir'at al-sharq*, August 21, 1935; "Nationalist girls' school," *al-Karmil*, July 2, 1932.

12. "The Amina Shufani school for girls," *al-Karmil*, July 29, 1928.

13. "The Amina Shufani school in Haifa," *al-Karmil*, August 26, 1928.

14. For a partial list of nationalist schools, and number of pupils, see "Schedule of Schools not provided by Government School Medical Services," December 31, 1941, CZA, J17/8356.

15. Government of Palestine, Department of Education, *Annual Report 1935–1936*, table XVI, "Moslem schools (non public) teachers and pupils classified by locality and sex," 82.

16. Government of Palestine, Department of Education, *Education in Palestine General Survey 1945–1946*, 8.

17. Tibawi, "Report on Education," 9.

18. Calculations based on "Schedule of Schools Not Provided by Government School Service," December 31, 1946, CZA, J17/8356.

19. Kupferschmidt, *Supreme Muslim Council*, 143.

20. Al-majlis al-sharʿi al-islami al-aʿla, *Bayan al-majlis al-sharʿi al-islami al-aʿla fi filastin le-sana 1340–1341 (1921–1922)*; al-Majlis al-sharʿi al-islami al-aʿla, *Bayan al-majlis al-sharʿi al-islami al-aʿla fi filastin le-sana, 1341–1342 (1922–1923)*.

21. About al-Najah school, see Matthews, *Confronting an Empire*, 50–51.

22. Government of Palestine, Department of Education, *Annual Report 1925–1926*, table III, "Government Schools," and table V, "Non-government schools: distribution by communities."

23. Head of the Local Education Committee to president of the SMC, July 7, 1926, IIRHR, 13/25/2,31/1/75.

24. Register of pupils, IIRHR, 13/1925/1,1/2/75.

25. Government of Palestine, Department of Education, *Annual Report 1930–1931*, 37.

26. Petition from Muslims in ʿAjami to president of the SMC, 1929, IIRHR, 16/29/2,12/1/75.

27. Inspector of Islamic schools to general director of *awqaf*, March 20, 1940, IIRHR, 15/44/1,6/1/75.

28. Woodsmall, Bound Reports, 325–326,. Also quoted in Woodsmall, *Moslem Women*, 196.

29. Woodsmall, Bound Reports, 325.

30. President of the SMC to governor of Jerusalem, October 1, 1925, IIRHR, 13/25/2,31/1/75.

31. "Muslim Girls' School, Herod's Gate," ISA, RG 10, 1540M, file 18/1/180.

32. About Munira Saffuri, see American University of Beirut Alumni Association, *Al-kulliya: The Alumni Journal of the American University of Beirut* 20, no. 3 (February 1, 1934): 96.

33. President of the SMC to the director of the Islamic Orphanage, August 2, 1931, IIRHR, 13/25/2,31/1/75.

34. See her employee registration, IIRHR, 13/39/1,20/1/75.

35. Nuzha, interview by the author and Khader Salameh, Jerusalem, June 14, 2000; Serene Husseini Shahid, *Jerusalem Memories* (Beirut: Naufal Group, 2000), 13.

36. Michelle Maskiell, "Social Change and Social Control: College-Educated Punjabi Women 1913 to 1960," *Modern Asian Studies* 19, no. 1 (1985): 61.

37. About these women, see Nuzha, interview by the author and Khader Salameh, Jerusalem, July 20, 2000; see also Melia al-Sakakini's employee file, IIRHR 13/39/1,17/1/75.

38. ʿAnbara Salam al-Khalidi, *Jawla fi al-dhikrayat bayn lubnan wa-filastin* (Beirut: Dar al-nahar lil-nashr, 1966), 66–67.

39. October 31, 1923, decision no. 285, Qism ihyaʾ al-turath al-islami, *Qarirat al-majlis al-sharʿi al-islami al-aʿla wa-qarirat lijan al-awqaf al-mahaliyya*, vol. 5 (Jerusalem, 1994), 134.

40. Daphne Tsimhoni, "British Mandate and Arab Christians in Palestine 1920–1925" (Ph.D. diss., University of London, 1976), 270.

41. Nuzha, interview, June 14, 2000.

42. Suʿad, telephone interview with the author, February 9, 2003; Register of pupils, IIRHR, 13/1925/1,1/2/75; Ilan Pappe, *Atsilat ha-arets: mishpahat al-Husayni* (Jerusalem: Bialik Institute, 2002), 321–322, 344.

43. Nuzha, interview, July 20, 2000.

44. Application of Naʿamati al-ʿAlami to study in Egypt, 1927, IIRHR, —/27/4,5/2/75.

45. Application of Ruwaida ʿUthman al-Shihabi for employment, IIRHR, 13/37/2,74/1/7; Headmistress Matilde Saʿad to inspector of schools regarding Suʿad al-Kazami, October 30, 1928, IIRHR, —/28/4,9/2/75.

46. See their entries in "Register of pupils Jerusalem 1927," IIRHR, 13/1927/1,2/17.

47. O'Donnell Commission Report, paragraph 131, CO 733/208/87330.

48. Inspector of Islamic schools to headmistress, Islamic Girls' School of Jerusalem, April 28, 1930, IIRHR, 13/30/2,17/1/75.

49. Salim Butrus Mikha'il to the mufti of Palestine, October 14, 1930, IIRHR, 13/30/2,17/1/75.

50. See, for example, list of thirteen girls from the Islamic Orphanage who had reached the age of marriage, circa 1930, IIRHR, 13/30/2,17/1/75.

51. Inspector of Islamic schools to Khalil Hamuda, October 16, 1930, IIRHR, 13/30/2,17/1/75.

52. Government of Palestine, Department of Education, *Annual Report 1929–1930*, 29.

53. Register of pupils, IIRHR, 13/1925/1,1/2/75.

54. Suʿad, telephone interview with the author, March 15, 2003.

55. Suʿad, interview, February 9, 2003.

56. Nuzha, interview, June 14, 2000, and July 20, 2000; al-Madrasa al-islamiyya lil-banat, *Barnamaj al-madrasa al-islamiyya lil-banat fi al-quds sana 1929–1930*, IIRHR, 13/30/2,16/1/75.

57. Rebecca Rogers, "Boarding Schools, Women Teachers, and Domesticity: Reforming Girls' Secondary Education in the First Half of the Nineteenth Century," *French Historical Studies* 19, no. 1 (Spring 1995): 161, 163.

58. Kupferschmidt, *Supreme Muslim Council*, 136–137, 179–182.

59. Pupils of the third secondary and first secondary classes from the boarding school to the president of the Supreme Muslim Council, January 10, 1931, IIRHR, 13/31/5,31/2/75.

60. Shahid, *Jerusalem Memories*, 13–17, 73–74.

61. See Register of Pupils, IIRHR, 13/1925/1,1/2/75. See also Shahid, *Jerusalem Memories*, 73–74. It appears that at some point the Islamic Girls' School reintroduced its boarding section, as some pupils who attended the school in 1940–1941 were listed in the Register of Pupils as residing in the "boarding section."

62. Director of the Islamic Orphanage to head of SMC, July 29, 1931, IIRHR, 13/25/2,31/1/75.

63. General director of the awqaf to the deputy of the SMC, August 16, 1933, IIRHR, 13/47/2,104/1/75.

64. See Okkenhaug, *Quality of Heroic Living*, 215. It is not clear if the Arab teachers at this school were Palestinian or hailed from elsewhere.

65. Samiha Rassas to inspector of ahliyya schools, February 25, 1935, IIRHR, 0/35/1,10/1/75,

66. Ishaq Darwish, inspector of Islamic schools, to director of awqaf, October 16, 1934, IIRHR, 0/34/2,14/1/75.

67. Ishaq Darwish, inspector of Islamic schools, to director of awqaf, November 23, 1935, IIRHR, 13/47/2,100/1/75.

68. Inspector of Islamic schools to director of awqaf, August 15, 1938, IIRHR, 13/38/2,76/1/75.

69. Headmistress to inspector of Islamic schools, April 17, 1939, IIRHR, 0/39/2,19/1/75.

70. Register of pupils, 1939–1940, IIRHR, 13/1925/1,1/2/75.

71. Headmistress to inspector of Islamic schools, May 13, 1939, IIRHR, 0/39/2,21/1/75.

72. Rochelle Davis, "The Growth of the Western Communities, 1917–1948," in *Jerusalem 1948: The Arab Neighbourhoods and Their Fate in the War,* ed. Salim Tamari (Jerusalem: Institute of Jerusalem Studies; Bethlehem: Badil Resource Center, 1999), 38–39.

73. Mahmoud Yazbak, "Muslim Orphans and the Shari'a in Ottoman Palestine according to Sijill Records," *Journal of the Social and Economic History of the Orient* 44, no. 2 (May 2001): 123–140.

74. Al-Majlis al-shar'i al-islami al-a'la, *Bayan al-majlis al-shar'i al-islami al-a'la fi filastin le sana 1340–1341 hijri (1921–1922),* 3.

75. Dar al-aytam al-islamiyya al-sina'iyya, *Majallat dar al-aytam al-islamiyya al-sina'iyya fi bayt al-maqdis,* nos. 1–2 (1932): 5.

76. Headmaster of the Islamic Orphanage to the president of the SMC, August 24, 1924, and November 30, 1924, IIRHR, 13/38/5,23/2/75.

77. Vice director of the Department of Education to president of the SMC, August 10, 1926, IIRHR, 13/26/5,27/2/75.

78. See, for example, "Picture speaks of the humanitarian efforts of our ladies," *Filastin,* January 13, 1940.

79. Members of the SMC to the general director of the *awqaf,* December 26, 1938, IIRHR, 13/38/2,31/1/75.

80. Headmaster of the Islamic Orphanage to inspector of Islamic schools, October 27, 1940, IIRHR, 13/39/1,20/1/75.

81. Ibid.

82. Inspector of Islamic schools to the members of the SMC, May 25, 1942, IIRHR, 13/39/1,23/1/75.

83. Medical officer to assistant district commissioner of Hebron, December 24, 1941, ISA, RG 10, 1537M, file 18/6.

84. Government of Palestine, Department of Social Welfare, *Annual Report 1944,* 16.

85. Tibawi, *Arab Education,* 250; "Jaffa School Lunch Scheme," *Palestine Post,* December 8, 1942.

86. Tibawi, *Arab Education*, 253. See also Government of Palestine, Department of Social Welfare, *Annual Report 1944*, 32.

87. Inspector of Islamic schools to the members of the SMC, May 25, 1942, IIRHR, 13/39/1,23/1/75.

88. Inspector of education of the Department of Education to heads of the Bakriyya and Musrara Schools, February 1, 1943, IIRHR, 13/43/5,12/2/75.

89. Headmaster of al-Najah School to inspector of ahliyya schools, July 24, 1927, IIRHR, 0/27/2,1/1/75.

90. Inspector of Islamic schools to headmistress, January 8, 1928, IIRHR, 13/28/2,9/1/75.

91. Inspector of Islamic schools to president of the SMC, June 14, 1928, IIRHR, 0/32/2,10/1/75.

92. List of weekly study hours, August 21, 1938, IIRHR, 15/38/2,6/1/75.

93. Government of Palestine, Department of Education, *Elementary School Syllabus, 1925*, 71–73. Christian students in both rural and urban government schools followed the same course of instruction in the principles of their own religions. See both Hukumat filastin, Idarat al-maʿarif, *Minhaj al-taʿlim al-ibtidaʾi fi madaris al-qura* (Jerusalem, 1929), 8–10, and *Elementary School Syllabus*, 74.

94. See Hukumat filastin, Idarat al-maʿarif al-ʿamma, *Minhaj al-din al-islami* (Jerusalem, 1947).

95. Hukumat filastin, *Minhaj al-taʿlim al-ibtidaʾi fi madaris al-qura*, 3, and "Barnamaj lil-kul al-sufuf fi madaris al-qura lil-banat," ISA, RG 8, 1011M, file 557/18.

96. Rema Hammami, "Between Heaven and Earth: Transformations in Religiosity and Labor among Southern Palestinian Peasant and Refugee Women, 1920–1993" (Ph.D. diss., Temple University, 1994), 79.

97. Ibid., 96, 100.

98. Woodsmall, Bound Reports, 326, box 25, Woodsmall Papers, SSC.

99. Nuzha, interview, July 20, 2000.

100. Suʿad, telephone interview with the author, February 12, 2003. In the interview, she used the word *nylon* for silk. Nylon, however, was not invented until 1940, and was not readily available until after World War II.

101. Al-madrasa al-islamiyya lil-banat, *Barnamaj al-madrasa al-islamiyya lil-banat fi al-quds sana 1929–1930*, IIRHR, 13/30/2,16/1/75.

102. Nuzha Darwish, interview, 20 July 2000.

103. "The first Palestinian woman's congress," *al-Jamiʿa al-ʿarabiyya*, October 28, 1929.

104. "Jerusalem: the great meeting of Arab schoolgirls," *al-Difaʿ*, May 14, 1936; "Ladies of Jerusalem examine the current situation," *al-Difaʿ*, July 15, 1936.

105. Fleischmann, *Nation and Its "New" Women*, 129–130; "The great meeting of Arab schoolgirls, *al-Difaʿ*, May 14, 1936.

106. Headmistress to inspector of Islamic schools, March 22, 1939; March 27, 1939; March 29, 1939; April 24, 1939; May 1, 1939, IIRHR, 13/35/2,21/1/75.

107. See, for example, headmistress to inspector of Islamic schools, thanking him

for the book *Ta'rikh ghazawat al-'arab* by Amir Shakib Arsalan, November 4, 1934, IIRHR, 0/33/2,12/1/75, and similar letter acknowledging the inspector for sending a book of *fatawa* issued by the mufti of Palestine against selling land to Jews, December 6, 1934, IIRHR, 13/38/2,34/1/75.

108. Inspector of Islamic schools to the Islamic schools, August 4, 1935, IIRHR, 0/35/1,2/1/75. About the development of the Palestinian flag, see Tamir Sorek, "The Orange and the 'Cross in the Crescent': Imagining Palestine in 1929," *Nations and Nationalism* 10, no. 3 (2004): 269–291.

109. Inspector of Islamic schools to the Islamic schools, February 1, 1936, IIRHR, 0/35/1,2/1/75.

110. Inspector of Islamic schools to the Islamic schools, February 24, 1936, IIRHR, 0/35/1,2/1/75.

111. For a description of school decorations, see IIRHR, 13/44/1,22/1/75.

112. About these teachers, see inspector of Islamic schools to director of *awqaf*, October 26, 1932, IIRHR, 13/32/1,10/1/75; List of teaching staff, 1938, IIRHR, 13/33/1,11/1/75; Certificate of study of Amna Rashid Sha'th and Husniyya Yusuf Sha'th, July 13, 1928, IIRHR, 15/28/1,2/1/75.

113. Zainat Nur al-Din to inspector of ahliyya education, December 25, 1928, IIRHR, 13/27/4,2/2/75, and inspector of ahliyya education to Zainat Nur al-Din, December 30, 1928, IIRHR, 13/27/4,2/2/75.

114. Lois Wilson to inspector of Islamic Schools, July 17, 1930, IIRHR, 13/30/1,12/2/95.

115. About the formation of the Girl Guides Movement, see Allen Warren, "Citizens of the Empire: Baden-Powell, Scouts and Guides and an Imperial Ideal, 1900–40," in *Imperialism and Popular Culture*, ed. John M. Mackenzie (Manchester: Manchester University Press, 1986).

116. V. M. Talbot-Rice to inspector of Islamic schools, March 28, 1929, IIRHR, 13/29/1,1/2/95.

117. Headmistress Matilde Sa'ad to inspector of Islamic schools, April 1, 1929, IIRHR, 13/29/1,1/2/95.

118. Teacher Munira al-Saffuri to inspector of ahliyya schools, March 17, 1929, IIRHR, 13/29/1,1/2/95.

119. "Praiseworthy zeal," *al-Jami'a al-'arabiyya*, February 21, 1927.

120. Report by inspector of Islamic schools, January 8, 1928, IIRHR, 13/28/2,9/1/75.

121. A. L. Tibawi, "Educational Policy and Arab Nationalism in Mandatory Palestine," *Die Welt des Islams*, n.s., 4, no. 1 (1955): 18.

122. Inspector of the Islamic schools, report on Islamic Girls' School, Jerusalem, April 21, 1930, IIRHR, 13/48/2,54/1/75.

123. Su'ad, telephone interview with the author, February 16, 2003.

124. Circular from inspector of Islamic schools to schools of the SMC, including the Islamic Girls' Schools, September 20, 1937, IIRHR, 16/36/2,26/1/75.

125. Ibid.

126. Swedenburg, *Memories of Revolt*, 179.

127. Inspector of Islamic schools to headmistress, Islamic Girls' School, September 10, 1940, and September 15, 1940, IIRHR, 0/40/2,26/1/75. The curriculum was published under al-Majlis al-islami al-aʿla, Idarat taftish al-madaris al-islamiyya, *Minhaj al-taʿlim al-ibtidaʾi* (Jerusalem: Matbaʿat dar al-aytam al-islamiyya, 1942/1361).

128. Al-majlis al-sharʿi al-islami al-aʿla, *Bayan al-majlis ʿan al-sanawat, 1361, 1362–1363 (1942–1944)*, table 10.

129. Headmistress, Islamic Girls' School in Nazareth to inspector of ahliyya schools, December 19, 1927, IIRHR, 15/28/1,2/1/75.

130. Headmistress, Islamic Girls' School in Jaffa to inspector of Islamic schools, July 25, 1938, IIRHR, 0/34/2,14/1/75.

131. Inspector of Islamic schools to assistant director of awqaf, August 1, 1944, IIRHR, 13/44/2,44/1/75.

132. Headmistress, Islamic Girls' School in Jaffa to inspector of Islamic schools, May 7, 1944, IIRHR, 13/44/5,14/2/75.

133. Secretary of the SMC to general director of awqaf, September 21, 1938, IIRHR, 13/38/2,76/1/75.

134. *Qadi* of Nazareth to president of the SMC, October 22, 1925, IIRHR, 15/28/1,3/1/75.

CHAPTER 5

1. "The mothers of tomorrow," *Filastin*, July 1, 1932, and August 24, 1932.

2. Raqib, "For all to be sincere in their work," *Filastin*, April 22, 1924.

3. Pollard, *Nurturing the Nation*, 128.

4. Seth Koven and Sonya Michel, "Womanly Duties: Maternalist Policies and the Origins of Welfare States in France, Germany, Great Britain, and the United States, 1880–1920," *American Historical Review* 95 (October 1990): 1077.

5. Anna Davin, "Imperialism and Motherhood," *History Workshop Journal* no. 5 (Spring 1978): 9–65.

6. Ibid., 26.

7. About health problems in historical Palestine, see Nira Reiss, "British Public Health Policy in Palestine, 1918–1947," in *Health and Disease in the Holy Land*, ed. Manfred Waserman and Samuel S. Kottek (Lewiston, NY: Edwin Mellen Press, 1996), 301–327; Iris Borowy, "Health in Interwar Palestine: Ethnic Realities and International Views," *Dynamis Acta Hisp. Med. Sci. Hist. Illus.* 25 (2005): 423–450; I. J. Kligler, "Public Health in Palestine," *Annals of the American Academy of Political and Social Science* 164 (November 1932): 167–177.

8. Erika B. Simmons, *Hadassah and the Zionist Project* (Lanham, MD: Rowman and Littlefield, 2006), 54.

9. Ibid., 21, 58–59; Mary McCune, "Social Workers in the *Muskeljudentum:*

'Hadassah Ladies,' 'Manly Men' and the Significance of Gender in the American Zionist Movement, 1912–1928," *American Jewish History* 86, no. 2 (June 1998): 147–148.

10. Dafna Hirsh, "'Anu mefitsim kan tarbut'—ḥinukh le-higena, ba-yishuv ha-yehudi ba-erets yisrael ba-tequfat ha-mandat ha-briti" (master's thesis, Tel Aviv University, 2000), 33–25, 41–42.

11. American Colony Aid Association, *Annual Report of the American Colony Aid Association for the Year 1929–1930*, 2.

12. Ibid., 5.

13. Ibid., 6–8.

14. Sadhij Nassar, "The woman's page: The home," *al-Karmil*, March 4, 1928.

15. "Women's education in Palestine," *Filastin*, September 20, 1927.

16. Muhammad al-Tahir, "The effects of the woman on the social system," *al-Difaʿ*, August 5, 1935.

17. Yusuf Haikal, "About the Palestinian woman," *Filastin*, April 9, 1927.

18. See, for example, ʾAref Abu-Rabiʿa, "Indigenous Practices among Palestinians for Healing Eye Diseases and Inflammations," *Dynamis Acta Hisp. Med. Sci. Hist. Illus.* 25 (2005): 383–401.

19. Dafna Hirsh, "'Almost Every Immigrant Child Is a Problem': School Hygiene and the Immigration of People and Ideas in Mandatory Palestine" (paper presented at the annual meeting of the Association for Israel Studies, Open University of Israel, June 2007), 2.

20. Government of Palestine, Department of Health, *Annual Report for the Year 1930*, 7–8.

21. Vester, "Moslem Girls' School, Draft of Chap. 26 of Our Jerusalem," p. 9.

22. Ibid.

23. Boyd, *History of Western Education*, 417.

24. "Instructions for the Medical Inspection of Schools and School Children," August 15, 1923, CZA, S2/448.

25. Government of Palestine, Department of Health, *Annual Report of the Department of Health for the Year 1921*, 47.

26. Woodsmall, *Moslem Women*, 331.

27. Acting director, Department of Health, to secretary, Palestine Zionist Executive, August 16, 1928, CZA, J1/3143.

28. See, for example, Government of Palestine, Department of Health, *Annual Report of the Department of Health for the Year 1927*, 43.

29. Ibid. See also "Instructions for the Medical Inspection of Schools and School Children."

30. "Instructions for the Medical Inspection of Schools and School Children."

31. Ibid.

32. Fleischmann, *Nation and Its "New" Women*, 49.

33. Inspector of Islamic schools to headmistress, October 18, 1933, IIRHR, 13/33/1,11/1/75.

34. Headmistress to inspector of Islamic schools, February 14, 1935, IIRHR, 13/33/1,11/1/75.

35. Su'ad, interview, February 12, 2003.

36. Palestine Sessional Papers, "Advisory Council Minutes," March 8, 1921, 7–8, National Archives, PRO, CO 814/6; Government of Palestine, Department of Health, *Annual Report for the Year 1923*, 47.

37. "Instructions for the Medical Inspection of Schools and School Children," August 15, 1923, CZA, S2/448.

38. Government of Palestine, Department of Health, *Annual Report of the Department of Health for the Year 1927*, 43–44.

39. Reiss, "British Public Health Policy," 309–310.

40. Sandra M. Sufian, *Healing the Land and the Nation: Malaria and the Zionist Project in Palestine, 1920–1947* (Chicago and London: University of Chicago Press, 2007), 250.

41. About Brachyahu, see Hirsh, "Anu mefitsim kan tarbut," 55–56.

42. Department of Education, *Annual Report for the Year 1924*, 20; Executive Committee for Health Week, Jerusalem, "Report Health Week, November 17–30, 1924."

43. Nahid, interview by Ellen Fleischmann, Amman, January 28, 1993.

44. Jasamin Rostam-Kolayi, "Foreign Education, the Women's Press, and the Discourse of Scientific Domesticity in Early-Twentieth Century Iran," in *Iran and the Surrounding World: Interactions in Culture and Cultural Politics*, ed. Nikki R. Keddie and Rudi Matthee (Seattle and London: University of Washington Press, 2002), 191.

45. Jamal Khalidi, district inspector of education to director of education, February 1, 1922, ISA, RG 8 1010M, file 412/EN.

46. About the incorporation of European styles in Ottoman wedding dresses, see Nancy Micklewright, "Late-Nineteenth-Century Ottoman Wedding Costumes as Indicators of Social Change," *Muqarnas* 6 (1989): 161–174.

47. Okkenhaug, *Quality of Heroic Living*, 112.

48. "Report on the Islamic Girls' School (Jerusalem)," December 29, 1927, IIRHR, 13/28/2,9/1/75.

49. For a description of this way of eating, see Jabra Ibrahim Jabra, *The First Well: A Bethlehem Boyhood* (Fayetteville: University of Arkansas Press, 1995), 11.

50. See, for example, an advertisement for Ovaltine, *Filastin*, March 21, 1926. See also Pollard, *Nurturing the Nation*, 183–184, about a political caricature depicting Egypt as a modern woman seated at a dining table, being served by England.

51. Espie Emery to her mother, July 21, 1941, MECA, Emery Collection, GB 165-0099, box 1, file 6.

52. Headmistress of the Islamic Girls' School in Nazareth to inspector of ahliyya schools, November 22, 1927, IIRHR, 15/28/1,2/1/75.

53. Headmistress of the Islamic Girls' School in Nazareth to inspector of Islamic Schools, January 11, 1928, IIRHR, 15/28/1,2/1/75.

54. John Welshman, "Physical Culture and Sports in England and Wales, 1900–40," *International Journal of the History of Sport* 15, no. 1 (April 1998): 54–75.

55. See, for example, medical officer to assistant district commissioner of Hebron, December 24, 1941, ISA, RG 10, 1537M, file 18/6.

56. Ridler, "Special Problems in the Training of Women Teachers," 30.

57. About physical education in London, see Kathleen E. McCrone, *Playing the Game: Sport and Physical Emancipation of English Women, 1870–1914* (Lexington: University Press of Kentucky, 1988), 61.

58. Tamir Sorek, "The Sports Column as a Site of Palestinian Nationalism in the 1940s," *Israel Affairs* 13, no. 3 (2007): 605–616; Issam Khalidi, "Body and Ideology: Early Athletics in Palestine (1900–1948)," *Jerusalem Quarterly* 27 (Summer 2006): 44–58.

59. Ishaq al-Husayni, "Sports," *Majallat rawdat al-ma'arif* 4, no. 1 (January 1932): 36–37.

60. "Sports curriculum," n.d., IIRHR, 13/?/2,80/1/75.

61. Okkenhaug, *Quality of Heroic Living*, 154.

62. Julia Baramki, "School Games," *Jerusalem Girls' College Magazine* (June 1931): 44.

63. Department of Education, *Annual Report 1933–1934*, 46.

64. See, for example, A. MacInnes, "Games," *Jerusalem Girls' College Magazine* (June 1933): 8; "Winners of the girls' schools in basketball," *Filastin*, April 8, 1940, for names of different schools that played against one another.

65. Su'ad, interview, February 12, 2003.

66. Sorek, "Sports Column," 613.

67. Ibid.

68. Woodsmall, Bound reports, 313.

69. Government of Palestine, Department of Education, *Annual Report 1923*, 9.

70. Netball is an offshoot of basketball, created specifically for women in Britain in 1895, and then brought to the British colonies by women schoolteachers. In netball, the court divides into three sections, rather than two as in basketball, and players are required to touch the ball in all three parts of the court, presumably making the game somewhat easier. About the gendering of sports in Britain, see McCrone, *Playing the Game*, 91–92.

71. Senior medical officer to secretary, District Housing Commission, April 7, 1927, RG 10, 1539M, 18/1/98.

72. American Colony Aid Association, *Annual Report*, 1931–1932.

73. American Colony Aid Association, *Annual Report*, 1933–1934.

74. American Colony Aid Association, *Annual Report*, 1929–1930.

75. Inspector of Islamic schools to heads of schools, September 6, 1945, and September 19, 1946, IIRHR, 13/44/2,44/1/75.

76. Inés Dussel, "When Appearances Are Not Deceptive: A Comparative History of School Uniforms in Argentina and the United States (Nineteenth–Twentieth Centuries)," *Paedagogica Historica* 41, nos. 1–2 (February 2005): 184.

77. Okkenhaug, *Quality of Heroic Living*, 133, 137–138.

78. Dussel, "When Appearances Are Not Deceptive."

79. Inspector of Islamic schools to SMC, October 1, 1940, IIRHR, 13/40/5,11/2/75.

80. Anna Davin, *Growing up Poor: Home, School and Street in London 1870–1914* (London: Rivers Oram Press, 1996), 137.

81. A. Goodrich-Freer, *Inner Jerusalem* (London, 1904), 63.

82. Inspector of ahliyya schools to headmistress, Islamic Girls' School Nazareth, June 9, 1927, IIRHR, 15/28/1,2/1/75.

83. Dorothy Norman to her mother, October 7, 1934, MECA, Norman Collection, GB 165-0219.

84. Winifred C. Coate to Mr. Bickersteth, December 7, 1929, MECA, J&EM, GB 165-0161, box 42, file 3.

85. Dorothy Norman to her family, February 8, 1944, MECA, Norman Collection, GB 165-0219.

86. "Report required by the Royal Commission," by Headmistress Ruth L. P. Clark, Christ Church Girls' School Jerusalem, January 5, 1937, MECA, J&EM, GB 165-0161, box 63, file 3.

87. Småberg, "Ambivalent Friendship," 235–238.

88. To the best of my knowledge, the only photographs taken of this school were by Khalil Ra'ad in 1929, of children in the kindergarten class and an exhibit of embroidered items. They were published in the school's program for 1929. See al-Madrasa al-islamiyya lil-banat, *Barnamaj al-madrasa al-islamiyya lil-banat fi al-quds sana 1929–1930*, IIRHR, 13/30/2,16/1/75.

89. Su'ad, interview, February 12, 2003, and February 16, 2003.

90. Inspector of Islamic schools to headmistress, Islamic Girls' School, January 8, 1928, IIRHR, 13/28/2,9/1/75.

91. Robert H. Eisenman, *Islamic Law in Palestine and Israel: A History of the Survival of Tanzimat and Shari'a in the British Mandate and Jewish State* (Leiden: Brill, 1978), 36–39.

92. Mahmoud Yazbak, "Minor Marriages and *Khiyār al-bulūgh* in Ottoman Palestine: A Note on Women's Strategies in a Patriarchal Society," *Islamic Law and Society* 9, no. 3 (2002): 390.

93. Judith E. Tucker, "Marriage and Family in Nablus, 1720–1856: Toward a History of Arab Marriage," *Journal of Family History* 13, no. 2 (1988): 173.

94. Margalit Shilo, *Princess or Prisoner? Jewish Women in Jerusalem, 1840–1914* (Waltham: Brandeis University Press, 2005), 38–41. About marriages during the same period in Haifa's Muslim community, see Yazbak, "Minor Marriages and *Khiyār al-bulūgh*."

95. Baron, "Making and Breaking of Marital Bonds in Modern Egypt," 281–282.

96. Frans van Poppel and Jan Nelissen, "The Proper Age to Marry: Social Norms

and Behavior in Nineteenth-Century Netherlands," *History of the Family* 4, no. 1 (1999): 51–75.

97. Padma Anagol-McGinn, "The Age of Consent Act (1891) Reconsidered: Women's Perspectives and Participation in the Child-Marriage Controversy in India," *South Asia Research* 12, no. 2 (November 1992): 100–118.

98. Eleanor Rathbone to J. B. Williams, Colonial Office, June 30, 1933 CO 733/277/75132, and other letters in this file.

99. Draft of memorandum enclosed in letter from high commissioner of Palestine to Philip Cunster-Lister, January 3, 1935, CO 733/277/75132.

100. "Criminal Code Ordinance 1936," section 182, *Palestine Gazette* no. 633, September 28, 1936; Eisenman, *Islamic Law in Palestine and Israel,* 103–104.

101. High commissioner for Palestine to secretary of state for the colonies, May 20, 1933, CO 733/238/17332.

102. Vashitz, *Ha-'aravim be-erets-yisrael,* 207.

103. Woodsmall, *Moslem Women,* 100.

104. Al-majlis al-shar'i al-islami al-a'la, *Manshur fi al-muhur* (Jerusalem: Matba'at dar al-aytam al-islamiyya, 1348). See also al-Majlis al-shar'i al-islami al-a'la, *Nida' bisha'n al-muhur min da'irat al-ma'had al-diniyya* (Jerusalem: Matba'at dar al-aytam al-islamiyya, 1353).

105. Stockdale, *Colonial Encounters,* 137–138.

106. "No. 13. Khadigie Ersas," listed in "Christian Herald Orphans Conducted by the American Colony, List of Children."

107. American Colony Aid Association, *Annual Report for the Year 1930–1931.*

108. American Colony Aid Association, *Annual Report for the Year 1929–1930.*

109. American Colony Aid Association, *Annual Report for the Year 1927–1928.*

110. American Colony Aid Association, *Annual Report for the Year 1930–1931.*

111. Woodsmall, *Moslem Women,* 194.

112. Ibid.

113. Fleischmann, *Nation and Its "New" Women,* 42.

114. Millicent Fawcett, *Easter in Palestine, 1921–1922* (London, 1926), 144.

115. Fleischmann, *Nation and Its "New" Women,* 84–85.

116. Ibid., 53–54.

117. See her employment file, ISA, RG 8, 1036M, file 1363/11.

118. Mabel C. Warburton to Mr. Bickersteth, September 16, 1927, MECA, J&EM, GB 165-0161, box 42, file 1.

119. Hilda Ridler, "Note on Female Education in Palestine," Appendix A in Government of Palestine, Department of Education, *Annual Report for the Scholastic Year 1925–1926,* 14.

120. Bowman, *Middle-East Window,* 260.

121. "Program for all the classes in the village girls' schools," January 28, 1929, ISA, RG 8, 1011M, file 557/18.

122. Government of Palestine, Department of Education, *Annual Report for the School Year 1936–1937,* 13.

123. Glenna Matthews, *"Just a Housewife": The Rise and Fall of Domesticity in America* (New York and Oxford: Oxford University Press, 1987), 145–148; Barbara Ehrenreich and Deirdre English, *For Her Own Good: 150 Years of the Experts' Advice to Women* (New York: Anchor Press, 1979), ch. 5.

124. Government of Palestine, Department of Education, *Annual Report for the Year 1931–1932*, 17; Government of Palestine, Department of Education, *Annual Report for the Year 1932–1933*, 20.

125. Su'ad, interview, February 12, 2003; Widad, interview by the author and Bassam Quttine, Jerusalem, May 27, 2000.

126. Government of Palestine, Department of Education, *Annual Report 1930–1931*, 12.

127. Ridler, "Special Problems in the Training of Women Teachers," 30.

128. Government of Palestine, Department of Education, *Annual Report 1933–1934*, 8. See also treasurer to crown agents, June 9, 1921, CO 733/9/32662, about hiring English women specialists.

129. Davis, "The Growth of the Western Communities 1917-1948," 36.

130. Baron, *Women's Awakening*, 155. About these changes, see Tewfik Canaan, *The Palestinian Arab House, Its Architecture and Folklore* (Jerusalem: Syrian Orphanage Press, 1933).

131. Ad for Boutagi's store, *Al-Karmil*, September 29, 1926.

132. Mary Hancock, "Home Science and Nationalization of Domesticity in Colonial India," *Modern Asian Studies* 35, no. 4 (2001): 881.

133. Within the context of the Middle East, see Pollard, *Nurturing the Nation*, 122–128; Russell, "Creating the New Woman," esp. ch. 5.

134. See, for example, "The women's awakening," *al-Karmil*, April 18, 1926; "Two hands of women," *al-Karmil*, July 1, 1928; "So and so," *Mir'at al-sharq*, May 16, 1929.

135. See, for example, "The women's page," *al-Karmil*, December 5, 1926, and Sabiha Miqdadi, "The woman's page: woman's education and her upbringing," *Filastin*, May 29, 1931.

136. Fleischmann, *Nation and Its "New" Women*, 83.

137. Okkenhaug, *Quality of Heroic Living*, 126–131.

138. Jamal 'Adawi, "Pe'ilut ha-quakerim ha-Amerikanim," 165, 211.

139. Madrasat al-frindz lil-banat, *Barnamaj Madrasat al-frindz lil-banat 1931–1932*, 17.

140. Okkenhaug, *Quality of Heroic Living*, 74.

141. Government of Palestine, Palestine Board of Higher Studies, *Matriculation Examination*, 1925.

142. Government of Palestine, Palestine Board of Higher Studies, *Palestine Secondary School Certificate and Palestine Matriculation Certificate*, June 1934; Tibawi, *Arab Education*, 108. About the Board of Higher Studies and the matriculation exams, see Tibawi, *Arab Education*, 102–127.

143. "List of weekly study hours," signed by Su'ad al-Asir al-Husayni, August 21,

1938, IIRHR, 15/38/2,6/1/75; List of lessons in the Islamic Girls' School, 1945–1946, IIRHR, 13/48/2,55/1/75.

144. Fleischmann, *Nation and Its "New" Women*, 32.

145. Inspector of Islamic schools to headmistress, Islamic Girls' School, May 15, 1930, IIRHR, 13/47/2,100/1/75; Government of Palestine, Department of Education, *Annual Report 1931–1932*, 18.

146. Director of Health G. W. Heron to Hilda Ridler, and to senior medical officer, Jerusalem, March 27, 1937, ISA, RG 10, 1615M, file 66/5.

147. The Haifa Social Service and Infant Welfare Association, *Sixth Annual Report*, 1931.

148. Director of Education Humphrey Bowman to deputy district commissioner, Jerusalem, September 28, 1927, ISA, RG 23, 853/3M, file 19/31; district officer, Jerusalem-Bethlehem-Jericho sub-district, to director of Lands Department, Jerusalem, September 29, 1934, ISA, RG 23, 853M, file 19/34.

149. Sharkey, "Christians among Muslims," 63.

150. Government of Palestine, Department of Education, *Annual Report 1931–1932*, 18.

151. Eva Cotching, *Infant Welfare for Women and Girls in Palestine* (N.p.: 1930), 3.

152. Ibid., 6.

153. "Children's illnesses," *al-Hayat*, July 2, 1931.

154. Baron, *Women's Awakening*, 158.

155. Leila El Khalidi, *The Art of Palestinian Embroidery* (London: Saqi Books, 1999), 35–49; Jehan S. Rajab, *Palestinian Costume* (London and New York: Kegan Paul International, 1989), 18; Iman Saca, *Embroidering Identities: A Century of Palestinian Clothing* (Chicago: Oriental Institute Museum of the University of Chicago, 2006), 13.

156. Stockdale, *Colonial Encounters*, 91–102.

157. Ibid., 92, 97–98.

158. Wilson, "School year in Palestine," 42.

159. Ridler, "Special Problems in the Training of Women Teachers," 29.

160. Sabin Shalfun, "Handicrafts," *al-Mar'a al-jadida* 1, no. 6 (September 1921): 187.

161. El Khalidi, *Art of Palestinian Embroidery*, 50–51.

162. Su'ad, interview, March 15, 2003.

163. Ibid.

164. S. Weir, *Palestinian Costume* (London: Trustees of the British Museum, 1970), 208, 224.

165. Ted Swedenburg, "The Palestinian Peasant as National Signifier," *Anthropological Quarterly* 63, no. 1 (January 1990): 18–19.

166. Hannie J. Iranie and N. Hannush, *Palestinian Embroideries* (Jerusalem, 1920); Azize Daoud, *Ramallah Embroidery and Ramallah Weaving* (Jerusalem: Palestine Government Schools, 1930), both cited in El Khalidi, *Art of Palestinian Embroidery*. The

Islamic Girls' School owned thirteen copies of Daoud's book. See "List of contents of Islamic Girls' School," 1944, IIRHR, 13/44/1,22/1/75.

CHAPTER 6

1. Speech of Augustine Tleel, "The Orthodox School in Jerusalem," *al-Mar'a al-jadida* no. 10 (October 1925): 390.

2. Najmabadi, "Crafting an Educated Housewife in Iran," 91–125.

3. Newton, *Fifty Years in Palestine*, 161.

4. See essays by Khaldieh El Khaldy, Naimeh Nashashibi, Jamal Saleem, Annig Khatchigian, Katie Abdo, and Wadad Nasr, box 24, file 6, SSC, Woodsmall Papers.

5. Ayalon, *Reading Palestine*, 49–64, 88–93.

6. Ibid., 97–101.

7. Accountant Saba to director of awqaf, December 8, 1932, IIRHR, 13/32/2,20/1/75.

8. Nuzha, interview, June 14, 2000. Newspaper reading was also popular in Jewish schools. The headmistress of the Evelina de Rothschild Girls' School gave the school copies of the English-language *Palestine Post* and the *Palestine Review*, as well as the Hebrew-language *Ha-Arets* paper, which pupils reportedly enjoyed. See Evelina de Rothschild Girls' School, Jerusalem, *School Magazine* 4 (1938): 3.

9. Kabha, *Palestinian Press*, 19; Ayalon, *Reading Palestine*, 52.

10. "Subscriptions," *al-'Arusa* 11, no. 6 (September 1925): 332.

11. "Subscriptions," *al-Mar'a al-jadida* 2, no. 5 (March 1922): 165.

12. Rabiha Dajani, "Aim of the girl," *Majallat rawdat al-ma'arif* 7, no. 1 (December 19, 1934): 40.

13. Na'amat Kamil, "The nation and morals: To my sisters, the girls of this generation," *al-Difa'*, June 21, 1935.

14. Sabine Shalfun, "Handicrafts," *al-Mar'a al-jadida* 1, no. 6 (1921).

15. See the "Beautiful babies," column *al-'Arusa* 4 (1928). For a discussion of the way photographs have been used for promoting the nation, see Baron, *Egypt as a Woman*, ch. 4.

16. Rushdi Shawwa, mayor of Gaza, to chief secretary, September 20, 1939; Jerome Farrell, director of education to chief secretary, November 1, 1939, and March 27, 1940; M. Tomlinson for director of education to chief secretary, July 6, 1946, ISA, RG 2, 126/6M file E/59/37.

17. Maisar al-Shawwa, "The education of the girl," *al-Ghad* 1, no. 4 (August 1938): 24–25.

18. Tawaddud 'Abd al-Hadi, "The woman's awakening," *al-Ghad* 1, no. 1 (March 1938): 22.

19. Andrea L. Stanton, "A Little Radio Is a Dangerous Thing: State Broadcasting in Mandate Palestine, 1936–1949" (Ph.D. diss., Columbia University, 2007), 69.

20. Ya'acov Shim'oni, *'Araviye erets-yisrael* (Tel Aviv: 'Am 'oved, 1947), 393.

21. Ibid., 35.

22. Ibid., 180–185.

23. Edwin Samuel, transcript of radio show "Between ourselves," August 15, 1947, RG 14, Broadcasting Dept, box 1879M, no file number.

24. Government of Palestine, Palestine Broadcasting Service, *Official Programmes*, 1936. See also ISA, RG 14, 1879M from 1946 to 1947.

25. Stanton, "A Little Radio," 180–192.

26. Shim'oni, *'Araviye erets-yisrael*, 394; Stuart C. Dodd, *A Pioneer Radio Poll in Lebanon, Syria and Palestine* (Palestine: Government Printer, September 1943), 29.

27. Hadiya 'Abd al-Hadi, *Al-wamid* (Jerusalem: Matba'at dar al-aytam al-suriyya, 1943), 5–8; Vashitz, *Ha-'aravim be-erets-yisrael*, 212.

28. Marilyn Booth, *May Her Likes Be Multiplied: Biography and Gender Politics in Egypt* (Berkeley and Los Angeles: University of California Press, 2001), 150.

29. Thompson, *Colonial Citizens*, 36.

30. Katie Abdo, "English Essay," June 26, 1929, box 24, file 6, SSC, Woodsmall Papers.

31. Khaldieh El Khaldy, "English Essay," June 27, 1929, box 24, file 6, SSC, Woodsmall Papers.

32. Badran, *Feminists, Islam, and Nation*, 165.

33. Booth, *May Her Likes Be Multiplied*, 128.

34. Nuzha, interview, July 20, 2000; Su'ad, interview, March 15, 2003; Widad, interview.

35. Widad, interview.

36. Government of Palestine, Department of Education, *Statistical Tables 1943–1944*, table I.

37. Jaussen, *Coutumes Palestiniennes*, 48; "Open letter to director of education," *Filastin*, June 11, 1923. See also Tsimhoni, "British Mandate and Arab Christians," 270.

38. Ihsan al-Nimr, *Ta'rikh jabal nablus wa-al-balqa'* (Nablus: Matba'at 'ummal al-matabi' al-ta'awuniyya, 1975), 4:102.

39. Badran, *Feminists, Islam, and Nation*, 175–177.

40. Ibid.

41. "[Female] teachers dance and [female] pupils sing," *al-Jami'a al-'arabiyya*, June 27, 1927.

42. See Karin van Nieuwkerk, *"A Trade Like Any Other": Female Singers and Dancers in Egypt* (Austin: University of Texas Press, 1995), 3–7, 46–47, who writes that belly dancing, in particular, acquired a negative connotation because of its popularity among foreign troops stationed in Cairo during World War I, and thus its association with prostitution.

43. Booth, *May Her Likes Be Multiplied*, 145.

44. Woodsmall, *Moslem Women*, 192.

45. Nadiyya, interview.

46. Moors, *Women, Property and Islam*, 201.

47. Uri M. Kupferschmidt, "The Social History of the Sewing Machine in the Middle East," *Die Welt des Islams* 44, no. 2 (2004): 201.

48. T. J. Edelstein, "They Sang 'the Song of the Shirt': The Visual Iconology of the Seamstress," *Victorian Studies* 23, no. 2 (1980): 183–210.

49. Judith G. Coffin, "Credit, Consumption, and Images of Women's Desires: Selling the Sewing Machine in Nineteenth Century France," *French Historical Studies* 18, no. 3 (Spring 1994): 763.

50. American Colony, *Annual Report of the American Colony Aid Association for the Year 1931–1932*, n.p.

51. Advertisement for Singer sewing machine, *Filastin*, July 8, 1932.

52. Advertisement for "National art school for girls," *Filastin*, September 21, 1930.

53. Sa'id Himadeh, *Economic Organization of Palestine* (Beirut: American Press, 1938), 269.

54. "Good work of the Arab ladies' committee," *al-Difa'*, April 16, 1937.

55. "Report of the Islamic Girls' School, 1944-1945," July 21, 1945, IIRHR, 13/39/1,23/1/75; Headmistress to inspector of Islamic schools, listing number of pupils registered in sewing workshop, April 29, 1947, IIRHR, 13/34/2,73/1/75.

56. Amna Sha'th to inspector of Islamic schools, May 5, 1947, IIRHR, 13/34/2,73/1/75.

57. Widad, interview.

58. "Girls of the charitable workshop of the Arab ladies in Jaffa," *Filastin*, April 17, 1946.

59. Adel Z. Zidat, "Western Medicine in Palestine, 1860–1940: The Edinburgh Medical Missionary Society and Its Hospital," *Canadian Bulletin of Medical History* 10, no. 2 (1993): 269–279.

60. See, for example, Marwa Elshakry, "The Gospel of Science and American Evangelism in Late Ottoman Beirut," *Past and Present*, no. 196 (2007): 173–214; C. Peter Williams, "Healing and Evangelism: The Place of Medicine in Late Victorian Protestant Missionary Thinking," in *The Church and Healing*, ed. W. J. Sheils (London: Blackwell, 1982), 271–287.

61. Melkon Rose, *Armenians of Jerusalem*, 48–54.

62. Zuhal Özaydin, "Upper Social Strata Women in Nursing in Turkey," *Nursing History Review* 14 (2006): 163-164.

63. Huda Abu-Saad Huijer et al., "Cherishing the Past: 100 Years of Nursing Education at the American University of Beirut," *Journal of Transcultural Nursing* 17, no. 4 (2006): 328.

64. Manfred Waserman, "Henrietta Szold: American Progressivism, Zionism, and Modern Public Health," in Waserman and Kottek, eds., *Health and Disease in the Holy Land*, 274–280; Nira Bartal, "Yisud bet-ha-sefer le-aḥiyot be-Yerushalayim 'al yade ha-mishlaḥat ha-refuit shel tsiyone Amerika be-shnat 1918: hemshekh o mah-

pekha," in *Ha-'Ivriyot ha-ḥadashot*, ed. Margalit Shilo, Ruth Kark, and Galit Hazan-Rokem (Jerusalem: Yad Ben Zvi, 2001), 274.

65. Government of Palestine, *Annual Report for the Department of Health for the Year 1921*, 36.

66. Government of Palestine, *Annual Report for the Department of Health for the Year 1925*, 23–24.

67. "Training School for Moslem Nurses," October 22, 1925, ISA, RG 10, 1654M, file 96/6.

68. G. E. Heron to Lady Storrs, May 3, 1923, ISA, RG 10, 1654M, file 96/6.

69. Government of Palestine, *Annual Report for the Department of Health for the Year 1926*, 31.

70. Ridler, "Note on Female Education in Palestine," 14.

71. Director of the Department of Health to senior medical officer, Jerusalem District, n.d. (c. 1926), ISA, RG 10, 1615M, file 66/5.

72. Badran, *Feminists, Islam, and Nation*, 181.

73. "Report on investigation of the dearth of Arab nurses," ISA, RG 65, 392 P, file 3118. See also Fleischmann, *Nation and Its "New" Women*, 55–56.

74. "Ramallah Themes," 7, box 64, file 13, SSC, Woodsmall papers.

75. Fleischmann, *Nation and Its "New" Women*, 56.

76. Marcella Simoni, "A Dangerous Legacy: Welfare in British Palestine, 1930–1939," *Jewish History* 13, no. 2 (Fall 1999): 94–95.

77. Based on my own survey of applicants for nurses' training, whose religion was usually noted. See ISA, RG 10, 1654M, files 96/4, 96/5, and 96/6 and ISA, RG 65, 368P, file 2395.

78. "Notes of interview with Hutim Zu'bi, official of United States Operations Mission, Jordan, conducted by Charlotte Johnson, assistant to Ruth Woodsmall," March 29, 1955, box 62, file 7, SSC, Woodsmall Papers, who contended that certain types of women were coerced into entering nursing.

79. Fleischmann, *Nation and Its "New" Women*, 55.

80. "Minutes of meeting for recruitment of Arab women nurses," July 4, 1947, ISA, RG 27, 2651M, file G.1070. See also "Report on investigation re dearth of nurses," late 1942–early 1943, ISA, RG 65, 392P, file 3118.

81. See, for example, the photograph of "The head Arab nurse in the Jaffa hospital, Miss Matil Kawjuk," *Huna al-quds* 2, no. 3 (February 9, 1941), and photographs of the nurse 'Afifa Najjar tending children in Tul Karim, *Huna al-quds* 2, no. 13 (July 8, 1941).

82. Anne Marie Rafferty and Diana Solano, "The Rise and Demise of the Colonial Nursing Service: British Nurses in the Colonies, 1896–1966," *Nursing History Review* 15 (2007): 151–152.

83. Fleischmann, *Nation and Its "New" Women*, 197.

84. Ibid.

85. "Recruitment of Arab girls for nurses training," October 25, 1946, ISA, RG 27, 2651M, file G.1070.

86. "Minutes of meeting for recruitment of Arab women nurses," July 4, 1947, ISA, RG 27, 2651M, file G.1070.

87. Woodsmall, *Moslem Women*, 287.

88. See, for example, Sean Lang, "Drop the Demon Dai: Maternal Mortality and the State in Colonial Madras, 1840–1874," *Social History of Medicine* 18, no. 3 (2005): 357–378; Sandhya Shetty, "(Dis)Locating Gender Space and Medical Discourse in Colonial India," *Genders* 20 (1994): 182–230.

89. Elise G. Young, "From Daya to Doctor: Health, Gender, and the Race for Control of Knowledge-Making in Mandatory Palestine," *Thamyris* 4 (1997): 347–358.

90. Hibba Abugideiri, "The Scientisation of Culture: Colonial Medicine's Construction of Egyptian Womanhood, 1893–1929," *Gender and History* 16, no. 1 (April 2004): 89.

91. Government of Palestine, "Midwives Ordinance, no. 20 of 1929," CO 765/4–49.

92. See, for example, Great Britain, Colonial Office, *Report by His Majesty's Government in the United Kingdom of Great Britain and Northern Ireland to the Council of the League of Nations on the Administration of Palestine and Transjordan for the Year 1932*, 121.

93. Fleischmann, *Nation and Its "New" Women*, 54.

94. "Institution to train Muslim midwives and nurses," *Filastin*, October 28, 1924; see also "Maternity and child welfare general correspondence Jerusalem," ISA, RG 10, 1615M, file 66/5.

95. Heather Bell, "Midwifery Training and Female Circumcision in the Inter-War Anglo-Egyptian Sudan," *Journal of African Studies* 39 (1998): 300.

96. Ibid., 298.

97. Hilma Granqvist, *Birth and Childhood among the Arabs* (Helsingfors: Söderströms, 1947), 60.

98. "Goodness and charity," *Filastin*, September 5, 1924; Government of Palestine, Department of Health, *Annual Report of the Department of Health for the Year 1924*, 29; Government of Palestine, Department of Health, *Annual Report of the Department of Health for the Year 1927*, 36.

99. Woodsmall, Bound reports, 146, handwritten comment in margins, in Box 25, Woodsmall Papers, SSC.

100. Government of Palestine, Department of Health, *Annual Report of the Department of Health for the Year 1930*, 54.

101. Acting director of Department of Health to chief secretary, July 14, 1928, CO 733/162/20.

102. List of nurses and nurse-midwives, n.d., circa late 1930s, ISA, RG 65, 3682P, file 2395.

103. Young, "From Daya to Doctor," 353–354.

104. Aleksandra Majstorac Kobiljski, "Women Students at the American University of Beirut from the 1920s to the 1940s," in Okkenhaug and Flaskerud, eds., 70.

105. Sabri, *Pioneering Profiles*, 294–295.

106. "American Junior College for Girls, Beirut," box 8, file 15, SSC, Woodsmall Papers.

107. Nuzha, interview, July 20, 2000.

108. Sa'ida, interview.

109. Kobiljski, "Women Students," 72.

110. "Statistics of Living AUB Alumni," *Al-kulliya* 20, no. 4 (March 15, 1934): 108–109.

111. 'Awda, *Yusra Salah*, 2–3.

112. Randi Deguilhem, "Gender Blindness and Societal Influence in Late Ottoman Damascus: Women as the Creators and Managers of Endowments," *Hawwa* 1, no. 3 (2003): 329–350. See also Amy Singer, *Constructing Ottoman Beneficence: An Imperial Soup Kitchen in Jerusalem* (Albany: State University of New York Press, 2002).

113. Baron, *Women's Awakening*, 169–170.

114. Fleischmann, *Nation and Its "New" Women*, 95–96.

115. Tubi, *'Abir wa-majd*, 116–117.

116. Baron, *Women's Awakening*, 176.

117. "Haifa Girls' School," *Bible Lands* 3, no. 48 (April 1911): 246–248.

118. Reeves-Ellington, "A Vision of Mount Holyoke in the Ottoman Balkans," 159–161.

119. Fleischmann, *Nation and Its "New" Women*, 102.

120. See, for example, Amnon Cohen, *The Guilds of Ottoman Jerusalem* (Leiden: Brill, 2001).

121. Baron, *Women's Awakening*, 168.

122. Ibid., 171.

123. Fleischmann, *Nation and Its "New" Women*, 104, 107.

124. Tubi, *'Abir wa-majd*, 122–124. See also Fleischmann, *Nation and Its "New" Women*, 104.

125. Tubi, *'Abir wa-majd*, 125–128. About the founder, Adele 'Azar of the association in Jaffa, see Fleischmann, *Nation and Its "New" Women*, 104–105.

126. "Statutes of the Society called (Nahdat al Fatat al Arabieh)" ISA, RG 23, 833M, file 3939/92.

127. Fleischmann, *Nation and Its "New" Women*, 97.

128. Ibid., 103.

129. Baron, *Women's Awakening*, 175.

130. Alice Meikhalian, "Service in the City," *Jerusalem Girls' College Magazine* (June 1933): 53.

131. Badran, *Feminists, Islam, and Nation*, 47; Fleischmann, *Nation and Its "New" Women*, 101.

132. Fleischmann, *Nation and Its "New" Women*, 113.

133. Ibid., 165–166.

134. "Arab Woman's League Association," n.d., circa 1938, ISA, RG 65, 392P, file 3117.

135. Ernestine Ghuri to governor, Jerusalem District, April 11, 1939, ISA, RG 23, 845M, file 3939/1324.

136. "Minutes of the representatives of institutions functioning for the relief of the orphan in Palestine," August 30, 1939, ISA, RG 23, 845M, file 3939/1324.

137. District commissioner to general secretary, YWCA, Jerusalem, October 21, 1946, ISA, RG 65, 392 P, file 3117.

138. "Propaganda," n.d., circa 1937, CZA, S25/22717.

139. Fleischmann, *Nation and Its "New" Women*, 194.

140. List of Organizations, n.d., ISA, RG 65, 392P, file 3117.

141. "The Women's Social Endeavour Society," n.d., ISA, RG 65, 392P, file 3117.

142. Fleischmann, *Nation and Its "New" Women*, 195.

143. Shim'oni, *'Araviye erets-yisrael*, 380.

144. "The Women's Social Endeavour Society," ISA, RG 65, 392P, file 3117.

145. Wafi'a, interview by Ellen Fleischmann, al-Bireh, March 21, 1993.

146. Sa'ida, interview.

147. Nuzha, interview, July 20, 2000.

148. Su'ad, interview, February 16, 2003.

149. Lila Abu-Lughod, ed. *Remaking Women: Feminism and Modernity in the Middle East* (Princeton: Princeton University Press, 1998).

150. Rosemary Sayigh, *Too Many Enemies: The Palestinian Experience in Lebanon* (London and New Jersey: Zed Books, 1994), 53.

BIBLIOGRAPHY

PAPERS AND ARCHIVES CONSULTED

American Colony in Jerusalem Collection, Manuscript Division, Library of Congress, Washington, D.C.
Central Zionist Archives, Jerusalem
Institute for Islamic Research and Heritage Revival (IIRHR), Abu Dis, Palestine
Israel State Archives, Jerusalem
Middle East Center Archives, St. Antony's College, Oxford University, Oxford, England
National Archives, Public Records Office
Ruth Woodsmall Papers, Sophia Smith Collection, Smith College, Northampton, Massachusetts.

INTERVIEWS

'Aliyye. Interview by Laila 'Abed Rabho. Bayt Safafa, Spring 2001.
Ibtihaj. Interview by Ellen Fleischmann. Acre, May 20, 1993.
Maryam. Interview by the author and Laila 'Abed Rabho. Silwan, January 16, 2001.
Na'ame. Interview by the author and Laila 'Abed Rabho. Bayt Safafa, January 30, 2001.
Nadiyya. Interview by Khader Salameh. Bethlehem, October 6, 2001.
Nahid. Interview by Ellen Fleischmann. Amman, January 28, 1993.
Nuzha. Interview by the author and Khader Salameh. Jerusalem, June 14, 2000, and July 20, 2000.
Sa'ida. Interview by Ellen Fleischmann. Jerusalem, April 19, 1994.
Su'ad. Telephone interviews by the author. February 9; February 12; February 16; March 15, 2003.
Wafi'a. Interview by Ellen Fleischmann. Al-Bireh, March 21, 1993.

Widad. Interview by the author and Bassam Quttine. Jerusalem, May 27, 2000.

NEWSPAPERS AND JOURNALS

Bible Lands. (Quarterly Paper of the Jerusalem and East Mission), 1904, 1908, 1911.
British Syrian Training College Magazine (Beirut), 1932–1934.
al-Difa' (Jaffa), 1935–1937, January–July 1940; few issues of 1942.
Filastin (Jaffa), 1911–1913, 1921–1932, 1935–1936, 1940.
al-Hayat (Jerusalem), 1931.
Huna al-quds (Jerusalem), 1940–1942.
al-Jami'a al-'arabiyya (Jerusalem), 1927–1931, 1934.
Jerusalem Girls' College Magazine (Jerusalem), 1931, 1933, 1938.
al-Karmil (Haifa), 1920–1936.
Al-Kulliya: The Alumni Journal of the American University of Beirut (Beirut), 1924–1935.
Majallat rawdat al-ma'arif (Jerusalem), 1922–1923, 1932–1935.
al-Mar'a al-jadida (Beirut), 1921–1922, 1924–1926.
Mir'at al-sharq (Jerusalem), 1929–1932, 1935–1938.
al-Nafa'is al-'asriyya (Jerusalem), 1909–1911.
al-Nafir (Haifa), 1926–1927.
Palestine Post (Jerusalem), 1935–1941, 1946.
al-Sirat al-mustaqim (Jaffa), 1930–1936.

PUBLISHED PRIMARY SOURCES

'Abd al-Hadi, Hadiya. *Al-wamid.* Jerusalem: Matba'at dar al-aytam al-suriyya, 1943.
'Ali, Rushdi. *Taqrir lil-mu'tamar al-islami al-'amm.* Jerusalem: Matba'at dar al-aytam al-islamiyya, 1350.
American Colony Aid Association. *Annual Report.* 1929–30/1930–1931.
Anglo-American Committee of Inquiry. *A Survey of Palestine, Prepared in December 1945 and January 1946.* 3 vols. 1946–1947. Reprint, Washington, D.C.: Institute of Palestine Studies, 1991.
Bowman, Humphrey. "Rural Education in the Middle East." *Journal of the Royal Central Asian Society* 26, no. 3 (July 1939): 402–414.
al-Bustani, Butrus. *Ta'lim al-nisa'.* 1849. Reprinted by Fu'ad Afram al-Bustani. Beirut: al-Matba'at al-kathulikiyya, 1929.
Cotching, Eva. *Infant Welfare for Women and Girls in Palestine.* N.p.: 1930.
"Criminal Code Ordinance 1936," section 182. *Palestine Gazette* no. 633, September 28, 1936.
Cuinet, Vital. *Syrie Liban et Palestine Géographie Administrative Statistique, Descriptive et Raisonnée.* Paris: Ernest Leroux, 1896.
al-Dabbagh, Mustafa. *Madrasat al-qarya.* Jerusalem: Matba'at al-'arab, 1935.

Da'irat al-ma'had al-diniyya, *Nida' ila al-muslimin 'ammatan bil-tahthir min al-madaris al-tabshiriyya.* Jerusalem: Matba'at dar al-aytam al-islamiyya, n.d.

Dar al-aytam al-islamiyya al-sina'iyya. *Majallat dar al-aytam al-islamiyya al-sina'iyya fi bayt al-maqdis* 1, nos. 1–2 (1932).

Dodd, Stuart C. *A Pioneer Radio Poll in Lebanon, Syria and Palestine.* Palestine: Government Printer, September 1943.

Eberhard, O. "Die Arabischen Volksschulen Jerusalem." *Palästinajahrbuch des deutschen evangelischen Instituts für Altertumswissenschaft des heiligen Landes zu Jerusalem* (1906): 80–122.

English High School for Girls. *Prospectus of the English High School for Girls Haifa,* 1931–1932.

Evelina de Rothschild Girls' School, Jerusalem, *School Magazine* 4 (1938).

Executive Committee for Health Week, Jerusalem. "Report Health Week, November 17–30, 1924." Jerusalem, 1924.

Great Britain. Colonial Office. *Report on Palestine Administration, July 1920–December 1921.* London: HMSO, 1922.

———. *Report on Palestine Administration, 1922–1923.* London: HMSO, 1923.

———. *Report by His Britannic Majesty's Government on the Administration under Mandate of Palestine and Transjordan for the Year 1924.* London: HMSO, 1925.

———. *Report by His Majesty's Government in the United Kingdom of Great Britain and Northern Ireland to the Council of the League of Nations on the Administration of Palestine and Transjordan for the Year 1930.* London: HMSO, 1931.

———. *Report by His Majesty's Government in the United Kingdom of Great Britain and Northern Ireland to the Council of the League of Nations on the Administration of Palestine and Transjordan for the Year 1932.* London: HMSO, 1933.

———. *Report by His Majesty's Government in the United Kingdom of Great Britain and Northern Ireland to the Council of the League of Nations on the Administration of Palestine and Transjordan for the Year 1934.* London: HMSO, 1935.

Great Britain. Colonial Office. Palestine Royal Commission. *Minutes of Evidence Heard at Public Sessions.* London: HMSO, 1937.

Government of Palestine, Department of Education. *Annual Report* Jerusalem, 1924–1943/1944.

Government of Palestine, Department of Education. *Education in Palestine General Survey 1945–1946.* Jerusalem.

Government of Palestine, Department of Education. *Elementary School Syllabus.* Jerusalem, 1925.

Government of Palestine, Department of Education. *Statistical Tables and Diagrams for the Scholastic Year 1943–1944.* Jerusalem.

Government of Palestine, Department of Education. *Statistical Tables and Diagrams for the Scholastic Year 1944–1945.* Jerusalem.

Government of Palestine, Department of Health. *Annual Report of the Department of Health.* Jerusalem: 1921, 1923–1927, 1930.

Government of Palestine, Department of Social Welfare. *Annual Report 1944.* Jerusalem.

Government of Palestine, Palestine Board of Higher Studies. *Matriculation Examination.* Jerusalem, 1925.

Government of Palestine, Palestine Board of Higher Studies. *Palestine Secondary School Certificate and Palestine Matriculation Certificate.* Jerusalem, 1934.

Government of Palestine, Palestine Broadcasting Service. *Official Programmes.* 1936.

Granqvist, Hilma. *Birth and Childhood among the Arabs.* Helsingfors: Söderströms, 1947.

Guérin, Victor. *Jérusalem: son histoire, sa description—ses établissements religieux.* Paris, 1889.

Haifa Social Service and Infant Welfare Association. *Sixth Annual Report 1931.*

Hukumat filastin, Idarat al-maʿarif. *Minhaj al-taʿlim al-ibtidaʾi fi madaris al-qura.* Jerusalem, 1929.

Hukumat filastin, Idarat al-maʿarif al-ʿamma. *Minhaj al-din al-islami.* Jerusalem, 1947.

[al-Husayni, Muhammad Amin]. *Khutbatan li-samaha al-mufti al-akbar wa-raʾis al-majlis al-islami al-alʿa al-sayyid Muhammad Amin al-Husayni fi muʾtammar al-ʿulamaʾ wa-fi ijtimaʿ wufud al-qura bi-shaʾn baiʿ al-aradi bi-filastin lil-sahyuniyyin waʾl-hath ʿala al-amr bi-l-maʿruf waʾl-nahy ʿan al-mufkar.* Jerusalem: Matbaʿat dar al-aytam al-islamiyya al-sinaʿiyya bil-quds, n.d.

Jaussen, Le Père J. A. *Coutumes Palestiniennes: Nablouse et son district.* Paris: Librarie Orientaliste Paul Geuthner, 1927.

Jessup, Henry Harris. *Women of the Arabs.* New York, 1873.

al-Khalidi, Ahmad Samih. "The System of Turkish Education." *Majallat dar al-muʿallimin* no. 1 (November 1925): 1–16.

Kligler, I. J. "Public Health in Palestine." *Annals of the American Academy of Political and Social Science* 164 (November 1932): 167–177.

al-Kulliya al-inkliziyya lil-banat. *Barnamaj al-kulliya al-inkliziyya lil-banat fi al-quds ʿan sana 1931–1932.*

Lane, Edward W. *An Account of the Manners and Customs of the Modern Egyptians.* 1842. Reprint, London, 1890.

Lee, Rosa E. *The Story of the Ram Allah Mission.* Board of Foreign Missions of the Yearly Meeting of Friends for New England, 1912.

Maʿluf, Anisa. *Muʾassasat jamʿiat al-asdiqaʾ al-amirkiyya fi filastin min sana 1869–1939.* N.p.: al-Matbaʿat al-ʿasriyya, n.d.

Madrasat al-frindz lil-banat. *Barnamaj madrasat al-frindz lil-banat 1931–1932.*

Madrasat al-islamiyya lil-banat. *Barnamaj madrasat al-islamiyya lil-banat fi al-quds sana 1929–1930; 1930–1931.*

al-Majlis al-sharʿi al-islami al-aʿla. *Bayan al-majlis al-sharʿi al-islami al-aʿla fi filastin le-sana* 1340–1341; 1341–1342; 1347–1348; 1361–1363 (1921–1922; 1922–1923; 1928–1929; 1942–1944).

al-Majlis al-shar'i al-islami al-a'la. *Manshur fi al-muhur.* Jerusalem: Matba'at dar al-aytam al-islamiyya, 1348.

al-Majlis al-shar'i al-islami al-a'la. *Nida' bi-sha'n al-muhur min da'irat al-ma'had al-diniyya.* Jerusalem: Matba'at dar al-aytam al-islamiyya, 1353.

al-Majlis al-islami al-a'la, Idarat taftish al-madaris al-islamiyya. *Minhaj al-ta'lim al-ibtida'i.* Jerusalem: Matba'at dar al-aytam al-islamiyya, 1942/1361.

Makariyus, Shahin. "Education in Syria." *Al-Muqtataf* 7, part 9 (1883): 529–537.

Miller, Ellen Clare. *Eastern Sketches: Notes of Scenery, Schools, and Tent life in Syria and Palestine.* Edinburgh, 1871.

Mills, E. *Census of Palestine.* Vols. 1–2. Alexandria, 1933.

Mogannam, Matiel. *The Arab Woman and the Palestine Problem.* London: Herbert Joseph, 1937.

Muqararrat al-mu'tamar al-islami al-'amm. Jerusalem: Matba'at dar al-aytam al-islamiyya, 1931.

Qism ihya' al-turath al-islami. *Qarirat al-majlis al-shar'i al-islami al-a'la wa-qarirat lijan al-awqaf al-mahaliyya.* Vol. 5. Jerusalem, 1994.

Reinicke, Dr. "Die evangelische Mission in Palästina." *Zeitschrift des Deutschen Palästina-Vereins* 6 (1883): 13–30.

Salname-i nezaret-i ma'arif-i 'umumiye 1318 (1900).

Salname-i nezaret-i ma'arif-i 'umumiye 1321 (1903).

Social Service Association. *Social Service Association Report* (1923–1924).

al-Tamimi, Muhammad Rafiq, and Muhammad Bahjat. *Wilayat bayrut.* Beirut: Matba'at al-iqbal, 1333–1335.

Woodsmall, Ruth Frances. *Moslem Women Enter a New World.* London: George Allen and Unwin, 1936.

World Mission of Christianity. *Messages and Recommendations of the Enlarged Meeting of the International Missionary Council held at Jerusalem, March 24–April 8, 1928.* London: International Missionary Council, 1928.

AUTOBIOGRAPHIES AND MEMOIRS CITED

Abu Rish, Said K. *Children of Bethany: The Story of a Palestinian Family.* London: I. B. Tauris, 1988.

Adıvar, Halide Edib. *Memoirs of Halide Edib.* 1926. Reprint, New York: Arno Press, 1972.

Bentwich, Norman, and Helen Bentwich. *Mandate Memories 1918–1948.* New York: Schocken Books, 1965.

Bowman, Humphrey. *Middle-East Window.* London: Longmans, Green, 1942.

Cromer, Evelyn Barin. *Modern Egypt.* 2 vols. London: MacMillan, 1908.

Farah, Najwa Kawar. *A Continent Called Palestine: One Woman's Story.* London: Triangle Press, 1996.

Fawcett, Millicent. *Easter in Palestine, 1921–1922.* London, 1926.

Goodrich-Freer, A. *Inner Jerusalem*. London, 1904.

Jabra, Ibrahim Jabra. *The First Well: A Bethlehem Boyhood*. Fayetteville: University of Arkansas Press, 1995.

Karmi, Ghada. *In Search of Fatima: A Palestinian Story*. London and New York: Verso, 2002.

al-Khalidi, 'Anbara Salam. *Jawla fi al-dhikrayat bayn lubnan wa-filastin*. Beirut: Dar al-nahar lil-nashr, 1966.

Melkon Rose, John H. *Armenians of Jerusalem: Memories of Life in Palestine*. London: Radcliffe Press, 1993.

Mills, Rev. John. *Three Months' Residence at Nablus*. London, 1864.

Musallam, Akram, ed. *Yawmiyat Khalil al-Sakakini*. Vol. 1, *New York, Sultana, al-Quds 1908–1912*. Ramallah: Markaz Khalil al-Sakakini al-thaqafi, al-Quds: Mu'assasat al-dirasat al-muqaddasiyya, 2003.

———. *Yawmiyat Khalil al-Sakakini*. Vol. 2, *al-nahda al-urthudhuksiyya, al-harb al-'uthma, al-nafi ila dimashq 1914–1918*. Ramallah: Markaz Khalil al-Sakakini al-thaqafi, al-Quds: Mu'assasat al-dirasat al-muqaddasiyya, 2004.

———. *Yawmiyat Khalil al-Sakakini*. Vol. 3, *ikhtibar al-intidab wa-as'ila al-huwiya, 1919–1922*. Ramallah: Markaz Khalil al-Sakakini al-thaqafi, al-Quds: Mu'assasat al-dirasat al-muqaddasiyya, 2004.

Newton, Frances E. *Fifty Years in Palestine*. London: Coldharbor Press, 1948.

Scrimgeour, Frederic John. *Nazareth of To-day*. Edinburgh and London: William Green and Sons, 1913.

Shaarawi, Huda. *Harem Years: The Memoirs of an Egyptian Feminist*. Translated by Margot Badran. New York: Feminist Press, 1987.

Shahid, Serene Husseini. *Jerusalem Memories*. Beirut: Naufal Group, 2000.

Tamari, Salim, and 'Issam Nassar. *Al-quds al-'uthmaniyya fi al-mudhakkirat al-Jawhariyya: al-kitab al-awwal min mudhakkirat al-musiqi Wasif Jawhariyya 1904–1917*. Jerusalem: Mu'assasat al-dirasat al-muqaddasiyya, 2003.

Tuqan, Fadwa. *A Mountainous Journey: A Poet's Autobiography*. St. Paul: Graywolf Press, 1990.

Vester, Bertha Spafford. *Our Jerusalem: An American Family in the Holy City 1881–1949*. Beirut: Middle East Export Press, 1950.

SECONDARY SOURCES

Abidi, Mahmoud. "The Arab College, Jerusalem." In *Arabic and Islamic Garland: Historical, Educational and Literary Papers Presented to A. L. Tibawi*, 28–35. London: Islamic Cultural Center, 1977.

Abugideiri, Hibba. "The Scientisation of Culture: Colonial Medicine's Construction of Egyptian Womanhood, 1893-1929." *Gender and History* 16, no. 1 (April 2004): 83–98.

Abu Hanna, Hanna. *Dar al-mu'alimin al-russiyya fi al-nasira "al-seminar" (1886–1914) wa-athariha ʿala al-nahda al-adabiyya fi filastin.* Nazareth: Department of Arab Culture, Ministry of Education and Culture, 1994.

Abu-Lughod, Lila, ed. *Remaking Women: Feminism and Modernity in the Middle East.* Princeton: Princeton University Press, 1998.

Abu-Rabiʿa, ʾAref. *Bedouin Century: Education and Development among the Negev Tribes in the Twentieth Century.* New York: Berghahn Books, 2001.

———. "Indigenous Practices among Palestinians for Healing Eye Diseases and Inflammations." *Dynamis Acta Hisp. Med. Sci. Hist. Illus.* 25 (2005): 383–401.

ʾAdawi, Jamal. "Peʿilut ha-quakerim ha-Amerikanim ba-Palestina, 1869–1948." Ph.D. diss., University of Haifa, 2000.

Ahmad, Feroz. *The Young Turks: The Committee of Union and Progress in Turkish Politics 1908–1914.* London: Oxford University Press, 1969.

Ahmed, Leila. *Women and Gender in Islam: Historical Roots of a Modern Debate.* New Haven and London: Yale University Press, 1992.

al-ʾAlami, Adawiyya. "Taʿlim al-banat fi al-quds." In *Al-quds madinat al-ʿilm: yawm al-quds: abhath al-nadwa al-khamisa yawm al-quds,* edited by Lajnat yawm al-quds, 39–55. Amman: N.p., 1995.

Almog, Oz. *The Sabra: The Creation of the New Jew.* Berkeley and Los Angeles: University of California Press, 2000.

Anagol-McGinn, Padma. "The Age of Consent Act (1891) Reconsidered: Women's Perspectives and Participation in the Child-Marriage Controversy in India." *South Asia Research* 12, no. 2 (November 1992): 100–118.

Anderson, Benedict. *Imagined Communities.* Rev. ed. London and New York: Verso, 1991.

al-ʾAnsari, Yaʿqub, and Ibrahim al-Husayni. *Jamʿiyat al-sayyidat al-ʿarabiyyat bil-quds.* Jerusalem: N.p., 1985.

Arai, Masami. *Turkish Nationalism in the Young Turk Era.* Leiden: Brill, 1992.

Ariel, Yaacov, and Ruth Kark. "Messianism, Holiness, Charisma and Community: The American-Swedish Colony in Jerusalem, 1881–1933." *Church History* 65, no. 4 (December 1996): 641–657.

ʾAwad, ʾAbd al-ʾAziz Muhammad. *Al-idara al-ʿuthmaniyya fi wilayat suriya 1864–1914.* Cairo: Dar al-maʿarif, 1969.

ʾAwda, A. Kafah. *Yusra Salah 1923–1993.* Nablus: N.p., 1995.

ʾAwda, Sadiq Ibrahim. "Al-kulliya al-ʿarabiyya fi al-quds 1918–1948: maʿlumat wa-dhikrayat," *Majallat dirasat al-filastiniyya* 40 (Winter 1999): 170–188.

Ayalon, Ami. *The Press in the Arab Middle East: A History.* New York: Oxford University Press, 1995.

———. *Reading Palestine: Printing and Literacy, 1900–1948.* Austin: University of Texas Press, 2004.

Badran, Margot. *Feminists, Islam, and Nation: Gender and the Making of Modern Egypt.* Princeton: Princeton University Press, 1995.

Baer, Gabriel. "The Economic and Social Position of the Village-Mukhtar in Palestine." In *The Palestinians and the Middle East Conflict,* edited by Gabriel Ben-Dor, 101–117. Ramat Gan: Turtlegrove Publishers, 1978.

Baron, Beth. "The Making and Breaking of Marital Bonds in Modern Egypt." In *Women in Middle Eastern History,* edited by Nikki R. Keddie and Beth Baron, 275–291. New Haven and London: Yale University Press, 1991.

———. *The Women's Awakening in Egypt: Culture, Society, and the Press.* New Haven and London: Yale University Press, 1994.

———. *Egypt as a Woman: Nationalism, Gender, and Politics.* Berkeley and Los Angeles: University of California Press, 2005.

Bartal, Nira. "Yisud bet-ha-sefer le-ahiyot be-Yerushalayim ʿal yade ha-mishlahat ha-refuit shel tsiyone Amerika be-shnat 1918: hemshekh o mahpekha." In *Ha-ʿIvriyot ha-hadashot,* edited by Margalit Shilo, Ruth Kark, and Galit Hazan-Rokem, 270–291. Jerusalem: Yad Ben Zvi, 2001.

Başcı, K. Pelin. "Shadows in the Missionary Garden of Roses: Women of Turkey in American Missionary Texts." In *Deconstructing Images of "the Turkish Woman,"* edited by Zehra F. Arat, 101–123. New York: Palgrave, 2000.

Bell, Heather. "Midwifery Training and Female Circumcision in the Inter-War Anglo-Egyptian Sudan." *Journal of African History* 39 (1998): 293–312.

Berg, Gerald M. "Zionist Women of the 1920s: The Voice of Nation Building." *Journal of Israeli History* 25, no. 2 (September 2006): 313–333.

Berkey, Jonathan P. "Women and Islamic Education in the Mamluk Period." In *Women in Middle Eastern History,* edited by Nikki R. Keddie and Beth Baron, 143–157. New Haven and London: Yale University Press, 1991.

Bernstein, Deborah. *Nashim be-shulayim: Migdar ve-leumiyut be-Tel Aviv ha-mandatorit.* Jerusalem: Yad Ben Zvi, 2008.

Booth, Marilyn. *May Her Likes Be Multiplied: Biography and Gender Politics in Egypt.* Berkeley and Los Angeles: University of California Press, 2001.

Borowy, Iris. "Health in Interwar Palestine: Ethnic Realities and International Views." *Dynamis Acta Hisp. Med. Sci. Hist. Illus.* 25 (2005): 423–450.

Boyd, William. *The History of Western Education.* 5th ed. London: Adam and Charles Black, 1950.

Boyle, Helen N. *Quranic Schools: Agents of Preservation and Change.* London: Routledge, 2004.

Braude, Benjamin. "Foundation Myths of the *Millet* System." In *Christians and Jews in the Ottoman Empire,* vol. 1, *The Central Lands,* edited by Benjamin Braude and Bernard Lewis, 69–88. New York: Holmes and Meier, 1982.

Brumberg, Joan Jacobs. "Zenanas and Girlless Villages: The Ethnology of American Evangelical Women, 1870–1910." *Journal of American History* 69, no. 2 (September 1982): 347–371.

Brummett, Palmira. "Gender and Empire in Late Ottoman Istanbul: Caricature, Models of Empire, and the Case for Ottoman Exceptionalism." *Comparative Studies of South Asia, Africa and the Middle East* 27, no. 2 (2007): 283–302.

Burgoyne, Michael Hamilton. *Mamluk Jerusalem: An Architectural Study.* World of Islam Festival Trust on Behalf of British School of Archaeology in Jerusalem, 1987.

Burrows, Mathew. "'Mission Civilisatrice': French Cultural Policy in the Middle East, 1860–1914." *Historical Journal* 29, no. 1 (March 1986): 109–135.

Canaan, Tewfik. *The Palestinian Arab House, Its Architecture and Folklore.* Jerusalem: Syrian Orphanage Press, 1933.

Chatterjee, Partha. *The Nation and Its Fragments: Colonial and Postcolonial Histories.* Princeton: Princeton University Press, 1993.

Cioeta, Donald J. "Islamic Benevolent Societies and Public Education in Ottoman Syria, 1875–1882." *Islamic Quarterly* 26, no. 1 (1982): 40–55.

Clancy-Smith, Julia. "Envisioning Knowledge: Educating the Muslim Woman in Colonial North Africa, c. 1850–1918." In *Iran and Beyond: Essays in Middle Eastern History in Honor of Nikki R. Keddie,* edited by Rudi Matthee and Beth Baron, 99–118. Costa Mesa: Mazda, 2000.

Coffin, Judith G. "Credit, Consumption, and Images of Women's Desires: Selling the Sewing Machine in Nineteenth Century France." *French Historical Studies* 18, no. 3 (Spring 1994): 749–783.

Cohen, Amnon. *The Guilds of Ottoman Jerusalem.* Leiden: Brill, 2001.

Colbi, Saul P. *A History of the Christian Presence in the Holy Land.* Lanham, MD: University Press of America, 1988.

Crombie, Kelvin. *For the Love of Zion: Christian Witness and the Restoration of Israel.* London: Hodder and Stoughton, 1991.

Danielson, Virginia. *The Voice of Egypt: Umm Kulthūm, Arabic Song, and Egyptian Society in the Twentieth Century.* Chicago and London: University of Chicago Press, 1997.

Davin, Anna. "Imperialism and Motherhood." *History Workshop Journal* no. 5 (Spring 1978): 9–65.

———. *Growing up Poor: Home, School and Street in London 1870–1914.* London: Rivers Oram Press, 1996.

Davis, Fanny. *The Ottoman Lady: A Social History from 1718 to 1918.* New York: Greenwood Press, 1986.

Davis, Rochelle. "The Growth of the Western Communities, 1917–1948." In *Jerusalem 1948: The Arab Neighbourhoods and Their Fate in the War,* edited by Salim Tamari, 32–66. Jerusalem: Institute of Jerusalem Studies; Bethlehem: Badil Resource Center, 1999.

———. "Commemorating Education: Recollections of the Arab College in Jerusalem, 1918–1948." *Comparative Studies of South Asia, Africa and the Middle East* 23, nos. 1–2 (2003): 1–17.

Davydov, Evgeniy. "Ha-peʿilut ha-ḥinukhit shel ha-aguda ha-imperialit ha-pravoslavit ha-falastinit be-erets yisrael ba-shanim 1882–1914." Master's thesis, University of Haifa, 2000.

Deguilhem, Randi. "Gender Blindness and Societal Influence in Late Ottoman Damascus: Women as the Creators and Managers of Endowments." *Hawwa* 1, no. 3 (2003): 329–350.

Dengler, Ian C. "Turkish Women in the Ottoman Empire, the Classical Age." In *Women in the Muslim World*, edited by Lois Beck and Nikki Keddie, 229–244. Cambridge: Harvard University Press, 1978.

Deringil, Selim. *The Well-Protected Domains: Ideology and Legitimation of Power in the Ottoman Empire, 1876–1909*. London: I. B. Tauris, 1999.

Dogramacı, Emel. "Education of Women in Ottoman and Republican Turkey: A Comparative Perspective." In *IIIrd Congress on the Social and Economic History of Turkey, 1983*, edited by Heath W. Lowry and Ralph S. Hattox, 213–225. Istanbul: ISIS Press, 1990.

Donaldson, Margaret. "'The Cultivation of the Heart and the Moulding of the Will . . .' The Missionary Contribution of the Society for Promoting Female Education in China, India, and the East." *Studies in Church History* 27 (1990): 429–442.

Doumani, Beshara B. *Rediscovering Palestine: Merchants and Peasants in Jabal Nablus, 1700–1900*. Berkeley and Los Angeles: University of California Press, 1995.

Doumato, Eleanor Abdella. *Getting God's Ear: Women, Islam, and Healing in Saudi Arabia and the Gulf*. New York: Columbia University Press, 2000.

Dussel, Inés. "When Appearances Are Not Deceptive: A Comparative History of School Uniforms in Argentina and the United States (Nineteenth-Twentieth Centuries)." *Paedagogica Historica* 41, nos. 1–2 (February 2005): 179–195.

Duvignau, Pierre. *Une Vie au Service de l'Église: S. B. Mgr. Joseph Valerga*. Jerusalem, 1972.

Edelstein, T. J. "They Sang 'the Song of the Shirt': The Visual Iconology of the Seamstress." *Victorian Studies* 23, no. 2 (1980): 183–210.

Ehrenreich, Barbara, and Deirdre English. *For Her Own Good: 150 Years of the Experts' Advice to Women*. New York: Anchor Press, 1979.

Eisenman, Robert H. *Islamic Law in Palestine and Israel: A History of the Survival of Tanzimat and Shari'a in the British Mandate and Jewish State*. Leiden: Brill, 1978.

El-Eini, Roza I. M. "British Agricultural-Educational Institutions in Mandate Palestine and Their Impress on the Rural Landscape." *Middle Eastern Studies* 35, no. 1 (January 1999): 98–114.

Elshakry, Marwa. "The Gospel of Science and American Evangelism in Late Ottoman Beirut." *Past and Present*, no. 196 (2007): 173–214.

Erhan, Cagri. "Ottoman Official Attitudes towards American Missionaries." http://128.36.236.77/workpaper/pdfs/MESV5-11.pdf (accessed September 16, 2008).

Erlich, Haggai. *Students and University in 20th Century Egyptian Politics*. London: Frank Cass, 1998.

Farah, Rafiq. *Ta'rikh al-kanisa al-usqufiyya fi matraniyyat al-quds 1841–1991*. 2 vols. Beirut: N.p., 1995.

Fleischmann, Ellen L. "'Our Moslem Sisters': Women of Greater Syria in the Eyes of American Protestant Missionary Women." *Islam and Christian-Muslim Relations* 9, no. 3 (1998): 307–323.

———. "The Impact of American Protestant Missions in Lebanon on the Construction of Female Identity, c. 1860–1950." *Islam and Christian-Muslim Relations* 13, no. 4 (2002): 411–426.

———. *The Nation and Its "New" Women: The Palestinian Women's Movement, 1920–1948.* Berkeley and Los Angeles: University of California Press, 2003.

Flemming, Leslie A., ed. *Women's Work for Women: Missionaries and Social Change in Asia.* London: Westview Press, 1989.

Fortna, Benjamin C. "Islamic Morality in Late Ottoman 'Secular' Schools." *International Journal of Middle East Studies* 32, no. 3 (August 2000): 369–393.

———. *Imperial Classroom: Islam, the State, and Education in the Late Ottoman Empire.* Oxford: Oxford University Press, 2002.

Frierson, Elizabeth Brown. "Unimagined Communities: State, Press, and Gender in the Hamidian Era." Ph.D. diss., Princeton University, 1996.

Gavin, Carney E. S., and the Harvard Semitic Museum, eds., "Imperial Self-Portrait: The Ottoman Empire as Revealed in the Sultan Abdul Hamid II's Photographic Albums." Special issue, *Journal of Turkish Studies* 12 (1988).

Gelişli, Yucel. "Education of Women from the Ottoman Empire to Modern Turkey." *South-East Europe Review,* no. 4 (2004): 121–136.

Ghanayim, Zuhayr Ghanayim 'Abd al-Latif. *Liwa' 'akka fi al-'ahd al-tanzimat al-'uthmaniyya 1864–1918.* Beirut: Institute of Palestine Studies, 1999.

Goitein, S. D. *A Mediterranean Society: The Jewish Communities of the Arab World as Portrayed in the Documents of the Cairo Geniza.* Vol. 2, *The Community.* Berkeley: University of California Press, 1971.

Goodwin, Isobel. *May You Live to Be 120! The Story of Tabeetha School, Jaffa 1863–1983.* Edinburgh: St. Andrew Press, 2000.

Graham-Brown, Sarah. *Images of Women: The Portrayal of Women in Photography of the Middle East, 1860–1950.* New York: Columbia University Press, 1988.

Greenberg, Ela. "Educating Muslim Girls in Mandatory Jerusalem." *International Journal of Middle East Studies* 36, no. 1 (February 2004): 1–19.

———. "*Majallat Rawdat al-ma'arif:* Constructing Identities within a Boys' School Journal in Mandatory Palestine." *British Journal of Middle Eastern Studies* 35, no. 1 (April 2008): 79–95.

———. "Between Hardships and Respect: A Collective Biography of Arab Women Teachers in British-ruled Palestine." *Hawwa* 6, no. 3 (2008): 284–314.

Grosvenor, Ian. "'There's No Place Like Home': Education and the Making of National Identity." *History of Education* 28, no. 3 (1999): 235–250.

Haddad, Mahmoud. "Syrian Muslims' Attitudes toward Foreign Missionaries in the Late Nineteenth and Twentieth Centuries." Columbia International Affairs Online, http://www.ciaonet.org/conf/mei01/ham01.html (accessed September 1, 2008).

Halaby, Mona Hajjar. "School Days in Mandate Jerusalem at Dames de Sion." *Jerusalem Quarterly* 31 (Summer 2007): 40–71.

Hammami, Rema. "Between Heaven and Earth: Transformations in Religiosity and Labor among Southern Palestinian Peasant and Refugee Women, 1920–1993." Ph.D. diss., Temple University, 1994.

Hancock, Mary. "Home Science and Nationalization of Domesticity in Colonial India." *Modern Asian Studies* 35, no. 4 (2001): 871–904.

Heggoy, Alf Andrew, and Paul J. Zingg. "French Education in Revolutionary North Africa." *International Journal of Middle East Studies* 7, no. 4 (October 1976): 571–578.

Herrera, Linda. "Downveiling: Gender and the Contest over Culture in Cairo." *Middle East Report* no. 219 (Summer 2001): 16–19.

Hewitt, Gordon. *The Problems of Success: A History of the Church Missionary Society, 1910–1942.* 2 vols. London: SCM Press, 1971.

Heyworth-Dunne, J. *An Introduction to the History of Education in Modern Egypt.* London: Luzac, 1938.

al-Hilali, ʿAbd al-Razzaq. *Taʾrikh al-taʿlim fi al-ʿiraq fi al-ʿahd al-ʿuthmani.* Baghdad: Ahliyya Press, 1959.

Hill, Patricia R. *The World Their Household: The American Woman's Foreign Mission Movement and Cultural Transformation, 1870–1920.* Ann Arbor: University of Michigan Press, 1985.

Himadeh, Saʿid. *Economic Organization of Palestine.* Beirut: American Press, 1938.

Hirsh, Dafna. "'Anu mefitsim kan tarbut'—ḥinukh le-higena, ba-yishuv ha-yehudi ba-erets yisrael ba-tequfat ha-mandat ha-briti." Master's thesis, Tel Aviv University, 2000.

———. "'Almost Every Immigrant Child Is a Problem': School Hygiene and the Immigration of People and Ideas in Mandatory Palestine." Paper presented at the annual meeting of the Association for Israel Studies, Open University of Israel, June 2007.

Hobsbawm, Eric J. *Nations and Nationalism since 1780.* Cambridge: Cambridge University Press, 1990.

———. "Mass-Producing Traditions: Europe, 1870–1914." In *The Invention of Tradition,* edited by Eric Hobsbawm and Terence Ranger, 263–307. 1983. Reprint, Cambridge: Cambridge University Press, 1992.

Hopwood, Derek. *Russian Presence in Syria and Palestine 1843–1914.* Oxford: Clarendon Press, 1969.

Hourani, Albert. *Arabic Thought in the Liberal Age, 1798–1939.* 1962. Reissue, Cambridge: Cambridge University Press, 1983.

Huijer, Huda Abu-Saad, et al. "Cherishing the Past: 100 Years of Nursing Education at the American University of Beirut." *Journal of Transcultural Nursing* 17 no. 4 (2006): 327–332.

Ichilov, Orit, and André Elias Mazawi. *Between State and Church: Life-History of a French-Catholic School in Jaffa.* Frankfurt am Main: Peter Lang, 1996.

Ilan, Yael. "Ha-peʿilut ha-tsarfatit be-sanjaq yerushalayim be-tḥum ha-ḥinukh ve-ha-siʿud be-shalhe ha-tequfa ha-ʿotmanit." Master's thesis, University of Haifa, 1987.

Jacobson, Abigail. "From Empire to Empire: Jerusalem in the Transition between Ottoman and British Rule, 1912–1920." Ph.D. diss., University of Chicago, 2006.

Jansen, Willy. "Visions of Mary in the Middle East: Gender and the Power of a Symbol." In *Gender, Religion and Change in the Middle East: Two Hundred Years of History*, edited by Inger Marie Okkenhaug and Ingvild Flaskerud, 137–154. Oxford and New York: Berg, 2005.

———. "Arab Women with a Mission: The Sisters of the Rosary." In *Christian Witness between Continuity and New Beginnings*, edited by Martin Tamcke and Michael Marten, 41–61. Berlin: LIT Verlag, 2006.

Kabha, Mustafa. *The Palestinian Press as Shaper of Public Opinion 1929–39: Writing Up a Storm*. London: Vallentine Mitchell, 2007.

Kark, Ruth. *Jaffa: A City in Evolution, 1799–1917*. Jerusalem: Yad Ben Zvi, 1990.

———. "Post Civil War American Communes: A Millenarian Utopian Community Linking Chicago and Nås, Sweden to Jerusalem." *Communal Societies* 15 (1995): 75–113.

———. "Sweden and the Holy Land: Pietistic and Communal Settlement." *Journal of Historical Geography* 22, no. 1 (1996): 46–67.

———. "The Impact of Early Missionary Enterprises in Palestine on Landscape and Identity in Palestine, 1820–1914." *Islam and Christian-Muslim Relations* 15, no. 2 (2004): 209–235.

Kark, Ruth, and Michal Oren-Nordheim. *Jerusalem and Its Environs: Quarters, Neighborhoods, Villages 1800–1948*. Detroit: Wayne State University Press and Jerusalem: Magnes Press, 2001.

Kayalı, Hasan. *Arabs and Young Turks: Ottomanism, Arabism, and Islamism in the Ottoman Empire, 1908–1918*. Berkeley and Los Angeles: University of California Press, 1997.

Kent, Eliza F. "Tamil Bible Women and the Zenana Missions of Colonial South India." *History of Religions* 39, no. 2 (Nov. 1999): 117–149.

Khalaf, Issa. *Politics in Palestine: Arab Factionalism and Social Disintegration, 1939–1948*. Albany: SUNY Press, 1991.

———. "The Effect of Socioeconomic Change on Arab Societal Collapse in Mandate Palestine." *International Journal of Middle East Studies* 29, no. 1 (February 1997): 93–112.

Khalaf, Samir. "On Doing Much with Little Noise: Early Encounters of Protestant Missionaries in Lebanon." Columbia International Affairs Online, http://www.ciaonet.org/conf/mei01/khs01.html. Accessed September 1, 2008.

Khalidi, Issam. "Body and Ideology: Early Athletics in Palestine (1900–1948)." *Jerusalem Quarterly* 27 (Summer 2006): 44–58.

El Khalidi, Leila. *The Art of Palestinian Embroidery*. London: Saqi Books, 1999.

Khalidi, Rashid. "Society and Ideology in Late Ottoman Syria: Class, Education,

Profession and Confession." In *Problems of the Middle East in Historical Perspective: Essays in Honour of Albert Hourani*, edited by John P. Spagnolo, 119–132. Reading, UK: Ithaca Press, 1992.

———. *Palestinian Identity: The Construction of Modern National Consciousness*. New York: Columbia University Press, 1997.

Khalidi, Walid. *Before Their Diaspora: A Photographic History of the Palestinians 1876–1948*. Washington, D.C.: Institute of Palestine Studies, 1991.

———, ed. *All That Remains: The Palestinian Villages Occupied and Depopulated by Israel in 1948*. Washington, D.C.: Institute for Palestine Studies, 1992.

Al-Khalidi, Walid Raghib. "Al-kulliya al-ʿarabiyya fi al-quds: khalfiya taʾrikhiyya wa-nathra mustaqbaliyya." *Majallat dirasat al-filastiniyya* 44 (Winter 2000): 136–144.

Khasawneh, Diala. *Memoirs Engraved in Stone: Palestinian Urban Mansions*. Ramallah: Riwaq-Centre for Architectural Conservation; Jerusalem: Institute of Jerusalem Studies, 2001.

Khuri, Yusuf Q. *Al-sihafa al-ʿarabiyya fi filastin 1876–1948*. Beirut: Muʾassasat al-dirasat al-filastiniyya, 1976.

Kiskira, Constantia. "'Evangelising' the Orient: New England Womanhood in the Ottoman Empire, 1830–1930." *Archivum Ottomanicum* 16 (1998): 279–294.

Kobiljski, Aleksandra Majstorac. "Women Students at the American University of Beirut from the 1920s to the 1940s." In *Gender, Religion, and Change in the Middle East: Two Hundred Years of History*, edited by Inger Marie Okkenhaug and Ingvild Flaskerud, 67–84. Oxford and New York: Berg, 2005.

Koven, Seth, and Sonya Michel. "Womanly Duties: Maternalist Policies and the Origins of Welfare States in France, Germany, Great Britain, and the United States, 1880–1920." *American Historical Review* 95 (October 1990): 1076–1108.

Kupferschmidt, Uri M. *The Supreme Muslim Council: Islam under the British Mandate for Palestine*. Leiden: Brill, 1987.

———. "The Social History of the Sewing Machine in the Middle East." *Die Welt des Islams* 44, no. 2 (2004): 195–213.

Kushner, David. "Zealous Towns in Nineteenth Century Palestine." *Middle Eastern Studies* 33, no. 3 (July 1997): 597–612.

Lang, Sean. "Drop the Demon Dai: Maternal Mortality and the State in Colonial Madras, 1840–1874." *Social History of Medicine* 18, no. 3 (2005): 357–378.

Langlois, Claude. "Les congrégations françaises en Terre Sainte au XIXe siècle." In *De Bonaparte à Balfour: La France, l'Europe Occidentale et la Palestine 1799–1917*, edited by Dominique Trimbur and Ran Aaronsohn, 219–240. Jérusalem: Centre de Recherche français, 2000.

LeVine, Mark. *Overthrowing Geography: Jaffa, Tel Aviv, and the Struggle for Palestine 1880–1948*. Berkeley and Los Angeles: University of California Press, 2005.

———. "The Palestinian Press in Mandatory Jaffa: Advertising, Nationalism, and the Public Sphere." In *Palestine, Israel and the Politics of Popular Culture*, edited by

Rebecca L. Stein and Ted Swedenburg, 51–76. Durham: Duke University Press, 2005.

Mahamid, ʿUmar. *Safahat min taʾrikh madaris al-jamʿiya al-russiyya-al-filastiniyya fi filastin bayn aʿwam 1882–1914.* Taybe: Markaz ihyaʾ al-turath al-ʿarabi, 1988.

Makdisi, Ussama. "Ottoman Orientalism." *American Historical Review* 107, no. 3 (June 2002): 768–796.

Mansur, Asʿad. *Taʾrikh al-nasira min aqdam azmaniha ila ayamina al-hadira.* Cairo: Matbaʿat al-hilal, 1924.

Maskiell, Michelle. "Social Change and Social Control: College-Educated Punjabi Women 1913 to 1960." *Modern Asian Studies* 19, no. 1 (1985): 55–83.

Matar, Philip. *The Mufti of Jerusalem: Al-Hajj Amin al-Husayni and the Palestinian National Movement.* New York: Columbia University Press, 1988.

Matthews, Glenna. *"Just a Housewife": The Rise and Fall of Domesticity in America.* New York and Oxford: Oxford University Press, 1987.

Matthews, Weldon C. "Pan-Islam or Arab Nationalism? The Meaning of the 1931 Jerusalem Islamic Congress Reconsidered." *International Journal of Middle East Studies* 35, no. 1 (February 2003): 1–22.

———. *Confronting an Empire, Constructing a Nation: Arab Nationalists and Popular Politics in Mandate Palestine.* London: I. B. Tauris, 2006.

McCarthy, Justin. *The Population of Palestine.* New York: Columbia University Press, 1990.

McCrone, Kathleen E. *Playing the Game: Sport and the Physical Emancipation of English Women, 1870–1914.* Lexington: University Press of Kentucky, 1988.

McCune, Mary. "Social Workers in the *Muskeljudentum:* 'Hadassah Ladies,' 'Manly Men' and the Significance of Gender in the American Zionist Movement, 1912–1928." *American Jewish History* 86, no. 2 (June 1998): 135–165.

Medebielle, Pierre. *The Diocese of the Latin Patriarchate of Jerusalem.* Jerusalem, 1963.

Melman, Billie. *Women's Orients: English Women and the Middle East, 1718–1918.* 2nd ed. Basingstoke: Macmillan, 1995.

Micklewright, Nancy. "Late-Nineteenth-Century Ottoman Wedding Costumes as Indicators of Social Change." *Muqarnas* 6 (1989): 161–174.

Miller, Ylana N. *Government and Society in Rural Palestine, 1920–1948.* Austin: University of Texas Press, 1985.

Moors, Annelies. *Women, Property and Islam: Palestinian Experiences 1920–1990.* Cambridge: Cambridge University Press, 1995.

Murre-van den Berg, Heleen. "Nineteenth-Century Protestant Missions and Middle Eastern Women: An Overview." In *Gender, Religion, and Change in the Middle East: Two Hundred Years of History,* edited by Inger Marie Okkenhaug and Ingvild Flaskerud, 103–122. Oxford and New York: Berg, 2005.

Naguib, Saphinaz-Amal. "Modelling a Cosmopolitan Womanhood in Egypt (1850–1950): The Role of Nannies and French Catholic Girls Schools." *Acta Orientalia* 62 (2001): 92–106.

Najmabadi, Afsaneh. "Crafting an Educated Housewife in Iran." In *Remaking Women: Feminism and Modernity in the Middle East,* edited by Lila Abu-Lughod, 91–125. Princeton: Princeton University Press, 1998.

al-Nimr, Ihsan. *Ta'rikh jabal nablus wa-al-balqa',* 4 vols. Nablus: Matba'at 'ummal al-matabi' al-ta'awuniyya, 1975.

O'Brien, Susan. "French Nuns in Nineteenth Century England." *Past and Present,* no. 154 (February 1997): 142–180.

Okkenhaug, Inger Marie. *The Quality of Heroic Living, of High Endeavour and Adventure: Anglican Mission, Women and Education in Palestine, 1888–1948.* Leiden: Brill, 2002.

Okkenhaug, Inger Marie, and Ingvild Flaskerud, eds. *Gender, Religion and Change in the Middle East: Two Hundred Years of History.* Oxford and New York: Berg, 2005.

Özaydin, Zuhal. "Upper Social Strata Women in Nursing in Turkey." *Nursing History Review* 14 (2006): 161–174.

Pappe, Ilan. *Atsilat ha-arets: mishpahat al-Husayni.* Jerusalem: Bialik Institute, 2002.

Parker, Rozsika. *The Subversive Stitch: Embroidery and the Making of the Feminine.* Rev. ed. London: Women's Press, 1996.

Pollard, Lisa. *Nurturing the Nation: The Family Politics of Modernizing, Colonizing, and Liberating Egypt, 1805–1923.* Berkeley and Los Angeles: University of California Press, 2005.

Porath, Yehoshua. *The Emergence of the Palestinian-Arab National Movement, 1918–1929.* London: Frank Cass, 1974.

———. *The Palestinian Arab National Movement: From Riots to Rebellion.* Vol. 2, *1929–1939.* London: Frank Cass, 1977.

Predelli, Line Nyhagen. "Sexual Control and the Remaking of Gender: The Attempt of Nineteenth Century Protestant Norwegian Women to Export Western Domesticity to Madagascar." *Journal of Women's History* 12, no. 2 (Summer 2000): 81–103.

Rafferty, Anne Marie, and Diana Solano. "The Rise and Demise of the Colonial Nursing Service: British Nurses in the Colonies, 1896–1966." *Nursing History Review* 15 (2007): 147–154.

Rajab, Jehan S. *Palestinian Costume.* London and New York: Kegan Paul International, 1989.

Reeves-Ellington, Barbara. "A Vision of Mount Holyoke in the Ottoman Balkans: American Cultural Transfer, Bulgarian Nation-Building and Women's Educational Reform, 1858–1870." *Gender and History* 16, no. 1 (2004): 146–171.

Reid, Donald M. *Cairo University and the Making of Modern Egypt.* Cambridge: Cambridge University Press, 1990.

Reiss, Nira. "British Public Health Policy in Palestine, 1918–1947." In *Health and Disease in the Holy Land,* edited by Manfred Waserman and Samuel S. Kottek, 301–327. Lewiston, NY: Edwin Mellen Press, 1996.

Richter, Julius. *History of Protestant Missions in the Near East.* 1910. Reprint, New York: AMS Press, 1970.

Rogers, Rebecca. "Boarding Schools, Women Teachers, and Domesticity: Reforming Girls' Secondary Education in the First Half of the Nineteenth Century." *French Historical Studies* 19, no. 1 (Spring 1995): 153–181.

Rostam-Kolayi, Jasamin. "Foreign Education, the Women's Press, and the Discourse of Scientific Domesticity in Early-Twentieth Century Iran." In *Iran and the Surrounding World: Interactions in Culture and Cultural Politics*, edited by Nikki R. Keddie and Rudi Matthee, 182–202. Seattle and London: University of Washington Press, 2002.

Rubin, Avi. "Ha-mizraḥ davar aḥad ve-ha-maʿarav davar aḥer: Muhammad Bahjat ve-Rafiq al-Tamimi be-wilayet bayrut." *Jamaʿa* 7 (2001): 54–81.

Rumman, Muhammad Saʿid Muslih. *Suba: qarya muqaddasiyya fi al-dhakira*. Jerusalem: Matbaʿat ʿAin Rafa, 2000.

Russell, Mona L. "Creating the New Woman: Consumerism, Education, and National Identity in Egypt, 1863–1922." Ph.D. diss., Georgetown University, 1997.

Sabri, Marie Aziz. *Pioneering Profiles: Beirut College for Women*. Beirut: Khayat Book and Publishing, 1967.

Saca, Iman. *Embroidering Identities: A Century of Palestinian Clothing*. Chicago: Oriental Institute Museum of the University of Chicago, 2006.

Salt, Jeremy. "A Precarious Symbiosis: Ottoman Christians and Foreign Missionaries in the Nineteenth Century." *International Journal of Turkish Studies* 3, no. 1 (Winter 1984–1985): 53–67.

———. "Trouble Wherever They Went: American Missionaries in Anatolia and Ottoman Syria in the Nineteenth Century." *Muslim World* 92, nos. 3–4 (Fall 2002): 287–313.

Sannu, ʿAbd al-Raʾuf. *Al-masalih al-almaniyya fi suriya wa-filastin 1841–1901*. Beirut: Maʿhad al-inmaʾ al-ʿarabi, 1987.

Sayigh, Rosemary. *Too Many Enemies: The Palestinian Experience in Lebanon*. London and New Jersey: Zed Books, 1994.

Schilcher, Linda Schatkowski. "The Famine of 1915–1918 in Greater Syria." In *Problems of the Modern Middle East in Historical Perspective: Essays in Honour of Albert Hourani*, edited by John P. Spagnolo, 229–258. Reading, UK: Ithaca Press, 1992.

Schleifer, S. Abdallah. "The Life and Thought of ʿIzz id-din al-Qassam." *Islamic Quarterly* 22, no. 2 (1979): 61–81.

Seikaly, May. "Haifa at the Crossroads: An Outpost of the New World Order." In *Modernity and Culture: From the Mediterranean to the Indian Ocean*, edited by Leila Tarazi Fawaz and C. A. Bayly, 96–111. New York: Columbia University Press, 2002.

Sharkey, Heather J. "Christians among Muslims: The Church Missionary Society in Northern Sudan." *Journal of African History* 43, no. 1 (January 2002): 51–75.

———. *Living with Colonialism: Nationalism and Culture in the Anglo-Egyptian Sudan*. Berkeley and Los Angeles: University of California Press, 2003.

———. "Arabic Antimissionary Treatises: Muslim Responses to Christian Evangelism in the Modern Middle East." *International Bulletin of Missionary Research* 28, no. 3 (July 2004): 98–104.

———. "Empire and Muslim Conversion: Historical Reflections on Christian Missions in Egypt." *Islam and Christian-Muslim Relations* 16, no. 1 (January 2005): 43–60.

———. *American Evangelicals in Egypt: Missionary Encounters in an Age of Empire.* Princeton: Princeton University Press, 2008.

Shaw, Stanford J., and Ezel Kural Shaw. *History of the Ottoman Empire and Modern Turkey.* Vol. 2, *Reform, Revolution, and Republic: The Rise of Modern Turkey, 1808–1975.* Cambridge: Cambridge University Press, 1977.

Shetty, Sandhya. "(Dis)Locating Gender Space and Medical Discourse in Colonial India." *Genders* 20 (1994): 182–230.

Shilo, Margalit. "Women as Victims of War: The British Conquest (1917) and the Blight of Prostitution in the Holy City." *Nashim: A Journal of Jewish Women's Studies and Gender Issues* no. 6 (Fall 2003): 72–83.

———. *Princess or Prisoner? Jewish Women in Jerusalem, 1840–1914.* Waltham: Brandeis University Press, 2005.

Shim'oni, Ya'acov. *'Araviye erets-yisrael.* Tel Aviv: 'Am 'oved, 1947.

Simmons, Erika B. *Hadassah and the Zionist Project.* Lanham, MD: Rowman & Littlefield, 2006.

Simon, Reeva S. "The Education of an Iraqi Ottoman Army Officer." In *The Origins of Arab Nationalism,* edited by Rashid Khalidi et al., 151–166. New York: Columbia University Press, 1991.

Simoni, Marcella. "A Dangerous Legacy: Welfare in British Palestine, 1930–1939." *Jewish History* 13, no. 2 (Fall 1999): 81–109.

Singer, Amy. *Constructing Ottoman Beneficence: An Imperial Soup Kitchen in Jerusalem.* Albany: State University of New York Press, 2002.

Småberg, Maria. "Ambivalent Friendship: Anglican Conflict Handling and Education for Peace in Jerusalem 1920–1948." Ph.D. diss., Lund University, 2005.

Smith, Jane I. "The Virgin Mary in Islamic Tradition and Commentary." *Muslim World* 79, no. 3 (1989): 161–187.

Somel, Selçuk Akşin. *The Modernization of Public Education in the Ottoman Empire 1839–1908: Islamization, Autocracy and Discipline.* Leiden: Brill, 2001.

Sorek, Tamir. "The Orange and the 'Cross in the Crescent': Imagining Palestine in 1929." *Nations and Nationalism* 10, no. 3 (2004): 269–291.

———. "The Sports Column as a Site of Palestinian Nationalism in the 1940s." *Israel Affairs* 13, no. 3 (2007): 605–616.

Stanton, Andrea L. "A Little Radio Is a Dangerous Thing: State Broadcasting in Mandate Palestine, 1936–1949." Ph.D. diss., Columbia University, 2007.

Starrett, Gregory. *Putting Islam to Work: Education, Politics, and Religious Transformation in Egypt.* Berkeley and Los Angeles: University of California Press, 1998.

Stock, Phyllis. *Better Than Rubies: A History of Women's Education.* New York: G. P. Putnam & Sons, 1978.

Stockdale, Nancy L. *Colonial Encounters among English and Palestinian Women, 1800–1948.* Gainesville: University of Florida Press, 2007.

Strohmeier, Martin. "Muslim Education in the Vilayet of Beirut, 1880–1918." In *Decision Making and Change in the Ottoman Empire,* edited by Caesar E. Farah, 215–241. Kirksville, MO: Thomas Jefferson University Press at Northeast Missouri State University, 1993.

Sufian, Sandra M. *Healing the Land and the Nation: Malaria and the Zionist Project in Palestine, 1920–1947.* Chicago and London: University of Chicago Press, 2007.

Swedenburg, Ted. "The Palestinian Peasant as National Signifier." *Anthropological Quarterly* 63, no. 1 (January 1990): 18–30.

———. *Memories of Revolt: The 1936–1939 Rebellion and the Palestinian National Past.* Minneapolis: University of Minnesota Press, 1995.

Syzliowicz, Joseph S. *Education and Modernization in the Middle East.* Ithaca: Cornell University Press, 1973.

Temelkuran, Tevfik. "The First Teacher Training College for Girls in Turkey." *Journal of the Regional Cultural Institute* (Tehran) 5, no. 1 (Winter 1972): 37–44.

Thompson, Elizabeth. *Colonial Citizens: Republican Rights, Paternal Privilege, and Gender in French Syria and Lebanon.* New York: Columbia University Press, 2000.

Tibawi, A. L. "Religion and Educational Administration in Palestine of the British Mandate." *Die Welt des Islams,* n.s., 3, no. 1 (1953): 1–14.

———. *Arab Education in Mandatory Palestine: A Study of Three Decades of British Administration.* London: Luzac, 1956.

———. "Educational Policy and Arab Nationalism in Mandatory Palestine." *Die Welt des Islams* n.s., 4, no. 1 (1955): 15–29.

———. *British Interests in Palestine 1800–1901: A Study of Religious and Educational Enterprise.* London: Oxford University Press, 1961.

———. "Russian Cultural Penetration of Syria-Palestine in the Nineteenth Century—Part One." *Journal of the Royal Central Asian Society* 53, no. 2 (1966): 166–182.

———. "Russian Cultural Penetration of Syria-Palestine in the Nineteenth Century—Part Two." *Journal of the Royal Central Asian Society* 53, no. 3 (1966): 309–323.

Tsimhoni, Daphne. "British Mandate and Arab Christians in Palestine 1920–1925." Ph.D. diss., University of London, 1976.

Tubi, Asma. *'Abir wa-majd.* N.p., 1966.

Tucker, Judith E. "Marriage and Family in Nablus, 1720–1856: Toward a History of Arab Marriage." *Journal of Family History* 13, no. 2 (1988): 165–179.

van Nieuwkerk, Karin. *"A Trade Like Any Other": Female Singers and Dancers in Egypt.* Austin: University of Texas Press, 1995.

van Poppel, Frans, and Jan Nelissen. "The Proper Age to Marry: Social Norms and Behavior in Nineteenth-Century Netherlands." *History of the Family* 4, no. 1 (1999): 51–75.

Vashitz, Yosef. *Ha-'aravim be-erets-yisrael.* Merchavia: Sifriat ha-po'aalim, 1947.

Vatikiotis, P. J. "The Greek Orthodox Patriarchate of Jerusalem between Hellenism and Arabism." *Middle Eastern Studies* 30, no. 4 (1994): 916–929.

Warren, Allen. "Citizens of the Empire: Baden-Powell, Scouts and Guides and an Imperial Ideal, 1900–40." In *Imperialism and Popular Culture*, edited by John M. Mackenzie, 232–256. Manchester: Manchester University Press, 1986.

Waserman, Manfred. "Henrietta Szold: American Progressivism, Zionism, and Modern Public Health." In *Health and Disease in the Holy Land*, edited by Manfred Waserman and Samuel S. Kottek, 263–299. Lewiston, NY: Edwin Mellen Press, 1996.

Waserman, Manfred, and Samuel S. Kottek, eds. *Health and Disease in the Holy Land*. Lewiston, NY: Edwin Mellen Press, 1996.

Weir, S. *Palestinian Costume*. London: Trustees of the British Museum, 1970.

Welshman, John. "Physical Culture and Sports in England and Wales, 1900–40." *International Journal of the History of Sport* 15, no. 1 (April 1998): 54–75.

White, Ann. "Counting the Cost of Faith: America's Early Female Missionaries." *Church History* 57, no. 1 (March 1988): 19–30.

Whitehead, Clive. "The Historiography of British Imperial Education Policy, Part I: India." *History of Education* 34, no. 3 (May 2005): 315–329.

Williams, C. Peter. "Healing and Evangelism: The Place of Medicine in Late Victorian Protestant Missionary Thinking." In *The Church and Healing*, edited by W. J. Sheils, 271–287. London: Blackwell, 1982.

Wollons, Roberta. "Travelling for God and Adventure: Women Missionaries in the Late 19th Century." *Asian Journal of Social Science* 31, no. 1 (2003): 55–71.

Yazbak, Mahmoud. "Nabulsi Ulama in the Late Ottoman Period, 1864–1914." *International Journal of Middle East Studies* 29, no. 1 (1997): 71–91.

———. *Haifa in the Late Ottoman Period, 1864–1914: A Muslim Town in Transition*. Leiden: Brill, 1998.

———. "From Poverty to Revolt: Economic Factors in the Outbreak of the 1936 Rebellion in Palestine." *Middle Eastern Studies* 36, no. 3 (July 2000): 93–113.

———. "Muslim Orphans and the Shariʿa in Ottoman Palestine according to Sijill Records." *Journal of the Social and Economic History of the Orient* 44, no. 2 (May 2001): 123–140.

———. "Minor Marriages and *Khiyār al-bulūgh* in Ottoman Palestine: A Note on Women's Strategies in a Patriarchal Society." *Islamic Law and Society* 9, no. 3 (2002): 386–409.

Young, Elise G. "From Daya to Doctor: Health, Gender, and the Race for Control of Knowledge-Making in Mandatory Palestine." *Thamyris* 4 (1997): 347–358.

Zidat, Adel Z. "Western Medicine in Palestine, 1860–1940: The Edinburgh Medical Missionary Society and its Hospital." *Canadian Bulletin of Medical History* 10, no. 2 (1993): 269–279.

INDEX

Page numbers in *italics* refer to photographs.